A good rifle, three cartridges, and three tails!

WOODCHUCKS
and
WOODCHUCK RIFLES

by C. S. LANDIS

Martino Publishing
Mansfield Centre, CT
2012

Martino Publishing
P.O. Box 373,
Mansfield Centre, CT 06250 USA

ISBN 978-1-61427-248-9

© *2012 Martino Publishing*

Cover design by T. Matarazzo

Printed in the United States of America On 100% Acid-Free Paper

WOODCHUCKS
and
WOODCHUCK RIFLES

by C. S. LANDIS

GREENBERG: PUBLISHER

New York

Author's Note: Neither author nor publisher
assumes any responsibility for the loads published in this book. They are to serve as guides
only.

Dedication

This book is dedicated to my grandfather

Adam Singer

And to my cousin

John W. Metzgar

the shooting mentors of my youth.

It is also dedicated to

Irvin Cooper

my shooting companion and hunting

associate for fifteen years.

These experienced hunters and splendid field and woods shots have all passed on.

Contents

Introduction

To DATE, a single work of about 140 pages, of which I do not
own a copy, seems to be the only other book exclusively devoted
to the hunting and shooting of woodchucks. Other books do contain
material on the woodchuck, but the present work has borrowed
from none of them. It contains a short, technical description of
the different varieties of North American woodchuck and their
habitat. Naturally, considerable space is devoted to woodchuck
rifles, cartridges, and rifle telescopes used in Canada and the
United States. It is in no sense a reloading book. Custom rifles
and commercial and wildcat cartridges and loads are discussed
by a wide variety of riflemen experienced in chuck hunting, many
of whom have not previously published anything on the subject.
These resourceful, skillful, and successful woodchuck hunters
present the most up-to-date data obtainable. In addition to the
above information, the book contains many detailed descriptions
of actual chuck-shooting experiences.

Woodchuck hunting has hundreds of thousands of devotees.
One state alone, and not the best chuck state by any means, recorded the bagging of more than 259,000 woodchucks in 1948 and
265,000 in 1949. In 1949 the same state recorded a total bag of
only 5181 quail, 36,304 ruffed grouse, 59,103 wildfowl, and 6885
turkeys. This is less than one-tenth of the annual kill of the first
two species in the same state fifteen to twenty years ago. The
total bags suggest either that game protection in this area has
been a failure in spite of the immense sums spent in the effort
to improve field shooting, or that previous estimates and counts
were indefensibly exaggerated.

In any event, we can be thankful for the relative abundance
of woodchucks. The sport of hunting them should continue to gain
in popularity for many years to come unless the landowning public becomes so abnormally selfish that they will not let anyone
hunt on their property. Most state game lands and public shoot-

ing grounds are on cut-over mountain areas in which, for perfectly obvious reasons, there are very few woodchucks. Their food does not grow there. Chucks are animals of hay fields, grown-up ravines, briar patches in fields, and pasture fields. It is there you will find them and it is there you must hunt them. Occasionally they inhabit rocky narrows. But these are usually flanked by fields on one side.

There is considerable debate over whether or not the flesh of the woodchuck is a tasty, tender, and suitable food. Some sportsmen think it is. I have attended two official woodchuck banquets. We had roast woodchuck in abundance — selected young chucks kept in cold storage — as well as roast turkey for those who wished to compare the two. Each time four or five out of a dozen or so guests definitely preferred the woodchuck. I had two splendid dinners, but mine were mostly turkey. There are few things I like better than woodchuck rifles and woodchuck shooting, but with me it stops right there!

In these pages you will find information about a goodly number of woodchuck cartridges which either have been designed (and rifles chambered) between 1946 and 1950, or have not as yet been widely advertised to the public. Many of them, I feel, have a great deal of merit. This new data concerns cases from the .170 Parkinson and the .70 Landis Woodsman to the three .25 caliber Donaldson bench-rest and woodchuck cartridges, with a trifle about a few that are still larger. It is quite likely that you have never heard of some of these cases and hence know nothing of their characteristics.

This is a practical, not a theoretical book. The results discussed are based on the shooting of thousands of woodchucks. I have seen as many as 500 to 600 woodchucks on one hunting trip, and our party has bagged 350 or more of them. Some of the contributors to this book have found even more woodchucks — or have hunted a greater number of times per year so that their bags were larger. Out of this wide range of experience comes the lore and advice contained in these pages — how, when, where and with what tools a rifleman shoots woodchucks.

Here's to Marmota Monax, then, and his whole clan. You will find him the same courageous and interesting animal that we have hunted in every locality, a grand little long-range target.

C. S. Landis,
Wilmington, Delaware

March, 1951

CHAPTER 1

The Woodchuck *

MOST of the sub-species of woodchucks differ slightly in size, but primarily in coloring and tints. The size is regulated by the abundance of food and the length of the feeding season, which is the year minus the total length of one or more hibernating periods. During hibernation the bodily functions of the chuck cease or are reduced to a very low level. The heartbeat goes down to a very low figure and the breathing to as little as once or twice in two minutes. No food passes the mouth or the anus, and for from two to six months the woodchuck is asleep or dormant. It remains so until the demands of nature, need for food intake, the arrival of the mating season, or a rise in temperature arouses him.

The woodchuck is a ground hog or marmot — in fact, it is a large, fat, ruggedly built squirrel as well. It has a heavy-set body, the general lines of which follow rather closely those of an alderman who has been on the public payroll for ten to twenty years. When aroused and irritated, it will fight viciously and will do in the average dog which may attack it. The woodchuck's head is broad and short and the brain cavity is small, although very well protected by the bones of the skull. The brain pan is slightly longer than high or wide, and because of its size requires the use of a very accurate rifle for uniform hits on that spot. The skull can be fractured completely and regularly by the .22 long-rifle, high-velocity, hollow-point bullet at distances of 100 to 125 yards and even more, and by any other more powerful cartridge at greater ranges.

---

*The author has been very graciously permitted to quote extensively in this chapter from The Field Book of North American Mammals by Harold E. Anthony, Chairman, American Museum of Natural History, New York City, and in turn, Mr. Anthony was materially indebted to Howell's Monograph on the species.

1

THE DISTRIBUTION OF THE SUB-SPECIES
OF MARMOTA MONAX

1. Marmota Monax Ochracea
2. Marmota Monax Petrensis
3. Marmota Monax Canadensis
4. Marmota Monax Ignava
5. Marmota Monax Rufescens
6. Marmota Monax Preblorum
7. Marmota Monax Monax

In this layout Mr. Howell took a map of Canada and the United States and, beginning on the left or west side, numbered the sub-species as above.

No. 1. Monax Ochracea inhabits a rather long, narrow area along the mountains of the west coast of British Columbia and southern Alaska. This woodchuck has a longer and narrower skull than the main variety of northern Canadian woodchuck. The color is tawny below and ochreous above. It is found most frequently in the interior mountain ranges of Yukon Territory and northern British Columbia from Fortymile Creek south to the Babine Mountains and Stuart Lake. This species seems to range mostly or possibly altogether westward from the Alaskan Highway.

No. 2. Marmota Monax Petrensis is the British Columbia woodchuck. This chuck also inhabits only a narrow area. It is found in the Interior ranges of southern British Columbia from Barkerville, south to Thompson Pass, Idaho, and through the extreme northwestern end of Montana. Its skull is larger and longer than the ordinary northern Canadian woodchuck, Monax Canadensis.

No. 3. Marmota Monax Canadensis inhabits a wide strip clear across the northern United States and southern Canada. The lower part of the strip extends from Newfoundland through the whole of the upper portion of Maine and a very narrow strip of northern New Hampshire and Vermont; it goes across the extreme northern part of New York State, westward to the upper shores of Lake Huron, then southward across the upper peninsula of Michigan and the upper part of Wisconsin and Minnesota, and then upward and northwestward across the provinces of Manitoba, Saskatchewan, Alberta, and northeastern British Columbia, plus a small bit of southern Yukon Territory. If there are any considerable number of woodchucks along the Alaskan Highway, they would belong to this variety.

The upper part of the strip starts at the Gaspe Peninsula at the mouth of the St. Lawrence and thence runs northwestward to the lower tip of Hudson Bay. Then the area extends westward along the southern shore of Hudson Bay to about the location of Fort Churchill, cuts southward and westward and then northwestward to Yukon Territory, takes in a small part of that, and then runs out close to the Pacific coast. This is much the largest area inhabited by any species of woodchuck in North America. Howell notes that this species is rather small, with a total length of 20 inches for both sexes. The coloring is strongly reddish above and below. Oddly, enough, in the thirty-four years during which I have been Gun Editor of the principal Canadian sporting magazine, Rod & Gun, practically none of my correspondents living in this chuck area ever said they were woodchuck hunters or that they had been shooting woodchucks; nor do I know of any friends from southern Ontario who went up that far to hunt woodchucks. Most of this area is essentially moose and bear country with numbers of deer here and there. It is quite likely that bears, foxes, wolverines, and possible lynx, wolves, and coyotes prey on these small northern chucks, particularly the young.

No. 4. Marmota Monax Ignava inhabits the southeastern extremity or tip of Labrador and the extreme eastern edge of Quebec out by the Atlantic Ocean. It is not an important subspecies, though oddly enough it is a trifle larger than the other smaller northern Canadian chucks. It has a broad nose and is reddish in color. Not many get to hunt this chuck because few persons live in the region.

No. 5. Marmota Monax Rufescens is the most important and the most common species of the woodchuck. It has a range which extends westward from the Hudson River and the Catskills in eastern New York State, approximately along the New York-Pennsylvania boundary, to the eastern tip of Lake Erie. Its southern range thence extends westward along the north shore of Lake Erie and across Michigan to a point about 75 miles above Chicago. From there it goes northwestward across Wisconsin, Minnesota, and for a short distance into North Dakota. On the northern side it curves west from about Troy, New York, mostly south of the Adirondacks, over across the northern portion of southern Ontario to the southern tip of Georgian Bay, takes in the Bruce Peninsula, all of the southern peninsula of Michigan, and then extends westward as mentioned in a strip 100 to 150 miles wide.

It includes the two most important woodchuck shooting areas in North America — New York State and southern Ontario. Chucks are there, even today, in greater numbers than anywhere else I know. A few of this species are also found in the higher country in western Massachusetts and on Long Island.

This chuck is reddish or reddish brown; rather frequent specimens are black on the outside of the legs and up onto the back, and a few are a solid mahogany color all over, or even coal black. In southern Ontario the young usually come out above ground during the last week of May. Not many of the adult chucks weigh more than 8 to 9-1/2 pounds, especially in the spring. I have never seen a gray woodchuck in Ontario and never shot a gray one there.

In the northern part of southern Ontario, these chucks were reported to me as habitually sitting insolently on the tops of immense stone piles, where they provided excellent targets. While I killed a few on such lookouts, most of the chucks were in flatter lands, sitting in patches of Canadian thistle, or feeding on the meadow lands and in the hay fields, or moving about their dens in the sides of the escarpment, from which they did not venture very far.

The richer parts of southern Ontario are flat farming country very much like Lancaster County, Pennsylvania. The chucks prefer the little hills and banks and thistle patches in the ravines of this country which is largely devoted to dairying, horse raising, and the growing of hay and mixed grains. (These last are oats and barley sowed together indiscriminately and growing densely to a height of 5 to 5-1/2 feet.)

The Ontario Department of Lands and Forests has had a drive on for the past two or three years to keep their own Canadian hunters out of the fields in summer. The Department claims that summer gunners shoot a good deal of game out of season. In 1948 only about 10 per cent as many woodchuck licenses were issued locally, as usual, so dealers told me. The idea was laudatory, but I do not feel the condemnation of the local men justified. I was there that summer and traveled 2500 to 3000 miles or more. We very rarely jumped a cottontail rabbit or a pheasant in the fields, and I saw but six or seven deer in the chuck

The woodchuck. CREDIT: HAL HARRISON FROM NATIONAL AUDUBON SOCIETY.

Whistling marmot in Yellowstone Park. CREDIT: EDNA MASLOWSKI FROM NATIONAL AUDUBON SOCIETY.

Eastern woodchuck found in woods and fields. CREDIT: HUGH M. HALLIDAY FROM NATIONAL AUDUBON SOCIETY.

districts. I saw no other organized chuck hunting parties whatever — only one to three boys a week, out with a .22, and never
did I see them with or shooting game. Nor did anyone else in
our parties do so. No one can shoot what they don't see.

At this writing, spring of 1951, special woodchuck licenses
are not being issued to tourists from the United States, on the
assumption that tourists would shoot everything they saw, regardless. Granted that during Prohibition thousands of our citi-
zens went up there for a two-weeks' drunk and thus gave us a
frightful reputation, most of our hunters are not that sort, and
certainly not the woodchuck hunters. If a man respects the game
laws at home, he'll be even more careful on a visit.

I have obtained my occasional woodchuck licenses through
the courtesy of friends and because the Department was interested in the design and production of woodchuck cartridges
which would not ricochet — a very important characteristic in
their flat dairy and horse-raising and cattle country. Also because I was interested in collecting information on unusual coloring in woodchucks and in scientific matters generally.

Do not write up and ask for a woodchuck license just now.
You won't get it until the ban is raised. In my opinion it would
be better to permit limited chuck-hunting licenses and to refuse
to issue small.game-hunting licenses to Americans in the areas
south and east of Lake Huron, in Ontario, for two or three years.
This would cut down the drain on their limited small game supply in the area. Some townships now require special licenses or
permits and that is developing into a racket rather than a game-
saving measure. Their chuck licenses expire about August 25,
as Ontario chucks hole up early. Spring starts late and summer
ends quickly. Then it is cold.

If you happen to find the right areas in central New York
State, Vermont, New Hampshire, or central Massachusetts or
Connecticut, you should be able to do quite well and have two
additional days to hunt.

There are reasonable numbers of Marmota Monax Rufescens in some parts of southwestern Wisconsin and Minnesota,
probably fewer in southern Michigan. I have had few correspondents out there who are chuck hunters.

No. 6. Marmota Monax Preblorum is found all over southern New England from Connecticut to southern Maine. There
are very few woodchucks in Maine these days. Samuel Clark,

Jr., confirmed this and also noted that most of the fields were small and would have provided little long-range chuck shooting had there been chucks in numbers.

Marmota Monax Preblorum is of an intermediate color and smaller than most other woodchucks. The land he grazes on is often poor land from which most of the topsoil has been washed. Clover crops are therefore poor and short. New England chucks are quite often found in flat meadows along streams, where hay is raised or pastures are common. A great deal more has been written about New England chuck shooting than the number of chucks still left warrants.

A New England field with sparse soil, covered with boulders and field stone and dotted here and there with chuck holes, is a discouraging thing to try to cultivate. But the chuck is patient. As soon as the farmer's back is turned, he holes up along the fence line stone pile and comes out to feed on the clover or whatever when the field is vacant. After his meal he may sun himself up on the stone fence. This is likely to be the pattern in central or western Massachusetts or in central or western Connecticut, back from the highways and the railroads. In northeastern Massachusetts, between Springfield and Worcester, and closer to Worcester, I have seen miles of country which is mostly short, worthless bush and small swamps containing a few inches to a foot of water. Much of it is rocky and there is considerable slate. Until I rode a slow passenger train across it, I had no idea there was so much completely worthless farm country in that area. It is simply so lacking in clover and other foods for chucks that the proportion of the area worthwhile traversing for woodchucks is negligible. On the higher knobs you will now and then see an old chuck den, but you can cross most of that part of the state off your hunting area. Even crows avoid it!

The proportion of varmint hunters and woodchuck rifle cranks in New England is quite high. This tends to thin down the existing chuck breeding supply, as a good rifle shot with the proper scope-sighted outfit will kill ten times as many chucks in a week of shooting as the average boy with a light .22 will bag in a season. What's more, he will kill a lot of the old timers who have waxed smart and watchful and who know to slide off the mound and go below before the boy arrives sufficiently close to start hostilities. On the other hand, the general terrain, climate, and food supply is such that Monax Preblorum will survive in sufficient remaining supply so that the naturalists' maps will be but little changed and persistent chuck hunters with a car will still bag a few now and then.

No. 7. Marmota Monax Monax is the southern woodchuck. The species has the longest feeding season of any and consequently often becomes quite large and heavy. When you bag a big old sow with pigs of about a pound (or maybe she is carrying a second litter), you'll pick up what at first, because of her size and weight, you may think is a bear cub or a black raccoon. Marmota Monax Monax is widely distributed and is a most important species. On the north, draw a line from Newark, New Jersey, westward to Erie, Pennsylvania, thence along south of Lake Erie to Sandusky, Ohio, and jump over to a point 50 to 75 miles above Chicago. Forget the lake and keep on going slightly northwest until you arrive almost the whole way across Iowa, then turn due south until you hit the large river which runs eastward across the state of Oklahoma, meanwhile crossing the eastern edge of Kansas, and then turn due east and swing northward as you go to the junction of the Ohio River with the Mississippi. Cut southeastward from there down through Tennessee well into Alabama; next, cut northeast so as to include the hilly part of Georgia and Tennessee. Include just the northwestern tip of South Carolina. (You won't get over nearly as far as Henry Davis' wild turkey swamps, which will probably please Henry because too much banging around with chuck rifles would chase those hermit gobblers right out of the ridges down into the swamps.)

Then go just east of the mountain ranges in North Carolina, northeastward through Virginia, including all of the central part of it, the Shenandoah Valley and all its surrounding hills and mountain ranges on the west, on until you strike the Atlantic coast and up to Newark, New Jersey, again. You have included all of Kentucky, West Virginia, Maryland, and theoretically, you have also included all of Delaware (there are few chucks south of the Delaware Canal). The hilly chuck country of New Castle County is now nearly all included in large estates which are posted against hunting. Many of them are patrolled by mounted, armed guards whose duty is to keep out the whole public. The hunt-club foxes eat up the pheasants, rabbits, and woodchucks which in most instances were formerly available to registered hunters. You can't have much small game, including chucks, when too many foxes are roaming the hills.

About fifteen years ago, there was a considerable migration of woodchucks down through central Pennsylvania into Dauphin, York, and Cumberland Counties. When I lived in Dauphin County and hunted in all three of these counties, woodchucks were a rarity. Our rifle game were gray squirrels, crows, and hawks, also geese and ducks on the river.

You will often find a southern chuck out as late as mid-October or even early November, if the day is warm. By that time the chucks are mostly gray in color and quite large and heavy. They have a length of 27 inches or more, of which 6 inches is tail vertebrae. The hind foot may be 3 to 3-1/2 inches in length. Southern chucks are often very determined and fearless when they are digging in or cleaning out their dens. I recall an occasion when I was hunting chucks about 20 miles below Wilmington. I was walking along a fence line surrounding a private race track. It was a sunny afternoon and no less than three woodchucks, sterns outward, in three different dens close together, were vigorously throwing dirt out of their holes. It came shooting out like a widely spread charge of shot. I walked right along toward them, close to the fence, stepping as quietly as possible, and so intent were the chucks on their engineering that the dirt kept on coming until I was almost on top of them. They were all then too close, and not in position either, for a Hornet bullet.

ENEMIES

Hunters kill a lot of chucks. Hoses strung from the exhausts of cars and tractors probably destroy more of them than any other type of varmint. Powerful and vicious dogs, as well as hounds, will kill woodchucks regularly. So will gray and red foxes, white foxes, gray and black wolves, coyotes (upon occasion), wolverines, large hawks and owls, and eagles (which are nearly all destructive in spite of the ballyhoo to the contrary). Bears of all sorts in North America feed off chucks and whistling marmots. In the north, chucks provide a supply of fresh meat the bears can readily dig out and eat.

Yet in spite of man, bird, and beast, the woodchuck continues to hold his own in easily found groups or individual dens over most of its range. The adult woodchuck is an unsociable and extremely scrappy householder when annoyed by an intruder. He rarely lays out the welcome mat. The female bears a litter of from two to five and keeps them with her until they come above ground and sit out now and then. At that first appearance, they weigh from about 1/2 pound to around 1-1/2 pounds, depending upon the locality. I have seen the very small ones (they are quite helpless, by the way) only in Ontario.

Woodchuck hunters today pay hundreds of thousands, yes, millions of dollars for gunning licenses to hunt woodchucks. Yet practically none of it is spent for the benefit of the chuck hunters as chuck hunters. A very few localities may allot a special season for the sport, but no Game Commission attempts to destroy the vermin which preys on woodchucks because it preys on woodchucks. They receive any protection they get only because they dig dens which are used by ringnecked pheasants and cottontail rabbits as hiding places. Woodchuck hunters should band together and insist either that chuck hunting licenses be abolished or that the total returns from those licenses be applied solely to the protection of chucks — which primarily means killing the varmints which prey on them.

WINTER DENS AND SUMMER DENS

Chucks always have winter dens in the hillsides. These face east or southeast — never west, north, or northwest. If you find dens on such slopes, either they are not winter dens or else those chucks never listened to their mother's tales about the cold north winds which blow and blow. They also build special spring and summer dens which are always out in a clover patch, in a bottom, or in a swale on the rear side of a pasture where visitors seldom come and where the chuck can look forward to one to five months of steady, strength-sustaining, fat-producing, self-satisfying eating. During those months all they do is eat, play occasionally, and sleep contentedly. Sometimes you will find one that seems annoyed and watchful, or perhaps an old chap with an itchy foot who is just wandering around. Maybe he is on his way over to see Mabel on the opposite hill and has cut through a woods on the way. Mabel may not live there any more, but the chuck won't take anyone's word for it. He goes over to look for Mabel — and she better be home!

You will always find woodchuck runways in grass fields or those with ground blackberries. There is always a den at one end of this runway, and often at both. Don't step into them unexpectedly!

CHAPTER 2

Selection of a Rifle

TO BE a successful woodchuck hunter it is obvious that you should be equipped with a rifle that comes close to being the perfect woodchuck rifle. It should be equipped with a telescope sight of outstanding optical qualities and suitable power that is fitted with rigid and sufficiently coarse crosshairs, or a Lee Dot, which you can see quickly under most field conditions; and it should be slung in the very best available grade of detachable micrometer mounts proportioned to carry a scope of that tube diameter. In addition, the scope itself should be of a length, diameter, and weight which provides both convenience and shooting accuracy.

The cartridge should be chosen, not because some recognized rifle or chuck-hunting authority recommended it for woodchuck shooting, but because it is the ideal cartridge in range, accuracy, killing power, and report in those areas in which you will most frequently hunt woodchucks.

THE IDEAL WOODCHUCK RIFLE

The specifications of the ideal woodchuck rifle should depend upon the age, financial ability, physical strength, technical ability and background, walking experience, and the shooting skill of the woodchuck hunter who will use it. Omit any one of these, and you have overlooked a vital consideration in choosing a suitable rifle. It is also necessary to consider the manner in which the rifle itself must be transported from the home of the rifleman to the field. A rifle can be so light as to be a ridiculous choice; likewise it can be so unnecessarily heavy as to soon exhaust most men.

The weight and size of the rifle should also depend upon

10

what type of shooting will be done. The shooting may be prone, with sling, or prone using a woodchuck rest, made either with vertical rod to be pushed into the ground and the grooved rest block adjustable for height, or with such rest made with small tripod and adjustable legs, the grooved rest for cradling the rifle barrel being on top of the center of the tripod. All these methods of firing suggest a fairly heavy and stiff rifle barrel which may be anywhere from 24 to 30 inches long. Any of them are very successful in open, flat, farming or stock-raising country, on which the grass is quite short at the time. If the grass is long, you cannot see over it while lying down to fire. Also, you can not often fire successfully up or down a steep grade, or at a chuck on a bench much higher than yourself, from any sort of prone position. Your body must be more or less parallel to the slope between you and the woodchuck.

The weight, stock-drop, length, down-pitch, and trigger-pull are the important specifications along with perfect balance, when you have to shoot kneeling, squatting, and offhand — especially the latter. When firing across fence posts, fence rails, rocks, blown-down tree trunks, or alongside a post, a rigid rifle with a very clean, sharp trigger pull and not too much drop in the stock, so that your right cheek is not of necessity raised from the rifle stock while aiming and firing, is the ideal weapon.

Each of the firing positions mentioned above is a thoroughly practical shooting position when one is afield hunting chucks. To be a consistently good woodchuck shot year after year, a man must be able to fire accurately, quickly, and with proper aim and sight setting for each of these firing positions. You will be called upon to fire from each of them time after time. The most vital requirement for good rifle shooting on chucks is to be able to shoot at least reasonably well from all of the firing positions, especially offhand. Here you need a rifle of perfect stock fit and balance, with a short, sharp, crisp trigger-pull. The rifle should be sufficiently heavy to hold well, but not so weighty as to tire one.

A 15- or 20-pound bench-rest rifle, made with a thick, heavy grip and a rather massive stock for rigidity, will perform well from a car, but in hilly country in hot weather you will likely not feel like carrying it very far. An excessively short and light rifle, especially if it has a trigger-pull that feels like the uneven travel of a wagon over a mountain road, is unsuitable. Add a $10 or $15 telescope with fogged and dirty lenses, plus a tendency to flinch unexpectedly, and you will soon find yourself quite discouraged.

A man with a medium-weight, nicely finished rifle fitted with a high-grade medium-power scope should get satisfactory results.

There are a few musts to bear in mind: The proper sighting for prone shooting makes a rifle shoot a bit low when fired from the sitting position and very definitely too low when it is shot offhand. You must add more elevation. A rifle barrel rested against the right side of a tree will almost always group to the right, even at 50 to 100 yards, and this jump-out is normally one to three inches. When a right-handed man rests a rifle barrel against the left side of a tree trunk, the jump-out may be as much as twice the right side deflection, yet it is better to use the left side of a tree which is leaning materially to the right and allow for the jump-out.

A rifle barrel invariably jumps away from a solid object; the lighter the barrel and the sharper the recoil, the greater the deflection.

A woodchuck hunter will ofttimes have an opportunity to fire at a chuck out in a field when he is in the cover of a woods and can shoot across the top of a fence rail or a post. In that instance, he should always rest the back of his hand, rather than the rifle barrel, because if the barrel is rested, almost invariably the shot goes high, and with a light barrel and a high-intensity cartridge, the shot may go very high.

FIRING AT THE HEAD OF A WOODCHUCK AT CLOSE RANGE

When changing from iron sights to a telescope sight, one almost always raises the line of sight from half an inch to an inch or more, especially with target telescopes of large diameter riding in target-type micrometer mounts. One reason for using bobtailed mounts on chuck rifles is to keep down the size of the graduated mount thimbles.

At close range any rifle shoots lower than the line of sight by the distance between the line of the bore and the line of sight. As you will sight your chuck rifle to shoot to center at a distance of from 75 to 250 yards from the muzzle, depending upon the power of the cartridge and the flatness of its trajectory, naturally the rifle will shoot low at all the ranges between the muzzle and the target until the bullet rises to meet the line of sight.

Suppose a chuck suddenly sticks his head up when you are walking across a grass field or paralleling a fence row, and the distance is but 50 or 100 feet. Where must you aim to strike the chuck's brain?

If you are using iron sights, the line of sight is probably 5/8 to 1-1/4 inches above the bore. In that case aim about an inch above the butt of the ear.

If you are using a scope sight, it is much more confusing. Your line of sight is probably 1-1/2 to 1.65 inches above the line of the bore so that at the chuck the bullet will still be probably 1.3 inches low. Suppose we say it is 1-1/4 inches low. That seems simple until we remember that the rifle is fitted with a 6-power telescope, and that both the head of the chuck and everything around the chuck appear to be about six times normal size. Probably the chuck is so close that it takes up almost the whole field of the telescope. If you are using a 6- or 8-power scope. a fairly safe rule on a close shot is to aim about as far above the spot you want to strike as the apparent distance between the center of the eye and the center of the orifice of the ear.

The head of a chuck nearly always sticks out of a den mouth at an angle. If you happen to shoot at the chuck without remembering to aim high and without remembering that your scope enlarges the image of the chuck by the power of the scope, you will very likely drive your bullet under the chin or the throat of the woodchuck, and down he goes as if he has suddenly forgotten something.

With iron sights, nothing is exaggerated except the apparent difficulty of shooting the woodchuck. But with a scope sight this magnified hold-over is necessary, or in goes your woodchuck. Remember you never aim low on a close shot unless you are so foolish as to sight your rifle for 400 yards or some such distant range.

THE WOODCHUCK CARTRIDGE

The cartridge to use in your favorite woodchuck rifle should be a standard factory cartridge that you can buy in any good-sized sporting goods store — unless, of course, you want to reload. Among the more suitable commercial cartridges are the following:

Factory Loads

For Close-Range shooting
.22 Long Rifle, High Speed, Hollow Point
.22 Hornet
For Medium-Range Shooting
.22 Hornet
.218 Bee
.222 Remington (not as yet widely distributed)
.25-20
For Long-Range Shooting
.219 Zipper
.250-3000 Savage-Spire Point Bullet

Wildcat — or Hand-Loaded — Specially Designed Woodchuck Cartridges

For Medium-Range Shooting
.170 Landis Woodsman
.22 K-Hornet (in which .22 Hornet ammunition may also be used successfully)
R-2 Lovell (.22)
K-.222 Remington
.22-357 Magnum, Ramsey
.22 Chucker (either the rimmed or the rimless version)
.219 Donaldson
.219 Improved Zipper (in which factory .219 Zipper may be used)
For Medium- and Long-Range Shooting
.219 Improved Zipper
.219 Donaldson
.22-250 (or .22 Varminter)
.22 Marciante Blue Streak
.228 Ackley
Lovell's No. 7, No. 8, or No. 9 in .22 Caliber
.22-303 Varmint-R (either the G. B. Crandall or the slightly shorter Ray Weeks version)
.250 Donaldson Ace
.250 Donaldson
.250 Don-Helldiver

In my opinion, for 95 per cent of woodchuck shooting in the eastern United States or in Canada, a .22-caliber wildcat cartridge which uses more than 30 to 38 grains of powder is unnecessary and inadvisable. If it has a greater powder capacity, it gives a report of such volume and high pitch that its general use will eventually bring complaints from landowners, dairymen, farmers, ranchers, and the women of their households. It is much better to select a charge of low or medium report and continue shooting than to select a Super-Magnum and lose your shooting grounds.

There are a few other factory cartridges and a large number of .22, .236, .240, .25, 7 M.M., and .30-caliber wildcats which would give accurate and efficient results, but the list given above includes most of those in the widest use, for which swaged cases are easiest formed and for which bullets, reloading tools, and factory cases for re-sizing are available in the most states. These are the ones, too, which have produced the best accuracy. With Sisk, Sierra, or other custom bullets, or with R.C.B.S. bullets made at home by the shooter himself, they are deadly and effective in the field.

The cartridge chosen for a custom-built rifle, whether factory cartridge or band-swaged wildcat (this latter also includes those wildcats made by firing a factory charge in an enlarged or "improved" chamber), must be of such shape (rimmed or rimless) and of such diameter of head, and have a case of such length that the existing bolt can be made to handle it and the magazine will receive the loaded cartridges. Otherwise, you'll have to use a bolt-action single-shot rifle.

Years ago, woodchuck cartridges were chosen for characteristics placed in the following sequence: (1) accuracy, (2) killing power, (3) flatness of trajectory, and (4) report. That was in the days of the .32-40, .25-21, .25-25, .28-30 Stevens and similar cartridges. Since then, such cartridges have gone through a number of evolutions.

Today we have two general conditions:

The thickly settled locality. There cartridges should be chosen for the following characteristics in this order: (1) low report, (2) accuracy, (3) flatness of trajectory, and (4) killing power.

The thinly settled locality. Probably quite hilly and containing a high percentage of worked-out, eroded, and abandoned farms. You can let a fellow loose in such an area with a .375 Holland & Holland Super-Magnum, necked to .236, a peck of 120-grain bullets and a keg of .50-caliber machine-gun powder (which is of the same chemical composition but of larger grain than the .30-2906 military rifle powder), and when he adjusts the 24-power telescope with 2-1/2-inch lenses on his 26-pound piece of ordnance and lets her loose, it won't make a bit of difference unless he shoots closer than the legal distance to the closely shuttered house of the two maiden ladies who keep a goat and 14 cats.

Unless you use a very low-report rifle and fire it only very occasionally and not closer than 300 yards to farm buildings or restless stock, you are not going to be allowed to shoot long on any farm today. Public opinion has changed in these matters. You've simply got to stay away off from whatever the farmer prizes.

THOSE 400- TO 800-YARD SHOTS AT CHUCKS

Another quick way to get yourself heaved off your favorite woodchuck grounds is to listen to the A.R. ballyhoo about the California or Colorado rock-chuck hunters who go out in gangs and shoot at every chuck they see at 450, 800 or even 1000 yards, and keep it up until someone claims he has hit one. Then they all go over to look.

Almost as soon as you started to shoot, ungodly long .22- and .25-caliber bullets would go whining over into the next township, and by the time you arrived at the spot where you claimed you had killed a woodchuck, you'd find a greeting committee consisting of four farmers, six state police, three state cars, a patrol wagon, and two ambulances in waiting. And everyone there would be in a fighting mood. The first thing they would do would be take your rifle, ammunition, and scope away from you and then two burly farmers and three cops would grab you by the coat collar and the seat of your pants and throw you into the back of the patrol wagon. . . . No, you just can't get away with that kind of Rocky Mountain rock-chuck hilarity here in the East. It isn't being done even in the worst circles. Even Parker Ackley couldn't get away with it!

Three miles back of beyond is the only place you can try out your ear-splitting, long-range woodchuck rifle. A few woodchucks still live there, but only the Creator knows how. Anyway, a ricochet simply thuds into yonder hill. You can test your rifle on granite, schist, limestone, sandstone, steel plates, stumps, or woodchucks; but I am inclined to agree with one of my friends who maintains that woodchucks get so discouraged trying to eke

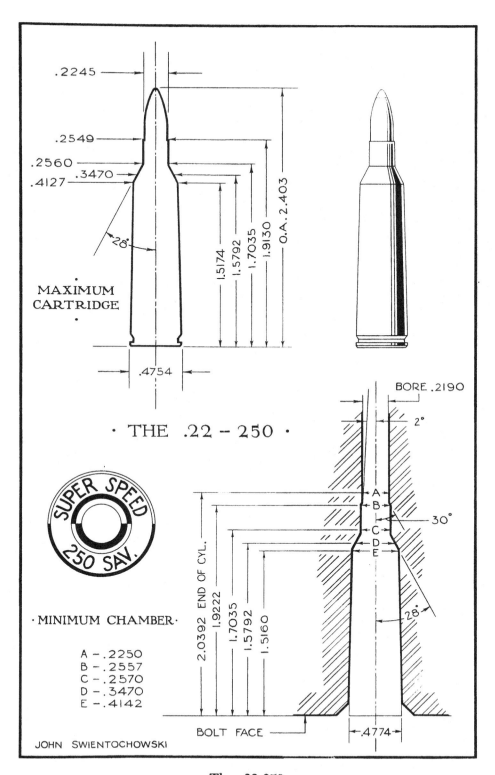

.2245

.2549

.2560
.4127 .3470

28°

MAXIMUM
CARTRIDGE

1.5174
1.5792
1.7035
1.9130
O.A. 2.403

.4754

· THE .22 – 250 ·

SUPER SPEED
250 SAV.

·MINIMUM CHAMBER·

A – .2250
B – .2557
C – .2570
D – .3470
E – .4142

JOHN SWIENTOCHOWSKI

BORE .2190

2°

A
B
C
D
E

30°

28°

2.0392 END OF CYL.
1.9222
1.7035
1.5792
1.5160

BOLT FACE

.4774

The .22-250.

The 200-yard firing line at Johnstown, N. Y., annual bench rest matches.

Outdoor reloading beneath the trees.

Edgar L. Warner and R. G. (Bob) Owen of Port Clinton, Ohio—expert woodchuck rifle stockers.

out a living from three small clumps of clover on four acres of stony land that they just don't care any longer, and that if a hunter comes toiling up the hill bearing an 18-pound bench-rest rifle, with his heart pounding up in his throat and his knees wobbling, those chucks simply sit there with their front paws hanging listlessly down on their chests and dare him to shoot. What do they have to lose? There's not another morsel of clover! How the two Wood brothers (who have some very interesting and helpful advice further along in this book) ever found 2100 woodchucks in such places, I don't know. But they did sound this note of warning that even in the back districts of central New York state where the land is often poor, if you hunt where there are hedges or grown-up fence rows behind which such cattle as are there have a habit of lying down and now and then sticking up a head or a rump so that you think you see a 14-pound chuck sitting back on a rock of that fence, and you let drive, there could be trouble. This 400- to 500-yard chuck shooting sooner or later poses the question: What is that over there on the dip in the field? Well, the hired man may have gone down behind that fence line and is just now arising and adjusting his belt. He is wearing an old felt hat pulled down over his face, he hasn't shaved recently, and his whiskers are red. A hunter should always look through his scope at least three times to be certain it is a woodchuck he is shooting at.

STYLES AND CALIBERS

Let's examine several styles and calibers of woodchuck rifles which, possibly with a few small modifications, might suit you perfectly.

My own rifle is a very lovely .22-250 woodchuck rifle which might be described as a .22-250 Springfield-Pfeifer-Bob Owen-Edgar Warner-John Unertl-Wurzer-Peterson job. That traces it back practically to the head of one of the topmost Scottish clans.

This rifle was actually conceived and the idea born one evening after I walked into a hut on Commercial Row at Camp Perry, about 1922, where Bob Owen, then of Sauquoit, New York (in the woodchuck country), had on display a .30-1906 Springfield Sporter which had been made up for Charles Nash, President of Nash Motors. The metal work on this rifle had been done by R. S. Risley. The rifle had been stocked by Bob Owen

with a piece of imported walnut that had the most beautiful pro-
portions and figure I have ever seen in a rifle stock. It was a
rich combination of reds and blacks with some streaks of gold-
en sunlight. The brilliant reds and deep blacks predominated,
while the grain was simply superb. I've never in my life seen a
rifle I wanted as badly as that rifle. The elaborate engraving
had been done, I believe, by Kornbrath of Hartford, Connecticut
who did equally well on a 10-inch S & W of mine (which Harold
Croft, the arms collector, has pronounced the handsomest pistol he has ever seen).

I have never forgotten that Risley-Owen-Hornbrath-Spring-
field rifle. Now I have one which is nearly the equal, except that
it is not engraved. It happens to resemble to a considerable degree the design of the better-grade Holland & Holland Mauser
sporting rifles. When a man once comes into possession of one
of these Hollands, he rarely sells it. It is like possessing a farm
which contains the richest land, the most desirable location, and
the handsomest trees in the valley. Something like that should
not go out of the family. It cannot be replaced. There is only one
precisely like it, and he who owns it is king.

SPECIFICATIONS OF THE .22-250 SPRINGFIELD

This .22-250 bolt-action has a handsomely tapered 26-inch
barrel, 1-1/4 inches in diameter at the breech, slightly swelled
from a true taper forward to a point about where the tip of the
bullet lies in the chamber, and then tapering evenly forward to
the muzzle which is 0.70 inches in diameter. The 26-inch barrel
and the Springfield long action put the muzzle blast out ahead of
one's ears. The muzzle is cut off square, is recessed, but is
not crowned. Pfeifer put the scope blocks 7-1/4 inches between
centers — a placement impossible for a man of my build to use.
In theory this gives a 1/4-inch movement at 100 yards for each
click of a target scope mount, but that is worthless if, when you
try to aim through the scope, the front mount is 1-1/4 inches
too far forward for prone shooting and almost 3 inches too far
forward for offhand. With such mount base attachment, a short,
broad, huskily built man can't use the rifle at all, because he
finds it impossible to see through the telescope even from the
prone position, much less from the offhand. Only an abnormally
tall man with long arms and fingers could use a rifle so set up,
prone. I wear a 16-1/2 to 16-3/4 collar, and a 32-inch sleeve,

and I have a moderate-size hand. I have a long body, but not long legs, neck, or arms. The tube length and focal length of a scope determine where it must be placed so that you can see best through it. I went up to see Martin Wurzer, the noted gunsmith of Philadelphia, Pennsylvania. We took the barrel and action out of the stock and put new scope base blocks on the barrel where they should have been — 6 inches ahead of the rear mount (on the receiver) for prone, another 4-3/8 inches ahead of the rear mount for offhand. We found my rifle stock well fitted in recoil shoulder and around the action, but the forearm, while lovely outside, was rough beneath the barrel, the result of rushing the job to get it to me quickly. The checkering was tops.

At Murta, Appleton & Co. in Philadelphia, Ed Flood, the manager of the gun department, and Harold Croft, the arms collector, who happened to be there, were especially pleased with the stocking job on my .22-250; and neither in that store nor in Wurzer & Peterson's place, with lots of rifles in for repair, did I see any rifle as handsomely stocked as mine.

So the big 8X Unertl varmint scope is now in target mounts on the rifle on the offhand bases, bore-sighted and ready for Canada. The rear end of this big scope should be just above the front end of the comb to be in perfect focus for a man of my build. If you ever take a scope-sighted rifle on a long trip for squirrels and chucks or either, and when you get there, find you cannot use the scope offhand because it is mounted on the prone bases, you'll be very certain you will never again go on a hunting trip with any short- or medium-length scope on your rifle which is not slung in target mounts placed definitely on the offhand bases you had put on the barrel, or barrel and receiver, to fit you exactly. And, so help you, you won't let anyone else go into the woods with a scope sight a good 2 inches too far in front of his face. To heck with the theory that your base centers should be exactly 7-1/4 inches apart. Those bases should be such a distance apart and ahead of the center of the butt—such a distance to each of them — that when the scope is on those bases, on the rifle, and you are ready to shoot, and have something to fire at, your scope will be in perfect focus for your eyes.

With scopes of short barrel, but different focal lengths, when the rear mount is placed about 20 inches ahead of the center of the butt, the front mount base 6 inches ahead of that, or 26 inches ahead of the butt, for prone; and 23-7/8 to 24-3/8 inches ahead of it, for offhand, then you have the proper placement for a man with a 32- or 33-inch sleeve length and not much neck, who keeps the butt of the rifle well in on the shoulder when aiming (which is where it should be). A gunsmith who turns out a rifle with the scope bases mounted to suit only a very long-armed and giraffe-necked rifleman and ships it to a man he knows, or has been told, is the opposite in build, uses the same logic which has always cursed the New England rifle and shotgun builders who have never turned out a standard model rifle or shotgun that will fit the average huskily built Pennsylvanian, for instance; yet 12 per cent or more of their gun business is in Pennsylvania.

There has been entirely too much gun and rifle designing in this country to suit and to fit the people who built the guns and rifles, instead of to fit the people they were making them for. Gun builders should forget the advantages of the 7-1/4-inch sighting placement. A turtle can retract its neck or shoot it forward to grab an insect. But the woodchuck shooter cannot change the length of his neck.

So that chuck hunters may get their scope sight bases mounted in the proper positions in relation to the center of the butt plate and the center of the trigger, I list this data:

For a man with a very long neck, 34- to 35-inch sleeve length, rifle fitted with stock having 13-1/4-inch trigger to butt measurement. For 13-1/2- or 13-3/4-inch stock, bring back forward bases 1/4 to 1/2 inch.

Distance center front base to center butt plate	Distance middle base from center butt plate	Distance rear mount base from center butt	Butt plate to center trigger
27 to 27-1/2 inches	25 to 25-1/4 inches	20-1/4 inches	13-1/4 inches

For a man with a very short neck, 32- or 33-inch sleeve length using 13-inch stock, these dimensions are correct. For 12-inch stock length, move forward the two forward bases, each 1/4 inch. For 13-1/4-inch stock, move them back each 1/4 inch.

Same headings as above:

26 inches	23-7/8 to 24-3/8 inches	20 inches	13 inches

You can always push your scope forward in the mounts, but you cannot bring it back more than the distance to the stop on the scope. If you have the scope mounted on the offhand bases and want to fire prone, using the same bases, and find this brings the scope too close to the eye, simply slide the scope forward 2 inches or whatever distance is required. For frequent prone shooting in the field, better have the front mount on the front base and resight the rifle.

These placement distances will be approximately correct for scope mounting on Springfield, 1917 Enfield, Winchester Models 54 and 70, Remington Models 30-S and 721. For rifles like Winchester Model 43, Remington Model 722, and Mausers with short bolt actions converted to woodchuck or varmint rifles, the bases will have to be placed forward a distance equal to the difference in length between the above long actions and the short ones. Also, any difference in stock length must be allowed for. This can readily be adjusted by fitting the scope on top of the barrel or barrel and receiver and holding it on with encircling rubber bands or string, then pushing the scope forward and backward until it is in exactly the right position for proper focus to the shooting eye. Then attach the bases to the rifle barrel.

This .22-250 Springfield sporter is 46 inches long, can be carried in a long canvas case, and is not a take-down. None of the military bolt actions are. Without iron sights, but with scope blocks, the rifle weighs 9-1/2 pounds. A rifle with a 23- or 24-inch barrel (0.70 inches at the muzzle) would weigh 9 pounds, if similarly stocked. The large Unertl 8X varmint scope I use on it (which sells for $75) weighs 1-1/4 pounds in use, and 1-1/2 pounds with its steel caps in place. This makes an outfit of 11 pounds in action and without sling. (I rarely use a sling on a chuck rifle because it is such a nuisance in offhand shooting. The sling swings beneath the rifle, as it is raised, and that interferes with aiming.)

Now I could reduce the weight of this rifle — in the field, for carrying on a train, or on long trips to Ontario — by using my lighter-weight 5-1/2X Fecker-Unertl scope, or my still lighter K-6 Weaver (the latter in its mounts and bases only — not on the Unertl scope bases); but the big 8X Unertl contains wonderfully good lenses. There is no more comparison between such a glass and the $9 to $30 scopes on the market than there is between the scope on a finest grade civil engineer's wye level and that on a cheap transit.

My rifle, as I mentioned, when fitted with its heavy scope, weighs 11 pounds. Imagine the weight of a heavy-barrel varmint rifle on a Springfield or Enfield action, or a military Mauser, if the barrel is 26 inches long and is made 7/8 inch (0.875 inch) at the muzzle, or is made a bull barrel and is left 1 to 1-1/4 inches at the muzzle. Lead the butt properly to balance the rifle, and you immediately have a gun which feels almost twice as heavy as an 11-pound rifle.

The weight of a man's rifle should always be governed by his physique, and by his known physical weaknesses. I doubt if any class of men carry as excessively and unnecessarily heavy rifles as do woodchuck hunters. Chuck shooting is a sport splendidly adapted to most men physically handicapped, but they should not overdo the weight of the rifle or telescope. They should sit still and still hunt as much as possible. Men who should avoid physical strain would be wise to use a rifle weighing not over 9 pounds complete, and let someone else or the car carry the rifle as much as possible. One of the best rifle and scope outfits to use afield is the Winchester Model 43 rifle fitted with Weaver 6X scope. The total weight is about 7 pounds.

The whole bolt action of the .22-250 rifle was worked in the white, by Wurzer & Peterson, and finished by Joe Pfeifer. Originally it was one of the roughest war actions I've ever seen, but no other Springfield action was available. Pfeifer damaskeened the whole bolt action, finished the bolt handle and chrome plated it, blued the barrel after turning to size, and blued the receiver. He fitted this rifle with a Carmer speed action and this was then also completely damaskeened. A special short striker was included and the action produced a short and sharp trigger pull when carefully adjusted. The arm contained the usual Springfield safety.

You've heard of Bob Owen, one of the top-flight custom stockers. For three years Bob had a younger understudy in Port Clinton, a man originally a die sinker, which Bob says is a splendid background for a top-flight stocker. This man is Edgar L. Warner, of Warner's Sales & Service, in Port Clinton, and both say he did all the work on my stock after receiving Owen's suggestions. Two blanks were obtained from England three years ago, sent out to Bob for a selection. The finished stock of my rifle deserves special mention and praise because of the design these two stockers used, and the good fitting of the wood along barrel and receiver. The front end of the black bakelite tip on the fore-end is 18-3/4 inches ahead of the trigger. I believe it is the rule or custom to lengthen the forearm one inch for each

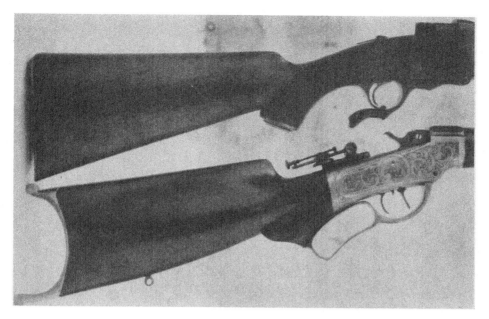

Top: Farquharson single shot, falling block, **English** action by Holland and Holland. *Bottom:* Ballard single **shot,** .25-20 caliber.
CREDIT: ELMER MC CONNELL. RIFLES FROM HIS COLLECTION.

Mauser Sporter chuck rifle with Monte Carlo P. G. **stock,** Damaskeened bolt, and Weaver scope.

Pfeifer model chuck rifle. Note well-fitting cheek piece, well-checkered stock, and long forearm.

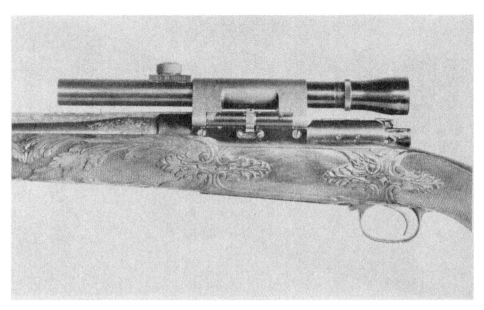

Pachmayr carved stock on a bolt action sporter.

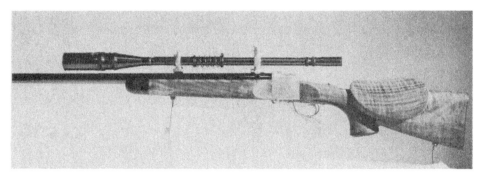

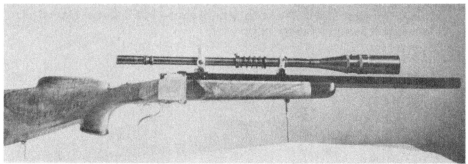

Left and right sides of the Bland Farquharson .270 falling block single shot varmint rifle. Note high cheek piece. CREDIT: PAUL E. WOLFE.

two inches of increase in barrel length, and to shorten it an inch for each two inches of reduction in length. A forearm can be too long or too short to be symmetrical with the remainder of the arm.

The forearm, about 6 inches in front of the breech of the rifle, measures 1-3/4 inches wide and 1-5/8 inches in depth. The wood of the stock is exactly 2 inches thick, through the receiver, and the wood itself has a thickness of 0.30 inch on each side of the receiver steel. This thickness is extremely important for producing accurate and uniform shooting. If the stock does not have sufficient thickness and strength where it cradles the steel of the receiver it will spring vertically on some shots and not on all, and you may have a rifle that shoots the first shot over the chuck, the second shot under the chuck, and the third shot may hit him somewhere but not where you had intended. A chuck shot where you did not intend, is generally quite badly mussed up inside, may make quite a fuss over it, and goes underground and sobs to himself. Then you feel like a heel, too. Above everything else, this sort of shooting from a woodchuck rifle is exactly what you don't want. Improper stock bedding is often the cause of it.

This .22-250 Springfield sporter of mine has very handsome fishtail type checkering on the forearm, extending for a distance of 8 inches forward and backward with a single large diamond figure in the center of the underside of the forearm. The pistol grip is most handsomely designed by Owen, and the execution of the checkering is possibly even better than on the forearm. The grip is so shaped that the length of hand hold from center of the trigger to the front end of the grip cap is but 3 inches, and the comb is undercut sharply on both sides, the checkering extending up as high as possible and out to the rear. The cheek piece is a slightly modified teardrop pattern, and extends to the rear 7-1/2 inches from the point of the comb beneath which it starts to sweep backward and downward as the large end of the cheek piece is of course to the rear. The butt is fitted with a Mershon, white line, red rubber pad. This rifle stock is of fancy figured imported walnut, apparently French walnut, of a very rich and beautiful deep golden color throughout. The grip has the grain in the right direction. The wood is fitted up to the various surfaces of the receiver steel most beautifully. The trip is capped. The barrel carries no metallic sights. The rifle was designed by Owen and Pfeifer and myself to be shot offhand and across various rests available in the hunting field, and with scope only. It balances perfectly.

The stock drop, measured from the top of the two prone telescope sight bases is 1-1/2 inches at the comb and 2-2/10 inches at the heel. Just about the same as that of my 20-gauge Ithaca field gun. I always could shoot that gun accurately without even looking at the sights. The faster I shoot it, the better I shoot it. This is exactly how a gunstock should fit a man.

For years I have been somewhat skeptical of the uniformity of shooting of a rifle barrel less than 0.75 inch in diameter at the muzzle. Yes, I know how splendidly most National Match service Springfields shoot with a barrel materially smaller than mine. I've had a number of them, and have fired thousands of rounds at 500, 600 and 1000 yards from them. But in a woodchuck rifle you need better accuracy than is obtained from the average National Match service Springfield. Consequently, I do not think a woodchuck rifle should be made with a barrel less than 0.75 inch at the muzzle unless the man who is to use the rifle is not too strong.

I really believe that for a fairly heavy sporting rifle to be used in the field by a healthy, fairly active and muscular man under 65 or so, this rifle would be difficult to excel. It also should shoot fairly well for bench-rest matches for rifles weighing under 12 pounds. Bob Owen had the forearm flattened a bit with that end in view, and also, so it would sit steadily for me when fired across a fence rail, the top of a fence post, or out a car window when you are on a back lane. But there are some who just couldn't handle such a rifle, and it did come through somewhat heavier than I expected for the barrel diameter.

CUSTOM MADE SINGLE SHOT CHUCK RIFLES

Most of us have gone rather thoroughly, through the single shot, set-trigger, squirrel, crow and woodchuck rifle craze. Twenty to fifty years ago these took mostly the form of modified Schuetzen rifles. I had my share of them. I had the No. 2, and the No. 6 Remingtons. Then came a model 12 Remington .22 repeater. Next a .25-20 Marlin repeater, and a poorly balanced heavy frame, hi-side, .25-20 Winchester single shot with 30-inch No. 2 barrel which was octagon. The rifle had a single set trigger and a rifle butt plate.

My favorite single shot was a Model 52 Stevens Schuetzen,

with the 44-1/2 action, two breech blocks, and .25-21 and two different .22 long rifle barrels, at various times. One was a very good Stevens barrel but that rusted badly in a very humid rainy spell. The solvent I had in the barrel ran or dried out of it and then it rusted badly before I could reoil it. I had this replaced by a very fine H. M. Pope barrel and shot a lot of squirrels and crows with that.

Today, a great many woodchuck rifles are still built, particularly in .219 Zipper and .219 Zipper Improved calibers, in Ontario. Some years back G. B. Crandall was turning out quite a good many of these in .22-303 Varmint-R caliber and in K-Hornet. The .22-303 Varmint-R is very accurate and dependable and a good killer on chucks at 300 to 450 yards. The K-Hornet however, in my hands, was nearly twice as accurate at 100 yards. But it did not have the range of the big rifle.

Various gunsmiths have made up most excellent woodchuck rifles with the various single shot actions. M. S. Risley, Earlville, New York; L. R. Wallack, Langhorne, Pennsylvania; and Wurzer & Peterson do this. The actions most preferred today, especially in Ontario, are the Winchester Hi-Wall, both the thick wall and the thin wall. In the States, however, the Sharps Borchardt, the Stevens 44-1/2, and a few others are preferred.

In Ontario most of these rifles are made up with a stock having a very high comb for scope shooting. These stocks fit well and the rifles shoot very well, but the stocks are not always too handsome. Wismer, however, has a very lovely one of Oregon myrtle, and Crandall made up another for himself in 1948 which had a very fine forearm. I do not recall what the stock itself looked like when finished.

The big trouble with fitting these single shots to the shooter is that the tangs of the Winchester and Stevens 44-1/2 rifles slope downward too much and that gets the hand hold down too far, and the comb then must rise too abruptly. Either bending up, or cutting off the rear ends of the tang straps just back of the screw holes, and brazing a metal bridge, vertically, between these ends, will help. Maurice Atkinson, of Streetsville, Ontario, or Elmer McConnell, at Delhi, Ontario, can each of them make a fine single shot rifle stock. In the States, Woerner Shelhammer at Dowagiac, Michigan, M. S. Risley, Earlville, New York, or Martin Wurzer of Philadelphia can make a rifle and stock it. On these rifles the cheek piece should be very high and the butt plate should be a shotgun butt plate. The firing pin in all cases must be bushed. Readily obtained short lengths of good walnut can be used.

LOCATING THE WOODCHUCK

Two things are necessary to successful woodchuck shooting, each of which is more important than the rifle or your shooting ability. The first is hunting skill. It includes where and when to look for woodchucks. You can fail on what would otherwise be a very successful hunt because you go in the middle of a hot, or a very cold day when the grass is too high, or in the wrong season. The second is good eyesight and spotting ability so that you will see the chucks that are out. They will be among rocks, in grass fields, along the edge of briar patches, and in Ontario, in thistles.

You cannot acquire good eyesight by reading about it, or merely by practicing. You must be born with it, and when you need shooting glasses, you should be fitted with these by a competent man who has been told exactly how you will use them. It is quite necessary, also, for you to get out into the country and make a practice of locating and spotting woodchucks, hawks, crows, squirrels, quail, grouse, pheasants, rabbits, deer, or other game.

The real problem of every woodchuck hunter is to discover small colonies or groups of dens of woodchucks, at some place where they can legally be shot where the landowner will permit or even encourage such shooting. In many square miles of good chuck country today, the most careful and quiet still hunting, and the firing of a single shot only from a low-report rifle at each woodchuck, is good judgment. A delay of a half-hour or so in walking up to the shot chuck will help too. A great many farmers or guards will permit occasional quiet shots when a volley from a very high pitched cartridge would result in your being chased off.

Remember that woodchucks are seen out at almost any hour of the daylight or dusk, but they are most likely to appear before the heat of the day in the morning, and then again after 3 to 5 P.M.

In Ontario, the very best shooting is almost always quite late in the evening. Even in the best chuck areas in Ontario you can drive for miles and see scarcely a woodchuck. Then you may run into a colony in the evening and for the next one to one and one-half hours you may shoot and kill a chuck every three to eight minutes. Ontario woodchucks have a penchant for digging holes in the sides of the escarpment or hill which runs diagonally across much of the southeastern portion of the province. They may also be found in small, brown-gray patches of thistle in otherwise relatively bare pasture fields or in grass fields containing small ravines along which patches of thistle may be seen. You leave the car and climb the barbed-wire fencing and walk slowly into a field. You assume a comfortable and partly screened shooting position in the cover of the shade of a tree, if possible, or along a fence line or a clump of high grass, an old building, or a pile of posts or rails. You see nothing for fifteen to thirty minutes and then they start to come out to feed and wander from hole to hole.

In the United States, most chucks, as you know, are found in or on old rail piles, post piles, old hollow chestnut stumps out in fields, under abandoned buildings or foundations. They are in timothy, clover and alfalfa fields, and also go into nearby grain fields at times, simply for temporary shelter. Chucks avoid clay, because water will not drain through it. They also do not often den in bottoms containing milkweed because there the soil is usually sour. In such choice they show far more judgment than man who will erect an expensive home on clay and then never be able to understand why he cannot drain his cellar when water gets in it from rains. Absolutely the only place I have ever heard of where the ground is clay and which is inhabited by chucks is along the northern line of the Canadian National Railway eastward from Cochrane and Hearst, in what they call the Clay Belt, which is southwest of James Bay. Many chucks up there live in drift piles and not down in the clay ground, and they are reported to me to be unusually wild there. Six or eight a day is a normal good bag. They are not as plentiful as farther south.

In New England they are often seen along old stone fence lines, and stone piles, and in rather barren fields containing rocks scattered here and there.

In the Middle Atlantic states, chucks are often seen along briar patches, either out in fields or along fences, in poison ivy, particularly along old worn fences.

Fields containing granite or limestone boulders are the likely places to hunt for chucks, also on the relatively bare hillsides of central and northeastern New York State and in the bottoms along the New York, New Haven & Hartford Railroad which runs northward through Vermont on its way to Montreal. The chucks are most often seen in the localities you pass through shortly after daylight and up to the serving of breakfast, while traveling north on the train called the Montrealer.

When hunting anywhere, and especially near your home, it is always a good plan to keep a map on which you carefully dot or X every known inhabited woodchuck den and where it is located. Then, with some other identifying mark, like a small circle or a circled X, every known kill is designated. Only those blessed with a photographic memory will otherwise be able to recall the exact location of all woodchuck colonies, dens, feeding grounds within a 20 to 200 mile radius of your home. Always keep a copy of this map (obtained by making white prints, blue prints or brown prints of it) in the pocket of the rifle case in which you carry your favorite woodchuck rifle; and plan to keep another copy in the glove compartment of your car or some other convenient place in case your first copy becomes lost or unusable.

WHERE THE WOODCHUCK IS HIT

In shooting woodchucks, I have used the .22 long, the .22 long rifle, the .25-21, .25-20 S.S., and the .250-3000 Savage. I have also used the .170 Parkinson Woodsman (with 15-degree shoulder slope), the .170 Landis Woodsman (with 28-degree slope), .22 Hornet, the .22 K-Hornet, .219 Donaldson, .220 Swift, .22 Varmint-R, .20-1906 Springfield, and various other calibers including the .22-303 Varmint-R, some with many different loads. By long odds, the .30-1906 with 150-, 170-, 172-, 180-grain bullets was found to be the least deadly and at the same time, the noisiest. I'd much rather have a .22 long rifle H.P. hi-speed any time.

The reason the .30-1906 cartridge, except with the new Spire Point bullets, is so lacking in killing power on woodchucks is that the bullets for it are designed to expand properly on game weighing 100 or 150 pounds up to about 1800 pounds, and not on a tough little animal of three to ten pounds. The 110-grain .30-1906 cartridge has higher muzzle velocity and does a better job on woodchucks, but the bullet is definitely lacking in the accuracy needed for an animal that small, and it usually is loaded to 3250 or 3300 f.s. muzzle velocity and not to 3500 f.s.m.v. as was first advertised.

Custom woodchuck rifles using cartridges of the range and the powder capacity of the .219 Zipper, .219 Donaldson, .22-250

Lightweight Warner stocked .270 Winchester-Mauser with short barrel, Weaver scope.

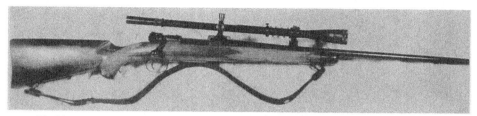

.22-250 woodchuck rifle, stocked by Warner, weighing about 10 pounds complete.

The author's Model 52 Winchester Hoffman heavy sporter, 5″ Winchester scope.

Springfield sporter rifle, cheek piece on right side of Warner stock, for shooting from left shoulder.

.220 Swift rifle by Bob Wallack of Langhorne, Pa., built on FN Mauser action. Weighs about 10½ pounds with Lyman Super Targetspot scope.

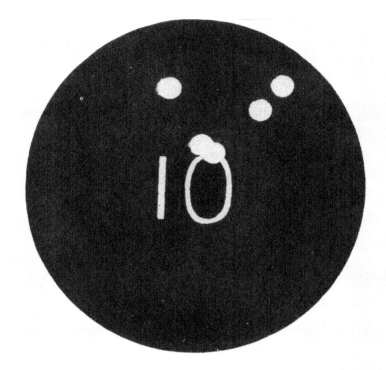

First group made by the author in setting the 8X Unertl Varmint scope on his .22-250 Springfield-Pfeifer-Warner chuck rifle. Shot from a bench rest at 118 paces.

The 5.6 x 61 M.M. Nimrod Mauser on the right killed this 12-pound chuck.

or .22 Varminter, .22 Marciente Blue Streak, .22-303 Varmint-R, are deadly chuck rifles and used extensively in Canada. However, the .219 Donaldson is not as yet too well thought of north of the International Line. One reason is that the men up there have plenty of chucks at which to shoot at ranges of 300 to 500 yards, when they want to try such shooting, and it is felt by some of them that the .219 Donaldson lets off where they start to shoot at them.

Canadians are partial to the .22-303 Varmint-R and to the .22 Zipper and the .22 Improved Zipper. When loaded with the 49-grain Sisk, or the 55-grain Sisk or Sierra or the Hornady or the Speer bullets, they will blast one-third to one-half of the body contents right out of the chuck, tear the body considerably, and throw the carcass one to four feet from where the chuck sat. Sometimes the chuck will just wilt down, but that is usually when the spine or brain is struck and possibly the bullet was hard and did not expand too much. In any case, the chuck will likely lie dead right there on the surface.

With cartridges of 16 to 27 grains powder charge, you must aim more carefully and squeeze off perfectly while keeping the cross hair intersection or the Lee Dot on the brain, the butt of the ear, the throat or high on the shoulder. On a shoulder shot, the bullet should drive through and break both shoulders. A shot from in front, breaking the one shoulder, will let the chuck get in and he may run fifteen to thirty feet before going down. His one idea is to make the den, regardless of how he is hit. Down in out of sight he goes. To some this suggests a woodchuck cartridge that blasts the chuck to kingdom come. The one shot, one chuck idea. This idea can be carried out in areas where the human inhabitants, also horses and cattle are extremely well distributed but in the more thickly settled districts it is just foolish and the quickest ticket to the first road home.

Chucks struck in the skull, with the skull shattered and burst, and hit nowhere else, will bleed like stuck pigs on the spot on which they sit. The .22 long rifle, high speed, H.P. cartridge will do this up to 100 — 150 yards almost as effectively as the far more powerful high power .22's. Chucks shot through the butt of the ear will also bleed very freely and may also bleed from the nostrils. It is bright, arterial blood, in most instances. Chucks shot directly into the center of the throat from in front, may turn around just once, or one-half way around, if too weak, and lie down and die on the spot on which they sit. In these cases the spine has been cut, also the jugular or the windpipe has been torn or penetrated. Those shot high through the shoulders sink down, totally paralyzed, and die on the spot. A chuck shot square-ly through the butt of the ear or hit so that he has a smashed skull or a broken neck, may sometimes slide very slowly and deliberately backwards down into the den, gaining speed as he slides because of gravity. This chuck will nearly always slide clear down out of sight. If he slides in head first, he will often double up and stick part way down and you can reach in and pull him out. Sometimes it is not too safe as he can be scrappy after being hit.

There may at times, be an occasional chuck which simply won't die. I recall one which was shot through the jugular, and ran in and out of the mouth of his den time after time. He was bleeding very freely in jets, from the wound in his throat but he would not give up.

Regardless of what anyone else tells you, train yourself to aim at the brain, butt of the ear, or throat of the woodchuck. On a side shot center the cross hairs between eye and butt of ear. Between eye and the orifice in the ear. On shots like those at 300 to 350 yards, most people would realize both their rifle and themselves would require a bit more leeway than an area this size, so they would aim a bit higher than the middle of the shoul-der. If you shoot to either side, and the chuck is down feeding, you get a throat or head shot or a lung shot. If the chuck is erect, with his paws hanging loosely over his chest, then aim about the collar bone, or on the head, if the range is beyond your normal sighting. To simply aim at the approximate middle of the brown blur which is the woodchuck (when using iron sights) is often to miss the woodchuck. Pick out some one vital spot on that chuck, and then make every possible effort to hit that exact spot. That is the one and only way to consistently kill chucks, so that you will now and then make long runs of twenty or thirty woodchucks. Ed. Burkins taught me this method of chuck shoot-ing.

If your rifle stock is made of well-seasoned, close-grain wood, the barrel is properly bedded in the forearm, the wood and metal meet squarely at the recoil shoulder, the tang screws are tight, the scope bases are firmly screwed or brazed to the bar-rel, or barrel and receiver, and the trigger pull is smooth, sharp, and even, from shot to shot and for shot after shot, and you continue to aim every shot at a given vital spot and then don't flinch as you fire: with proper sighting you are certain to kill chucks consistently. After some months of shooting, you will reach the point where you can tell within an inch or two, without ever going over to examine the chuck, exactly where your bullet struck from the way the chuck acted immediately after being hit, and from your let-off. No high power .170 or .22-caliber woodchuck rifles using up to 55-grain bullets and 40 grains of powder or less, for the .22's, and 25- or 30-grain bullets and 15 to 16.5 grains for the .17's, will give more than 1-1/2 to 4-1/2 ft. lbs. of free recoil, especially in a 10- to 12-pound rifle. So, there is no need to flinch.

HUNTING THE DENS

In Spring always hunt the spring and summer dens, which usually are in meadows, in creek bottoms, in the edges of ravines grown up with briars or high grass, these usually being adjacent to green clover patches. The dens may also be in sharp, steep little hills, not more than five to twelve feet above the grassy bottoms or fields. Such dens are usually just out of but very close to clover or grassy fields. In all cases, they will be found well above the high water mark of nearby streams.

After very prolonged and unusually severe floods, where normal high water marks are exceeded by several feet, the chucks may be found sitting out on small raised hummocks in generally level ground, most of which is flooded. Here they sit only a few inches to a foot above the water level, much like ring-necked pheasants roost in a swamp on the grass hummocks. Most of the dens found very freshly and newly dug into rather open hillsides in April or May have apparently been prepared by the old chucks for sole occupancy by the young chucks after the latter mate and prepare to raise their first kits. I have had extremely poor luck trying to find old chucks at work in the digging of these dens. Apparently most of these dens are dug out very early in the morning and two or three morning's work suffices to provide the young couple with a new fifteen-thousand-dollar home. These all seem to be strictly new holes into solid banks and are not old dens cleaned out and turned over to the kids. When you do find a chuck occupied in digging one of these dens, he is usually completely inside the den mouth, which looks very fresh, while dirt comes out in a shower from between his hind feet propelled by the front paws. I have discussed this matter with numerous veteran chuck hunters and usually they are in agreement that their experiences have been similar.

In late summer or early fall, always hunt the winter dens which always face the east or the southeast and are usually well protected from west and northwest winds.

THE BEST RIFLE SIGHTING FOR WOODCHUCK SHOOTING

Remember: you do not sight your rifle point blank for too great a range or distance. I'd suggest that with a flat shooting varmint rifle, you sight it for not more than fifty yards farther than the average distance at which you are killing woodchucks. In theory you should sight it to strike center at exactly that range. But we can safely add fifty yards. I've computed and averaged this time and again. In Ontario for three trips, each of the first two for one week, and the third for two weeks, during which I killed 282 woodchucks, the average shot lay between 103 and 108 yards. This shooting included the use of two different Woodsman .17-caliber cartridges, one with 15-degree, the other with 28-degree shoulder; the .22 Hornet — the old standby; the .22 K-Hornet; .219 Donaldson for a few shots only; the big heavy .22-303 Varmint-R; and two rifles in .220 Swift caliber (one in standard weight barrel by myself, one in .220 heavy target barrel type, by a companion on one shoot). The one Swift burst its bullets repeatedly, the other gave very irregular verticals. All the other calibers were extremely satisfactory.

Rifles of calibers like the .22 Hornet, .22 K-Hornet, .170 Parkinson or .170 Landis Woodsman, and the R-2, should all be sighted so as to group one inch above the line of sight at 100 yards. Rifles of the .219 Zipper, .219 Zipper Improved, .219 Donaldson, .22 Marciante Blue Streak, .22 Chucker and similar calibers, most of which have about a 2-1/2-inch trajectory over 200 yards, with some loads a trifle less, should be sighted to group 1/2 to 3/4 inch above the line of sight at 100 yards, and cartridges like the .22-250, .220 Swift, and similar, 1/4 to 1/2 inch above the line of sight.

Far too many people sight their Zippers and Swifts to group one inch high at 100 yards and shoot over everything from 75 to 250 yards. Remember the factory 48-grain Swift has a 1.5-inch trajectory over 200 yards, and a 3-1/2-inch trajectory over 300 yards, and remember also, the bullet must rise 1-1/2 to about 1.65 inches above the bore to get up to the line of sight in most good sized rifle telescopes when the mount bases are both on a fairly heavy barrel, or one on the top of the receiver and the other on a high base 6 to 7.2 inches ahead of the center of the rear mount. With a medium long stock and a long action like that on the Mauser military 98, the Springfield or the Enfield 1917 actions, many persons of ordinary build will not be able to mount the front mount base more than 3-7/8 to 4-3/8 inches ahead of the base on the receiver or they will not be able to see clearly through the scope to take aim when shooting offhand and sitting. So, for rifles like the Swift, one really ought to sight the rifle to hit the point of aim at 100 yards, or possibly about 0.15 inch below the point of aim for the cross hair intersection to have perfect sighting for 200 yards. If you get any of these long range rifles sighted too high, then you'll have the most unexplainable misses between about 75 to 250 yards and won't know why. Other unexplainable misses are caused by bullets going to pieces before they reach the mark. Some do, especially in a cold, dry barrel usually at higher than 3850 f.p.s.

The K-Hornet is a particularly deadly woodchuck rifle up to about 225 to 250 yards considering the charge, cost of ammunition, report, lack of recoil, and other characteristics. At 100 yards, some of these rifles, even on the Winchester Hi-side single shot frame, will group at least twice as well as many of the larger case .22's at that range. I've shot them side by side. In both the .22 and .25 calibers you can more easily overdo the size of the cartridge on the upside than on the down, ·or small side or size.

This business of setting the sights on a flat shooting rifle of considerable powder capacity for about 400 yards with the idea of aiming a bit low at ranges between 150 and 350 yards, is too indefinite to produce good results in the field. Raise your sights or hold high on the long shots rather than attempt to hold low at all the shorter ranges at which you will actually kill 85 to 95 per cent of your woodchucks. For shots away off in the distance, possibly 100 yards past your regular sighting, hold from the top of the back when the chuck is down eating, to anywhere between the top of the head and one to three inches over the top of the head when the chuck is sitting up. When using the .22 Hornet, or even the K-Hornet, you may need to add a bit to these higher holds, but even so, with the horizontal wire of the scope to judge by, this is not difficult.

You can have an additional Lee Dot of contrasting size

placed on the vertical wire below the center Lee Dot, if using a dot, and have this adjusted for 350 to 400 yards range. This lower dot is always made a bit smaller than the center dot. The extra dot is never placed above the center dot or the cross hair intersection.

WHAT IS THE TOTAL DROP OF YOUR BULLET?

This seems to intrigue thousands of sportsmen. The total drop of your bullet, from a .22-caliber high velocity woodchuck rifle, or any other rifle for that matter, is four times the mid-range trajectory height. For instance, if your .219 Zipper Improved has a 2-1/2-inch trajectory over 200 yards, the bullet drops 10 inches from the line of the bore — not the line of sight, it would be about 8-1/2 inches from the line of sight. At 300 yards the total drop would be about 32 inches because the mid-range trajectory is 8 inches. If you sight a .219 Zipper Improved for 300 yards, at 150 yards the bullet will be approximately 8 inches above the line of the bore or 6-1/2 inches above the cross hair intersection. Different bullets, different charges, different cases or different primers, will all introduce small variations from these figures.

 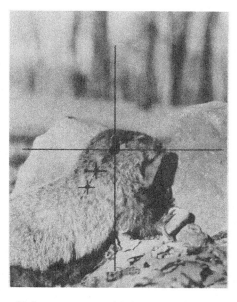

Telescope cross-hair aligned for a fatal brain shot.

Taking aim with the Lee Dot on the butt of the ear. Any of the shots marked on the curved line should paralyze the chuck.

This wary chuck must be hit squarely in the brain.

The author firing his lightweight Model 61 hammerless Winchester .22 long rifle with K-4 Weaver scope.

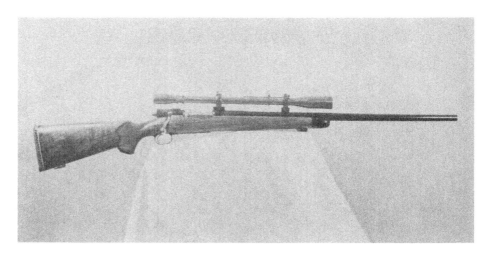

The author's long-range Springfield-Pfeifer-Warner, with 8X Unertl Varmint scope, Damaskeened Cramer speed action, Mershon butt.

CHAPTER 3

Sights and Scopes

THE SELECTION OF TELESCOPE SIGHTS
FOR WOODCHUCK SHOOTING

THE high grade rifle telescope is the most important item in the equipment of the chuck hunter, excepting the rifle itself. It is an investment that should last for twenty to thirty years. Today a really good scope will cost $50 to $125 with its mounts and bases and base screws, but that is only a few dollars a year over its lifetime.

A telescope is likely to be used longer than any of the chuck rifles upon which it may be mounted. Chuck rifles come and go! Almost any day a rabid rifle crank is likely to buy himself a new model and if there is not sufficient money in the savings bank or under the bedroom rug, something violent but effective is likely to happen to Junior's piggy bank.

Although a rifle may look like a perfect varmint rifle, it needs to be fitted with the proper sort of varmint scope, properly mounted. After a man uses a scope for some months, he discovers what it needs to make it suit him exactly. If he needs a target type glass, he then has it fitted with coarser single cross hairs or a medium hair and a Lee Dot. The dot should cover one to one and one-quarter or even one and one-half inches at 100 yards, because in a fog, in the shadow of a deep woods, in late evening or very early morning, or when crawling through waving grass, it takes too long to locate and place a very small dot. It is too difficult to see it instantly in the field of the scope. A dot covering one-half to three-fourths inch at 100 yards is fine for testing ammunition or for bench-rest target shooting, but when lying down in grass a foot high, with irregular clumps of grass waving in the wind, you have to hunt around too much for the dot

35

when you are in a hurry. So many chucks have the very exasperating habit of suddenly withdrawing the head back into the den, or of moving the front portion of the body ahead a couple of feet and directly back of a fence post or a rail. A lot of chucks have been lost for good because the shooter had to spend too much time taking aim.

Each scope you get, including the better ones, needs to have the parallax taken out by careful adjustment and the cross hairs readjusted to your vision. The cross hairs must be adjusted for perfect focus, and so they can be seen sharply. This is done by screwing the eyepiece lens cell forward or backward. There is a locking ring to be loosened first. After focusing the cross hairs properly, you can see them sharply in the scope. The cross hairs are your sight. Focusing for distance is done by turning the barrel of the focusing sleeve, usually on the front of the scope, but on Fecker scopes near its middle.

Bear in mind that the most important feature connected with the mounting and use of a rifle telescope is that the bases be so placed and securely screwed to the rifle that the scope is in perfect vision for the shooter. These include offhand front mount, 3-7/8 to 4-3/8 inches in front of the rear mount. If the scope should be slid forward or backward in the mount rings, the binding screw in each ring should be loosened and this adjustment made. Be sure to retighten the screws.

The focal length of the scope should be sufficiently long so that you are not whacked in the eye, on the eyebrow, or you do not have your glasses broken, when raising the rifle to the shoulder to take aim — or by recoil. Shooting glasses with heavy enclosing frames are seldom broken, but the thin lens office type of glasses are easily broken.

RIFLE TELESCOPE MANUFACTURERS

Today there are four very well known rifle telescope sight manufacturers and eight or ten others of some note. Among the leaders are John Unertl Optical Company, 3551 East St., Pittsburgh 14, Pa.; J. W. Fecker, Inc., 2016 Perrysville Ave., Pittsburgh, Pa.; Lyman Gun Sight Corp., Middlefield, Conn.; and W. R. Weaver Co., El Paso, Texas.

UNERTL

I have two makes of Unertl on my chuck rifles now. The latest, which came in almost three years ago and which I have been saving for my latest heavy chuck rifle, the .22-250 Pfeifer-Warner, is an 8X Varmint scope having a 7/8-inch tube in dehorned or bobtailed mounts regularly, but which on my scope I had replaced by the target mounts, so that definite records can be kept in a small notebook carried on the person while hunting, of the proper sight setting for each range.

VARMINT SCOPES

The size of field of the Unertl Varmint scopes, which are made in 6, 8 and 10 power, is about the same as in high-grade target-type scopes, or a trifle greater. However, the Unertl Varmint scopes have what Mr. Unertl refers to as "wider field and optical characteristics of big game scopes."

Unertl says that from his experience in supplying scopes to chuck hunters and others, Varmint scopes in powers of 6X to 10X are the most popular and the most practical. I consider the 6X the most practical for the most hunters, especially those who have not as yet learned to hold a rifle in full control of the shooter at the exact moment of let-off. The 10X and the 8X are better if you wish to do considerable rest shooting or prone work in testing different woodchuck loads or different makes and lots of bullets for accuracy.

The $75 Varmint scope made by Unertl, is listed as having a 12-foot field at 100 yards in 10X, 14-foot in 8X, and 18-foot in 6X, which of course means that you can catch the chuck quicker in the field of the scope in the lower powers. Its weight is listed as 1 pound 2 ounces. However, mine weighed 1 pound 7 ounces (according to a grocer's large scales) with the dehorned mounts and the two steel dust caps in place, and now weighs 1 pound 9 ounces with the target mounts and the dust caps. On the Varmint scopes, the objective cell is 1-1/2 inches in diameter and the eyepiece cell and tube 1-1/4 inches. The eye relief is 3-1/2 inches and the scope 19-1/2 inches in length. This is both heavier and longer than the Weaver K-6 scope, and is somewhat longer and heavier than the 7X Fecker Woodchucker. As a further comparison, the Unertl Condor big game scope has a 17-foot field at 100 yards, an eye relief of 3 to 4 inches, is 13-1/2 inches in length, and weighs between 8 and 9 ounces without mounts. To a scope add weight of the mounts and blocks, and its screws and all these to the weight of the rifle. If you use a sling, add that.

SMALL GAME SCOPE

Unertl makes other good target and game scopes which are suitable for chuck hunting. Among these the small game scope is made with 3/4-inch tube, weighs 3/4 pound and is 18 inches in length. It costs $40 with mounts and is put out in 3X, 4X and 6X. In 6X it has a 17-foot field at 100 yards.

Unertl also makes a one-inch scope in 6X, 8X and 10X, which costs $58 with target mounts. It has a 16-foot field at 100 yards in 6X. The 1-1/4-inch scope is quite practical for the average shooter. This one is made in 8X, 10X, 12X and 14X. It is longer ——24 inches, the tube 3/4 inch, and the scope weight 1 pound 3 ounces. It costs $78 with mounts and has 2-1/4-inch eye relief. It differs from the Varmint scope in being longer and slimmer. In use it is rather similar to the Lyman Targetspot Jr. and is of about the same general style but possibly somewhat higher grade. In appearance it is still more like the 1-1/4-inch Fecker scope. As a matter of fact, the Unertl and the Fecker lines resemble each other more than any other two makes.

COMBINATION SCOPE

The 1-1/2-inch Unertl combination scope is 25-1/2 inches in length. The objective cell is 1-13/16 inches in diameter, the eyepiece cell 7/8 inch and the main tube 3/4 inch. The scope is made in 10X, 12X, 14X, 16X, 18X and 20X. It sells for $72 without mounts or $90 with Unertl mounts of target type. This scope weighs 3 ounces more than the Varmint scope, is longer, and the objective cell is larger, which makes it look larger in front. Never forget as you increase the size of the scope——get it up farther off the center of gravity of the rifle and get it heavy out front——just so much more do you increase the tendency of the rifle to roll around with the scope underneath, when carried in the hand or on the shoulder. Also, one seems to increase the tendency to catch the scope in brush or bang it against anything hard.

Focusing for ranges under 200 yards is accomplished by moving the objective lens only. This method is claimed to be the most satisfactory way of focusing a target-type scope and presumably it is. The scope is equipped with a Pope rib on its top, as is the Varmint, and has a clamp ring recoil absorber which can be removed if you don't like it, and screw dust caps for both ends. Interchangeable eyepieces to raise or lower the original

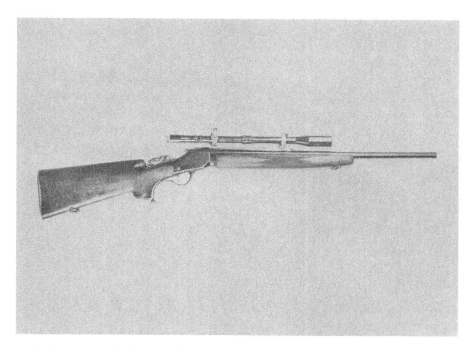

Sedgley stocked Winchester Hi-side rebarreled by Wallack for .22-3000 R-2 Donaldson with 7X Fecker "Woodchucker" scope.
CREDIT: DENSHAM & SCHILL.

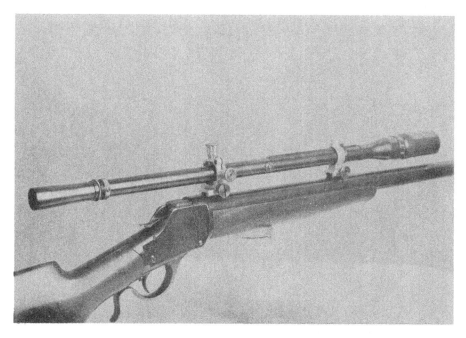

The author's .170 Winchester Hi-side Woodsman with 5½X Fecker-Unertl scope, fitted with a Lee Dot.

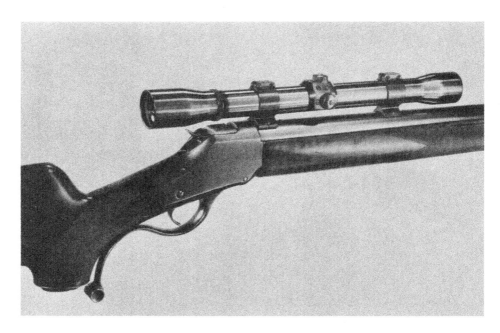

Weaver K-6 telescope on a Winchester heavy hi-side single shot with special finger lever. CREDIT: LARRY DARST.

Pachmayr Swing Out scope and mount.

Pachmayr Swing Out scope ready for use.

magnification of this scope by 35 per cent are available from the manufacturer. When this scope is mounted on receiver and prone base on barrel it sticks back nearly to the point of the comb, and forward to about 6 inches in front of the end of the forearm on a bolt action sporter with custom stock.

TWO-INCH SCOPE

The Unertl with the 2-inch objective is the sort of scope chosen by the man who does not mind weight, and demands a precision in the instrument and optical qualities which are un-surpassed.

These big glasses balance and handle best on a rifle with a short, very heavy barrel which is shot more frequently from a car or a fence line than from a hilltop 400 yards inland. For such purpose they are superb.

The 2-inch Unertl scope is available in 10X, 15X, 18X, 20X, and in 24X, is equipped with 1/8-inch Pope rib on top of the tube, clamp ring, recoil absorber and screw dust caps for both ends. It is supplied only with oversize 1/4-minute click target-type mounts and bases. It must be mounted on bases 1/16 inch or 0.0625 inch higher than the standard height base. The scope is 24 inches long, has a tube 1 inch in diameter. The objective is 2-1/4 inches in diameter — meaning the larger diameter front portion is that size and the eyepiece cell is 1-1/8 inches in di-ameter.

Now just what do we get for $125 which is the cost of this scope and its mounts? The scope weighs 2 pounds 2 ounces, and would likely weigh 2 pounds 8 ounces to 2 pounds 10 ounces with steel caps and mount bases. The luminosity of this scope is 25 in 10X. The luminosity of the 10X Varmint scope is 9.6, although the luminosity of the 8X Varmint scope is 15.2 and that of the 6X Varmint scope is 28. That of the 6X Condor big game scope is 40. On the other hand, the luminosity of the 1-1/2-inch 10X Unertl scope, a very fine glass indeed, is 14.4. The 1-1/4-inch glass in 10X is rated at 9.6 in luminosity, the one-inch at 6.25, so you notice that the luminosity of the 2-inch target glass of quality type is four times that of the one-inch scope of the same power, 10X. That is what you receive for the difference between $58 and $125.

Woodchucks do not seem to like chuck hunters looking at them through 2-inch Unertl telescopes while they are contentedly nibbling clover. But if you want to quietly observe the table manners and the home life of Marmota Monax, regardless of the distance, and will pay the price in toil and sweat to lug the heavy scope to where you must take it, one of these 2-inch rifle telescopes will show you. Right here I would like to warn against using a 20X to 33X spotting scope held in the hands, or against a car window frame, for the spotting of chucks, especially when the auto is moving. You will develop severe eyestrain which may prove highly dangerous.

If you purchased your Unertl scope early in the game, and you want to change the small game scope with 3/4-inch tube, to one-inch objective size, you can have this done for $18. You can also have the 1-1/4-inch glass changed to 1-1/2-inch objective for $20. You cannot change to the 2-inch because the scope barrel of that is one inch and the front portion would be too large to fit.

THE FECKER TELESCOPES

The J. W. Fecker telescopes have been made in Pittsburgh, Pennsylvania, for many years. The late Mr. Fecker at one time worked in the Bausch & Lomb plant at Rochester, then went into the rifle scope manufacturing business for himself. He should receive credit for probably the most outstanding improvements in rifle telescopes over the years, of anyone in the scope manufacturing industry in this country, and for his insistence on maintenance of quality in all his scopes.

As in general, Fecker and Unertl scopes are very similar (for years John Unertl worked for Fecker), it would scarcely be worth the space to go into elaborate detail regarding all the Fecker scopes. Today Fecker supplies a target scope with 3/4-inch tube, 3/4-inch eyepiece and 1-1/4-inch objective, which is made in 6X, 8X, 10X, 12X and 14X. This scope is 23 inches in length and weighs 1 pound 2 ounces.

THE 1-5/8-INCH FECKER

Fecker also has a very fine large size target and hunting scope with 3/4-inch tube, 3/4-inch eyepiece, and 1-5/8-inch objective. The scope is made in 10X, 12X, 16X, 20X and 24X, the powers higher than 10X being better adapted to target shooting than to field shooting. It would be nice to have a glass like that in 6 power, but the manufacturers seem to feel this is unnecessary. The 1-5/8-inch Fecker is 26-1/4 inches in length and weighs 1 pound 3 ounces.

THE WOODCHUCKER

This scope was introduced early in 1948. I examined one of the first in 7X. It is made today in 4.5X, 5.5X, and 7X. The scope is 16-1/2 inches in length and weighs 15 ounces. It has coated lenses, a 3/4-inch tube and a 1-1/4-inch objective. When coated lenses first appeared, I tested an uncoated scope and a similar coated scope from rest, from an upstairs back window, across a long flat area. Over there was a village of freshly painted houses of different colors. I found the coated scope much less effective on dark brown colors and some medium browns, than the uncoated scope. On other colors it was better. Remember woodchucks often show up as medium to dark brown, red, or grayish brown. Repeated glances gave identical results.

The Woodchucker has external windage and elevation screws, and is one of three very good models of Fecker scopes for woodchuck shooting. It is excelled optically only by their 1-5/8-inch glass.

THE LYMAN RIFLE TELESCOPES

Lyman Gun Sight Corporation, of Middlefield, Connecticut, has been making metallic rifle sights since 1878. The best of their early telescopes was the 5-A which they improved somewhat in details and also in mounts.

JUNIOR TARGETSPOT

Their most practical scope for woodchuck shooting is the Junior Targetspot which has a 3/4-inch tube, mounted in Lyman 1/4-inch mounts of target type. The glass is made today in 6X, 8X and 10X, with cross hair or other graticules. It is 20-1/2 inches long, weighs 1 pound 4 ounces and is a surprisingly good glass for its diameter. It is quite reliable as a hunting and target scope and the definition is much better than one expects in a scope of this size. The 6X is, in my opinion, one of the best woodchuck scopes on the market. The eye relief is rather short, being but 2 inches, but because of the considerable length of the scope, it can usually be mounted so that you can get the eyepiece right where you want it.

THE LYMAN SUPER TARGETSPOT

This is one of the outstanding rifle telescopes on the market, in regard to quality, durability and the excellence of the lenses. The regular Targetspot in 10X was a very fine glass optically, but it is not now on the market.

The Super Targetspot is definitely a high grade target glass of large size. It is made in 10X, 12X, 15X, 20X and 25X, is 24-3/8 inches in length, is quite heavy, weighing 1 pound 9 ounces, has a 3/4-inch tube and a 3/4-inch eyepiece, which seems to be standard for Lyman target scopes. It has an objective about 1.35 inches in diameter. The Lyman target scopes are nicely graduated on the front portion; the mounts are three-point suspension of high grade. They also have a special attachment which can be used, called the Lyman Known Ranger, which consists of hinged gauges permitting quick adjustment of sight from 50, 100, and 200 yards. The eye relief of the scope is short, being but 2 inches. This is common with the large target scopes, many of which have but 2-inch to 2-1/4-inch eye relief. Optically the Super Tragetspot is a wonderful rifle telescope and is quite practical for woodchuck shooting, especially where much carrying is not required or you fire from a steady rest. Some use the higher powers for chucks, but personally I do not care for such a large scope nor so high a power for field shooting.

Redfield makes a good safety for use on the Springfield action, with a telescope sight. These sell for $5.75 each. Buehler has a somewhat different low safety also for use with a large scope sight on a Springfield action. Lyman in more recent years has snapped up their metallic sights and loading tools; they have scrapped their old and cheaper telescope sights and have gone in altogether for the higher priced hunting and target scopes.

WEAVER RIFLE TELESCOPES

W. R. Weaver of El Paso, Texas, is a scope manufacturer who has come along very rapidly during the last 10 or 12 years, mostly by producing a simple, rugged, strong line of hunting telescopes at very reasonable figures. Weaver helped his business materially in its earlier days by making scopes for the Savage Arms Company who supplied them on Savage and Stevens rifles in .22 caliber under their own name. Weaver's 29-S was the top grade inexpensive Weaver scope for years, while the Savage .22 L.R. and .22 Hornet sporters were the best-fitting of the less expensive woodchuck rifles. This helped to introduce Weaver scopes.

Then came the 330 and 440 Weaver scopes. The first a three power and the latter a four power glass. For some reason the 330 was much the better scope, mine of that grade being a fairly good glass, small and practical.

THE K SCOPES

Weaver's ten strike was the K line of telescopes. These are short, light, rugged, simple quality telescopes of 2.5X, 4X, and 6X. There is also a 1X for use on shotguns and for running deer shooting. The K-4 and K-6 glasses have first class lenses and good bright fields.

Weaver has good substantial detachable mounts for both of them now, but you can also use the Redfield Jr., or the Stith.

I have the K-4 on my Winchester hammerless .22 repeater. It is a nice size and has good lenses for woods hunting on that sort of squirrel rifle. Within 125 yards it will kill woodchucks right along with any of the big varmint rifles provided you will memorize where to hold.

The K-4 is 11.9 inches long, hangs in ring mounts, weighs 9-1/2 ounces, has a one-inch tube diameter, has a 1.30-inch front lens cell and objective and a 1.30-inch rear or eye lens tube. The windage and elevation knobs are near to the middle of the scope and the whole scope and mounts give one the idea of a compact, substantial and splendidly designed scope. It is marked "up" and "left" to make it easier for the hunter in setting for any one range. This is an important part of the design. I like my scope mounts legibly lettered to show which way the thing is going to move. In my neck of the woods, when you turn the mount in the wrong direction, even if it is the exact proper number of quarter clicks, you miss by undershooting; and both the woodchuck and you are annoyed.

On the K-4 Weaver the eye relief is said to be 3 to 5-1/2 inches. To those like myself whose eyes are farsighted from gathering years, I think there is less perfect focus than 1-1/2-inch variation in head placement. It sells for $45.

The K-6 scope is just over 13 inches in length, weighs 10-1/2 ounces, and otherwise is about the same as the K-4 except that the object in the scope seems much plainer at 100 yards and your field is 20 feet compared to 31 feet in the K-4. Unless you are going to shoot running deer or moose, I'd get the K-6. You'll like it better for chucks. Its price is about $48.50.

OTHER WEAVERS

I took a K-2.5 along to Canada for deer, but found the brush so thick where I hunted, and so much of the day was dark in the brush, that I left the scope in the cabin.

I now have a Weaver 2-3/4 and 5X KV convertible scope on that rifle. This scope is 11-3/4 inches in length of tube which is slightly short for those with short necks and wide shoulders, but it is quite usable. The cross hairs can be focused perfectly and the lenses are large, clear and sharp. The mounts are of a unique design. A round rod runs across the underside of the mount and fits into a U-groove on the top of the mount base on the bridge of the Model 70 receiver. That keeps the chappies from putting the scope base on any other than the right spot on the block.

I had a J-4 Weaver for about a year, and found it one of the best inexpensive scopes on the market. It is well suited to a 12- or 14-year-old boy who is not too careful with expensive scientific equipment.

WHAT YOUR BOY NEEDS

Your boy should be supplied with a well-made, thoroughly safe rifle, fitted with at least one of the best of the medium grade 4-power rifle telescopes. He should be placed under the instruction of a rifleman. I mean a rifleman, not merely a National Guard instructor. Most times the two are by no means synonymous. Remember that most boys of twelve to twenty are physically incapable of holding a rifle offhand as steadily as when forty or fifty. Their nervous system is more highly keyed up; the kid can't sit quiet; he has to be doing something all the time. Don't get the power of the scope too high simply because you worry about the boy and want to get him the most expensive equipment you can. Get him the brightest and clearest 4-power scope you possibly can afford.

OTHER CUSTOM TELESCOPE SIGHTS FOR WOODCHUCKS

There are numerous additional hunting scopes, most of them of rather recent introduction. Most of these scopes have been produced since 1946 and are in the main of 2-1/4 to 4 power, with

The author with a pair of chucks.
CREDIT: DICK NOEL.

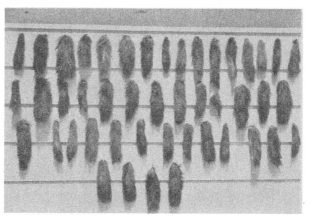

One day's bag in Ontario—54 chucks.
CREDIT: STANLEY ADAMS.

Stocker Maurice Atkinson, of Streetsville, Ontario, working on one of his handsome stocks.

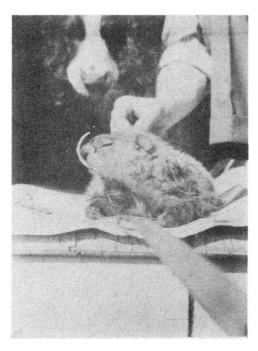

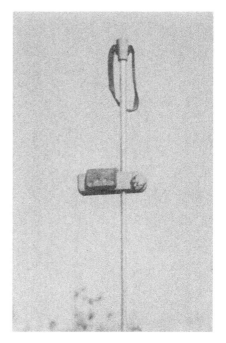

This chuck was starving to death. Abnormal grown-out tooth prevented cutting of food. CREDIT: RAY WEEKS.

The Weeks chuck and crow rest. Rod is a No. 2 golf iron, rest has a sponge rubber pad with clamp fastening.

Ray Weeks firing prone from his crow and woodchuck rest. Note position of left hand under toe of stock.

short tubes, designed primarily for big game shooting. But not all are of that type. The four powers will do for chuck hunting provided the mounts can set the center of impact just above the center of aim, at 100 yards.

Among these scopes are the Bausch & Lomb Balfor of 4X, and the B & L Balvar of 2-1/2X and 4X. Each is 11-1/2 inches in length and weighs 7-1/2 ounces. The tube diameter of these is one inch, and the eyepiece diameter is 1-9/32 inches. The B. & L. mounts are recommended for these scopes and the elevation and windage adjustments on these are external.

Other scopes are the Litschert, the Edwards, Norman-Ford Texan, the Stith Bear Cubs in 4X and 6X, with either external or internal movements; these latter scopes being 11-1/2 to 13-1/2 inches in length and weighing 7 to 11 ounces. There is also the splendid Hensoldt 8X Ziel-Dialyt, a 14-inch scope, having a tube of slightly over 1 inch in diameter and an eyepiece of 1.53 inches. The objective is just over 2 inches. The Hensoldt Dur-alyt is a 6X, is 12-1/2 inches long and weighs 14 ounces. The Leupold-Stevens is another good one, made in two models, but both only 2-1/2X.

The Lyman Challenger 4X is one of the best 4X scopes on the market. It is 11-1/4 inches long, weighs 13 ounces, has a tube diameter just over 1 inch, an eyepiece of 1-11/32 inches and an objective of the same size. The lenses are very fine. In Lyman or Unertl target mounts it might have chuck possibilities. In fact, it would have them, due to its clear field that is 30 feet across at 100 yards. The Edwards Model V weighs 15 ounces in a 14-inch length, in 4 power, and they make 6X, 8X and 10X scopes an inch longer and of the same weight.

CARE AND USE OF THE SCOPE

Woodchuck hunters should understand that an unsatisfactory scope cross hair or post can always be replaced readily and usually quite cheaply. A complete cleaning job on the lenses, and the remounting of the lenses may cost up to ten dollars or so, but unless the scope tube is badly dented, or mashed, this should result in a scope about as good as new. Most lenses can be re-cleaned — and are, when you put in a Lee Dot, or similar sighting device.

It is extremely important to keep a small notebook in your shooting shirt pocket in which is recorded the elevation and windage readings for each range normally shot on. Especially that giving a group 1/2 to 1 inch above the line of scope sight at 100 yards.

Learn where your rifle groups when firing from the side of a tree; — remember that a right shoulder shooter will find his rifle bouncing out about twice as far to the left when rested against the left side of a tree or post as when rested against the right side of it where it bounces out to the right. This bounce-out will normally be at least as much as 1 to 3 inches at 100 yards and sometimes much greater.

Learn to fire accurately across the top of a post or a fence rail. The "know how" is that you start to let off your shot before the cross hair intersection or the front bead comes onto the mark from the side, especially if the post or rail is loose and moves.

It is far more important to know the direction you move the mounts than the distance.

In the field you should have metal or leather scope caps and some very soft tissue like that used to remove dust from camera lenses, to wipe the scope lenses free of mist, drops of water, dust, grit, oil or any scummy accumulation. A rifle scope is only 100 per cent efficient when its lenses are clean and the bases rigid.

PORTABLE ROD WOODCHUCK RESTS FOR FIELD SHOOTING

In various sections of the United States, — mostly in New York State, Vermont, Massachusetts, also Southern Ontario, a number of riflemen use portable rests for prone or sitting shooting at woodchucks, and also at crows.

Most of these have been homemade. They consist essentially of a vertical cylindrical rod upon which a horizontal rest is fastened, or slipped. This horizontal rest is usually topped or covered with soft sponge rubber or a pad of cloth. It is held by one or two clamps and is usually of two pieces or of a hollow center single piece so that the clamp or clamps, when tightened, press the two sides against the barrel of the vertical rod. The rifle barrel is rested across the middle of the rubber rest pad, which may be flat, or U-shaped on top, and is moved up or down the vertical rod before aim is taken.

In action, in the field, the rod is jammed into the ground until it is rigid or leaned against a fence, a rock, or a log. The rest, if it then requires moving, is slid up or down as needed, and clamped in proper position. The shooter then assumes the lowest position comfortable to him consistent with the height of the grass over which he must fire, takes aim and lets off the shot. This gives a reasonably consistent point of aim for each shot fired. The vertical screw of the scope mount is adjusted for elevation so that the rifle shoots to the desired point of aim.

Ray Weeks, of Tillsonburg, Ontario, whose principal hobby is crow shooting, made his crow and chuck rest from a No. 2 golf iron which is light and readily carried. The sliding rest has a sponge rubber pad. When firing prone he places the forearm of his rifle on the rubber pad, the left hand under the butt of his rifle, and fires with the right trigger finger.

A close-up view of the chuck rest with the point driven into the top of a stump, is also provided for use in this book. This shows the thong at the top for carrying the rod, the rest, the clamp in the right side of the rest for gripping it to the rod, and the sponge rubber pad. Either a right-handed or a left-handed rifleman can use such a rest as the pad can be placed on either side of the upright.

Murphy's of 236 West Locust St., Butler, Pennsylvania, makes up and sells for $3.50 plus 10 cents postage, a Varmint Shooter's Gun Rest. It measures 11 inches high when closed, 17 inches high when open and weighs 7 ounces. The rest portion of the Murphy rest is a U- or V-shaped top and carries but little soft or padding material. It is of approximately the same length and weight as a K-6 or one of the 2-3/4- or 5-power Weaver convertible scopes.

Descriptions and photos of chuck rests have been included in this book to enable you to properly outfit yourself with a rest, if you want it.

CHAPTER 4

Woodchuck Hunting in Ontario

A TRIP to the thistle clumps and the pasture fields of southern Ontario to hunt the numerous woodchucks to be found there is without question a most remarkable and enjoyable experience. Even now, after the passing of four years, the whole hunt seems like a rose-colored dream. Nine days by the calendar passed within seemingly a few hours.

Many will not believe anything exists which they have never seen. If they have never shot more than five to ten woodchucks in a season, and probably have not seen more than twenty in a year, it is useless to tell such people you killed forty-three woodchucks within a week, or that you saw more than fifty dens in one field.

Provincial riflemen discuss, as a matter of course, the bagging of fifty to one hundred woodchucks in a single day. They talk, almost continuously, when shooters are gathered in a group, of where they can take you where you can bag a hundred woodchucks between the break of dawn and dark, and of how they disdain to fire at the close ones, and how they shoot most of their chucks at 300 to 450 yards.

Since admission limit in Canada is 60 loaded cartridges, this is not nearly sufficient for a woodchuck hunt lasting a week or two weeks. But if you take in 60 to 100 rounds of loaded varmint ammunition and 200 to 300 additional bullets and primers and have someone like Parkinson reload for you, you can often convince customs officials of your actual requirements. You can also convince them that you are not going to sell any of your equipment in Canada and that you are a tourist and a hunter, not an importer or a sporting goods dealer. The important thing is that you declare each rifle, telescope and camera or binoculars you have with you, and get them checked off when you return.

Local Canadian riflemen are, at times, so pleased to have you visiting that they drive fifty or sixty miles just to greet you and sit and talk for a half-hour. In the morning the bunch of you may motor along for three to six hours, everyone soon talking at once, and almost constantly, about how many chucks you should see in this township and that one. And, why it is not worth stopping to fire at twelve to fifteen healthy looking woodchucks along the road, these usually being in groups of two to five. You, of course, register immediate and violent objection to passing up these shots, but your objection gets you exactly nothing. The gang keeps right on; the driver steps on it; no one but you looks back; and someone holds your arm tightly to keep you from falling out. It is all just a trifle disconcerting.

The group motors along at almost breakneck speed for three to five or six hours, remarking that if the hay were either very short or all cut, you would have seen twenty-five to fifty chucks by this time, but they would not have been worth stopping for. You are on your way to where there are woodchucks. They do not intend to stop even for a sandwich until they get you there in the real woodchuck hunting country where there are a couple of hundred chucks on one farm.

After you have discussed nothing for three or four hours but woodchucks by the dozen and by the hundred, even a chuck kitten looks as large as a small black bear cub, and a really good-sized Ontario woodchuck of eight or ten pounds reminds you somewhat of a grizzly bear digging out marmots. You look around hurriedly to see if there are any autoists up or down the highway and whether your personal gun bearer has bolted with your double express rifle. One never knows when he may be attacked by woodchucks en masse.

The woodchuck country of southern and central Ontario is in many places a farmer's paradise. It contains mile after mile of wonderfully rich, rolling farm lands which stretch away far into the distance. The view looks more like that in central Indiana than any other part of the United States I have visited. The crops stand thick and high in mid-summer with mixed grains being the most popular, and even considerable tobacco being raised in southern Ontario near the lake around St. Thomas and Tillsonburg and down toward the orchards and vineyards from there.

Such is the agricultural setting for some of the finest woodchuck shooting in North America. With it you find thousands and thousands of acres of pasture and hay lands dotted here and there by small clumps of Scotch thistle (they prefer to call it

Canadian thistle) which is the favorite cover for chucks along the whole of the hilly escarpment which stretches from near Detroit and Windsor to near Ottawa on the northeast. On some parts of this long range of hills, in the month of May before the grass gets too high so as to blot them out, or in August after the hay is cut, the old and the young chucks can be seen feeding on the barren and sun dried stubble. It is then and there probably possible to shoot the rumored ''100 woodchucks a day'' a pair of local men were reported to have killed, although we never found any actual proof. The small gray-green and dense thistle patches are not of themselves particularly striking or easily noted. A stranger will not immediately sense their importance in the whole plan of woodchuck hunting and shooting. From a distance they slightly resemble ragweed or nettles, the latter more than the former.

The thistle clump looks like something the cattle encouraged to grow by grazing a bit too long in one spot and fertilizing that spot as they loafed and switched their tails. The Canadian thistle is a tough, scratchy combination of colors which include forest green, German field gray, dead sticks, a pile of brown dirt, and some drying cow dung. It is particularly effective in camouflaging the head and neck of a chuck. In Ontario, the chucks, especially the immature animals, appear to sit much more in the mouth of their burrow, with just the head and a bit of the neck showing, than in most other localities and these thistle patches and the cut-over hay fields are the places to locate the chuck dens. Thistle clumps very frequently grow five to fifteen feet down from the upper end of a wash, or out in groups in pasture lands, also up on slightly higher ground near small streams. All you have to do is to sit down 100 to 400 yards or so from such thistle clumps and it won't be long until, like an enemy sniper, you will see a chuck, or three or four chucks, peering out at you cautiously from such cover. Note the details in a thistle clump and before long, there in plain sight to you but unseen by others, is Marmota Monax and he considers himself quite perfectly hidden. You should shoot that chuck squarely in the brain pan because generally his den goes down vertically from where he sits. The Canadian frost line is so deep his den seems to go right down to China, and he is not easy to pull out.

THE HUNTING BEGINS

Mr. G. B. Crandall, veteran gunbuilder, was my host all week except when we were hunting far up the province. The rifle, which was the heavy gun in our party, was a G. B. Crandall Hi-side .22-303 Varmint-R as designed and built by Mr. Crandall for his version of the .22-303 cartridge. This powerful rifle was owned by Phil Wismer who very kindly placed it at my disposal. My targeting of the Crandall rifle was at Mr. Crandall's range outside Woodstock, at which place I also sighted in the relined K-Hornet which grouped so well I used it more than the heavier rifle. This K-Hornet was a heavy BSA liner having four grooves fitted by Mr. Crandall into a barrel blank on a Winchester single shot action. I used mostly factory loaded .22 Hornet ammunition in that rifle.

Mr. Philip Wismer of Jordan Station got up about 3 A. M. to drive more than 100 miles to Mr. Crandall's residence to meet me early on the morning of the second day and drive us to the shooting area. Because of the long drive, things had to move fast, but not too fast to enjoy the rail fence perch on the way.

By way of explanation I should mention that among the thousands of miles of barbed-wire fencing in southern Ontario, you occasionally find some man of agriculture who still relies on rail fencing. Most gratefully does your battle-scarred tail seat regard this rail fence. You are attracted to it like a fly to molasses. It is a place where you can sit down in comfort and look things over. Only a man who has tried to sit down comfortably on ten thousand miles of barbed-wire fencing knows the soul-satisfying feeling that permeates your whole being when you gaze in rapt contemplation on at least three sections of good solid rail fencing.

Phil Wismer introduced me to a good high, hard, but wide rail fence just on the P.I. of two tangents at the apex of a curve on a back road, and said most innocently, "Hop up on that rail fence and rest your back" — it wasn't my back, brother, not my back; but I climbed up stiffly and rather painfully and settled myself and started to look around. Mister, that fence felt just fine, even to the barbed-wire scratches.

Right here I learned that brother Wismer is a man who never forgets the location of a woodchuck hole. I looked down, and there right beneath my feet were at least ten different woodchuck dens. I counted twenty-five to thirty chuck holes within 90 yards and would likely have searched out more dens when a young chuck popped out and sat up just 83 paces directly in front of me. I shot him, then walked out, hacked off the brush and traveled on down the fence row counting six dens beneath a clump of large trees and eight more down along the edge of a field of mixed grains. I also saw a road or path which the chucks had worn in foot-high grass which was a good twice the width of a chuck.

Since it was early in July, wild strawberries were growing here in profusion, most of them short and covered with a few white blossoms. There was a dense bog nearby covered by a very thick growth of hemlock and Norway Spruce, called "bush" by the Canadians. Just to the left were two chuck paths leading into it; but it was illegal to shoot across the road from the top of a cliff, the only place where one could station oneself, so we went back to the car and drove on.

When you deliberately drive away from at least forty to forty-five chuck dens, most of them very fresh, to go and shoot in some other place where you have a better opportunity to get some shooting, you are in chuck country. I never expected to live to experience the sensation of purposely driving away from forty to forty-five woodchuck dens.

Two or three farms in this general area actually had been left lying idle for a few years because during that period they contained so many woodchucks that farming them was definitely dangerous. Field after field was honeycombed. I think this "100 woodchucks a day" got its start in that place.

When you are in Ontario and in the company of friends who have planned for two or three years exactly what you will do every minute of a week-long shooting vacation, it is a certainty that there will be action.

So we went on, and there one after the other, both of them in thistle patches were two woodchucks. I happened to shoot each of them through the right eye. I noticed the others looking rather peculiarly at each other and then one murmured, "Ho hum — so he shoots them all through the right eye!"

A resume of the first day's shooting using the .22 K-Hornet showed that two chucks had been shot in the right eye. One chuck was shot offhand at some 40 yards as he ambled unconcernedly on his way to his home thistle patch and as I topped a rise in the hill. I shot that one purposely through the heart area, and he never even kicked. Just collapsed on his nose.

One chuck was shot in the mouth from in front on a prone shot as it was facing me. Another was shot in the head. Both were killed instantly, the back of the skull being blown out in each instance. Three were shot in the forehead just above the eyes as they faced me. The neatest shot of the day was the seventh chance, and was about 80 per cent of the way across a very wide and very flat hay field containing a dense stand of grass. This chuck suddenly stood up his full height on a small knoll in the deep green grass and I fired across a fence rail with arm rest. The chuck, which was very large, went down as if poleaxed. The range was estimated by the president of the local Game and Hunting Association, who was there as host, as just over 200 yards. Lorne Crandall thought it was about 175 yards. It paced out as just 181 paces. This chuck lost much blood on the spot. A skull fracture at both ears will give exactly this result. It will do it with the .22 Hornet, the K-Hornet, or the .170 Woodsman. This Marmota Monax was almost coal black on the outside of all four legs and for half the distance up his sides. The upper parts were a very rich chestnut red. This was the blackest woodchuck out of 60 or 65 knocked flat on the trip. The only completely black woodchuck seen was a very large coal black animal that suddenly ran across a back road in front of the car and disappeared in a field high with mixed grain.

It is impossible to see a woodchuck which has gotten well into a field of mixed grains, in fact, you will find it extremely difficult to force your way into such a field because of the density of the grain as it stands on the rich ground. Even a wounded chuck will keep right ahead of you in such cover and searching for him is just a waste of time.

Of the eight chucks bagged the first day, two were abnormally large and also unusually dark. Seven of the eight were large chucks, one shot by a companion being about a 9-pound animal. The largest I had opportunity to weigh on this trip tipped the scales at 11 pounds. The last one killed that day was stopped at 95 paces and was struck a half an inch back of and below the butt of the ear. The bullet emerged through the top of the skull after severing the skull from the top vertebra of the neck.

THIRD DAY'S SHOOTING

Now for the shooting on the long trip. This was the journey on which it was stated one could kill "100 woodchucks in a day,"

conditions as to height of grass, weather, and season, of course
being favorable. The importance of all three factors can scarcely be overemphasized. During the hot or very warm weather,
especially during a dry spell, the chucks do not come out well
and sometimes do not appear at all. In a field dotted with dozens
of chuck dens, and this is relatively common in the better areas,
you may sit for two or three hours and not see a whisker. You
might as well be in a cemetery. During the very hot or warm
parts of a high temperature day they simply stay underground.

This, the third day of the week, was the day of the big bet.
One man suddenly proposed that the man shooting the most
woodchucks that day should treat the crowd. The bet was accepted but a time limit of 5 P.M. was put on that one. How important the time of day can be in this northern woodchuck shooting will be seen when it is mentioned that at 5 P.M. the loser of
that wager had four chuck tails. His companion had two. The
other pair of riflemen had five chuck tails, one having bagged
two and the other three. Up to 5 P.M. four chucks was, therefore, high gun among four woodchuck shots, all of considerable
experience.

Balance that, if you will, against 100 woodchucks a day.
Eleven chucks against an advertised 400 woodchucks. How would
you like to travel 800 miles to find such a shrinkage?

But the evening shoot put an entirely different tint on the
picture. The loser of the bet, who had four tails by 5 P.M., cut
the tails off sixteen woodchucks by quitting time. That happened
to be me. My companion bagged nine woodchucks. That made a
total for the pair of us of twenty-five woodchucks, nineteen of
which were shot during the evening.

The day's shooting began under rather peculiar circumstances. A chuck was seen away out on a bare hill across a shallow ravine. Then he went in. One chap thought he could bring
him out and did so. But the chuck raced back over the top of the
hill and did not present a shot so the shooter walked back down
a lane to the vicinity of an old abandoned barn. He walked over
there cautiously, as he expected to find a very wild woodchuck
around the barn foundation. Suddenly he saw a chuck stick its
head out of a hole and killed it with an offhand shot at fifty yards.
Then he shot and killed another and a very large chuck which
was lying sound asleep on a rafter. The previous report of the
Hornet cartridge had not awakened him. This sleeping chuck
was knocked fifteen feet out into space and landed motionless on

an open spot of turf and was not found for fifteen minutes or so
as the shooter was in the meantime carefully looking for it in
the debris in the bottom of the building.

After these two chucks had been carried back to the car, a
farmer came along and insisted that the hunters drive onto his
farm as he had a large colony of woodchucks and wanted to get
them thinned off. Can you imagine anything like such an invita-
tion being extended here in the States? On the way down his
farm lane, a chuck was seen squatted motionless on the top of
his hayfield hill, sitting there in a thistle patch. The shot was
almost directly toward the setting sun, which brought the top of
his profile into sharp relief, but even so, only his ears were
plainly visible. The shot would have been impossible, due to re-
flected light, if a telescope had not been used. At the crack of
the rifle this chuck simply flattened down into the thicket in
which he was sitting as the bullet landed at the base of his ear.
Another equally inquisitive animal was shot at the mound in front
of his den. The pair were carried to the farmhouse and weighed
on small spring scales. One weighed 5-1/2 pounds and the other
7-1/2 pounds.

As I had seen a smaller chuck at a den when we had passed
the field, so I went back up into the cut-over hayfield escorted
by the farmer's wife and his daughter who had a truck patch and
were determined to point out every woodchuck on the place. This
included the abode of what they termed the "old granddaddy." A
rather difficult offhand shot of medium distance, but downhill,
resulted in a clean shot which struck the neck just back of the
ears. About this time a good-sized chuck was seen moving along
rapidly toward his den, far down along the edge of the orchard.
I made a quick dash up over the top of the hill. Seeing me in an
unexpected location the chuck stopped momentarily and then
started again for the den. The result was a quick offhand shot
from hilltop to valley, the bullet striking directly in the butt of
the ear for the best long-range, offhand shot made during the
week.

Soon a regular and evenly spaced number of shots sounded
back over the farm. It came so regularly I wondered for a time
whether some trapshooting had been put on for our entertain-
ment. I found, however, that my friend had gone to work with
his long range rifle (a .219 Zipper hi-side with set trigger and
scope) on a colony of chucks which were denned up in a small
hillside with an almost vertical bank. In all, he bagged seven

chucks there and totaled nine for the afternoon and evening.

I crossed over to the far side of the farm, to the east, and soon saw two chucks playing around in a hayfield. After climbing the usual three or four fences and wading a weed grown bog, I arrived at the edge of the hayfield near a large pile of posts and fence rails. A chuck suddenly rushed out of the cover of the grass, backed up against the pile of rails and showed definite defiance at my trespass. I shot this one offhand with a bullet through the throat. Next was a shot across the rails and through the wires of a fence at a chuck crouched rather low down and feeding in the hayfield.

Three jack rabbits were gamboling around in the cut-over hayfield. They galloped around much like lambs or goats, dashing around the chucks and once around my feet, and by the time I had shot five chucks, it kept me busy distinguishing which were moving chucks and which were wildly carousing jacks. The jackrabbit seems to have the characteristics up there, of the jitterbug fanatic. He careens and bounds and bounces and gyrates around like something that is half insane. Late afternoon or early evening seems to be his pet time to put on a show.

REFLECTIONS ON THE TRIP

The week of the 1946 chuck trip ended on a Saturday morning hunt with five straight kills with five cartridges from Wismer's heavy hi-side .22-303 Varmint-R. For years this caliber has been the most common long range woodchuck and coyote rifle in Canada. The case is made by cutting off and necking down the heavier cases made for anti-aircraft machine gun ammunition. In these, the body of the case appears nearly twice as thick as in ordinary .303 British commercial hunting ammunition.

The charge is generally a 50- or a 55-grain Sisk, Sierra or Speer bullet pushed along by 30 to 36 grains of IMR No. 4320, 3031, 4064 or 4350 powder. Muzzle velocities are usually between 3200 and 3800 f.s. Toward the end of World War II, there was considerable difficulty in Canada in obtaining bullets which would expand uniformly and which were really accurate. Copper tubing to make such bullets was difficult to obtain and so was lead wire of the proper diameter. Empty .22 rim fire cases could be used for jackets, but they rarely gave the same degree of accuracy as copper tubing. The firing pin indentation always showed on the butt, and this also tended to give a slightly un-

Charles Parkinson, of London, Ontario, admires son Buddy's outsize chuck. Unaided, Junior bagged the largest of the trip.

Author Landis and George B. Crandall take time out to swap stories.

L to R: Phil Wismer, Frank Bacon, Charles Parkinson, and Mr. Bacon's father—expert Canadian chuck hunters. CREDIT: C. S. LANDIS.

A pair of varmint rifles from Ellwood Epps' shop. Top arm is a medium weight sporter; lower has heavy sporter stock.

Mausers made up by Epps. Top is left side view of lower gun in photograph above; lower has German double set trigger and Fecker scope.

balanced bullet. I saw shots on this trip, mostly by G. B. or Lorne Crandall, using these bullets, in which the bullet seemed to fail to expand at all and gave little or no tearing effect visible on either side of the chuck. It might take five or ten minutes of most careful examination of a carcass to find any evidence of either the hole of entrance or the hole of exit, and some of the chucks, most solidly and centrally hit, simply refused to lie down and die. At other times the heavy rifle would blow a hole through the chuck that two fists could enter. So long as lead wire is available, the expansion appears prompt and uniform. But if hard scrap lead must be used for cores and empty .22 rim fires for jackets accurate results are often uncertain.

In Ontario, it pays to hunt away from a car if the colonies are properly located for such hunting. You can shoot anywhere away from the main highways if you are not in a "Red Area" which is simply a Provincial Game Preserve identified by red signs posted along its boundaries.

I had enough chuck tails to bring along home to fill two 12 gauge shotgun shell boxes, but before the week was ended, the host's cat, which had been having quite a time for herself playing with the tails, began to carefully avoid that side of the room and we had to throw them out.

On a two or three weeks' trip of this sort, you can, with luck and a local hunter or two who know the location of the different chuck colonies for 100 to 150 miles in all directions, obtain as much chuck shooting as you would obtain at your home district, possibly within the following ten to twenty years. But remember, until Ontario is opened generally to American tourists, you can legally hunt big game or small game there, but you'll have to be satisfied with reading about their grand woodchuck shooting. It is the best shooting they have, and it will be worth $75 to $150 of any man's money to enjoy it when and if the time comes that it is generally and publicly available.

Some of the local woodchuck hunters have a sense of humor. One night a local man came home from a very long drive and did not reach the place where we had stopped until about 1:30 A.M. Two chucks weighing 9 and 11 pounds were in the back of his car. They were forgotten until the next afternoon when, as he was passing a cemetery, he thought of them and it seemed most fitting they should be deposited near the main gateway. A short time later someone, who will forever remain nameless, phoned the leading undertaker and in very agitated tones let it be known that there were two bodies lying near the cemetery—possibly the work of some hit and run driver who failed to look after the dead. Could the undertaker pick up and embalm the bodies? It is reported the undertaker's ambulance was heard clanging down the highway soon afterward.

As I write this, I have my Ontario licenses for 1951. The Indian had to die to reach his Happy Hunting Grounds but all a white man needs is gasoline money or carfare. That and friends, who know their way around among the woodchucks.

Readers will come to different conclusions as to whether we shot too few or too many woodchucks, but the number of chucks shot should always be considered in regard to the available supply and whether chucks in a locality are a rarity, reasonably plentiful, or the farmer's worst curse. The farmer is almost helpless to protect his crops from their ravages. In view of the plentiful supply in Canada, a bag of fifty or sixty chucks for half a dozen riflemen, all of them experienced chuck hunters and all armed with .22-caliber high velocity varmint rifles sighted with quality telescopes, did not seem high to us.

A matter which gave me considerable concern before the journey was whether some of the most expert rifle shots in all Canada, most of them twenty or thirty years my junior, would shoot much better with their own rifles to which they were accustomed, than I could with rifles I had not previously fired. They knew the country, the type of terrain in which the chucks were mostly located, the physical conditions, average wind drift, and similar things which affect accuracy of rifle fire. All were strange to me when I arrived there. All these give a visitor to any hunting country problems which he must be able to solve quickly and at times almost instantly to hunt successfully. But the unusual concern of each Canadian rifleman I gunned with as to my personal success showed a true hospitality and added greatly to the enjoyment of the whole trip.

THE 1947 WOODCHUCK HUNTING TRIP IN ONTARIO

It can rain forever, at least there are times when it seems so. When Dick Noel and I made our 1947 shooting trip to Ontario, it had rained there continuously for 25 days. But such a small matter does not often stop a pair of enthusiastic woodchuck hunters, so we left home on a Saturday in high spirits and with high hopes of fine shooting.

The trip started out well enough! We had nothing but slightly overcast skies and a few denser clouds here and there, until we reached Rochester, New York. While we were eating breakfast on Sunday morning, it started to pour, and kept it up with what seemed like increasing intensity for the next eight days. Then the sun came out.

But the rain had left its mark and the thirty to fifty mile winds, common in southern Ontario, did not improve the prospects for chuck shooting. Most of the chucks were pretty well drowned out in the bottomlands where the richer hay fields lay, while in many instances, two to eight inches of water was lying on flat fields, even those at considerable altitude. The chucks were denned up on small mounds and the hills which dotted the countryside. These chucks had been kept in too long by the rains and they were hungry.

On my firearms permit I had listed five different rifles, three of which I shot. This was to be a hunt on which we would try all available rifles, including numerous wildcats, and note the differences in results. I also hoped to explode the oft-repeated but fallacious theory that the .22 Hornet rifle is not an effective woodchuck rifle.

The grass was still but three to eight inches tall in the richer fields. Spring comes late in Ontario and this year it had been abnormally wet and cold. The growing season is really May to August, not March to November. This short grass permitted chuck shooting at much greater ranges than we would have had during June and July.

On this trip we used about ten different rifles. The make-up of the party changed some from day to day, as we visited one friend or another. In six days we shot in five different districts and had good shooting in all of them. We used two .22-303 Crandall Varmint-R rifles, a combination of great range and power. The Crandall rifle is made by necking down the .303 British heavy machine gun cartridge to .22 caliber, after first cutting off part of the length. One of these rifles weighed 12 pounds. Stanley Adams used a .22-250 with deadly effect. A very accurate R-2 Sharps-Borchardt was in the party but wet and flooded rifle ranges delayed sighting it in. One .250-3000 caliber Model 70 Winchester was used now and then but not too successfully. There appeared to be no practical and observable difference in accuracy between the heavy, high side Winchester single shots and the bolt actions.

Two rifles were used extensively by myself and Dick Noel. A standard weight, Model 54 Winchester .220 Swift, was shot by me, taking most of the long shots presented during the first four days of the week. A targetweight, heavy barrel, Model 70 Winchester in .220 Swift caliber, was shot by Dick Noel. My .220 was fitted with a 4-power Fecker hunting telescope while his was fitted with a 10-power Unertl target scope.

Other rifles included a .22 K-Hornet High Side Winchester single shot fitted with Parkerifled 8-groove barrel, a comparatively light single shot of some 8 or 8-1/2 pounds, used by Lorne Crandall on the one day he was able to hunt with us. This is the same rifle with which I shot 23 straight on chucks the previous year, and which performed very well for Mr. Crandall this season. It was fitted with a 9-power Parker-Hale rifle telescope which has been described by some as a rather poor replica of the Fecker. It is not exactly the same, neither are the mounts. It can be purchased reasonably in Canada.

Another rifle shot considerably by me — in fact, it killed more woodchucks than any other rifle used on the trip, was my old reliable "Meat in the Pot" — "Old Sal," my Model 54 Winchester .22 Hornet, fitted with Malcolm 3-3/4 power first-grade hunting scope in Mann V-type mounts. This rifle made a long run of 19 kills out of 21 consecutive shots, all witnessed and spread over parts of three days. Of the other two shots, one chuck was hit in the right shoulder, while facing me, on a long range shot in a strong wind, and the bullet blew out a bit more than expected on a puff. That one pulled in, badly hurt. We may have been able to get it out, but it was not advisable to attempt a retrieve. The one actual miss was undershot beneath the chin on an otherwise easy chance, in an attempt to get a photograph of both the shooter and woodchuck at the exact instant of shooting. It just didn't work out. There were too many distractions.

Then we had a rifle made up by Charles Parkinson, of London, Ontario, on a high side Winchester single shot action. It consisted of an Ackley .170 caliber, 24-inch barrel chambered by Parkinson for the .170 Woodsman Special cartridge but made with a more gentle slope of shoulder than the original design, in this instance 15 degrees; in the original design, 28 degrees. This rifle and cartridge combines more that is desirable, and less that is undesirable in a small caliber, medium power woodchuck rifle than any previous rifle I have shot. The report isn't a report, it is simply a surprisingly soft "plop." The recoil is but one foot pound——only one seventeenth that of the service rifle cartridge. The ballistics recently given for this cartridge, as a result of chronograph tests made on the range of C. C. Meredith, at Streetsville, Ontario, gave m.v.'s of 3000 to 3500 f. s. and with a selected load listed to give 3600 f.s. m.v.

I had an opportunity to shoot this particular rifle and its cartridge most of one day, Friday, May 30, 1947. I killed eight woodchucks instantly with the first eight cartridges fired. Each one went down as if struck by lightning and died, apparently without kicking. Then I shot a big 12-pound jack rabbit with it, and that went down without kicking. In all, I killed twelve woodchucks and one jack with it that day, the longest kills being at 220 and 250 paces. It seemed to get its tiny 25-grain soft point bullet out to the game quicker and faster than the .220 Swift. I had killed 20 woodchucks with the Swift the previous four days, and while the Swift tore a bigger hole in the chuck, it did not kill so instantly and uniformly.

The penetration in steel of this .170, suggested a very high f.s. m.v. Remember, Ackley obtained 4935 f.s. repeatedly with a .170-250-5000 cartridge I had designed and he had made up six months previously. Noel and I were so impressed with the remarkable killing power of this cartridge as demonstrated in this public test held a year previously by Parkinson, that each of us ordered and purchased a rifle in this caliber. We had it made up with this cartridge, but with the sharper shoulder to hold a little more powder, and reduce possible erosion by burning the powder more completely in the case and on a straight line up the bore.

Parkinson had killed 30 crows and 50 woodchucks with this rifle, which is his own personal weapon, and he killed a crow neatly with it at 100 yards the day I shot it. Never has this rifle thrown a ricochet in the hands of anyone. This is the most remarkable and useful quality in a woodchuck rifle which can be added to those already possessed by the best of the special varmint rifles used for chuck shooting. There is little left of 25- and of 30-grain soft point bullets after they have landed at a striking velocity of around 300 f.s. or more. They seem to impart a degree of nervous shock rarely witnessed.

On this trip Noel and I came to a number of conclusions. One being that the .220 Swift cartridge is not ideal for woodchuck shooting in farming communities. It makes too sharp and too loud a report. This attracts attention, which is never desirable.

Our two Swift rifles, using the best soft point factory ammunition, and later some slightly more accurate hand loaded .220 ammunition by Parkinson, were at least 50 to 100 per cent less accurate than my .22 Hornet rifle used exclusively with factory loaded ammunition of the same make. The heavy barrel Swift, in addition, varied materially in its grouping vertically from day to day and also from one time of day to another. However, in the years 1948 and 1949, the .220 Swift settled down and shot more accurately.

On one occasion, I shot a chuck with the .220 Swift, down along a rocky fence line. It was sticking its head out of a den mouth. I held a bit low as the shot was downhill, and I didn't intend to overshoot. At the report, that chuck was knocked out of the hole, a distance of three or four feet, it spun around on its back, like a turtle, whizzed its tail frenziedly in the sure sign of death, then rolled over onto its feet again, got up and rushed a distance of fifteen feet — which was paced — and ran headlong and stuck in the V of a rock wall where two stones were upended so as to form a V orifice about eight inches high on both sides with a two-inch wedge-shaped opening. That chuck was dead when I reached there. It had lost its whole head, throat, and whole neck, except a thin strip of skin on the back of the neck, and the upper flat section of the skull and upper half of the right eye. That chuck could not see, breathe, swallow, or think yet it got up and rushed for fifteen feet and almost made safety. Had it turned around and rushed, it would have gone in.

Of the rifles doing exceptionally well, the .22-250 lost two hit chucks down holes and bagged 17 tails, one afternoon and evening. I do not know how many misses were scored. A heavy 12-pound .22-303 Varmint-R made some excellent shots on Tuesday. Most of these were very long range kills. The .170 made the most instant kills consecutively at an average range, for it, of 150 yards. The .22 Hornet killed the most woodchucks. Its longest kill was 202 paces. The heavier rifles were used at longer distances when both were immediately available. Every one of the .22 wildcat rifles used on the trip was a consistently accurate, deadly, and efficient woodchuck rifle.

We hunted with a majority of the most experienced and skillful woodchuck hunters in Ontario. Our party killed 140 to 150 woodchucks during the week. The two of us from the States shot and killed 108 of these. My hunting partner got 44, and I myself 64.

I was wearing high rubber arctics over Bean's Maine Shoe

Packs, well oiled, it was that sopping wet down in those fields. Even so, my trousers were soaked almost to the knees.

The most annoying thing in Ontario chuck shooting is the tens of thousands of miles, more or less, of wire fencing, most of it topped with rusty barbed wire that you have to climb to hunt in the fields, and to bring back your woodchucks. Much of this fencing, due to lack of repairs during the war, has posts loose at the bottom, and, as you cannot crawl under such fences, you hang there on that top barbed wire, suspended between heaven and hell, caught fast where it is hardest to wrench loose. By mid-afternoon you wish some of those fences were eight thousand miles farther down in the ground and by dusk maybe you just don't give a hoot and you let someone else crawl over the fences, while the fences stretch ahead of you, mile after mile. In a comparatively mildly settled area, you wonder how anyone found time to build so many high fences and to string all the barbed wire.

Then you drive back to the house where the group drifts in, one by one, and you sit and talk rifles, ballistics, varmint cartridges and trajectories until midnight or later. By that time you are too sleepy to bother with barbed wire scratches and you go to bed, crawl between the covers — for normally, it is cool at night in Ontario. When you roll into bed, the barbed wire fence scratches bite and sting, and sting and bite. For that, you have travelled 2200 miles! But for some odd reason, the creator willing, you will be back again!

Sixty-four woodchucks in the rain. Twenty with the Swift, 32 with the Hornet, and 12 within a few hours, with the .170. There was that run of eight straight and the kill of 19 in 21 chances. Such shooting beckons! A man must keep in training for those fences. All the good shooting is on the other side of the wire. Over there the fields are greener, the chucks are thicker, and one always expects to get another shot. In the middle of the next field you think you see a big woodchuck that sits up two feet tall, or so he looks! No — it isn't just one big chuck, there are eight woodchucks in that field, and every one of them is now sitting up like a picket-pin wondering, probably, what that hunter with the scope-sighted rifle is up to now. With eight chucks in one field, and fourteen up at once, as reported from another, who would let small matters like barbed wire scratches and five weeks of rain, keep you home? Tomorrow the sun may shine, and then, out those chucks will pop!

THE 1948 WOODCHUCK HUNTING TRIP IN ONTARIO

Most riflemen are inclined to judge what is good woodchuck shooting, and the size of probable bags, by the chucks they have shot in the localities they have visited. Such places may never have been good woodchuck districts. Many times one may shoot more chucks within a day or two, in a really good chuck district, than he may see in a year in some locality having only fair chuck shooting. Charles Parkinson wrote me May 20, 1950, from Ontario, ''We have had no rain for two weeks. Conditions very dry. We went out today where we saw about 75 woodchucks a month ago and the farmer told me some boys were out last Saturday with Lovell (R-2) rifles and they shot 61 chucks.'' Persons never having seen anything like this, will have difficulty to visualize such shooting.

Upon my return from the 1947 woodchuck hunt in Ontario, I determined to have a .170 rifle built in the smallest practical cartridge efficient for use in thickly settled districts. We would then, if possible, take this rifle to Ontario in 1948, and give it an extensive trial.

An order was placed through a custom gunsmith for seven .170 rifle blanks with P. O. Ackley Inc., of Trinidad, Colorado. These were to be chambered and fitted for a group of Ontario, New York, Pennsylvania, Delaware, and Alaska sportsmen. These barrels were bored by Koozer, in Ackley's plant, and my blank was stamped with my name when it arrived in the shop of the gunsmith. A few went direct to the ultimate owners, but most of them went to Parkinson.

We had planned in advance that Harold Wood of Allentown, Pennsylvania, and I would go up together and each of us would have a .170 along. He would also take his .220 Weatherby Rocket, and I would take my .22-250 Pfeifer Springfield, but since this rifle had not arrived yet, I would also take my .22 Hornet. At the last moment Mr. Wood cancelled his trip due to sickness in his family, and I went up alone by train. All I could take with my baggage was the one .170 rifle.

Phil Wismer had one of the .170's chambered by Parkinson with his latest chambering reamers, made in Detroit with my suggested 28-degree shoulder. Mine had the same chambering. Parkinson had his .170 then chambered by the same tools, after having used it successively with 15- and 40-degree shoulders for testing purposes. The barrel had been cut off at the breech and rethreaded and refitted with each chambering.

This shooting excursion was laid out carefully for the sole purpose of testing the .170's. Phil Wismer was to take and shoot, as occasion warranted, his new .170 Woodsman; Charles Parkinson, who fitted up most of them, would take his. So with Wood's rifle and mine, that would have made four .170 rifles to be tried on the one chuck shooting excursion, all four of the .170's to be of the same caliber and for the same cartridge.

It would be thus, the first trip of its kind ever held in North America in which four .170's would be shot in part, together, and in all four units on the same shooting excursion — but possibly on different days. Thus the accuracy of four different barrels and of four riflemen would be employed which should give a good general average of the results normally to be expected with the .170 Woodsman cartridge. Unfortunately, we did not have Mr. Wood along, but continued our plans with the three remaining rifles.

The rifle was to be tested in the presence of W. B. Elliott, Philip Wismer, G. B. Crandall, Lorne Crandall, Charles Parkinson, Ray Weeks, Maurice Atkinson, Elmer McConnell, Ellwood Epps and such others as might join the party. This group included many of the most skilled chuck hunters in Ontario. Weeks and Parkinson are the best-known rifle shots on crows in that Province. Shooting in such company, probably unexcelled anywhere as chuck shots due to the amount of chuck shooting they can obtain in a season, is a challenge to the skill of any rifleman. You must be able to dope wind, estimate distance, and shoot offhand, be a good stalker and be able to kill chucks from almost any shooting position.

Something, now, about the men with whom I hunted. W. B. Elliott, BSC, is General Manager of Engineering, Tool and Forgings, Limited, of St. Catharines. He is the designer of two versions of the .25-303 British woodchuck cartridge. He has shot the .25-303 extensively on crows and chucks in past years and also has an R-2 and a .219 Zipper Imp., now. Bill Elliott is an excellent host, and an agreeable shooting companion in the field. According to my observations, he is also a darned good rifle shot. Bill shot and killed a crow, on this trip, using an R-2 rifle, from the top of a considerable hill down into a creek valley. The distance paced 199 yards on the way down with the grade, and 214 yards back which was uphill. The wind was blowing practically a gale at the time he shot the crow in the presence of Wismer and myself. The only day we could be together, he shot a nice bag of chucks and a very good bag of crows with Wismer.

Bill has quite a battery of good chuck rifles and a number of fine shotguns. He had expected to shoot a .219 Improved Zipper on a hi-side action on this trip, but the rifle wouldn't group better than 3- to 3-1/2-inch groups at 100 yards, for either him or Ray Weeks, so they sent it back to Ackley for a new barrel. He had to use his R-2, and complained "It was only good for 150 yards or so, in the wind." They have more wind in southern Ontario than seems to be the case even in the United States south of the Great Lakes.

Philip Wismer, good-hearted and generous fruit grower of Jordan Station, is probably the most widely known chuck hunter in the Province. He and his brother are both experienced and successful chuck hunters and talk of "100 shots in a day" as a matter of course. Unfortunately, in the three years I hunted in those districts, 25 or 30 shots in a day was the best we could do. Phil has a very accurate .22-303 hi-side by Crandall. Also a .170. He has a K-Hornet and has owned or tried out a lot of .22 Hornets and other woodchuck rifles. In all, he kills a good many chucks over the course of a year, at such times as his fruit-growing and berry business permits excursions farther up the Province.

In 1947 he wrote Mr. D. P. Noel essentially as follows: "I want to thank you for the shipment of loading components. I had just finished my 50-grain Sisk bullets on Saturday, August 19, 1947, as I was hunting with my brother in the area where you, Landis and I went on the last day we were together early in 1947.

"About 5:30 P.M. on August 19 (1947), I made 26 shots in the two fields without moving from one shooting position. I made 24 hits in the 26 shots at ranges of 150 to 300 yards. I was using my .22-303 heavy single shot Winchester Hi-side made by G. B. Crandall of Woodstock, Ontario, the rifle you shot the first of the last week you were here. My brother took the shots closer than 150 yards, using his K-Hornet, making 23 kills in the same two fields. We then moved on to the hills we passed this side of ———. You will recall where you took a long shot at a chuck at the mouth of his den, using your target weight Swift." Note that this was 47 hits within two fields, by two men, the same evening.

Mr. Crandall was belatedly working on the forearm of his new .22-303 Varmint-R rifle to take chuck shooting with me,

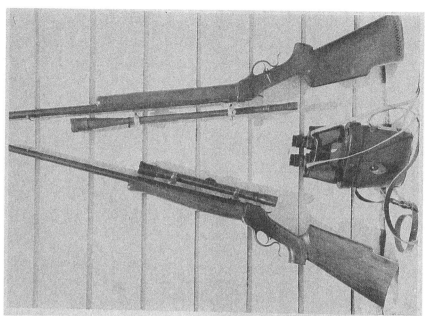

Left: Stanley Adams' .219 Zipper Winchester Hi-side, single set trigger, Weaver scope. *Right:* Adams' .22-303 Varmint-R with single set trigger —a G. B. Crandall job.

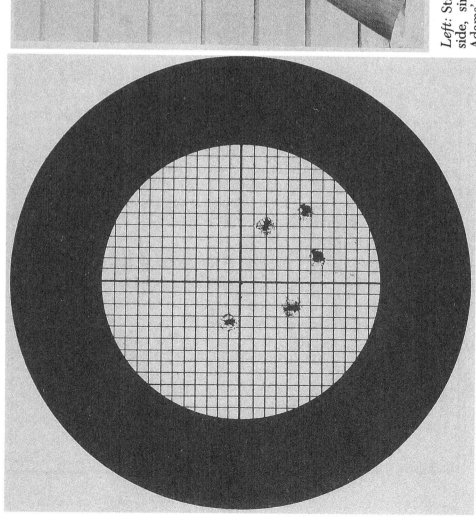

Group fired by the author with a Winchester Hi-wall.

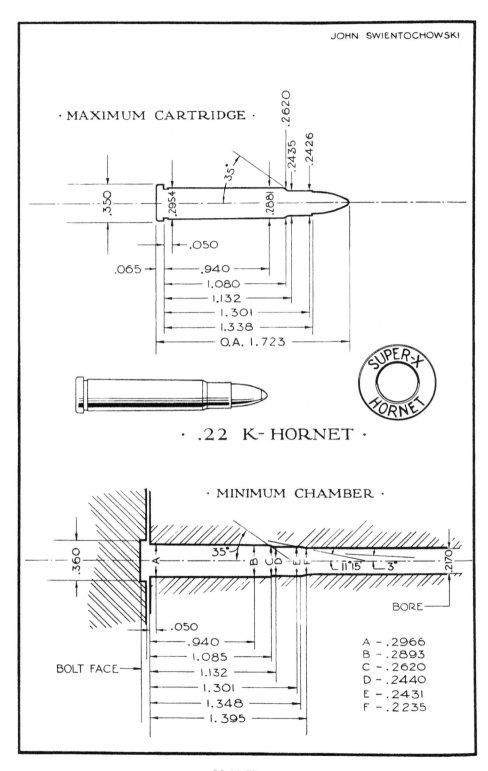

.22 K-Hornet.

when I arrived in Woodstock. He was not ready to go out for another day or two, so I did not get out with the Crandalls on the 1948 trip, as I did not get back to Woodstock.

Charles Parkinson, of London, Ontario, has long been a shooting companion and protege of Ray Weeks. About a year before this was written Charley went into the custom gunsmithing business, in a shop on his property. Parkinson fitted and chambered most of these .170 Marksman barrels. During the 1948 shoot, he and I spent two days together and he made a number of abnormally good long range shots on crows at 200 to 350 yards or so, making a few very spectacular kills using a .219 Zipper caliber rifle — a hi-side single shot of his own manufacture. His son killed 11 woodchucks on one day when seven of our group were out together, and was "high man" that day. The boy was only about 11 years old.

Practically everyone has heard of Ray Weeks of Tillsonburg. Mr. Weeks is an agent for the Prudential Insurance Company, and with his car travels over a considerable area of the tobacco country of Ontario. He is generally credited with being probably the best field shot in Ontario, and one of the best at rest shooting matches. While we were together for the two days, Ray bagged 20 chucks with the .219 Donaldson, while I killed 19. He shot a number of crows at very long range, using the .219 rifle — his old Winchester single shot rifle, formerly in R-2 and then in short .22-303 calibers, now in .219 Donaldson for less report.

The .219 Donaldson cartridge is an almost ideal woodchuck cartridge, insofar as killing power is concerned, up to 250 or 300 yards. It is a 30-grain case holding twice the powder charge of the .170 Woodsman and handles a 55-grain bullet to splendid advantage. It is not too noisy or too long ranged for most Ontario chuck shooting, but it does give some loud ricochets and it is too noisy for much thickly settled shooting in the States. It develops 3500 to 3750 f.s. muzzle velocity with a pressure that seems to be fairly high, although not often excessive.

Stan Adams, who hunted with us again part of the second day, is one of the most expert woodchuck shots in Ontario. He has been a District Insurance Manager in Tillsonburg for many years, but recently moved onto a farm a good distance from there where he will devote most of his time to developing and selling Christmas trees. He usually uses a .219 Improved Zipper in a hi-side Winchester Schuetzen double set-trigger action. He will be one of the high shots on almost any chuck hunt. This year, while hunting with Wismer and myself, he made a most astonishingly long kill.

I was making my way up a swampy hollow and was stalking a big chuck sitting up in a field a quarter of a mile to the south, when I saw someone come out into the field, lie down in the grass, and shoot at what I thought was the chuck I was stalking but which chuck, in the meantime, unknown to either of us, had "gone down." It proved to be Adams making the stalk, and when he fired he killed a woodchuck sitting along a bare fence row, clear across the very wide far field and he shot across about two thirds of the field he was in, and in a diagonal direction. The chuck was probably 350 to 400 yards from Adams. He picked it up and laid it on a fence post but forgot to pace the distance either going up or coming back.

Elmer McConnell, who might be described as "the big silent man," one of the most lovable characters I have met on any of the Canadian trips, is described at length in the long range shooting described farther on.

Ellwood Epps, of Clinton, Ontario, has a sporting goods business with wide ramifications. Much of it is mail order, but he also sells much hunting equipment and fishing tackle to local residents. Clinton is 10 or 15 miles east of Lake Huron, and is a town of 5000. The country for 100 or 125 miles in every direction was abnormally dry while I hunted in Ontario in 1948, grass was short, and the hills were relatively bare. At a glance, few would take it to be good chuck country. Years ago, Epps drove a truck in a transportation business, and knows that part of Ontario like a book. He does more big game hunting than woodchuck shooting, but he seems to know all of the back roads once taken to dodge traffic. And there is where the chucks live, in the adjacent fields. A few of the hills in the territory provide good farming and are green and covered with thick stands of grass, but most of the small hills are dusty and dry and have very little cover. A chuck hole and mount will stand out on the surface of such bare hills, but it is not always too easily seen due to the dull gray color of the earth.

Epps is a relatively young man, who has built up a successful sporting goods business. He is a woodchuck shot of far more ability than most riflemen in Ontario credit. I personally saw him kill a skunk, at what both of us very conservatively estimated to be 500 to 550 yards, across in the third wide field on a small hillside. The animal was centered on the second shot, and the first bullet struck within four to six inches of it. I saw him kill two and three chucks successively at 250 to 350 yards, time and again. On a number of occasions he killed five or six straight at 200 to 350 yards, taking the shots as they came. Most of these shots were straight prone, prone across a wire or a rail, or sitting with arm rest.

His rifle, which had been obtained on a trade with one of his customers, was a C. C. Johnson, using Johnson's version of the .22 Marciante Blue Streak cartridge. These are made up from the .25-35 necked down, or the .22 Savage H.P. He shot the 55-grain Sisk bullet with a fair load of powder. In Epps' hands this cartridge was consistently deadly at 100 yards beyond the average range at which most persons consider this cartridge effective. On every shot the bullet landed with a resounding "thwack." The numerous chucks I examined that Epps shot, were killed uniformly outside the den mouth and were torn two or more times as much as by the little .170. The sighting seemed to be almost the same from 200 to 350 yards, much to the surprise of the shooter. He was more inclined to overshoot than to undershoot. The hitting and killing power of this charge was ample for all old and tough chucks at muzzle to 350 or 400 yards. But this rifle could, and at times did, give a howling ricochet.

When I left for Canada, I had only 160 or 165 loaded cartridges. These were put up by the late Bob Bley, and were all case-forming loads. I was worried about how I would get along with no more than that number of cartridges. But this was solved readily by sending my empties — as soon as I had a box or more fired — on to Parkinson who loaded them with full charges in the expanded cases and sent them on to my next stopping point. Obviously, having chambered the rifle, he had a duplicate set of reloading tools for it. In this manner he loaded for me three additional lots, all of them of moderate numbers, and I was thus able to get a reasonable amount of shooting for eleven days, and to bring 125 loaded cartridges along home with me. But on the last day of shooting, I was counting my cartridges on hand and was picking my shots. Also, the fly of the set trigger, a small irregularly shaped piece, about one quarter as big around as a dime and a sixteenth of an inch thick, had come loose again, and so completely blocked the hammer upon occasion, that I could not fire the rifle at all on six occasions which included most of the best shots I had that day. A normal expectancy would have been at least five, and possibly six kills, on those chances. One of these chucks was standing up straight, facing me, within a foot or a foot and a half of the body of a large chuck I had shot at the same den, the evening before. It was a perfect offhand shot.

I had little opportunity to do target shooting or even to sight in properly while in Canada and none at all before I went up there. I did a bit of sighting on Wismer's 100-yard range, after which Phil reported a group of seven or eight shots — all that were fired — in a cluster approximately 5/8 by 1/2 inch, allowing for windage correction made on the mounts. I fired a few shots at 100 and at 200 yards on Weeks' range below Tillsonburg, and Elliott, Wismer and myself each wasted a half dozen shots or so at a chuck across a valley, in a hollow, firing across a very strong, tricky wind drift. None of us hit it.

I suppose I saw 550 to 600 woodchucks in all, some of them from railway car windows. Many were along the numbered and paved King's Highways, where you do not shoot unless you wish to siesta for a while in the King's Pokey. I suppose the group killed 300 to 300 woodchucks all told, on this excursion, but no one considered the bags excessive, and friends who had been in the group went out again later on, and shot just as many.

There is no disputing the fact that with the little .170 Landis design of Woodsman I killed 16 chucks a day for 11 days, and that is successful chuck shooting any place and any time. It was high because I did not have to hunt in the same areas day after day, and because, when the wind was not too strong, I shot consistently.

STORY OF A WOODCHUCK DOG

Ray Weeks and I hunted mostly in the back fields, away from the roads on this trip. Kim, or Kimmie, the Weeks' 12 year old spaniel, often had hard going. Kim is what you might call a real woodchuck dog. He has accompanied Weeks on countless hunting trips and, although he is an old dog now and not as active as he used to be, Kim still has the know how of retrieving. Weeks says of his dog:

"My old Springer Spaniel's official title is 'Bluewater Kim of Avandale.' Avandale is a well-known line of spaniel pedigree. We call him Kim or Kimmie, as the fancy strikes us, although most people think that we say 'Timmie.' The name 'Kim' came of course from Kipling. I regret to say that the poor old fellow is failing rapidly and the recent hot weather appears to be taking a lot out of him. After all, he is 12 years old, which for a dog is an age comparable to that of an 84-year-old man. Twice, recently while taking him out for a little jaunt through the woods and the field, he has bogged down in a marshy spot while quenching his thirst, and would surely have stayed there to perish if I had not been on hand to pull him out. . . .

"When he was younger, he was a most enthusiastic woodchuck retriever. He would stand tense and rigid while I was aiming the shot, but at the crack of the rifle would be off like a shot. If he couldn't readily locate the chuck he would keep looking back over his shoulder for me to wave him on to the proper direction. When he found the animal, he would trot back with it — no matter how heavy the chuck — and lay it at my feet with an expression of profound pride on his face. Once, however, he came back with such a chuck, laid it down to crawl under a fence along the road, when the chuck, only stunned momentarily by the bullet, suddenly reached up and bit him on the lip.

"I'd estimate that Kimmie jumped two feet straight up in the air with his face wearing the most ludicrous expression of pain and surprise. When he came down again, onto the ground, he seized the chuck and shook it until I feared those big ears of Kimmie's would fly right off his skull. After this onslaught he placed the animal on the ground and chewed it from stem to stern with such thoroughness that you could hear every bone in its body snapping. While ordinarily the gentlest of dogs, from that day on, Kim was death on chucks and liked nothing better than to corner one away from its den. He developed an effective safety-first method of attack. First, he would closely circle the chuck for a few moments at high speed. When he believed that the animal was sufficiently bewildered by this procedure, he would dart in, seize the marmot in his jaws and toss it several feet into the air. The instant that it touched the ground it would be seized and tossed again. Six or eight of these heaves seemed to take the fight completely out of his antagonist. The chuck was then quietly, methodically, and most thoroughly crunched from head to tail. It was most amusing to see the manner in which he literally puffed out his chest once the obliteration was completed to his satisfaction. I doubt if any chuck ever succeeded in biting him in such a scrap.

"The old fellow could sure make me feel like a heel. Nothing could stop him from the dash to the chuck's den after the shot had been fired. If the result had been a miss, he would snoop around the burrow with an air of extreme puzzlement and would keep looking back at me for more explicit directions. When I would finally induce him to return to me, his attitude would suggest that he was thinking to himself, 'What a heck of a fine rifle shot you are turning out to be!'"

Kimmie has slept by, or on the foot of the Weeks' bed since he can remember. He always went along as a companion on the hunts to retrieve the chucks and crows. But today, when he has to be left at home, his spirit rebels. He rushes angrily to the refrigerator, jams his head as far as it will go beneath the refrigerator, and with rump raised and eyes rolling, he remains there in that most uncomfortable position for hours, actively engaged in a one-dog "sit down" strike. On one occasion, while with Ellwood Epps, I rode back to the Weeks' home in Tillsonburg, and as no one answered the bell, unlatched the kitchen door and left a note on the table. There was Kim, still fully as aggrieved as ever, sulking, broken-hearted beneath the refrigerator.

ONTARIO WOODCHUCK HUNTING LICENSES
NOT BEING ISSUED GENERALLY TO AMERICAN TOURISTS

The small game supply of southern Ontario is at a precariously low level. This is due to overshooting by local hunters, to a number of abnormally severe winters during the last ten, to poaching out of season for food and for sale to hotels or to non-resident hunters, and to a lower income level. The game supply is also lower due to a lack of any systematic system of educating the local hunters to protect their own game. They have never had a large program of raising game on game farms and liberating it in the hunting fields. A lack of effective, modern firearms by many of the local hunters, and the presence of many small cedar swamps and bush districts, are all that helps preserve most of the game they still have.

However, there is no question that the average farmer, in chuck country, does not want so many woodchucks. Time and time again, farmers have come out on the road and invited and implored us to come in and kill off the chucks which were honeycombing their timothy and alfalfa fields and pasture fields. There are places where for miles the land is not suitable for chuck dens and there one finds no chucks whatever, or very few dens. In other places, chucks even today are relatively in good-ly numbers.

Woodchuck licenses are issued by the Provincial Department having charge of such matters, by the game wardens, and by local sporting goods dealers and gunsmiths. During 1948 only about 10 per cent as many woodchuck licenses were issued to local residents of Ontario as during 1947. This was because of a campaign to keep hunters out of the game fields in the breeding seasons.

For the present, the average American will not be able to obtain a woodchuck license. A Firearms Permit is necessary to anyone going to Canada to shoot anything. For Ontario, the Firearms Registration Officer — who for years has been Mr. W. H. Boyd, an archery enthusiast, a pistol shot, and a hunter of experience, located in the Provincial Police Office, Toronto, Ontario — is the man who issues them. He will need the description of each rifle or shotgun, its serial number, and gauge or caliber. You carry this permit on your person while carrying a firearm or hunting. Don't try to go anywhere in Canada with firearms without first applying by mail for a permit. Be sure to tell the truth when you apply.

Ontario, to my knowledge, is the best place in existence to test out firearms and new cartridges on woodchucks. Never fail to realize, however, when hunting in Canada that you are a foreigner there, enjoying yourself by their sufferance and hospitality. Like every other country, the people have their own national and local laws, customs, feelings and problems. Respect them and be invited to return!

CHAPTER 5

.170 Landis Woodsman

PART II — THE 1948 HUNTING TRIP IN ONTARIO
PRACTICAL BALLISTICS OF THE .170 WOODSMAN

So that readers may visualize more clearly the potentialities and various possibilities, also both the good qualities and the drawbacks of the little .170 Woodsman, I will make a few comparisons.

Parkinson, Ackley, Wismer, Noel Wood and others have made a few tests of the .170 with 30-grain Sisk bullets. The method of drawing and applying the bullet jacket is such that sometimes quite a few 30-grain bullets are found having air pockets in the base between core and jacket. This detracts somewhat from accuracy, but is solely a defect of bullet manufacture, not of rifle or cartridge. I have never observed such with 25-grain bullets which so far have given much the better accuracy of the 25- and 30-grain sizes. Phil Wismer has been the most outspoken against the 30-grain bullets. But he says they kill better on shoulder shots, although less certain in accuracy. Penetration is better. Ackley made our barrels with 12-inch twist and a groove diameter of .172 inches. With a 2-inch sharper twist, they might be superior in accuracy if made so as to exclude air pockets.

WEIGHTS OF BULLETS IN SMALL CALIBER CARTRIDGES

Suppose we begin with the B.B. cap. This tiny cartridge shoots an 18-grain bullet at 780 f.s. m.v. It has 24 ft. lbs. of muzzle energy and retains 13 ft. lbs. of it at 100 yards. The C.B. or Conical Ball cap now shoots the 29-grain bullet at 720 f.s. m.v.

and with 33 ft. lbs. muzzle energy and 24 ft. lbs. remaining at 100 yards. Few would consider these woodchuck cartridges, although they are relatively quiet and will kill a chuck on a brain shot at close distance.

The .22 Short and the .22 Long we can pass over. We find the .22 Long rifle giving 1100 to 1400 f.s. m.v. to 37-grain hollow point and 40-grain solid bullets. The muzzle energies are 108 to 168 ft. lbs. and with 80 to 104 ft. lbs. of energy remaining at 100 yards. When properly hit, woodchucks were cleanly killed with these cartridges within moderate ranges and sometimes far beyond. They are unsatisfactory for average long distance chuck shooting but I have killed many dozens of chucks with the .22 Long rifle.

THE .170 WOODSMAN

The 25-grain bullet is smaller in mass and weight by four grains, than that of the C.B. cap; is 37-1/2 per cent lighter than the .22 Long rifle bullet and has but 62 per cent of its mass. A bullet of this size, driven at 3500 f.s., tiny as it is, develops 680 ft. lbs. of energy at the muzzle. The energy is calculated thus: E, (or KE), equals $1/2\frac{MV^2}{g}$. It equals also $\frac{MV^2}{2g}$. The mass or M, is 25 grains. There are 7000 grains in one pound avoirdupois. Now then, divide $\frac{25 \times 3500 \times 3500}{2 \times 32.16}$ by 7000, as the result must be expressed in foot pounds, not in foot grains, as it would be if the bullet weight were not reduced to pounds. Multiplying we find that $25 \times 3500 \times 3500$ equals 306,250,000 which in turn is divided by the divisor resulting from $2 \times 32.16 \times 7000$ equaling 450,240.00. Be sure to point off the two decimal points or you will think your .170 is sure to be ineffective.

Divide 450,240 into 360,250,000. The result is 680 ft. lbs. of muzzle energy. This is delivered very quickly, and with abnormally high rotational velocity of the bullet. Thus the boring effect is greater. At 3500 f.s. m.v. the 25-grain Sisk bullet would develop 604 ft. lbs. at the muzzle, a 30-grain bullet at 3200 f.s. would give 682 ft. lbs. of muzzle energy.

Possibly you have never worked out the muzzle energies of any of the larger .22 wildcats, firing the 55-grain bullets as most of them do, for better control of wind drift. A comparison, of muzzle energies of two rifles each giving 3500 muzzle velocity, may be made or given as being directly proportional to the respective bullet weights. For instance, if your .170 caliber with 25-grain bullets is giving 3500 f.s. m.v. with its 16 grains of powder, and you want to compare it with the .219 Donaldson or the .22 Varminter, each giving 3500 f.s. with proportionate loads, to their 55-grain Sisk bullets, then the two or three cartridges compare in muzzle energy as 25 is to 55. If the .170 develops 680 ft. lbs. then the .22 wildcat develops $\frac{55}{25}$ of 680, which is 2.2 as much, or 1496 ft. lbs. This is just under what the .250-3000 Savage develops with 87-grain and 100-grain bullets. These produce 1740 ft. lbs. and 1730 ft. lbs. of energy, the .25-35 gives 1350 ft. lbs. and the .25 Remington, 1375 ft. lbs. with factory ammunition. The 219 Zipper with 46-grain and with 56-grain bullets in factory loading, gives 1175 and 1155 ft. lbs. of muzzle energy. The little .170 therefore gives 58 per cent as much energy as the fast 46-grain bullet of the Zipper and almost 60 per cent as much energy as the heavy 56-grain Zipper load — this with a bullet weighing much less than half as much.

Another thing to bear in mind is that the 12-inch twist, and the very small caliber of the .170 Woodsman gives much higher rotational velocity to the .170 bullet than is given to any of the .22 caliber bullets at 3500 f.s. m.v. or less and gives as much as with .22 loads of considerably higher muzzle velocity.

This has a tendency, in some .170 rifles, to bore a hole through the woodchuck and completely empty it of flesh. I do not know why Parkinson's .170 rifle of 1947 with only a 15-degree shoulder slope gave much more of this hole drilling effect than did my rifle in 1948 with its sharper shoulder and greater confining effect upon the burning powder gases, more of a churning effect upon the gases while being consumed, and with its louder and sharper report than the Parkinson 1947 rifle. He may have used faster loads with 4198 in some instances. I was shooting 4320, a moderate charge then, according to Parkinson's comment. He loaded the ammunition.

Chronographed results with Marciante's own .22 Blue Streak, using 55-grain Sisk bullets and 31 grains of 4084, gave 3526 f.s. m.v. while 30 grains of 3031 and the same bullet, gave 3780 ft. seconds.

OTHER RIFLES USED ON THE TRIP

The Johnson Blue Streak rifle that Epps was using was an extraordinarily accurate and consistent shooting piece, yet otherwise it had little to recommend it to most as a woodchuck rifle. It weighed probably 12 or 13 pounds, was rather clumsy; the stock was neither too neat nor did it fit too well. The rifle did not balance well for offhand or sitting shooting. The Fecker target scope had a very small field and was quite dirty.

You could, as a matter of fact, find fault with that rifle in just about every particular as a practical field shooting piece. Yet I advised Epps to not even try to improve it because if anything upset that perfect balance which produced such a high degree of accuracy, it almost certainly would not have killed as uniformly at long range. Maybe the thing just fit him, and he had gotten used to it. He did complain of the difficulty of finding the woodchuck in the scope, which made the rifle slow to get into operation in the field. A chuck might go in while he was searching for it, but I have never seen anyone do more consistent killing on woodchucks between 250 and 350 yards with any rifle. And it killed them clean as a whistle, above ground, shot after shot. Of course the rifle had plenty of report, and in many districts that would soon bar the rifleman.

THE .219 DONALDSON IN ONTARIO

The 55-grain Sisk bullet and 28.0 grains of 3031 gave 3600 f.s. in the .219 Donaldson rifle with 14-inch twist. Weeks, in 1949, was doing considerable shooting with two .219 Donaldson rifles. Both were chambered and fitted by Maurice Atkinson, of Streetsville, Ontario. Maurice is an expert toolmaker and metal man in a plant in Streetsville, and while I was with Weeks, brought down a new .219 Donaldson caliber Springfield-Sporter rifle for Weeks. He had done both the metal work and the very fine stocking on this rifle. The stock looked very much like a Bob Owen or a Frank Hoffman job and was very neatly done. These two Weeks' rifles were neat and handsome heavy sporting rifles. They were fitted, balanced and outlined like sporting rifles and were not the clumsy 15-pound benchrest shooting rifles which some of the gunsmiths who specialize on the .219 Donaldson cartridge produce.

Ray Weeks is not a particularly large man, nor especially rugged. But he is wiry, strong for his size, and very active and quick in his movements. A rifle weighing 9 to 10-1/2 pounds will be much more comfortable for his use in field shooting than will a 15- or 16-pound rifle, particularly those with 27- to 30-inch pressure barrels. For muzzle rest match shooting he is now breaking in the .219 Springfield which is heavier all over but still not a club.

Today, Maurice Atkinson and Elmer McConnell definitely have the edge on any other gunsmiths in Ontario in the making of beautifully proportioned varmint and sporting rifle stocks. Some of the United States gunsmiths are sending poor grade work to Canada but some very well-bored barrel blanks by Pfeifer and by Buhmiller are now being imported there. I saw quite a nice stock of Pfeifer blanks in G. B. Crandall's shop in Woodstock, in May of 1948, and they were running uniformly good in workmanship and appearance.

SHOTS TAKEN UP TO 140 YARDS

So far as I know, no one has ever set down in print, or in a book on shooting, the results of a very considerable amount of woodchuck shooting with a .170-caliber rifle — a rifle in which the normal bullet weights are 20, 25 and 30 grains. I have written a few articles about this subject and now wish to make available the following itemized data for a considerable number of shots.

In this section, I have lumped all shots as short range or medium range chances for a cartridge of this type and size and have set the dividing line at 139 yards. Beyond that they have been classified as "long range shots," and these have been listed in the next chapter.

My shooting was done with my own Winchester Hi-side s.s. rifle with P. O. Ackley barrel chambered for the 28-degree Landis Woodsman cartridge. The work was done by Charles Parkinson. The rifle is fitted with a Winchester single set trigger.

May 17, 1948. Ontario, Canada. Hunting with William Elliott of St. Catharines (formerly President of their Fish & Game Association) and with Philip Wismer who has been present, according to his count, "at the death of 10,000 woodchucks."

Shot No. 1. I was using case-forming loads, consisting of 15.0 grains of 3031 and the 25-grain Sisk soft point bullet. The chuck stuck up his head from the grass in a hay field. I shot it through the brain. Distance, 50 yards.

Shot No. 2. Range 60 yards. Struck at butt of ear resulting in instant death.

Shot No. 3. The range was 130 yards. The chuck sat up and was shot in side of head. A good clean kill.

Shot No. 4. Range 45 yards. I took this one in the shoulder to see what would happen. Chuck fell over, a clean kill. The bullet usually gives maximum laceration or bone smashing results on this sort of shot.

Shot No. 5. Range 60 yards. This was a body shot out in a grass field. No other chance presented itself. The 25-grain bullet laid this one out neatly.

Shot No. 6. Range 135 yards. This would sound like a real long shot for a 25-grain bullet to many, but the chuck died quickly. Up to this distance you often find that you have shot your woodchuck before you are fully aware that you have fired. This little rifle shoots flatter than the .30-1906 Springfield, with service loads, up to about 250 yards.

Shot No. 7. Range 60 yards. Body shot. I was taking many body shots at this distance because the wind was blowing strongly, and the country we were hunting in was hilly in some sections.

Shot No. 8. Range 50 yards. An offhand shot. Bullet went through both shoulders.

Shot No. 9. Range 70 yards. Shot in the throat from in front. A good clean kill.

Shot No. 10. Range 60 yards. Another shoulder shot which was quickly fatal.

Shot No. 11. This one was purposely shot through the lungs. It bled considerably and was a good clean kill.

Shot No. 12. This one was shot in the head at 45 yards. The little rifle was killing well in the wind. It was hitting the chucks right where it was aimed. Then I shot a skunk offhand, across from one little hilltop to another hilltop, 50 yards off and someone remarked, "that was a good offhand shot." The wind was blowing quite strongly where I stood. Had fine long range kills the same day, which are described in next part.

Bill had an unexpected long range shot, that same day, at a fox as the fox vaulted a fence. We thought he had scored, but the fox got up and dodged into cover.

May 18, 1948. Hunted with Phil Wismer and Stanley Adams. We were pretty far up the Province where they get temperatures of 35° to 45° below zero in winter, as a fairly regular performance. The chuck dens are deep and often straight down in this area. We had high winds most of the day.

Shot No. 1. When we drove out a lane from Adams' house there was a nice fat chuck sitting on the bank above a pot hole which was full of water. The water was deep and the chuck looked very defiant and unconcerned. When I got out of the car it seemed the wind would almost blow me down. I shot this one and hit the butt of the ear, which, at 35 yards in that gale, was definitely difficult to hold on. This chuck bled over a space 18 inches long by 3 inches wide down into the hole. It was an instant kill, with the chuck lying dead, head downwards in the den and it was rather difficult to pull him out on the sloping bank without plunging into the pool. This was a red, pot-bellied chuck, and must have lived there quite a long time.

Shot No. 2. Range 135 yards. Shot in chest from in front. Wind was strong.

Shot No. 3. Range 118 yards. Paced. Shot in throat, and the bullet came out the shoulder. The hole of exit was 1-1/2 inches in diameter and was blown fairly free of flesh. Wind was blowing a gale. This one was sitting up looking at us.

Shot No. 4. Range 75 yards. Chuck was shot in the chest as he faced us.

Shot No. 5. Killed at 125 yards across a swamp. They call them muskegs. This one was facing us and was shot in the middle of the chest.

Shot No. 6. Shot at 85 yards. In the chest. Wind was still lamming across the fields and I was taking body shots. As I recall, I climbed up on a fence and shot this one out in an abnormally bare field, near a pot hole. He was in a cut bank which faced the other way, and I had to get up on the fence to see him plainly. It took two men to get me off the wire on the fence.

Shot No. 7. This one was killed at 90 yards with a bullet in the front of the throat. These throat shots are very deadly with the tiny 25-grain soft point bullet.

Shot No. 8. Killed at 60 yards with a shot in the chest. Regardless of whether the tiny bullet went into the front of the chest from one side or the other, or struck about the kidneys from the rear and tore up through the lungs, for me this chest shot was effective.

Shot No. 9. Range 75 yards. Bullet struck butt of ear. A clean kill. It is surprising how much a large woodchuck bleeds on such a shot. Normally the chuck does not get off that spot.

Shot No. 10. This one was out in a plowed field. He climbed up on a post to look at me and then climbed down again. This one was shot at 125 yards, through the chest. It bled a small amount externally.

Shot No. 11. Shot at the base of throat from in front. Shot offhand and a very clean kill. Range 50 yards.

Shot No. 12. Shot in chest at 45 yards. A good kill in the wind.

Shot No. 13. The old hard luck shot, number 13. The bullet pulled out of the cartridge case when unloading the rifle. One and a half grains of powder was spilled and not recovered. Then I killed a large chuck at 125 yards with the remainder of the charge and a second insertion of the cartridge. This was a chest shot. You may begin to see here why I have mentioned that a long neck to this tiny cartridge is necessary, to keep the bullet in the case.

Shot No. 14. Chuck shot in the face from in front, at a distance of 60 yards. This is always quite an upsetting occurrence to the woodchuck.

Shot No. 16. Aim was taken during an unusually hard blast of wind. Rifle fired at exactly the wrong moment. It was a very large chuck and the bullet landed low and far back and chuck got into the hole with only two feet to go. Had one long range kill that day. Extremely poor day for shooting with a very light bullet. Yet, note number of kills.

May 19, 1948. Hunting with Charley Parkinson.

Shot No. 1. Brain shot into left side of head at the ear orifice. Range 125 yards. This was a real nice shot.

Shot No. 2. This shot was taken prone. The chuck was facing me, shot squarely in the throat. Almost invariably such a shot anchors the chuck in a once-around circling movement. Other times it goes down on its face or its back.

Shot No. 5. This one was killed at 125 yards, the bullet striking at the base of the brain, but going through the spine instead of through the brain which was slightly higher. Such shot causes immediate, total paralysis and usually almost immediate death.

Shot No. 6. Range 85 yards. Shot this one in the throat while it was standing up along a fence row.

Shot No. 7. Shot at 85 yards. Hit at the base of the brain, but coming in from the throat in front. These shots are carrying along about one inch below the brain pan. They are uniformly clean killing.

Shot No. 9. This one was shot under the chin. It fell down a vertical hole about seven feet in depth, and then there was a right angle turn of a foot or so back of which the chuck lay. Repeated efforts to haul him out failed. I did not count this one. We had no wire chuck snagger with us.

SPECIAL NOTE: Of the last fifteen shots fired with the .170 thirteen were instant kills with the firing of but fifteen cartridges. It is assumed at least one of the others died quickly.

May 20, 1948. Hunting with Parkinson.

Shot No. 1. A group of us went out to a nearby quarry to sight in a .257 Roberts caliber woodchuck rifle for one of Parkinson's friends and customers. Back of the rifle range across the quarry a chuck stuck up his head and I shot him in the brain. Range 75 yards. Windy that day, too.

Shot No. 5. This chuck was shot in the neck from the side, directly at the base of the brain. It was, of course, killed instantly. Spine cut off.

Shot No. 7. This was a small chuck. A head shot at 65 yards.

Shot No. 8. Range 135 yards. Made a chest shot. Killed eight that day. Chucks not too plentiful in that neighborhood.

May 21, 1948. Hunting with Ray Weeks.

Shot No. 1. Shot Weeks' .219 Donaldson Wasp Hi-side Winchester single shot for two shots only. This chuck was at 65 yards. Shot directly in butt of ear. Used Weeks' sighting. Then one long range shot with same rifle and a kill.

Shot No. 3. Using .170 Marksman again. Next chuck was at 125 yards. A high shoulder shot and a very clean kill. This was an abnormally large chuck.

Shot No. 4. This woodchuck had absolutely no tail. Killed at 75 yards with a bullet directly into the butt of the ear. Notice the way this rifle makes a brain, neck or shoulder shot time after time.

Shot No. 5. Chuck killed offhand at 50 yards. Shot through butt of the ear.

Shot No. 6. This woodchuck was killed from the prone position. It was shot through the brain at a distance of 125 yards. A nice clean kill.

Shot No. 7. A very large chuck shot from standing position,

firing over top of fence post, chuck hit exactly in the butt of the ear. Range 65 yards.

Shot No. 8. A small chuck this time. Also shot over the top of a fence post.

Shot No. 9. Chuck shot through throat and bullet went through spine at base of brain. Most throat shots were at chucks raising the head out of a grass field looking at the shooter.

NOTE: It is best to give yourself some leeway, so hold carefully, with the cross hairs or dot held just above the top of the grass. Unless you are at very close range, the trajectory rise then helps to keep the bullet in the clear, and so low it gets little wind drift. All of a sudden lightning strikes the woodchuck and he goes down. Then there is nothing but a sea of waving grass stems and not a thing to mark the location of the dead chuck. There might be a dozen or more dens within a small radius of the spot when you get there. Estimate carefully before you fire, lining up a tree in the distance, if possible, then pace carefully to where you think he lies. Add three paces, and then mark the spot carefully with a handkerchief tied on the grass. He might be in the front den hole, the rear one, just lying on the ground, or he might be farther or nearer than you estimated. Walk slowly back and forth on your line of shot, not over five yards to either side, until you find him, or find blood or a bullet gash in the dirt. He may be close but you probably can't see the spot more than four or five yards away from the dead chuck.

One long range shot followed this one, and closed the shooting for the day.

May 22, 1948. Another day with Ray Weeks. Maurice Atkinson came down and brought a new heavy Springfield Sporter for Weeks, and the three of us went out together.

Shot No. 1. This chuck was shot through the lungs with the 25-grain Sisk S.P. bullet. Frothy pieces of lung were blown out on the ground. Range 60 yards. Bullet opened up a good deal for a long shot, and the animal died quickly from hemorrhage of the lungs.

Shot No. 2. Shot in the brain, offhand, at 50 yards.

Shot No. 4. This one was killed at 135 yards, with a shot in the neck, while standing up in fairly high grass.

Shot No. 6. Shot in the brain, from side of head. Range 35 yards. Unexpected shot.

Shot No. 9. Another close shot obtained by stalking. Bullet in the brain from 35 yards. Killed instantly.

During the short time we hunted together, Mr. Weeks killed 20 woodchucks with his single shot .219 Donaldson. This same action and stock has at different times been fitted with two different R-2 barrels, a short type .22-303 version of the Varmint-R, and a .219 Donaldson. With his rifle I killed two woodchucks while the set-trigger fly had fallen out of my rifle, and I also killed 17 woodchucks with the .170, making a total bag for the two of us, of 20 and 19, or 39 chucks, in an area in which they are not exceptionally plentiful. The .219 Donaldson, of course, had more range than the .170. It is more effective beyond 250 yards in open country shooting, but it uses twice the powder charge of the .170 Woodsman and makes far more noise, hence would be unwelcome in many neighborhoods. Our bags were almost identical. I am making this comparison so that the reader will see that you can kill plenty of chucks with either type of cartridge, or with both of them, but each is a specialized cartridge in a definite field. The opinion is general and firmly held in Ontario that the .219 Donaldson is not equal in range, in flatness of trajectory, and in long range killing power on chucks to the .219 Improved Zipper, the .22-250, or the .22-303 Varmint-R — the latter in either the long or the shorter case length. The Donaldson is a cartridge of greatest use between 175 and 300 yards as compared to both larger capacity and smaller case cartridges.

May 24, 1948. Hunting with Elmer McConnell. Elmer is the local forestry and corn borer official in his neck of Ontario, a constable. He also has the longest and most muscular pair of legs in southern Ontario, I am sure. We drove out to a farm and looked down an expanse of fields nearly a mile long. The farmer said, to Elmer, "There are woodchucks scattered all the way down across those fields until you cross that woods and trout stream in the far distance. Don't go any further. The chucks are right there and have been busy eating everything edible on this farm."

Elmer suggested that we move as rapidly as possible down toward the creek and go to work on the woodchucks who, as it was a hot, dry morning, were probably feeding on the green grass which grew down near the run. So we walked and walked and walked. A mile or so seemed to lengthen at Elmer's pace to two or three miles. The ground was too flat, too rich and too much covered with manure, here and there, to be in my opinion, a proper garden spot for woodchucks. It was quite a challenge for short legs like mine to keep up with long legs like Elmer's. I would rather meet a man rifle to rifle.

Shot No. 2. I saw a woodchuck backed up against a tree and shot him in the left side of the throat, the bullet raking the body. An instant kill at 65 yards, out in a field of standing wheat. He was on a sort of grassy oasis containing one tree, which stood in the wheat.

Shot No. 3. Range 120 yards. I shot this one in the butt of the ear and the bullet came out the right eye. Skull completely smashed.

Shot No. 4. Shot in the neck and out through the lungs. An instant kill at 116 yards. One of these was on one side of the trout stream and the next on the far side. I could see from the gleam in his eye, that my companion was thinking much better of me than he had been when he was leading me by fifty yards on the race across the three long fields. Three long kills followed described later.

Shot No. 8. Killed cleanly at 50 yards, offhand. Bullet blew a 1-1/2-inch clot of blood and a chunk of the lungs out on the far side. At 50 yards the tiny 25-grain bullet is traveling more than 3400 f.p.s. when it strikes and in addition it is revolving much faster than a kid's top. Result is that on a lung shot, it throws things and at times bores a tunnel right through the woodchuck that you could stick a banana in.

Shot No. 10. This chuck was sitting on a fence post top in a hot sun, probably asleep. It was killed at 90 yards, with a bullet in the neck, after closing the distance gradually. This one seemed greatly surprised, but he was very, very dead when I got there.

Shot No. 11. Shot in the butt of the ear at 75 yards.

Shot No. 12. Drilled high in the shoulder, also at 75 yards. A clean kill.

Shot No. 14. Killed at 104 paced yards with an offhand shot. The bullet went squarely through the lungs.

Shot No. 15. The rifle misfired. The chuck went in before I could get it to fire.

Shot No. 15-A. Killed at 50 yards with an offhand shot. Bullet went through the chest. On an offhand shot at 50 yards and beyond, I usually aim at the lungs or the high position on the shoulder — the vital area is larger.

May 25, 1948. With Ellwood Epps. After a memorable day with McConnell, and a good night of rest, Ellwood Epps arrived and after a lengthy examination of the very complete McConnell collection of high grade British shotguns, some rifles, and a very fine Ballard which had been converted to .25-20 caliber, we started northwest.

We drove practically all day, through wind storms, dust to a degree of density which I have seldom experienced, and which covered all clothing with a coat nearly an inch thick, even in a closed car. We saw less than half a dozen chucks on the way up. As I recall we did not stop for shooting.

After unloading the baggage we took a long drive for an evening of chuck hunting. It was abnormally dry, uncontrollable forest fires were raging on a 70-mile front farther north but the smoke was worse 1000 miles south than where we were.

Shot No. 1. Taken from the car while far down a farmer's lane back of a barn. At 110 yards the bullet cut the jugular in the neck and that chuck bled all over the place, even though its neck was broken. It was difficult to find him in the high grass of even height. Finally I picked him up, dead, on the edge of the vertical rear opening of the burrow, some 20 yards farther off than I had estimated.

Shot No. 2. Killed this one at 85 yards, out in a field, with a neck shot.

Shot No. 3. Broke the spine in the neck at 60 yards.

Shot No. 4. Killed at 120 yards with a bullet in the butt of the ear. These first four shots had been kills, with the bullet landing within 1 to 1-1/2 inches of the same spot on the chucks. One is fortunate to do such shooting after riding for six or eight hours through blinding dust and heat.

Shot No. 5. This was an offhand shot at 60 yards. The bullet struck in the ribs and disabled the chuck at once.

Shot No. 6. This shot at 110 yards struck at the butt of the ear and practically blew the head off. Why a .17-caliber bullet, or any other bullet, will at times create far more than the usual or average amount of damage given on that sort of hit, is one of the unanswerable mysteries. You never can foretell when it will not occur before the shot is fired and the animal examined. It is a fact which I have personally experienced in more than two dozen occasions, that either the Remington Hi-Speed Hollow Point, or the Western Super-X hollow point .22 Long rifle bullet, striking the side of the skull of a large woodchuck by penetrating the chuck's tough hide somewhere between the eye on that side and the orifice in the ear on the same side, will shatter the skull completely into at least four to six large fragments and some smaller ones. The bullet itself will be fragmented and seldom will the largest fragment weigh more than 15 to 23 grains. How much more certain therefore that a soft point bullet as heavy or heavier than the largest remaining fragment just mentioned (but traveling at approximately 3350 to 3425 f.s. remaining velocity when it strikes while revolving about its lengthwise axis at very high rotational velocity), shall blow the similar woodchuck skull to fragments. A woodchuck's skull which has been cleanly penetrated by such projectiles, without at the time also having been subject to such stresses that it is simply shattered, is rare. This could occur, however, with a solid lead bullet of a hard alloy traveling at a very low remaining velocity when it struck. Especially if the rounded point of the bullet resisted deformation at that velocity.

Shot No. 8. This chuck was shot by the same .170 rifle, using the same ammunition and bullet, at a distance of 45 yards, which is 65 yards closer to the muzzle, in exactly the same spot, the butt of the ear, yet the head was neither blown off nor blown to pieces. The chuck almost invariably bleeds very excessively over an area of 10 to 18 inches in diameter, and the blood is bright scarlet arterial blood. Sometimes the bullet blows upward and shatters the skull as its major accomplishment. Other times it strikes a bit lower and shatters the spine just below the rear portion of the skull. Sometimes there is also considerable damage to the rear portion of the mouth and throat. In any case the shot normally kills the chuck instantly, or practically so. There are exceptions but these are more likely to occur in the instance of chucks being shot through the side of the skull, between eye and ear, or just a trifle below that. I do not recall ever having shot a chuck through the nose, or through the jaws from the side, although I have an idea that some of the chucks I have shot at fairly long range, and which tore around considerably before holing, may have been so hit.

A butt-of-the-ear shot is nearly always immediately disabling and fatal within a very few moments. Actual death, however, may occur from profuse hemorrhage. In a few cases the animal will fall head first down the hole, in which instance he will usually lodge within one to four feet of the surface. In some cases the animal will slide slowly down into the earth, backwards, in which instance he is likely to slide down out of sight. The butt of the ear shot is so uniformly disabling or fatal that it is my favorite hold whenever practical.

Shot No. 9. This chuck was 130 yards out in a clover field. He was moving around a good bit and I put the bullet high up through both shoulders. Provided you have complete penetration of both shoulder joints, or complete shattering of both shoulders or the spine at that point, instant paralysis or lack of ability to move forward may be expected. He will often be dead when you arrive. You must always consider the possibility, however, that on a wet and slippery bare-ground, or wet-grass surface, the animal may slide backward due to gravity pulling his heavier end downward; and then of course there is always the natural reaction of any struck woodchuck to "hole."

Shot No. 9-A. Killed a crow out of a tree at 100 yards. The .170 simply "busts" a crow at this distance. I did not have sufficient ammunition along, or in immediate prospect to do crow shooting with the .170. As I recall, in all, I feathered one crow hard, and killed the other two out of three fired at on the trip.

Shot No. 12. Next chuck was shot at 55 yards (of the short range chances), the bullet went in the throat and broke the neck.

May 26, 1948. Also with Epps.

Shot No. 1. This was shot prone in a grass field. The range was 101 paced yards and the chuck was shot in the back when sprawled on a heap of sand. He was immobile and refused to move, so I shot him in or along the spine just above the kidneys, and the bullet ranged up through the lungs and shoulders. It was the sort of shot I rarely take but it was that or nothing and the chuck was killed instantly.

Shot No. 2. This was a prone shot at 80 yards, the bullet entering the throat as the chuck faced me. Two holes of exit were found in the neck and another two in the shoulders, making four holes of exit. The chuck was facing me and the bullet raked the forward portion of the body only, then emerged in small pieces. The average weight of these fragments could not have been more than six grains each, yet these small bits of jacket and lead core came right out through the hide. This animal looked rather shot up because he was bleeding from all four small holes.

Shot No. 3. This combined both the most unfortunate, and thus the worst, with some of the best rifle shooting I displayed during the trip. Epps and I were driving along a dirt road in back country and as we were passing a high rail or board fence, or a combination of both, we both noticed an old chuck traveling irregularly but rapidly up and to the right through an old apple orchard containing a few trees at that end and more toward the right. It was difficult to see through the fence; the grass was high for May; and there were scattered clumps of brush.

I got out of the car hurriedly, had trouble climbing the bank and getting my rifle and scope between the rails. But I made it and by that time the chuck had seen me and was making time. He was bounding along on uneven ground, and was quartering sharply and moving toward rising ground. The field above the orchard was open and materially higher.

I was using the hi-side single shot, had the rifle loaded by then and also an extra cartridge between my fingers. I started shooting and the first and second shots, fired rapidly, cut off first the right hind leg at the knee and then the left hind leg at exactly the same spot. The animal paused a moment and rolled around by which time I was soon over the fence and running after the chuck, meanwhile reloading the rifle. I aimed at the chuck a number of times, but he always either started in an unexpected direction or else got down out of sight into a grassed-over furrow.

The chuck was slowed up, but he was still faster than I when he was moving. I gained when he would stop. I shot him again through the lungs, and he moved only a few feet after that, but actually the animal died from excessive hemorrhage from the stubs. I went back over his trail, in the grass and could clearly see where the arterial blood had spurted first from one shattered knee joint, then both of them. He was mashed up inside, but bled but little from the shot in the lungs, although he then bled also from the nostrils, but not freely. Not much blood was then in him. It was simply that this shot shortened his breath.

The first shot at the running chuck was at 120 yards, the second at 150 yards and the third was offhand at 80 yards. His legs were so completely shattered and blown off that no one could feel happy over such an episode. These details are gruesome, but they are given to show two things: First, that due to irregular or rapid movement of the target you will at times hit a chuck where least intended; and second, that if you can really shoot a rifle at game, in the field, you can at times hit it repeatedly regardless of what it is doing.

Shot No. 4. I shot this chuck offhand, in the right shoulder, at 102 paces. It was an instant kill. The old high shoulder shot. This is good shooting on woodchucks, any time and any place.

Shot No. 5. This was a prone shot at 82 paces. The chuck was shot directly in the butt of the ear and killed instantly. In all my shooting in 1948 in Canada, I did not use a sling and I did not use a portable chuck rest. It was straight position shooting with a sporting rifle.

Shot No. 6. Shot directly in the butt of the ear, at 106 paces. This chuck was shot just once, but was badly torn with half a dozen holes of exit, lead coming out through neck and chest on the far side. The chuck was a bloody mess, being covered from nose to tail. You wouldn't think you could hit a chuck in so many places with 25 grains of anything, even gold, but there it was. How he got shot in the chest from a bullet at the butt of the ear, I don't know but he must have been on all fours, angling toward me, and with his head turned slightly to one side, which position could have presented such path to bullet fragments. Good thing this chuck was big and tough, or the ricochets would have sounded like a machine gun burst.

Shot No. 7. This was at 35 paces, on a kit which stuck its head out of a hole. I shot it in the back of the neck shortly after making the other and longer shot in the same field. The larger chuck went down so instantly that I thought I had shot over him. He was due south of me, and behind a single mound in rather high grass.

Shot No. 10. Fired over a post. Made a high shoulder shot at 110 paces. A good clean kill.

Shot No. 13. Shot directly in center of throat and out butt of ear. This was an angling shot. A clean kill at 121 paces.

Shot No. 15. Two shots at this one at 110 yards. One through entrails and second through shoulder. Second was a clean kill. When a chuck is moving around, feeding in the clover, this is what happens at times.

Shot No. 15. Crow at 65 yards. A shoulder shot and a clean kill. On almost any sort of hit the little .170 Woodsman really bursts a crow and often drills a clean hole, 1 to 1-1/2 inches in diameter, right through the crow.

Shot No. 18. This one was shot in head, offhand, at three yards, as he suddenly stuck his head out of the hole after I had killed No. 17 for this day, out of the same den, at long range.

Shot No. 19. Range 70 yards. A nice offhand shot which struck the heart. This chuck bled profusely.

Shot No. 20. An offhand shot at 50 yards on an abnormally large chuck. Bullet struck butt of ear and it also cut the throat of the chuck going through at an angle. This animal bled profusely of arterial blood.

Shot No. 23. A 60-yard shot through the lungs.

Shot No. 24. Drilled through the shoulders. A clean kill.

Shot No. 26. Bullet struck in the base of the ear right in the orifice. Range 135 yards. This was a nice shot and a clean kill.

Twenty-five woodchucks totalled the kill for the day. Mr. Epps had nearly as many. A lot of these chucks were shot off dry, dusty, sun-baked hillsides which from a distance did not look very promising. A great many of the chucks killed this day, in the southern portion of the shooting grounds, were badly afflicted with eczema. The infestation also extended to the north of the central section but not to the same extent. I saw this outbreak in no other section of the Province.

May 27, 1948. Hunting with Epps.

Shot No. 1. This was a 90-yard shot which struck the spine, in the back of the neck. A clean kill.

Shot No. 2. Chuck was shot in the head at 70 yards.

Shot No. 4. A shoulder shot at 60 yards. Also an instant kill.

Shot No. 5. A kill at 114 paced yards due to a bullet in the butt of the ear. An instant kill.

Shot No. 7. This was a really large chuck, for May in Ontario. A center of the shoulder shot and a clean kill. I did not have the recoveries and escapes on shoulder and lung shots spoken of elsewhere by Wismer. Range for this kill, 85 yards.

Shot No. 8. This chuck was down feeding and facing me. Range 111 paces. The bullet struck the throat on the left side and angled back through the lungs. This killed well.

Shot No. 9. A body shot and a kill. We were moving right along here, the shooting coming fast with little opportunity for bookkeeping.

Shot No. 10. This was an 85-yard throat shot which raked the body, threw lungs and pieces of flesh more than four feet. Quite a few of these shots were with a full case of 4895 in the expanded cases, Parkinson loadings.

Shot No. 11. An unexpected, close range offhand shot. Distance 25 yards. Bullet went through shoulders and killed well.

Shots No. 14 and No. 15. These were 40-yard and 30-yard shots at chucks which stuck their heads out of den mouths. Both shot in neck. Chuck moves fast at such close ranges when he decides to do anything, and a neck-shot aim will usually drill the brain if he decides to withdraw his head, and land on the shoulder if he decides to risk it and come out. We were shooting in a region of rather sparse population and chuck hunters were an object of curiosity rather than fear.

Shot No. 16. A chest shot from in front at 60 yards.

Shots No. 17 and No. 20. Each was a chance at 110 yards. First one was hit in ribs and killed instantly. Second in the neck.

Shot No. 22. Distance was 135 yards. Bullet struck the side of the neck and broke the spine. You feel quite well satisfied with every shot of this kind, as it is a sort of long range dry-fly fishing on woodchucks. The smallest possible tackle, as to bullet weight, which is practical. You toss that bullet out there with a sort of snap, put it right on the target, and down goes Mr. Woodchuck.

This was evening shooting. Chucks were out plentifully and I bagged one every three to ten minutes. One was too busy shooting chucks and retrieving them now and then to put down or even remember each minute detail.

Shot No. 24. Shot in the neck. Distance 75 yards.

Shot No. 25. A 65-yard shot to the shoulder.

Shot No. 27. This one was another very large chuck. It was shot through the spine, over the heart. It bled very profusely as the bullet blew up completely on the vertebrae. The result of this sort of shot is total paralysis back of the bullet strike and severe hemorrhage both internal and external. The larger the chuck, the tougher the bones and the more complete the bullet expansion or disintegration.

Shot No. 29. Chuck stuck head up out of grass, at 35 yards, and was shot offhand, in the butt of the ear.

Shot No. 30. Shot through chest into spine, breaking it.

These chucks I think were a bit tamer than in some other localities, but at the same time one obtained many long range shots. The cover in a few fields was green and high, but in others there were simply holes here and there, with a head coming out or a feeding chuck moving around. At times one saw six or eight chucks at once, either completely out or with their heads out.

Friday May 28, 1948. Hunting with Ellwood Epps.

This was the last day of the woodchuck hunt for 1948. We got an early start on the morning of May 28 because I had to leave for London late that afternoon. The rifle was giving trouble again, the set-trigger fly was loosening and blocking the fall of the hammer on some shots and I was nearly out of loaded ammunition. But Parkinson would load more for me in London, where he would work on the set-trigger fly.

Shot No. 1. Shot in the middle of the stomach from in front, at a range of 128 yards. That doesn't sound so good, but the chuck was killed instantly.

Shot No. 6. Range 65 yards and shot in the front end of stomach or rear portion of the lungs. Another dead chuck!

Shot No. 7. Range 45 yards. Shot in the butt or lower part of the neck breaking the spine.

Shot No. 8. Range 75 yards. Bullet struck exactly in center of the throat from in front. Bullet went on through and tore a hole of exit, 2 inches in diameter in the right side of the chest.

Shot No. 9. This one stuck his head out of the hole and took a neck shot at 60 yards.

Shot No. 10. Chuck stood up straight and faced me. Was a clean kill at 105 yards. Bullet went in front of chest.

Shot No. 13. This was a combination head and neck shot. The bullet hit in the neck at 65 yards and went up and out through the head. Killed.

Shot No. 14. Shot low in right chest at 35 yards. Killed.

Shot No. 15. Shot through both the throat and heart with one bullet. Chuck was down and facing me. Range 65 yards.

Shot No. 16. Drilled through the throat sidewise, at 110 paces.

Shot No. 17. Also shot through throat, sidewise, at 115 yards.

Shot No. 18. Chuck shot at butt of ear at 70 yards.

Shot No. 19. Shot at butt of ear at 45 yards. These offhand shots are always a source of satisfaction when you hit the chuck exactly where you aimed.

From here we will go to the long range shots, which to many may seem more truly indicative of the worth of the rifle or cartridge, and so more meticulous care was used in the field in pacing and estimating and in examining each chuck shot.

CHAPTER 6

Long Range Use of 25 Grain Bullet
in .170 Woodsman and .219 Wasp

PART III — THE 1948 HUNTING TRIP IN ONTARIO
LONG RANGE SHOOTING

THE following compilation gives the results of all the 60 long range shots which scored kills with the .170 Landis Woodsman cartridge at ranges greater than 140 yards. The cartridge has 28-degree shoulder and is made by swaging down to .17 caliber the empty R-2 cases. It is then loaded with 15.0 to 16.5 grains of powder behind the 25-grain Sisk S.P. bullet. The case holds a little over one grain more powder when fully expanded to fit the Parkinson-Landis chamber by previous firing. The first eight days shooting recorded here was done with case-forming loads, the last three, in part, with the full charges. Loads were 15 grains of 3031, and then 16.0 grains of 4895.

The first three days of this trip were abnormally wet and rather cool. The last four days were spent in abnormally dry, dusty country. During the time in between we had almost perfect weather conditions.

The .170-caliber rifle averaged 16 chucks per day for 11 days which were consecutive weekdays. On three of the days long trips were taken, consequently the kill is on eight full days of hunting and parts of three other days.

In 1948, chucks were found to be relatively plentiful everywhere, but the daily bag is fairly indicative of the numbers seen in different districts. Because of requests from the persons with whom I hunted, the actual areas in which we shot have not been mentioned and will not be given upon inquiry. A chuck hunter is entitled to keep the location of his pet colonies a secret.

Insufficient ammunition was on hand to permit taking favorable shots beyond 275 yards, which appeared to be the reasonably certain-kill range of the cartridge. The chucks were much wilder in some areas than others, showing where they had been hunted the hardest. In those wilder areas it took much longer to shoot half a dozen or a dozen woodchucks because it took each of them much longer to come out. Everyone pronounced chucks extremely hard to kill instantly, in Ontario, during this season. Consistent shooting for the butt of the ear, or the neck, or throat, seemed to be good policy under such conditions. The unusually small percentage of chucks shot too far back in the body was quite gratifying, and when so hit they seemed to be as readily killed as with any other caliber.

In each instance the point of aim was determined by the position of the woodchuck when seen and stalked, the firing position required, the distance, and the velocity of the wind at the moment.

May 17, 1948. Hunting with W. B. Elliott and Phil Wismer.

Shot No. 3. Range 165 yards. Result was a high chest shot at the base of the throat. Instant kill. Bullet struck about the level of the collarbone.

Shot No. 4. Another shot at the same distance, although not on the same spot. The bullet landed high in the chest and killed the woodchuck.

Shot No. 5. By an odd coincidence this shot was also at 165 yards and struck the chuck in the face, making a clean kill. That was three straight kills at 165 yards each.

Shot No. 7. This shot was at 190 yards, a high chest shot. The chuck kicked a bit and then died. Then followed a considerable number of shots at shorter distances.

Shot No. 18. Shot directly through the heart at 185 yards. In a bag of 18 woodchucks, I had five kills that day each beyond or at 165 yards.

May 18, 1948. Hunting with Wismer and Stan Adams. This was a very windy day to hunt or shoot woodchucks.

Shot No. 15. Shot in the chest at 150 yards. A good kill.

May 19, 1948. Hunting with Charley Parkinson. The country was open and fairly grassy where we were.

Shot No. 3. Range 175 yards. I shot this one in the brain. It was an instant kill.

Shot No. 4. Shot at base of brain. Range 145 yards. When

you get two to four of these in succession, everything seems mighty fine.

Shot No. 8. Range 160 yards. Shot this one in the throat from in front. This one was at the mouth of a den, near the sky-line. The chuck fell over on its back, lay there quietly for a few moments with its feet spread out like a turtle, then, being on muddy earth, it slid slowly, on its back, tail first, back into the den, just out of reach. Sometimes, when shooting chucks, you need your sky hooks to get over the barbed wire, then an excavator to get the shot chuck out.

May 20, 1948. Hunting with Parkinson and his group of shooters.

Shot No. 4. Range 145 yards. This chuck was shot in the spine just below the brain. Total paralysis is the result, and quick death, as in this case.

Shot No. 6. Range 165 yards. This chuck was shot directly in the butt of the ear. Instant kill. This was a very large chuck.

May 21, 1948. Hunting with Ray Weeks.

Shot No. 2. A shot with Ray Weeks' .219 Donaldson. Range 175 yards. Shot in butt of ear. The bullet went through spine and, of course, fractured the vertebrae. Both chucks I shot with the Donaldson were kills. The rifle impresses one as having a fair jump, a sharp report, although not excessively so, and is a good all-around chuck cartridge. But making the cases is consider-able work, including the cut off of the original case. The .219 Donaldson is unnecessarily powerful and noisy when used at less than 175 yards unless a reduced load is used. Beyond 300 to 350 yards the general opinion among most chuck shooters in Ontario is that it is inferior to the slightly longer and larger cases handling 33 to 40 grains of powder.

Shot No. 10. Range 165 yards. This was a shot in the spine at the base of the brain.

May 22, 1948. Hunting with Ray Weeks and Maurice Atkin-son.

Shot No. 3. Killed a large chuck while firing from a farm-er's lane down past his grass field. This was 181 carefully paced yards across his hay, which was then about shoulder high on a big chuck. The bullet struck directly in the butt of the ear. This chuck was found in the mouth of a den, at least 35 yards farther off in the field than I thought it was. This is the common error in a large field of grass with nothing to use as a marker. It took me half an hour to locate this one after the shooting. Chuck had bled profusely and had only moved about two feet. It was dead and within a foot of the opening of the rear part of his den. It was also on higher ground than it appeared from the shooting position.

Shot No. 5. This chuck came out on a mound, about 15 yards inside a short-grass field along edge of woods. I was sitting backed up against a tree, out in a bare wheat field, where I could see in all directions for some distance. I was the full diagonal distance across a large field from the fence near the chuck. I was on the skyline, watching three dens down the opposite side of the hill. The wind was blowing rather strongly across the fields, nearly at right angles to the proposed line of fire. A herd of steers was bunched in the far field, 100 yards to the left of the chuck and greatly to my left. The bullet, from a half-sitting, half-prone shot across the root of the tree, struck the chuck in the spine about the middle of the body, as it faced away from me and started to feed. I was trying for the maximum area in elevation and in windage from the point of aim which was a spot just back of the shoulders on the spine. This chuck rolled around a good bit after being shot. When I went over to pick up this chuck, a young steer detached itself from the herd and came over to my part of the fence and became quite belligerent, keeping me on my side of the fence for quite a while. I shot a chuck through the brain, at 35 yards, on the steer's side of the fence, when it stuck its head up in the grass, back along a swale, after the steer had again retired. When I went over and got that one, the steer came back and followed me for more than 200 yards down the fence line. At that point I almost stepped on a chuck in a fence corner in the edge of a good sized woods. This was a large chuck which then dodged into a worm fence line and got away without offering a shot. That steer interfered with the shooting of three chucks.

Shot No. 7. This woodchuck stuck his head up above the grass, back along a fence line parallel to that along which I shot the chuck at 214 yards. It was, however, about 15 yards out in the field, I killed this one at 165 yards. Even that distance, on a quiet evening, the 25-grain bullet made quite a report when it struck.

Shot No. 8. Range 175 yards. Shot struck at the butt of the

ear and went into the brain. This chuck bled very profusely onto the surface of the ground and for two feet down into the den.

May 24, 1948. Hunting with Elmer McConnell, the firearms collector.

Shot No. 1. Instant kill on shoulder shot at 150 yards.

Shot No. 5. Range 175 yards. Cut jugular vein and the result was very free bleeding.

Shot No. 6. Chuck out near far side of a very wide field. Bullet plainly struck about one inch inside 3 o'clock edge of the body while the chuck was low down, facing me. This bullet apparently struck just back of the edge of the shoulder and went on through the animal. Chuck could not enter the den but fell down the rear entrance after threshing around a great deal on the surface. The shot paced exactly 225 paces. Such a shot is rarely immediately fatal above ground with any caliber of rifle or weight of bullet. The bullet drifted two or three inches more than I expected or else I had a flyer out to the right side. Likely the former.

Shot No. 6-A. Range 175 yards. Bullet struck exactly in the butt of the ear. Last two shots were each an instant kill.

Shot No. 7. Range 180 yards. Chuck shot directly at the butt of the ear. Both eyes blown out on top of the skull and the skull fractured.

Shot No. 7-A. Range 185 yards. Hit a bit too far back in the body. The wind was blowing strongly across line of fire. Chuck was bagged and gathered in, but was not killed instantly.

Shot No. 9. Range 140 yards. Chuck shot while sleeping, sprawled on a sand pile. Shot through the spine from the back.

Shot No. 13. Range 147 paced yards. Bullet struck at butt of ear and blew out both eyes onto the top of the skull. Skull was completely fractured and crushed. Sometimes on such a shot most of the disruptive force is directed upward and forward, other times downward or backward. It depends upon the angle of the strike.

Shot No. 16. This was a prone shot at 152 yards, paced. Bullet struck the chuck in the neck, and as usual with such shots, was quickly fatal.

This day's shooting with Mr. McConnell provided nine vital hits at chucks at farther than 139 yards with the 25-grain bullet. The first five kills were in a shallow ravine with a stream in the middle, mentioned previously in this section but on shorter range shots. The ravine was about 200 yards wide, dotted with occasional very large trees. The stream was meandering in tobacco country, and the chucks had denned in the banks on both sides as far out as 100 yards or so.

May 25, 1948. Hunting with Ellwood Epps.

About two-thirds of the day was taken up by the long dusty trip into Epps' hunting grounds. We saw very few chucks on the way. In the evening of the 25th we went along until the seventh kill before one was shot beyond 140 yards.

Shot No. 7. Killed with a shot in the butt of the ear while feeding out in a hay field. Range 150 yards. Then shot a crow at 100 yards.

Shot No. 10. Range was 160 yards. Animal killed with a shot in the shoulder. This one was dropped away down in a pasture field, hunting far back from the car.

Shot No. 11. Range 251 paced yards. They were long paces. This chuck was shot from the sitting position diagonally across a hay field, and well down into a second hay field near a woods (Canadians call it "bush"). This chuck was struck by the first shot directly in the butt of the ear, believe it or not, and was found dead, after a considerable search, lying about two feet from where it had been feeding when shot.

The trait of many Canadian hunters to not always bother too much about hunting out and finding a shot chuck in a difficult area is not due to cruelty, but is well founded upon discretion and much experience. The spot may be two fields width distant, the intervening fences topped by very sharp barbed wire and difficult to scale. This hunting out of the chuck can be too time-consuming.

Shot No. 12. A good sized chuck was shot here with a bullet in the throat at 220 yards. This is a common shot when the chuck stands up above the level of the grass and regards you. Firing the small, high velocity expanding bullet into the tops of the grass never seems to produce anything but a puff of dust or pollen. Keep your bullet above the grass if you want to score. Don't try to land your bullet in the chuck's chest four inches below the level of the grass, or it will likely never reach the chuck.

If a mist rises off the chuck himself, it is dust plus vaporized blood and liquids from the body. This mist is more likely to occur if the bullet has above 3700 or 3800 f.s. remaining velocity when it strikes.

May 26, 1948. Hunting with Epps.

Shot No. 3. This was the 150-yard stage on a chuck, killed with three shots, as described in the short and medium range portion of this hunting trip.

Shot No. 8. This was a prone shot at 182 paces. The chuck was standing, facing me, on the mound in front of his den. He had gone in once, came out cautiously, and finally sat up for a look. I had crawled on my hands and knees and stomach across a slight ridge of ground, six or eight inches above the slope of the remainder of the field. The rifle was not fitted with a sling, or swivels, consequently all prone shooting was same as shooting a hunting rifle. This chuck was shot through the left side of the throat, the butt of the ear, and the base of the brain, all by the same bullet. It was knocked backward off the mound, and I thought had gone in since it went out of sight so suddenly; but there it lay about two feet from where it had been. This was a large, heavy chuck and bled very profusely.

Shot No. 9. I rested my arms across the top of a very large fence post and killed this woodchuck out in the middle of the second field. The bullet struck exactly one inch below the butt of the ear and the range paced out on level ground to 254 paces. I covered some 50 square yards of grass field very thoroughly, before I found this one. In most of the States, one is likely to find his den very quickly when walking up on a chuck out in a field, but in Ontario this may be complicated no little by unexpectedly coming across a group of 6, 8, 20, or 30 holes, some of which you will discover suddenly by falling into them. The question then is, which hole was your woodchuck feeding away from, and did he break for the front or the rear entrance, if not killed immediately? This woodchuck was lying out on the top of a small furrow, covered by growing grass. I then picked up a chuck which had been killed at 104 paces from the top of the same post.

Shot No. 11. This woodchuck had been seen at intervals, for about an hour across a bare, plowed field. He would come out and then go in. He was the only woodchuck along that fence row on the far side. Two others were seen feeding 400 yards off, across the second field and out into it at the lower end of the field. One was running aimlessly around on bare ground.

I had retired for half an hour or so of rest, in the shade of a large tree, out in the middle of a grass field, to get away from the black flies which were bad to the east where I had made several long shots.

Then that chuck came out again down along the bare fence. I crawled out to the edge of a small ledge on the grass field, lay prone and eased off the shot. There was a fair wind down over that bare plowed field. And it was hot and the mirage was running. For some reason that chuck looked to be at least 50 per cent farther off than I knew he must be, and I was shooting somewhat down hill. The rifle's center of impact might be anywhere within two feet of what you anticipate. If you don't think such a variation can occur, think back over the center of impact locations of rapid-fire groups at 200 yards at Camp Perry, and recall a few dozen of them. Lovely groups away down or away up, in the white of the target. I thought of all those before I calculated my wind drift and eased off the shot. I intended to hit the middle of that chuck, and did. Such calculation and aiming would allow the widest variations and at least hit the chuck. Or, at least could possibly hit it!

The report of the impact of the bullet came up from the dusty ground very pronouncedly — from my prone position, shooting low through the grass, with my head down to prevent being seen from the far fence, the chuck looked most darned small and a quarter of a mile off. My knees were raw when I finally got into the prone position, the black flies settled on the back of my neck, a hornet or a yellow jacket was buzzing around in front of my nose, and my heart was hammering from exertion. It hadn't looked so far from the shade of the tree to the firing position on the rump of the hill, but it was work, prone, getting there.

I had lain there a few moments, taking things easy, before shooting. Otherwise, I could hardly have hit an animal the size of a calf. Every black fly in the whole field always seems to sense this immediately and goes to work on the shooter.

I got up, dusted myself off, and paced down the hill and across the field. The shot came out to 184 yards, with downhill pacing, and then across the flat field, but anyhow it was a tough shot.

The bullet had hit him almost exactly in the middle, went in the ribs on the right side and came out through the spine in the middle of the back and blew out the guts on the far side. The woodchuck was dead and hadn't moved over a foot. Looking back through the mirage, to the shade tree, it appeared to be 275 yards, and somehow I was more proud of that shot than of some others a hundred yards farther off. I had earned that woodchuck.

Shot No. 12. This one came out of a den to the south, far from the shade tree, and in a different direction from all of the other shooting. I had rested up by the time this one showed up. I took this one prone, over the roots of the tree, and hit him directly in the butt of the ear at 154 paces. Blew out the brains and popped both eyeballs. That 25-grain bullet certainly goes to work on the skull of a woodchuck. Sisk seems to have the bullet jacket of just the right strength to require a bit of bone penetration before complete expansion when the 3200 to 3500 f.s. muzzle velocity has fallen off a bit at mid-ranges.

Shot No. 14. The next long range shot was at a pair of chucks which had come out of the same den across a considerable swale. The range was mutually estimated at 155 yards. The first was shot in the chest from in front, and the second in the stomach, after it had gone in and come out again and started to feed along the small hill which was covered with green grass.

Shot No. 17. The next long range shot was at 170 yards across on a hill. This one was shot in the head as he stuck his head out of the den for a moment. I misjudged the location of the den on this one, and had to hunt around for a time before I found it. There was a dead woodchuck.

Shot No. 21. I shot at a chuck on top of a hill at a considerable distance, and this one went in. When I went down to look around for blood, I saw a chuck stand up on a hillside clear across on the farthest hill, with a very wide, gradual slope in between.

I slipped down to the fence and sat down and took a rest along side of a fence post which was reasonably solid. Phil Wismer says that one cannot shoot accurately at long range from such a shooting position off the posts, but often you must hold and get off your shot from this shooting position or lose your shot. This was one of those shots. I had to time any small movement of the post, the wire, and my left hand touching both.

When the rifle cracked its spiteful little "splat" with the 16-grain charge of 4895, which makes more report than the 15 grains of 3031 or of 4320, the chuck wilted right down, shot in the middle. It paced out a good long 260 paces. I killed a long offhand shot on a bullet through the heart on the way over. One came out down the field to see what was going on. He probably never found out!

This was a nice pair of shots. I carried both chucks back to the car, and Epps took photographs.

Shot No. 22. The next longer ranged chance was at 174 paces. It was shot in the stomach or back portion of the lungs, and he stayed "put." Such a shot with the .170 rarely gives external bleeding, even enough to prove a hit, but if the paunch is full of grass, or the shot is cutting through the lungs as well, the chuck is often killed cleanly. If shot a bit farther back, he will very likely go in.

Shot No. 25. Killed at 155 yards standing up in a clover patch. With another at shorter range, that made 27 kills for the day.

Epps, shooting a .22 Marciante Blue Streak, killed 26 chucks. This Marciante Blue Streak, turned out by Charles Johnson of Thackery, Ohio, seems to be an abnormally good killing cartridge on woodchucks. It weighs about two pounds more than my rifle. It kills consistently up to 450 yards or more in the hands of Epps, and tears the chuck about twice as much as the worst mangled jobs from the .170. The Marciante Blue Streak was using a fast load with the 55-grain Sisk bullet. The cartridge is about the same size as the Savage .22 Hi-Power, Those cases, and others from the .25-.35 can both be used.

May 27, 1948. Hunting with Epps.

Shot No. 3. A shot into the center of the body from the rear right. This is a shot not attempted often by the woodchuck hunter unless the chuck just won't turn around. It wouldn't in this instance. The shot was a clean kill. It struck the spine and drove up through the body cavity. Range 143 yards.

Shot No. 6. 175 yards. This was an instant kill on a shoulder shot. Phil Wismer made eleven such shots with the .170 Marksman and nine of the chucks so hit got down into the hole. Some, recovered later, showed excessive surface laceration and not sufficient penetration; others of them, excessive penetration without expansion. I had no observable results of this type on shoulder shots, and, so far as I know, lost no such shots. But there was observable variation in expansion on lung shots. Some blew open the chuck to the extent of a one to one and a half inch hole, and others showed no surface expansion and no particles of lung blown out. I do not think that on the average, a lung shot killed quite as well as a shoulder shot, for me, with the .170; but generally it did kill either instantly or quite soon after the animal was struck. I found one chuck of about three pounds, which I shot in plain sight of me at moderate range. After a ten-minute careful examination of the animal, I couldn't find any blood or any sign of a bullet wound although obviously I had just shot it.

I had no experiences at all of making abnormally severe surface wounds with the .170 on shoulder or lung shots, or on any other shots. Neither did I lose a large number of consecutive shots which were obviously well hit. Occasionally, a chuck obviously shot in the neck or butt of the ear would bleed all over a couple of square feet of area, sometimes from one to three feet within the opening, and at times down well out of sight. Out of 175 kills, I only had very few animals make any sort of sound after being down the hole. Three shot in the butt of the ear made a slight sound, also one which was shot in the throat, and one shot in the head while it was in the hole.

Shot No. 12. 180 yards. A shoulder shot and a clean kill. There was no difficulty with these shoulder shots with my .170.

Shot No. 13. 180 yards. Shot in the throat. A clean kill.

Shot No. 18. 176 paced yards. Shot under the chin, in the throat. A good kill.

Shot No. 19. 165 yards. Shot in the shoulder. Another good kill.

Shot No. 21. 160 yards. Shot in the chest from in front.

Shot No. 23. This was a very large woodchuck in comparison with the others. We had no scales, but it probably weighed 10 pounds. This chuck was shot in the chest at 175 yards, and again in the neck at the same distance. It bled hard of both dull and of bright arterial blood. Both bullets expanded sufficiently to give a good blood lane through the hide, and yet this animal got down in the hole a couple of feet before it died.

Shot No. 26. 140 yards. This animal was shot in the deep shadows of a wood, downhill in the edge of a pasture field, from my shooting position on a hilltop back of a line fence. The chuck just had his head out and then when he reached out farther for a moment, I aimed low and shot it through the heart. It was the sort of shot in which one might readily overshoot the mark as much as a foot due to downhill shooting. This chuck was abnormally wild and it took him more than half an hour to come out. It was killed right in the den mouth and could not be seen until I had walked down and pulled him out.

That day I killed 30 woodchucks and Epps shot 31. In two

consecutive days we each killed 57, or 114 for two rifles. It was the high tide of the Canadian shoot of 1948 but in no instance did we kill a very large number on a very small area. Sometimes we would drive for 20 miles and not see a chuck. Then would come a farm, back from the roads, which supplied good shooting. We hunted long hours and hunted hard. We covered hundreds of acres, and missed comparatively few chucks.

Friday, May 28, 1948. Hunting with Ellwood Epps.
Shot No. 2. This kill was at 204 paced yards. This chuck was up a few yards on the hillside above a level field which paced an even 200 yards across. The bullet landed in the lungs with quite a "plunk." This was an early morning shot, and the day was getting quite hot. I had slept soundly in the hardest bed in a hotel in Ontario, the previous night. We reached that town about 9:30 or 10:00 P.M. after driving for miles on a back road between tremendous Norway spruce which overlapped above the car and which seemed to tower to the sky. It was dark as the inside of an infidel's chest. Newly peeled or cut logs were piled here and there on the edge of the left side of the narrow road, and were difficult to see so late in the day. The road curved here and there; on its right side were occasional clearings, but few dwellings of any sort. Smoke was in the air from the tremendous forest fires farther north. The woods and fields were as dry as tinder. I had never been along there before, and, at least in recent years, neither had Epps. By the time we hit the town, I didn't think my proposal and insistence that we go up there to hunt was as brilliant as it had seemed at first. A man gets a yen to go hunt a certain place because he has heard this and that about it, and on the map it appears to be a likely center of chuck colonies. When he gets there even barbershop gossip about local shooting conditions proves totally unreliable. It's like a man pioneering to the North Pole and finding nothing when he gets there but another endless and featureless sheet of snow and ice.

One consolation for that trip was that those "Santa Claus" trees were the most wonderful I have ever seen anywhere. It was like driving through fairyland at night with 60 to 80 feet of browse above your head.

But we had driven 125 miles, almost without stopping, to find almost no holes and fewer chucks. Three holes were spaced at intervals along the lower edge of a bluff about 50 feet high.

Shot No. 3. A bullet in the base of the neck, from the side, at 160 yards.

Shot No. 4. At base of the neck, at 165 yards. Epps killed a close one with a .22 pistol, near a back-field lane. Then we left the whole area in discouragement.

How good the Ontario shooting can be, when you hit exactly the right farms at the right time, is seen from quotes from letters from Dr. J. K. Kirk and from Bill Elliott, quoted in part here, to illustrate.

Dr. Kirk had tried to tell us where to go, but apparently someone got the ball just past the edge of the plate. Wrote Dr. Kirk: ''I have heard from Mr. Epps of your little-result hunt in the areas in question. We went up to the district I spoke of. There seemed to be quite a few chucks. There were several of us in the car, and we hunted only a portion of one farm, by walking into the fields from 4 P.M. to 7:30 P.M. We carried out to the car, 51 chucks and one fox. We could have had twice that many, but refused to take the little ones. They were all intended for fox feed and this year's chucks were not worthwhile. The chucks were almost all in hay fields, and could be seen only when they sat up. This necessitated taking many of the shots offhand. A few were shot from the line of the road. Because they were to be used for fox feed, we had to be careful to take mostly head shots, otherwise the bullet often tore them up.

''Some of these chucks were as large as I've ever seen. They seemed very fat for this time of year. Perhaps next year or in 1950 we can get together for a hunt in that area. I only hunt the district about once a year and could not direct you more accurately by letter. J. G. Kirk, M. D.'' (Apparently the area was 20 or 25 miles southwest of where Epps and I were directed from the small town we stayed in over night.)

A letter from W. B. Elliott to me, May 3, 1950, is quoted here in part to show conditions and chuck numbers.

Wrote Bill: ''Weather here has been so cold (up to May 3, 1950), that we have only been able to visit the chuck areas twice, April 22nd and April 29th. With the roads just breaking up we had very difficult traveling and had to get a tractor to pull us out once. Keeping to the main roads, due to snow and mud and poorer roads farther back, we saw comparatively few chucks. It is now hard to believe that two of us once got 237 chucks in one day and could get over 100 any day. I think Phil Wismer has done better than this. I shall make every effort to be with you again on part of your next trip, and shall write you as soon as my plans are definite. Sincerely, W. B. Elliott.''

Shot No. 5. This was one of the shots on the long hunt. This chuck was shot in the upper portion of the skull. One of the few shots so placed. Range was 145 yards. Instant kill.

Shot No. 6. Range 165 yards. This chuck was one of the relatively few which had to be shot through the spine from the rear. These shots do not show much exterior bleeding, but the bullet goes forward through the lungs and shoulders and sometimes strikes the heart or cuts off the aorta artery. In any case, the bullet then fragments and causes immediate, serious damage.

Shot No. 11. This was the following long range chance; distance 165 yards. Shot through the heart from the left rear. This was an unusually large animal but the bullet tore on through and made a good sized hole at the point of exit.

Shot No. 12. This was one of the few which took two bullets; at a range of 180 yards, which is not excessive range for this little rifle. It was an abnormally large chuck. It was shot twice through the front end of the body, the last time through the shoulders.

We then drove down a back road which apparently had been little hunted for some years, and which provided shots on both sides, almost as soon as we left the car to hunt the adjacent fields. Most times the chucks would stand up in the grass and offer a head shot or a neck shot, or either. Most of these chucks were out feeding some distance from the den. Then they were moving around more and sticking up and taking down the head quite often.

Shot No. 20. Range 250 yards. The shot was across a long, narrow swamp, too deep and too wet to wade, and was also on the far side of a barbed wire fence. There comes a time, especially along toward dusk when you are dog tired, when you look at each other and after a time someone suggests, ''We better just let that one lie, peacefully right where it is.'' Then you pool estimates as to distance. The motion to do this that way is carried unanimously. This chuck was shot almost exactly in his geometrical center. The puff of dust showed the strike.

Shot No. 21. Paced out at 214 yards. The chuck was shot high in the back. It left a large pool of blood. I had been after a shot at that pair of den mouths for three days as Epps and I went past there a number of times, and this time after shooting half a dozen around the adjoining fields. I finally caught one out and let him have it. By an odd coincidence, this was the last shot of the 1948 woodchuck hunting trip to Ontario.

My total bag was one skunk, two crows and 175 chucks. Mr. Epps' count for the last three days, later confirmed in a letter, was a little higher than that of which I kept written record. He had 80 for himself and 83 for me. He was using his .22 Marciante Blue Streak Johnson rifle. He shot a few with the pistol, which were included, one of these being killed when entering a pipe. There are always a few chucks of which no one can be certain either way. When Charles Parkinson was with me, he pulled out quite a few for me, each one being shot through the brain. Most people would have scored these as chucks which holed after being shot at, but not surely instantly dead chucks. Otherwise, my score would have been lower.

Sometimes, too, one walks around a kill in a den mouth for half an hour or more before you find it unexpectedly. You may have thought you shot at it on the main mound or entrance and find it dead in the rear entrance, farther in the distance.

This hunting trip covered somewhere between 2500 and 3000 miles by train and auto plus the numberless miles of walking.

WOODCHUCK HUNT BOOKKEEPING

The woodchuck hunt game register recording or bookkeeping you do on a hunting trip is not as simple as it sounds. Out in the car, on the back road, miles from anywhere, when you are tired and hungry, your eyes are inflamed from all day shooting and looking for chucks, and the sweat is down your neck and the black flies humming, you wish you had not counted upon taking any notes or any photographs. You wish you had induced some sweet and simple redheaded steno with lots of pep and a yen to see Canada, and who had a neat chassis and a good pair of legs (so that she would not get too tired tramping after you in the fields), to come along and take down the notes while you did nothing but shoot.

But, this having been overlooked, you discover that you have broken off the point of your third lead pencil, the automatic pencil is by now out of order, the fountain pen is without ink, you are still 30 or 40 miles from any town, and you must get the information down on paper.

So it is that the records of two chuck hunters, out shooting together, are likely to vary by two to half a dozen killed chucks, although both are determined to be accurate and conservative.

SUMMARY

So far as I know, this is the most complete and systematic test of a .17-caliber rifle and cartridge ever made on woodchucks. In no other way than by writing a descriptive account of a hunt, shot by shot, could I place the story of the .170 rifle and cartridge before you. I hope it has demonstrated what a rifleman, using "dry fly" trout tackle on woodchucks, in the matter of rifle and ammunition, can produce in the way of results.

I am surprised that this cartridge was as uniformly effective as it was beyond 160 yards. Any well-designed .170 made from short, medium or the full length..250-3000 Savage cases, or from the Zipper or Improved Zipper necked down, or the .219 Donaldson necked down, will have greater range and a higher degree of effectiveness at ranges beyond 200 yards, provided bullets are made available which will stand such velocities and not go to pieces in the air. The specific gravity of .22-caliber bullets of 45 to 55 grains is not as great as that of .25-caliber bullets of 87 to 101 grains because the mass and thus the weight of the jacket material is greater in proportion to the mass of the lead cores in the .22's. In the .170's the jacket needs to be fairly thick or the core would tend to melt quickly in the .170. Thus the bullet has a lower specific gravity in the .170's than in the .22's and of course still greater is the difference compared to the .25 calibers.

I think a medium-short .250-3000 Savage case, or a .219 Donaldson, a .25 Remington, or a .22 Chucker case of Lindahl's design, would any of them make a very fine and most satisfactory case for a .170 of greater powder capacity than the .170 Woodsman of either 15- or 28-degree shoulder slope. But each and all of these suggested would have a greater report which would be sharp pitched and of a high tone due to the very small bore and the considerable relative necking down from shoulder to neck. The fatter the case at the shoulder, the worse this would be in relation to other cartridges. Nevertheless, these larger capacity cases would give still fewer ricochets even than the present .170's because the still higher muzzle velocity developed would create greater energy and have a greater tendency to dash the bullet to pieces on the smallest or softest object. The use of a properly made 30- or 32-grain bullet in these larger cases with a 2-inch faster twist would give greater accuracy at 300 yards and beyond with less wind drift. However, we have still to make these developments and experimental rifles and try them out in field shooting experiments.

In the past twelve years there has been little or nothing really new except the .170 and the most recent .25-caliber Donaldson jobs which are merely in large measure stepped up .219 Wasps, but nevertheless developments of promise.

If we work in either direction, up or down, from the .22-caliber, we at once encounter both advantages and disadvantages. As we go up, we get less wind drift, more noise and more ricochets, and the fragments in each ricochet are larger.

As we go down, we get materially less report, far fewer ricochets, and the fragments are rarely over six grains in weight, except possibly for the largest, which likely is of 12 to 15 grains. In a .25, the largest fragment would likely be of 60 grains or more.

My rifle action was a new one in my hands. I had no idea it would shed its set-trigger fly on this trip, and had it not done so twice, I could have without a bit of difficulty, upped my 11-day bag to 200 to 210 woodchucks. Quite a few shots were lost because the hammer could not be made to fall at all when the trigger was pulled, or because it stopped suddenly at the half cock notch. In either case the rifle could then not be fired. By the time I got it to fire, the chuck had likely become aware that something was wrong and gone in.

I like Canada and I like Canadian hunting. You get a glimpse here and there, of the world as it was 200 or 300 years ago in some places. You find occasional evidence of what the ice cap did to the land. You find whole streams still unsullied by mining or manufacturing, and full of bass or trout. You can travel for miles without meeting a cop. You can get a place to stop over night, or a good cooked meal in a restaurant almost any place you go. Their beef tastes like beef used to taste in this country when I was a boy.

To some, a 600- to 800-mile journey to shoot woodchucks may seem excessive and overly expensive. But the trip is definitely worth it when you are an enthusiast of good hunting.

On the first trip I averaged eight woodchucks a day in a series of strange neighborhoods mostly in the central part of the chuck area where they are less plentiful.

In two years I doubled the average daily bag by becoming more familiar with the areas in which chucks were most plentiful, the daily average wind drift, light changes to be expected, and the hunting customs of my companions.

I never had sufficient ammunition along in any one year, to permit firing at every possible long range opportunity. This reduced the total bag somewhat. On the other hand, it increased the percentage of kills and the number of long runs of three to twenty chucks without a miss.

In 1946 I shot the K-Hornet with Hornet ammunition, the same rifle, for a few shots, with K-Hornet ammunition, and a .22-303 Varmint-R. In 1947, the .220 Swift and the .22 Model 54 Hornet, also, for one day, a .170 15-degree Parkinson. In 1948 the .170 Woodsman and a few shots with a .219 Donaldson. In three trips, totaling four weeks, in none of which was the weather especially favorable, I killed 282 woodchucks, and a few jack rabbits and crows. That is 70-1/2 woodchucks per week. Four days were lost each trip going up and coming home. We never hunted on Sunday. In southern Ontario it is not permitted. I hunted in all, parts of 21-1/2 days. That is therefore an average of 13.1 woodchucks a day, including many rainy days. Every one of these chucks was shot in company with experienced local hunters. In that time I never came across another organized party of riflemen hunting woodchucks. But we heard of much larger bags than ours, although never did we see them.

I hunted in areas covering a district probably 150 by 200 miles in extent, on dozens of different farms. I was never told to get off while actually hunting woodchucks, and in more than a dozen instances, farmers came out and begged us to come in and kill the woodchucks. In this regard it may be well to state that accurate and expensive rifles are rather rare among farmers in southern Ontario. Not more than one or two real rifle cranks armed with scope sighted varmint rifles live in most of the smaller cities or larger towns, and these were almost invariably all too willing to sponsor a hunt and hunt with me. By going around from locality to locality, more variety was introduced, I met many people with whom I wanted to hunt, most of them were old correspondents of mine. In no instance did we kill off the chucks too closely in any one district, as might have been done had we spent two weeks of steady shooting within a limited part of a township.

The only real handicaps to hunting chucks in southern Ontario are occasional herds of salt-famished cattle which at times are resentful of intruders and are vicious. There are relatively few farm dogs — the government discourages dog ownership to protect people walking along the roads at night, and to prevent the spread of rabies among cattle. Roads are everywhere. There are a few muskegs but not many large ones. Meals and lodging can be obtained in almost every district. As I go hunting for the enjoyment of the shooting, I consider Ontario woodchuck shooting an ideal way to spend a vacation or to try out a new varmint cartridge or rifle.

I appreciate the hospitality and courtesies shown to me on my trips in the field. I wish to express my thanks to Canadian officials who assisted in making the trips possible, because they too were interested in having quieter, safer and more efficient cartridges developed for use in their flat, settled, dairying and farming areas.

I do wish that more ammunition has been available, especially 16- to 16.5-grain loads, so that I could have done shooting at ranges of 300 to 450 yards to see exactly what would occur. But with limited rounds of cartridges, you cannot accept 225 chances or so, and maybe another 50 to 75 at greater ranges.

So this brings us up to the early summer of 1951. I have my four licenses for 1951, for Ontario and the woodchucks. I get letters from all over asking, ''Are you going to Ontario for chucks this year?'' My answer is that I have a new .22-250 rifle and a couple of new scopes. Ontario beckons as probably it has not beckoned before.

THE WOODCHUCK WHICH WAS CHARMED BY BAGPIPES

Truth is often stranger than fiction. If you see the event occur, you will remember it longer than if you read a tale which was composed on a typewriter.

Of all the amusing, unusual and extraordinary occurrences that I have witnessed in woodchuck hunting with a rifle, the most unexpected and astonishing occurred along the bank of the Maitland River in Ontario, a few miles due east of Lake Huron. Ellwood Epps and I were idly watching the spawning of black bass beneath a bridge over the Maitland River. It was may of 1948, and the river was full of bass at that point. I suppose we had been watching those bass, with much interest, between thirty and fifty minutes, when we heard bagpipes up a hill to the south. Whoever was playing those Scottish "pipes" certainly was expert. The music was beautiful, and along that little valley traversed by the gurgling stream it sounded almost heavenly.

Before long two gents dressed in full Scottish clan regalia, kilts and everything else, hove into view near the top of the rise. They were weaving and swaying from side to side. All of a sudden my companion murmured, "Those chaps are carrying quite a cargo! Especially the one with the bagpipes!" After a more careful look he mentioned, "I know one of them, he lives about fifty miles from here, and he is a very nice fellow too."

As they came closer and wove around from one side of the road to the other, it was apparent that but one was carrying a full cargo of panther sweat, the other was capering around, just enjoying himself.

We introduced ourselves when they reached the bridge, and I mentioned that probably I was almost related as my mother's mother was of direct Scotch descent half a dozen generations back, however. They immediately announced that truly I was one of the clan and they would salute me with a bagpipe serenade. This was then performed with considerable ceremony and skill.

It seems that there had been a large Scottish picnic or gathering a few miles away. About one third of the population of that section of Ontario is settled with men and women of Scottish descent; and each year they have their Scot gatherings in full regalia, kilts and bagpipes.

So, there at the bridge at Maitland River, the two Scots stood stiffly at attention and the piper played one selection after another of what was truly the very finest bagpipe music I have ever heard. Right in the middle of this serenade, a woodchuck came rushing angrily down off a hill just to the left of the macadam road, tore wildly across the road, into a field to the right and there sat on a chuck mound and chattered and scolded and wickered either in great excitement or considerable anger. We had not previously seen or heard this woodchuck, and in fact, had not seen any woodchuck dens or woodchucks within a few hundred yards of the Maitland River.

We decided that the Scots would shoot the chuck, but the next problem was to get the shooter across the barbed wire fence into the field, and also across a small but deep gulley.

Imagine the predicament of this gent who is thoroughly saturated with the fumes of panther juice, and who has been cele-brating since dawn with the descendants of the people who in-vented Scotch whiskey, and, according to report, have also im-proved it. Getting him up and over was something of a struggle amid the sounds of the ripping of good Scotch plaid. This may be the atomic age, but splitting the atom is no help to a man suspended between heaven and hell on the tines of a barbed wire fence anchored 50 to 100 yards on either side of him. With everyone present helping, pulling, pushing, giving good advice and twisting out tines too deeply imbedded, we finally got him over into the field.

One would think any chuck able to sit up and take notice would have left that quarter section under a full head of steam, or else have holed. But not this woodchuck. Seemingly, he had never seen, heard or smelled anything like those bagpipe cele-brants and he apparently never before heard bagpipe music of such class. So the Scot found the woodchuck still sitting there, giving vent to his feelings on the subjects of bagpipe music. chuck hunters and celebrants trying to get over the wire into his field.

This Scot put his borrowed rifle to his shoulder and made as perfect a head shot on the woodchuck as you will see in many a moon. Someone went over and retrieved the chuck; Epps took the photo shown in this book; and the two Scots gave us both a final and very formal serenade.

CHAPTER 7

Experiments by Charles E. Travis, Jr.

DIFFERENT RIFLES AND CARTRIDGES ON WOODCHUCKS

MR. CHARLES E. TRAVIS, JR., of West Chester, Pennsylvania, is one of the most enthusiastic and experienced of the younger generation of chuck hunters in southeastern Pennsylvania. He is also interested in bench-rest rifles and rifle shooting with 20-pound heavy barreled target rifles. He has his own 100-yard bench rest and varmint rifle range on his property about three miles from West Chester. The range is partly protected from wind by a cut bank and a woods, has good light and provides a most excellent place to test for accuracy and uniformity of grouping the half-dozen different woodchuck cartridges for which he has done extensive reloading and with which he has killed several hundred woodchucks.

Mr. Travis has a fine battery of varmint rifles, all of which I have seen and examined.

With the introduction of the .22 Hornet, a new world was opened to the serious varmint shooter. Here seemed to be the ideal chuck, crow and hawk rifle; it combined excellent killing power, moderately high velocity, flat trajectory and superb accuracy. All too, in factory ammunition. Another factor in its favor was the relatively low cost of the cartridges and its mild report. The latter is of utmost importance if much of your hunting is done in a farming section or on outlying sections of large estates. The majority of farmers or estate owners do little or no shooting of the varmint type hence are somewhat alarmed when a rifle of the .220 swift or .30-1906 class is fired on their property. This can at times be overcome to some extent by first calling on these folks in advance of the actual hunting and by assuring them that you are a safe hunter. When a person has cattle or horses valued at a thousand dollars each and upwards he doesn't care to have some trigger-happy lame-brain firing around—what he considers to be—recklessly on his place.

I had been hunting woodchucks for a number of years with an excellent .30-40 Krag fitted with a Winchester A5 scope and a remodeled military stock to give a high comb and close pistol grip. This rifle accounted for a goodly number of chucks but when the .22 Hornet appeared I immediately laid plans to secure one. At that time the splendid custom jobs on Sharps-Borchardt, Winchester Single Shot, Springfield and other fine actions were out of my reach financially. I did obtain a Savage Model 19H with target weight barrel and modern type stock well suited for prone shooting with a scope sight. Upon receiving this rifle I reworked the stock a bit, fitting in a block of walnut to give a closer grip. I rasped this down in the field till it fitted perfectly, then oiled the stock. I mounted the Winchester A5 scope and repaired to my range with it and some Western Super-X fodder. This load had the hollowpoint bullet and while it shot nice groups at the target, it allowed several large chucks to get into their dens. I wrote to the Western Cartridge Company commenting upon this and received a nice letter stating that they believed that the jackets were a little too tough to expand properly on animals the size of chucks but would be perfectly satisfactory upon somewhat larger animals such as coyotes. They sent along a hundred cartridges loaded with a 45-grain soft point bullet and asked me to give them a trial and send a report back on their performance. These bullets proved to be most excellent killers both on chucks and crows.

At this stage I decided to hand-load for the .22 Hornet and with this in view I ordered a thousand of these 45-grain soft point Western bullets and used them ahead of 10.5 grains Hercules No. 2400 powder and the Winchester No. 116 primer. I sighted the rifle to print an inch high at 100 yards and was then ready to try out this load on chucks.

That evening found me seated with my back against a large walnut tree overlooking a field of freshly harvested clover. Several dens were visible out in the field and I knew there were several more along the fence rows. After a short wait I spotted a slight movement in the mouth of a hole 100 yards distant. Peering through the scope I made out the head of a chuck staring back at me. I slowly slipped into a prone position as I already had the sling on my arm, as I usually do when watching a field. When the scope picked up the den, the chuck was still there. The crosshairs settled on his nose and at the crack of the Hornet, the head disappeared but I had heard the satisfying "plop" that means a solid hit. I sat up and put the fired case in my pocket. I never retrieve the shot chucks until I am ready to leave as sometimes you scare other chucks that are watching from under cover of the fence rows. Then you have a long wait. A minimum of movement is a must if you are hunting chucks that are being shot at often. Here in this section of Pennsylvania, a field may be worked over by as many as five hunters in one afternoon, most of these are not skilled riflemen but mostly youngsters with .22 rimfires and older men with shotguns. This type hunter usually sits and watches one den from a very short distance, perhaps 15 to 30 yards, or slowly walks along the fence rows. This practice tends to keep the chucks alert and educated.

To get back to the hunt: I had hardly settled myself when another chuck appeared. This one came from one of the dens hidden back in the fence row. He moved into the field cautiously and started to feed at 125 yards. As the report of the .22 Hornet died away, he simply collapsed and as I watched through the scope I saw his tail stand erect and wave vigorously a few times. This is a sure sign of a kill. I waited for another half hour and nothing else showed so I decided it was time to pick up.

Upon reaching the first chuck, I found he was in what we call a "drop hole." In this section, this is a hole straight down for two or three feet with no dirt showing around the entrance. I am of the opinion that these are used as back doors by the chucks in case they are caught away from the main entrance by a pair of foxes — they usually hunt chucks in pairs — or by a dog. Other chuck hunters share my belief that these holes are dug from the inside and the dirt thrown out the main entrance. The hole my chuck was in was barely large enough for me to pull him through for he was a large boar, well fattened from the clover he had been feeding upon.

I found upon examination, that the 45-grain bullet had entered between the eyes and these were bulged out of the eye sockets quite perceptibly. The skull had been reduced to a shattered mass and later upon skinning this specimen, I found the butt of the bullet and a small piece of jacket under the skin at the base of the skull. The other chuck was shot from the side, just under the ear and the story was the same, everything was found to be chewed up as if it had gone through a meat grinder. I was indeed well pleased with this bullet's performance. I shot quite a large number of chucks with this load and in all cases it gave perfect satisfaction. Another splendid load was made up using the 35-grain soft point bullet made by Mr. R. B. Sisk of Iowa Park, Texas. This bullet has a sharp point and when driven by 11.0 grains of Hercules No. 2400 it develops in the neighborhood of 3000 feet a second muzzle velocity. However, I do not like this load as well as the 45-grain bullet charge as that bullet seems to have quite a bit more energy left at 100 yards and beyond. I shot this .22 Hornet rifle with perfect satisfaction for a couple of years as a standard "Hornet."

THE .22 K-HORNET

When Mr. Lysle D. Kilbourn of Whitesboro, New York, announced his .22 K-Hornet—being like most riflemen, unable to resist something new—I decided to have my rifle rechambered for this new case. Accordingly, I sent my rifle to Mr. Kilbourn for this alteration together with $3.00, that being what he charged at that time. In a short time the rifle was returned and upon inspection of the chamber it proved to be a fine job. I fired my standard load of 10.5 grains Hercules No. 2400 and the 45-grain Western soft point bullet in the new chamber to form the cases to the K-Hornet with 35-degree shoulder slope and found that while thus fire-forming the cases the load was still as accurate as the standard case.

For the K-Hornet case I decided to use DuPont No. 4227 powder and the Sisk 41-grain Lovell bullet. Starting at 12.0 grains, I gradually worked up to 13.5 grains of this powder with fine accuracy resulting. This load increased the effective range of my rifle by 50 to 75 yards. The report seemed to be sharper but not objectionable to the landowners over whose property I hunted. The first chuck I killed with this load was spotted lying on a large, flat-topped rock sunning himself and was apparently asleep. He was at 125 yards and as I slipped into the prone position he awoke and turned his head but didn't move otherwise. The scope cross hairs settled on his chest at the base of the throat. When I pressed the trigger he just dropped his head and never even twitched as I watched him through the scope. This was a large cream-colored chuck and upon opening him I saw quite a mass of shattered body tissue. The bullet had gone in just about where I held and completely wrecked the lungs and cut off the top of the heart going through the diaphragm and into the liver and the stomach which was tightly packed with alfalfa. The stomach had a large hole blown into it and the contents well spread around inside the chuck.

Shortly after shooting this woodchuck I crossed a pasture on my way to a hayfield and as I crawled through a barway, I sighted a chuck racing towards a den under a stone wall at the other end of the pasture. Loosening my grip on the chuck I was carrying, I dropped to the ground slipping into the sling as I did so. When the chuck reached the den he stopped for another look and the K-Hornet bullet took him through the shoulder rather high up and breaking the spine. He never moved from the spot. My notebook shows that I killed fifty-one woodchucks that summer with the K-Hornet at ranges from 60 yards to 225 yards, all prone, as I either shoot prone or from a good rest of some sort or not at all. Some men are good offhand shots, but that does not seem to be among my accomplishments. When I am firing at a target of flesh and blood I want to kill it as quickly and humanely as possible so I take every means to place the bullet in a vital spot on the first shot.

THE .22-3000 R-2 DONALDSON

I thought it would be time to try another rifle that would permit the taking of shots a little farther out and would allow the use of a heavier bullet. The .22-3000 R-2 Donaldson was getting quite a bit of favorable comment in shooter's magazines and from veteran woodchuck hunters. I corresponded with several of these men and found this cartridge was giving a good account of itself. I decided upon Mr. Charles C. Johnson at his then address of Thackery, Ohio, but more recently of Springfield, Ohio, to do the barrel and action work. Mr. Johnson is a top mechanic and does work at a reasonable figure, which is an important item with many.

I had a fine Winchester Hi-Wall single shot with a single-set trigger and a No. 3 octagon barrel 30 inches long that had started in life as a .32-40 but its former owner shot out that barrel and had it rebored and rerifled by the J. Stevens Arms & Tool Company to .38-55 caliber. It is so stamped on the barrel by Stevens. I never understood why he did not send back the barrel to Winchester but perhaps they couldn't undertake the work at the time.

Mr. Johnson said this would make a fine R-2 with 16-inch

twist and that he could reline the barrel at about one-half the cost of a new barrel and it would prove just as accurate. This was later found to be true on both counts. I have a letter from my file before me at this time, in reference to this relining job. It may prove interesting to others, so I am quoting the last paragraph: "Referring again to the relining tubes. These tubes are drilled from solid stock and turned to size, fitted in the old barrel and then reamed to size and rifled right in place. The breach end is tapered for a depth of about 4 inches, so that the extreme breech is about, or slightly over 1/2 inch in diameter. This tapered portion is accurately fitted to a taper that has been reamed in the barrel and is driven in very tight." These liners were made and bored by Mr. Charles Diller. Mr. Johnson altered the extractor, bushed the breech block and fitted a firing pin with a spring that kept it away from the face of the breech block. Several people who have seen this alteration say it is a splendid piece of work. A hardened case-forming die was sent along with the completed job. So it was a simple matter to take the Winchester .25-20 single shot case and slip it into the die and press it all the way in a vise; this reduced the neck to .22 caliber and it was ready for loading and fire-forming. I had obtained a hundred Winchester .25-20 S.S. cases and one thousand 50-grain Lovell bullets from Sisk. My notebook shows that I used 14.0 grains of DuPont No. 4227 for fire-forming the cases. I had obtained a new Fecker telescope sight with 1-1/2-inch objective in 12.5X and when the R-2 was unpacked, the big Fecker was immediately slipped onto the blocks and carefully tightened on to them. The ocular definition of this fine scope was almost unbelievable. For the present I used the old stock with a piece set into the comb to raise it to a firm and comfortable height for use with scope. I also made a beaver-tail fore-end. I used this for the chuck season that was coming up and it proved satisfactory.

This R-2 proved to be very accurate from the bench rest, especially for the first shot fired from a cold, clean barrel. This matter of a rifle being able to deliver its first shot from a cold, clean, slightly oiled bore to the exact center of its normal group, or quite close to it, can scarcely be overstressed. The rifle which kills invariably with its first shot is this sort of rifle. No other can ever be depended upon to accomplish it. This R-2 rifle proved to be one of the most accurate I have ever fired or owned, and I still own it, and always expect to own it as I consider the R-2 the finest cartridge available of medium power, and in .22 caliber. Before I had opportunity to try this cartridge on chucks I had fired all my cases once so they were then the R-2 shape.

I had been corresponding quite a bit with a chap who had a relined Sharps-Borchardt of R-2 caliber, made by Jerry Gebby of .22 Verminter fame. This man was getting good accuracy from DuPont No. 4198 by simply scooping the case full and seating the 50-grain bullet on top of this, compressing the powder. I tried this myself and it proved so accurate and such a good killer that I never used any other powder or charge after this for the R-2. This would be about 16.5 grains if you just ladled it in with a spoon as I did, but you could get in 17.5 grains if you tamped it with a little rod and funnel. I could not see any advantage of this extra bit of work as the former loading performed as well and was a lot easier to assemble.

The first chuck killed with the R-2 was taken at 140 yards. The chuck had been scared in as I entered a field that was new to me and I did not have the dens located as yet. He ran for the den mouth and didn't hesitate on the doorstep for a last look as some do; almost immediately after he disappeared I saw his nose show, then the hair on top of his skull. I was already prone and in the sling so I cocked the hammer and set the trigger when his whole head showed in the big Fecker. I touched the set trigger and was rewarded by a loud "plop." I flipped out the empty case and reloaded. Nothing else showed in twenty minutes so I went over and picked him up. The Sisk 50-grain bullet had entered a little below and behind the ear from the side blowing a hole of exit about the size of a silver dollar.

It was a chuck of this year's litter and they weigh around five to six pounds for this age in my section. I have weighed hundreds of chucks and the woodchucks of the current year usually averaged around that figure. Their meat and hide and, of course, bone structure are a lot more tender than an older animal and the bullets seem to do a lot more damage on them. On the same hunt I killed two chucks with one shot. I never did this before or after but have seen my shooting partner kill two crows at once on a couple of occasions with the .220 Swift.

I had been sitting in the shade of a big elm tree watching through the scope the antics of four half-grown chucks down the slope from me. They had been rolling and playing like so many fox cubs. Almost as one they popped into the den, so glancing to my left I spotted a large shepherd dog making his way along the other side of the field. Evidently these chucks had had some experience with him, at any rate they lost no time going to earth. Soon one showed his head and shoulders. I was shooting down a slope so I took him through the neck. When I went to retrieve him I was surprised to see another chuck kicking around next to him — this one had been hidden on the far side of the first chuck and had been shot through the shoulder.

While he was still alive, he was unable to crawl down the den. I don't believe this would have been possible if the first chuck had been full grown as the bullet has a lot more resistance in a tough old chuck and in most cases does not come out the other side except maybe small pieces of the jacket. While cruising down a back road, a chuck was spotted from the car far out in a field of soy beans about three or four inches high. This chuck was down on all fours busily feeding. Pulling the car to a stop by some wineberry bushes, I slipped out, being careful not to slam the door as sometimes this frightens the chuck and he runs for the den before a shot can be gotten away.

It is illegal in Pennsylvania to have a loaded gun or rifle in a car or to fire out of a car from a road or highway. Many times, though, where it is permissible, a shot could be taken from the side of the road without trampling down any of the farmer's crops. As the thing stands, it is cheaper to obey the law.*

The chuck spoken of, just previously, was still feeding when I topped the bank. I either underestimated the range, or got the shot off poorly. A puff of dust this side of the chuck showed the bullet strike. I flipped out the case and slid in another cartridge. The chuck was facing away and when the crosswires came to rest between his ears, I touched the set trigger and he dropped instantly. It was a long walk over to Mr. Woodchuck but when I

*Author's Note: One reason why Game Departments encourage the passage of such laws is to prevent jacklighting of deer or cottontail rabbits at night. Another is to reduce shooting accidents. An excited rifleman may climb back into a car and overlook the removal of cartridges. A set trigger which is set is jarred or touched accidentally, and the car driver is struck in the back of his head or he shoots himself under the chin if it is his rifle. Sometimes a rifle discharges and a bullet goes up through the roof or down through the floor. Then the law does seem like a good law. In most other instances, it is simply an annoyance to the hunter. In any case, the chuck hunter should bear in mind that such law gives the game warden or a police officer the legal right to make an arrest.

arrived there I noticed the 50-grain bullet had broken the spine just back of the shoulders. When I skinned him out there was a large hole in the spinal column and two ribs cut off on each side where they joined the spine. Lungs, liver and heart were well shot up. A few days later I made a long shot on a chuck that was not killed instantly. This chuck was spotted across a meadow in a field of wheat stubble. I hesitate to state the distance as it was plenty distant for an R-2. From the prone position I held the crosshairs about six inches over his head while he was sitting erect facing away from me. At the crack of the rifle he dropped in a heap. I lay there and watched him through the scope. Feeling sure he was dead I started to get to my feet. About that time he got up too and raced towards a stone wall bordering the field. Another fellow was along with me but he did not have a rifle. He went over and started looking for the chuck. He was lying about forty feet from a den, under a stone wall. He died running because he had just stretched out while in a running position.

The bullet had entered to the left of the spine and had cut off the short rib. The stomach had a good sized hole in it and a large portion of the bullet jacket was found in the chewed up grass in the stomach cavity. He had bled badly internally and the abdominal cavity was full of blood. This was the longest shot made with the R-2 in my hands, on woodchucks, and if he had been nearer his den I would not have retrieved him.

THE T. K. LEE "DOT" GRATICULE

With the close of the chuck season I sent the scope to T. K. "Tackhole" Lee of Birmingham, Alabama, to have a dot graticule (or reticule) installed. I had found that on some shots, particularly where the chuck was in a shadow or shaded area such as under overhanging bushes, the crosshairs faded out while the chuck was still visible, making an accurate shot unlikely.*

With the dot, I specified that it cover an inch at 100 yards. Fading out was eliminated as the dot showed up clear and black under any conditions or background. I also sent the rifle to the late Otis Stapleton of Greenville, Texas, to be restocked. This was carried out in a most satisfactory manner using a beautiful piece of burl walnut. Stock was heavy target type with a close grip, high comb, and with cheek-piece. The forearm was beaver-

*Author's Note: This is much more likely to occur when fine, target-style crosshairs are used than when very coarse single crosshairs are installed.

tail. To get the grip as close as I wanted, Mr. Stapleton altered upper and lower tangs and made the lever conform to grip. I now had a handsome as well as a fine shooting rifle. I used the R- 2 for quite some time after this, always with satisfaction, and still consider it the ideal rifle for the majority of varmint hunting in a farming district.

THE .22-250

In the winter months I do quite a bit of crow and hawk shooting and like to use a 55-grain bullet between 3650 and 3750 f.s. m.v. The .22-250 seemed to be what most of the boys were using then, so I went about getting a rifle made in that caliber. I had a Mauser 1898 action that had the bolt altered and also was fitted with double-set triggers. This was shipped to Mr. J. R. Buhmiller, then of Eureka, now of Kalispell, Montana, to have a target weight barrel 26 inches long fitted and chambered for the .22-250 cartridge. When this work was completed barrel and action were sent to Mr. Hervey Lovell then of Indianapolis, Indiana, to be restocked. I sent along sketch and measurements for a target type stock with high comb slotted for removal of bolt and to have a cheek piece of my design. Mr. Lovell made me a fine stock of Circassian walnut. When the rifle arrived I had a batch of hulls waiting and lost no time in getting to the bench.

At this time it was impossible to get .250-3000 brass to neck down to .22-250 so I had 200 made up from .30-1906 brass. This gave a good strong case and worked fine. My first load to form cases was 32.0 grains of DuPont No. 4320 powder, 54-grain Sisk wartime bullet and F.A. No. 70 primer. This load shot one-inch groups so I set the scope to center group one inch high at 100 yards and was ready to try it on chucks.

The first chuck was spotted at 160 yards in a clover field. This chuck had not emerged from the den but was just looking the situation over from his doorstep. Dropping prone I held the Lee Dot about on his ear. When I touched the set trigger he just slumped forward and lay still. The .22-250 made quite a racket in that little valley in comparison to the R-2 which I had been used to shooting. Later, on examining the chuck I was surprised to see that the top of the head was blown off. The shot struck a little higher than I had held.*

*Author's Note: A rifle bullet having the velocity of that provided by the full charge in a .22-250 rifle, when the rifle is sighted to group one inch above the

Moving over to another field, a second chuck was noticed running toward a fence row. When he stopped I took him behind the shoulder, wishing to note what effect this shot with a .22-250 would have on a chuck. The bullet made a loud "plop" upon impact and the chuck simply died right there. I learned by more extended experience with this and similar size cartridges that the average body shot with the full charge will result in the bullet blowing a hole and forcing out of the body cavity enough of its contents, that about a third or a quarter of the animal will be exploded or mangled. Normally too, the chuck will be thrown a couple of feet and will lie right there, having suffered such amount of shock to its brain and nervous system and to its normal ability to move around, that it will rarely attempt to get back into the den. Sometimes when using a bullet which has a hard core and a thick, tough jacket, or which is propelled by a charge less by a material amount than the full charge, or when all these factors are in operation or when the bullet strikes only the jaws or the forepart of the head, the lacerated area will be less.

After further experiment, I concluded that it would be unwise to use this rifle on shoulder shots on chucks intended for the table. I shot forty chucks and a number of crows with this load while fire-forming the brass. Primers at that time were selling practically for their weight in gold when anyone had a few for sale, and extra primers were not expended in tests at the target. After the brass was formed I used the load recommended to me by the late J. Bushnell Smith, of 36.0 grains of DuPont No. 4320 powder and the Sisk 54-grain wartime bullet. This load proved to have quite a bit more remaining energy at 300 yards and would anchor the big chucks for keeps.

At this time an acquaintance connected with the federal government and working with me, and who was in process of transfer to Alaska, needed a rifle of the type of the .22-250. He wanted to buy my .22-250 badly so he could use it on eagles and hair seals while stationed there. I was busy with my work and had hardly any time to shoot, also gasoline and tires were in short supply, so I let it go. I later heard from him several times while he was getting a lot of splendid shooting. After selling the rifle

point of aim at 100 yards, using a scope sight of normal height, will shoot higher than the rifleman anticipates at 125 to 200 yards as the bullet is still rising for much of this distance. Where it is falling the amount that it has fallen below the line of sight is small.

I took steps to have another one built for the day when shooting could easily be indulged in. I secured a heavy barrel blank from Mr. Buhmiller and as he was not fitting barrels but was concentrating on barrel blanks only, I sent the blank to "Pop" Eimer, at Joplin, Missouri, together with a Model 1898 Mauser action with double set triggers. He fitted the barrel and altered the bolt for scope use. The barrel was turned to the same dimensions as Winchester's target weight and chambered for the .22-250 cartridge. When this work was completed, I sent barrel and action to Mr. Keith Stegall of Gunnison, Colorado, to have him make and fit a target type of stock of Oregon myrtlewood. He used a beautiful piece of wood with fine grain and turned out a very shapely stock but the checkering was not equal in symmetry of design on both sides of the stock, to later work. The stock fitting, however, was most excellent. I used this rifle with the same load as for the other .22-250, and it performed as well. With the ending of the late war I secured a thousand each of Sisk 55-grain Express and 55-grain Wotkyns-Morse 8-S bullets, using these and the Winchester No. 115 primer and 36.0 grains Du Pont No. 4320 powder. The accuracy of the rifle was doubled over that using the wartime bullets. This rifle and load accounted for two hundred chucks all killed above ground. There were apparently no crippled ones left to crawl into the hole and die.

THE .220 SWIFT ON WOODCHUCKS

My shooting partner, Harman Rogers, started his woodchuck hunting while a youngster using the .22 rim-fires. From these he went to the .22 Hornet and finally to the .220 Swift. He has been using the Swift since it was first announced by Winchester and is very well satisfied with its performance. He now has a Model 70 with target weight barrel and fitted with a Bishop stock of target type, the work being done by a local stocker. This is a fine, comfortable stock and when fitted by a good stocker leaves little to be desired. He uses a 10X Lyman Jr. Targetspot scope with a Lee Dot for sighting equipment and has the action fitted with a Miller set trigger. Like other serious varmint hunters he hand-loads all his cartridges. His rifle seems partial to a load consisting of the Sisk 55-grain Express bullet pushed by 33.0 grains of DuPont No. 3031 ignited by Western No. 8-1/2 primers. He uses a graphite wad at all times. Like myself he has a shooting range on his own property and finds it handy for rest shooting or testing loads as he loads for other calibers too, including the .30-1906 and the .270 W.C.F.

We were watching a field together one evening and as it was Harman's turn to shoot I was doing the spotting using his 7 x 50 Bausch & Lomb binoculars. If you are not used to carrying these binoculars they may seem bulky but that objection and that of weight are far outweighed by your ability to see chucks in shadow and in other darkened areas, such as those in the middle of dense stands of anything or between trees which contain much foliage and cut out light even if a shadow does not fall upon the chuck.

The field we were watching had a gentle slope from where we were sitting, against a fallen wild cherry tree, to the far fence row which was 225 yards away (we had measured it in the days when we were both using Hornets). At the fence row the ground rose rather sharply away from us and on this slope there were a number of good chuck dens as well as a goodly number along the fence rows in the field in which we were sitting. All of these dens could be taken care of from our stand. In the process of glassing the fence rows and the dense cover in plain view, a large chuck was spotted on the far bank. This was a cautious chap who just had his head showing. As the glasses examined the rest of the dens another chuck put in his appearance at the far edge of the field we were in and about 50 yards closer than the first chuck. Harman decided to take the one that was feeding for the first shot. He uses a Donaldson chuck rest too and already had the barrel resting on it. I put the glasses on the chuck selected and saw the 55-grain Sisk bullet knock it over onto its back. The other chuck never moved as the shot roared in that little valley. Harman shifted his position and took the chuck through the neck. When the bullet hit him he jumped right out of the den and his tail came up and he started to wave or buzz it in the manner that all chuck hunters like to see. As it was near dusk and too late to expect any more shots we went down to pick up. The first chuck was a large boar and had been hit at the base of the throat and it had made quite a mess of the chuck as the bullet went endwise through him. I went over and picked up the other one and he too was very large and in splendid condition. The bullet had hit him just about where the skull joins the upper vertebra in the neck, the bone mass was blown into small pieces and meat was shredded all around the wound, similar to the way wounds are from .22-250 and .219 Donaldson ammunition.

About a week later we had an odd experience with the Swift that might be of interest. We spotted a chuck at 300 yards out in a clover field. He was sitting erect facing us, the top half of the chuck showing above the clover. Taking a rest over a large rock, Harman let off the shot while I watched the chuck through the binoculars. I could not spot him as the clover was a little too high. Taking his Swift, Harman went over while I sat in the car. After a time he appeared carrying the chuck by the tail. The animal was still alive with not a mark on him but he looked really sick. We examined him thoroughly and couldn't make it out. The chuck just stood there and made no effort to get away. Finally, we turned him over on his back, then we saw it. In the paunch, about three inches behind the normal location of the stomach, was a small piece of intestine like a fishing worm sticking out of a cut about a half inch long. I got the Colt's Officer's Model out of the glove compartment and took the chuck over to the side of the road and put a bullet through its head. Then Harman opened the chuck and what a mess we saw. You would wonder how the chuck lived. The intestines were cut here and there and all the waste matter from the body was loose inside that chuck. Also the stomach had a hole cut in it and some of the contents was mixed up with the rest of the mass. We found a large piece of bullet jacket lodged in the flesh of the flank.

Our theory was this: the bullet had struck a thick clover stem a short distance in front of the chuck, the bullet then blew up and only the piece of jacket had hit the chuck. No doubt it ricocheted around inside the poor animal from the way he was cut up. This was just a flesh shot, however and could have happened with any of the very high velocity .22's — commonly called "hot" .22 varmint cartridges.

Again, we were out on another trip and were located in a pasture that at the time contained no cattle as it is the practice in this part of Pennsylvania to rotate the pasture fields about every two weeks. At the edge of the field (about 175 yards), was a creek and past this creek was an alfalfa field that contained a number of good dens. They usually do. Shots could be taken up to 300 yards. Just past the creek a chuck came out to feed, he was about two-thirds of the way out looking the field over, with his back to us. Harman put the Lee Dot on his neck and the Swift threw the chuck out of the den. Explain it — I don't think anyone can explain it so that it sounds rational. It's like a train starting to run away wildly from a standing start with the engine shot completely away with the trainmen insensible and no down grade.

I got the next chuck with the .219 Donaldson when one came out of the fence line. While we were using the binoculars on the field a chuck was spotted away up at the far end. The Swift barrel was laid on the chuck rest and the shot taken as the chuck sat up facing us. A satisfying "plop" was heard, then the usual tailwaving ensued as we both watched. We got five chucks from this stand, then went to pick up. The first chuck killed by the Swift had his head nearly taken off, in fact there was little left to identify that it had been a head. The one taken at near 300 yards was hit in the chest and the bullet did not come out the other side. Everything inside was well blown up and a piece of the jacket was found in the hide between the shoulder blades. The third chuck that evening was taken at about 175 yards. The bullet went through the shoulder and took off the far leg at the elbow. Very, very seldom does a chuck get in the den after being struck by the Swift; what it does to a crow is something to see. A little over 6000 rounds have been fired through this Swift but few of them have been factory loads or near to the muzzle velocity and the pressure of factory charges for the .220 Swift. Consequently they developed nothing like the heat of an equal number of factory loads.

Harman gets fine accuracy and good killing power with the load of a 55-grain Sisk Express and 33.0 grains of 3031. As Harman puts it, "I'm plenty satisfied!"

THE .219 DONALDSON

Always on the lookout for the most desirable cartridge for my needs, I was attracted to this creation credited by many to Harvey Donaldson. This cartridge made from the shortened and expanded .219 Zipper case seemed to be the most efficient one yet developed for shooting woodchucks in my section of Pennsylvania. With this case you can get near to Swift or .22-250 velocities with eight or ten grains less powder, using the same bullet. This cuts down the report materially which is an item when hunting in a farming district. I sent a 1898 Mauser action with double set trigger to Mr. L. R. Wallack, of Langhorne, Pennsylvania with instructions for fitting a bull barrel and making a case-forming die and a bullet-seating die. In due course of time this was finished in a fine manner and the rifle was sent to Mr.

Morgan Holmes of Montvale, New Jersey, to have the stock bedded. While this was being done, I was forming the cases. This was accomplished by pushing the .219 Zipper case into the die until the end protrudes. This is cut off with a hack saw and filed down flush with the mouth of the die. This work leaves a lip on the inside of the case neck. The lip is removed with a pocket knife blade while case is still in the die. When the case is pushed out of the die, a little burr is sometimes left on the outside of the case neck. The burr is removed with steel wool.

For a fire-forming load I chose 24.0 grains of No. 4198 and the 55-grain Sisk Express bullet. When the rifle arrived I mounted my 1-1/2-inch 12.5X Fecker scope on it and went out to the bench rest. I sighted it to group one inch high at 100 yards. I fired 20 shots at the two targets I had put up, ten on each, and these ran 3/4 and 7/8 of an inch center to center of widest holes. While fire-forming the 100 loaded cases all shots were under one inch. I then loaded 28.0 grains of DuPont No. 4320 into 20 cases behind the Sisk 55-grain Express and the 55-grain Wotkyns-Morse bullets. These did not do so well. By that I mean they did not group within less than one inch groups, but they grouped quite well enough for woodchuck shooting.*

So I loaded up 20 more using the Wotkyns-Morse bullet as it gave the smallest group. My wife and the children were anxious to see what the new rifle would do on a woodchuck so we set about finding one. We cruised along some back roads looking for a clover field, as this section was new to us. We had built a new home the summer before, quite a little distance from our former home and as yet had lacked the time to scout out our new territory. My wife was driving the car and spotted the first chuck in a clover field along an abandoned railroad bank. We looked the field over before taking the shot and saw two more chucks at distances of approximately 200 yards.

Slipping out of the car, I decided to take the chuck which we had seen first as he was then about 100 yards from and in plain sight of my eager audience. I poked the barrel through some tall grass along the fence line and from the prone position took the first chuck under the ear as he sat erect and sidewise to me. Working the bolt I put in another cartridge and shifted my posi-

---

*Author's Note: Four additional grains of a different powder, probably not so well suited to that barrel and with a case now having only a grain or so more normal capacity of charge. Many of the .219 Donaldson rifles shoot much more accurately with the reduction in charge, especially at a range of 100 yards.

 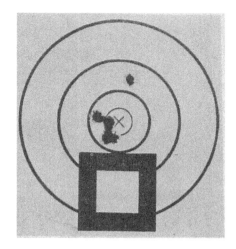

Two 5-shot groups at 100 yards, each ⅞″ in diameter, shot by Charles E. Travis, Jr. with his Charles C. Johnson, Winchester Hi-side single shot R-2 rifle sighted with a 5-A scope. Load was Winchester No. 116 primers, Sisk 50-grain Lovell bullets, and 16.5 grains of DuPont No. 4198.

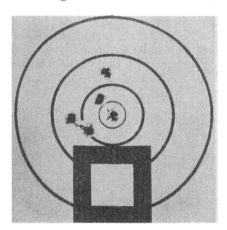 

5-shot group at 100 yards, measuring 0.45″ center to center, by Travis with .219 Wasp chambered rifle. Temperature was 15° F. Load was 30.2 grains of DuPont No. 4320 and R. B. Sisk's 55-grain soft-point Express bullet. Vertical spread is only 0.18″.

Two groups by Travis shot on bench rest 100-yard range with inexpensive factory-made rifle, the Savage Model 19-H Hornet (converted to a K-Hornet and stock remodeled). Load was 40-grain Lovell bullet ahead of 13.0 grains of 4227 ignited by Winchester No. 116 primers. One group measures ⅞″, the other ¾″.

Three of Travis' super-accurate woodchuck rifles. *Top:* .219 Donaldson Wasp, '98 Mauser action, Gregoire barrel by L. R. Wallack, Jr., stock by Keith Stegall, 12.5 Fecker scope. *Middle:* Savage 19H Model .22 Hornet, rechambered by Lysle Kilbourne, stock reworked and trigger fitted by Travis. *Bottom:* .22-3000 R-2 Winchester Hi-wall, barrel relined by Charles E. Johnson, Winchester A5 scope with 1⅛″ Lee Dot.

Large Pennsylvania chuck killed with Travis' Gregoire-Wallack rifle, .219 Donaldson-Wasp caliber. Bullet was a 55-grain Sisk.
CREDIT: CHARLES E. TRAVIS, JR.

Charles E. Travis, Jr. using a portable rest in the field.

tion a bit to get at the other two chucks. These had run at the shot and one went into his den but the other stopped for a final look and was right on his own doorstep when shot. Upon examination of these first two chucks shot with my new .219 Donaldson-Wasp I found that the wounds were of about the same severity as those caused by my .22-250, using the same bullet, but eight grains less powder was used in the .219.

A couple of evenings later I was watching some chuck dens far out in a clover field. The sun was at my back and I was in the shadow of a couple of large elderberry bushes. This was an ideal position as I could see everything that moved in that field while I could not readily be seen by the game I was after. I had a wait of perhaps twenty minutes before a chuck put in his appearance. This was a large mature chuck and as fat as a butter ball. He was down on all fours, busily feeding but just before I set the trigger he sat up facing me. He didn't seem alarmed, just watchful and I could see the small pieces of clover in his mouth as I watched him through the Fecker scope.

When the bullet hit him it knocked him over backwards and he lay there for perhaps a minute or two with all four feet sticking up into the air, then the muscles relaxed. This load had more shocking power than expected, out where the chuck sat, which is what really counts regardless of the initial velocity. When I went over to pick up the chuck the small pieces of clover were still in his mouth, showing instant paralysis of the muscles of the jaws. The bullet had entered just under his chin in the throat and completely shattered the spinal column in the neck and also pulped the surrounding flesh. This shot was taken at 220 yards.

After getting the chuck out I made my way over to another field about a quarter of a mile distant. This clover field was bordered on one side by a corn field and it was from this side that I approached. I stood in the first row of corn and looked the field over. The clover had been harvested about a week before and several good chuck dens were in plain view. Soon I had three chucks located; all were over 200 yards, and one big fellow was near 300 yards distant. I had my chuck rest set up just inside the cornfield.

I lay down prone and rested the barrel on the rest and got the first chuck lined up in the scope. I rest the toe of the stock on my left fist and in this manner I can raise or lower the rifle until everything is in proper position for shooting.

I set the trigger, and with the chuck facing directly away

from me, was ready to touch off the shot. This chuck was sitting erect and as the bullet struck he just fell forward. I lay there watching him through the scope and soon saw his tail buzzing, a sure sign of a solid hit. Both of the other chucks had run in at the shot so I just lay there and waited for one to appear.

After a wait of perhaps ten minutes a head appeared about 20 yards beyond the fallen chuck. I was still hidden by the corn, so I again got into shooting position with the .219 Donaldson. By this time the chuck had come out of his den and had started to feed. He was moving his head so rapidly that it was difficult to settle the Lee Dot at the butt of the ear so I held for a shoulder shot. When the bullet struck, which with the .219 Donaldson is almost immediately as one senses it, it landed with a pronounced "plop." Then I was not worried about the chuck going elsewhere. I waited twenty minutes longer for the big chuck to come out and show himself, but he stayed underground.

Upon picking up the first chuck I saw that the 55-grain W.M. bullet had entered the neck where it meets the shoulder, had ground up the bone quite a bit and had then come out the throat in front. The second chuck had been hit just behind the shoulder at an angle, the bullet ranging forward and nearly taking off the far leg. I was quite satisfied, so far, with the work of the .219 Donaldson. It killed as well as my .22-250 and used less powder per shot, and what was still more important for firing in some areas, it made materially less report. The crack of the rifle was sharp, but less loud.

I lacked the time to use the Donaldson very extensively during the summer of 1949, but did manage to kill 17 woodchucks very dead with it, all at nice ranges. As yet I have failed to obtain any of the desirable 1/4 or 3/8 inch groups one often reads of in connection with this cartridge. This of course has been disappointing, like pan-washing for gold and finding "traces" but no nuggets. However, while I visited at the Bench Rest Shooters Matches over Labor Day, 1949, I talked to several of the finest bench-rest shooters in the east and picked up quite a store of helpful information. Now I feel that with a bit of attention to detail in loading ammunition and in firing, and some rifle tinkering, I'll make the Johnstown information pay off. I had my bull barrel rifle made up specifically for the most accurate of bench-rest shooting and for the hunting of hawks and crows during the winter. Each requires a superaccurate rifle and a very uniform delivery of shot after shot to the normal center of impact of that rifle and charge. I do quite a lot of winter hunting of hawks and crows and it takes an extremely close shooting rifle to hit them at long range, or even at medium ranges, for that matter. The ordinary sporting rifle is of little actual use and is not very deadly for such specialized hunting. It not only lacks superaccuracy at a distance, but it is too difficult to keep its normal group centered on such targets from various firing positions. Also, the vital area of such game is most extremely small, much of the bird being nothing but feathers.

I have a fine, line-engraved commercial Mauser, with a splendid pair of double set triggers and a release lever on the magazine floor plate, also a Buhmiller barrel blank with 14-inch twist. I'm going to have this made up into a target weight .219 Donaldson and stocked with a beautiful piece of stump walnut that I have been saving for the past twelve years. It should be well dried by this time! This should make a fine chuck rifle and will be a lot handier than the before-mentioned .219 Bull Gun where a lot of walking and carrying in the game fields is in order.

I have used the collection of hot .22 center fires that I have described for shooting a goodly number of woodchucks. Quite a few hundred of them in fact. Frankly, each caliber has a niche to fill in some type of country. From my own personal experience I would choose the .22-3000 R-2 Donaldson and the .219 Donaldson cartridges for the type of country I hunt over. It should be remembered in this regard that either or both can be made up in a very widely differing lot of rifles of various makes and models of actions. Even the variations in stocks may make two rifles of either of these calibers vary quite widely in weight, balance, accuracy and in handiness of carrying and shooting. It does not do to take an R-2 rifle and say this rifle is representative of all R-2 rifles. It isn't. Changing the stock bedding, the headspacing, modifying the vibrations of the barrel while it is being fired, and especially changing the load or the bullet, the quantity of the powder charge or its granulation, or using a different primer will immediately have an effect upon accuracy.

DRESSING WOODCHUCKS AND USING THE FLESH

You may have wondered at times, why I dress my woodchucks. The reason is that every one shot is brought home. The young ones make splendid eating — a formal woodchuck banquet has been held annually, for years past, at a hotel not many miles from my home. Some eat the turkey course, others prefer the roast woodchuck, while more than half try both.

We prepare and consume the young chucks — and regard them as splendid eating. The old chucks, which are tough, are used as dog feed. They also are turned into small amounts of cash in some localities where there are fox farms and the carcasses are disposed of for fox feed.

In Pennsylvania the woodchuck is given the protection accorded a game animal and normally the season opens July first. Chucks are in splendid condition then from feeding on clover and alfalfa and some feel that it is a shame to dispose carelessly of the meat without obtaining at least some benefit from each carcass.

Skinning out carefully and dressing each animal means of course opening it the full length of the cavity of the body, and permits at the same time a most careful examination of the whole course of the bullet as it blew up in or passed through the woodchuck. I know some fellows who never even go over to look at the chuck after it is shot. While such action results in less attention being paid the shooter in some instances, I personally am more interested in this superb mark for the varmint rifle — Marmota Monax, the eastern woodchuck. If it were not for having the woodchuck as a target, I doubt that we would have today, most of the fine, superaccurate, flat-shooting varmint rifles that are being made up by gunsmiths which so many of us have spent hard-earned money to possess. The American woodchuck rifle stands today at the top, the prize jewel among all the types of special varmint rifles which have appeared since breech-loading rifles became common.

Nothing in practical shoulder arms has ever been as accurate over 100, 200 and 300 yards, and no rifle appears on the horizon which seems likely to equal or supplant them which would be suitable for long range shooting at woodchucks.

1949-1950 SHOOTING WITH THE .219 DONALDSON

Bull Gun — The Winter Hunting of a Pennsylvania Rifleman

Now we come to the most recent work with the heavy barreled bench-rest rifle by Wallack in .219 Donaldson caliber. Previously I spoke of the early work on late-season woodchucks during 1949. During the winter of 1949-1950, we had further hunting in the field with this rifle. The reader will understand of course that our local woodchucks are all denned up and hibernating at this winter season, so we used the rifle on crows and hawks. They are, if anything, more difficult to hit and kill instantly than woodchucks because of their small vital areas. The only really small vital area of the chuck is the brain pan, and that is the most vital of all.

My gunmaker is L. R. Wallack, of Langhorne, Pennsylvania, nearly opposite Trenton, New Jersey. I was not quite satisfied with the groups my rifle was making so, while at the bench-rest matches at Johnstown, New York, over Labor Day, 1949, I discussed this matter with Wallack, and he suggested I leave the heavy rifle with him so that he could look into the matter and try to tune it up.

He soon had it grouping better by tuning up my loads slightly and using Sierra bullets. When the rifle was returned to me, he sent along a 5-shot group of 3/8 inch that he had shot with it at 100 yards. This was obtained using the following load: Sierra 55-grain semi-round nose bullets ahead of 30.2 grains of No. 4320 DuPont powder and the Winchester No. 115 primer. This charge was in Winchester cases. When the rifle arrived I mounted my 1-1/2-inch 12.5X Fecker scope on it, and taking some ammunition along, I went out to my bench rest. My scope has a Lee Dot that just covers the aiming point of the official bench-rest target.

I adjusted the scope from my note book readings as I had been using this scope on my fine Winchester—Johnson R-2 Donaldson and, of course, had changed the settings. I put two targets on the butts, settled myself at the bench and fired ten shots, five on each target. It was very cold (15° F) and my fingers were so numb that I could hardly feel the set trigger by the time I had fired the first five shots. Upon going forward to the targets I saw two nice groups. The first was under 1/2 inch with four in 3/16 inch, the second was 3/4 inch with four in 3/8 inch. This was at 100 yards.

The next day (Saturday) was so windy that it was useless to take a .22-caliber rifle out of the gun cabinet. Monday morning before going to work I saw three crows along the edge of my woods in a tall maple tree, at 150 yards. I got the .219 Donaldson and pushed a patch through the bore. Opening the cellarway door a crack I eased out the muzzle. I sat on the step and rested my left hand on the sill. I touched the set trigger and exploded one crow, the other two wheeled around cawing and raised quite a fuss. Soon one came down a bit and sat on a limb, bobbing up and down, cawing for all he was worth looking down at the dead crow. Just then the 55-grain Sierra bullet struck him dead center in the breast. The third crow decided things were too hot around there and left right then. I went up to examine the two crows as these were the first I had shot with the Sierra bullets.

The first crow was hit from the side and was cut practically in half. The second was struck from in front and was split wide open. The whole front of him from the crop down, was shot completely away. His back was cut in half and it and the tail still hung up there in the tree. This load was indeed potent on crows!

The following Saturday morning my shooting partner, Harman Rogers, and I set out at 7 o'clock to cruise out a section of country we had mapped for hunting a few nights before. I have a large, detailed map of the area we hunt. This section includes 760 square miles. This means a section 25 by 30 miles in extent and slightly irregular in outline.

In the evening after such a hunt, while putting notes and entries in my shooting note book, I go over this map and trace out all of the route we passed over earlier in the day. This makes it most interesting and it is surprising to see how much ground is covered in a four- or five-hour cruise. While driving slowly down a back road, I sighted something out of place on one of the lower limbs of an old buttonwood tree. Putting the Fecker on it showed a Cooper's hawk resting there, hunched up with his back to us. This buttonwood tree stood on the edge of a nice little trout stream in the shadow of a large stand of Norway spruce. This accipiter was no doubt waiting for his breakfast to come along in the person of a bobwhite quail or a ringnecked pheasant. I put the Lee Dot on him and touched the set trigger. At the report of the .219 Donaldson the hawk flew apart. One wing was blown completely off and a very large hole torn in his back between the wings where the bullet had struck. This was with the load of 30.2 grains of DuPont No. 4320, Winchester No. 115 primer and the excellent Sierra 55-grain round nose bullet at 175 yards. A little while and a few miles later Harman killed two crows with his heavy barreled Model 70 Swift using that day a load consisting of the Sisk 55-grain Express bullet ahead of 34.0 grains of 4895 powder, lot unknown, and the Western No. 8-1/2 primer. This load treated a crow very rough, too. Later, while searching the edge of a woods about 300 yards away for hawks with the Bausch & Lomb 7 x 50 binoculars, one was sighted sitting back a little from the wood's edge. He was partly screened by small branches, but I decided to take the shot and see if I could get the bullet through. I put on my padded shooting glove and as Wallack had removed the sling swivels from the stock, I lay down prone and rested my gloved hand on the bottom rail of the fence and touched off the shot. I either missed or the bullet blew up on the branches. Anyway, the hawk took off and soared straight towards us across an open field. There was a lone oak tree about 75 yards from the road and darned if he didn't light right in it. I put the Lee Dot smack on his breast and this time there was a loud "blop" and the hawk came down in a heap. Upon going up to him, we found that the bullet had struck him full in the breast and had come out the back between the wing butts and left an area of nonexistent feathers, skin and meat about as large as my fist. The next chance came at a crow. He was sighted at about 125 yards and was walking around and searching the ground for something to eat. This kind of a shot can get on your nerves a bit at times, as the crow is walking about and is always changing direction exactly when you are about to press the trigger. After four or five tries I touched the set trigger and raked him across the back. It was of the nature of a scratch hit and he flopped around a bit before lying still.

On this trip we killed thirteen crows and five hawks, or a total of eighteen and with the exception of the one hawk taken at 75 yards, the rest of the shots were at distances of 125 to 250 yards. I was very much pleased with the results obtained with my .219 Donaldson, especially since it was equal in killing power and flat trajectory, or nearly so, to my .22-250 and other rifles using six to eight grains more powder. On the other hand, there is considerably more work in preparing the cartridges of the .219 Donaldson caliber due to having to cut off the necks and chamber them. This is fairly hard, tedious work, and requires time. So there are advantages and disadvantages both ways.

The report of the .219 Donaldson, while sharp, is somewhat milder and that is an important item and a factor for consideration in the country we hunt over. While the .22 rim-fire is far more dangerous in the hands of many hunters, it is the loud report of the .22-250, the .220 Swift, and the .257 Roberts type of rifles that stirs up the majority of the land owners who object to you hunting over or near their lands. Of course, if your hunting is confined to the farming districts, this will not apply to you, nor be of special significance. You can then use any caliber or type of rifle your heart desires.

This matter of being overgunned as far as report is concerned is very important if you have to hunt the same farms year after year. If the landowner objects to the report, and you cannot convince him that the rifle is not dangerous or unduly objectionable, it is then best to use the K-Hornet or the R-2 or else, if possible, find another place to hunt where you do not stir un antipathy. I have hunted the same general area for over 20 years and find that most of the real farmers, that is the ones that farm for a living and not just for a hobby, are pretty reasonable fellows and easy to get along with once they are convinced you are a safe hunter. This loudness of report concerns the chuck hunter more often than the crow and hawk hunter because during the time of year we do the most crow and hawk shooting it is either cool, or very cold and the farmers and their families are for the most part indoors, with the windows down, and do not hear the rifle being fired. When they do, the report seems soft. The majority of livestock are in the barns and the fields lie empty at this period of snow, ice and cold rains.

ANOTHER CROW SHOOTING TRIP

Getting back to the performance of the .219 Donaldson, another raid was planned into the haunts of the crow. Harman, Henry Wahls and myself were to go this time. I was ready at 6:30 A.M. and awaiting their arrival at my place. A trio of crows had been trading back and forth between my woods and two tall wild cherry trees about 200 yards from the woods.

I expected the fellows any minute so put off taking a shot, in fact the crows sort of decided that for me by not staying put long enough in one place to enable me to get ready for a shot. Finally they settled in a tree along the edge of the woods. I picked up my .219 and went down in the cellar intending to take the shot from the cellarway doors. All my windows have storm windows and can not be raised. At the moment I heard the car coming up the lane, the crows turned and took off. They only flew a few yards and settled again offering a good open shot at close to 175 yards. A rest was taken across the rear of Henry's car and the trigger set. I looked at the three crows through the big Fecker and selected the one offering the most open shot. When the trigger was pressed, there was a loud "blop" and the crow dropped to the ground. The other two didn't bother to come back for a second look. I particularly like the way the heavy Donaldson places the first shot from a cold barrel.*

Previous to taking the above shot on crows, the rifle hadn't been fired for two weeks. Keeping a uniform center of impact for the successive cold barrel shots from a rifle is very important from a varmint hunter's point of view because it has been my experience that very rarely do you get a chance for sighters or warmers when shooting crows. It's either connect on the first shot or mark a miss on the score card. I am a firm believer in the use of very heavy barrels. I know that some standard barrels will shoot splendidly; but day in and day out, consistent hits from all sorts of crazy positions and methods of resting in the field are best obtained from the very heavy barrels.

Getting back to this hunt: After killing the crow, I put the rifle on the back seat, went into the house and collected the remainder of the equipment. I carry a little leather bag with two compartments in it. This contains on one side loaded cartridges and on the other two screw drivers, one small and one medium (they come in mighty handy in the field at times, as do a pair of pliers), a pair of Bausch & Lomb shooting glasses, my Pennsylvania Hunting License, a copy of the Pennsylvania Game Laws. This is a book of 181 pages and contains the why's and wherefore's of most everything pertaining to hunting and shooting in Pennsylvania. Also in the bag is an Olt's crow call and a spare extractor for the rifle, also a score card properly filled out for the day's hunt—than all you have to do is to mark clearly and accurately the hits and the misses and the ranges. Also, a half-dozen targets are carried in case the scope is whacked, or the rifle dropped. In the car of each of us who hunt together is a steel, one-piece cleaning rod, just in case a shell sticks in the chamber or an extractor rides over a rim. This rod is never taken from the car. It is not a bad idea to also carry in the car, at all times, twenty extra cartridges. It would be very embar-

---

*Author's Note: This is common to other styles of somewhat similar cartridges also used in very heavy barrels because such barrels are not subject to wide differences of barrel flip. Changing loads also has the same tendency to uniformity of delivery and to fire to the common center of impact.

rassing to have a cartridge stick in the chamber and the extractor slip over it, and you many miles from home. An extra pair of shoes, with socks, in the car, is a wise measure.

About a mile from my home the next shot was presented. This was a Cooper's hawk at 150 yards. Henry was using the .22-250 that day and made the shot and also made short work of that hawk. This rifle is on a Model 1898 Mauser action and is fitted with a target weight barrel put there by Paul Jaeger, of Jenkintown, Pennsylvania, and has a Marksman type stock with Monte Carlo cheek piece. Henry made this stock himself from a nice piece of walnut. He also altered the Mauser bolt for scope use. The rifle is fitted with a Lyman Jr. Targetspot scope in 8X and is equipped with a cross hair.

The load he was using that day was 34.0 grains of 4895 powder, lot unknown, and the Sisk 55-grain Express bullet ahead of Remington No. 9-1/2 primers in cases made from .30-1906 brass. He has been using this outfit for quite some time and finds it quite satisfactory for chuck, crow and hawk shooting.

Harman got the next crow with his old standby the Model 70 Swift, described elsewhere in this chapter. It was a splendid day and the flocks were starting to break up preparatory to the nesting season. Crows were sighted in pairs and trios quite often and this makes most excellent shooting as they seem to lose most of their former alertness at this time of year and stay put better thereby giving you a shot. We had gotten around nine shots apiece and most all were hits so we were feeling pretty good.

Around my home it is very good shooting to obtain 27 or 30 shots in a couple of hours merely by hunting the countryside. We use another system too but that is only good when the snow has been on the ground for at least three days. There are about five places within a radius of about twenty miles that raise hundreds of pigs annually. The crows come in there by the hundreds to feed on the pig field. We select a place about 100 to 150 yards from the tallest trees and are set for as long as we care to stay. If the snow has been down for a week or more and you are alone, as many as fifty shots can be taken in four hours. The main trouble with these places is that sometimes a lot of trap and skeet shooters come out and do much shooting and show themselves so often that the crows won't light for the hidden riflemen. Of course you have to obtain permission from the piggery owner before any shooting is attempted.

We had been cruising slowly down a back road when a flock

of crows were sighted diving on a small thicket with a couple of tall oak trees towering over it. We couldn't see the reason for the disturbance but it might well have been a fox, or an opossum, an abandoned house cat turned wild, or one of the buteos or soaring hawks such as the Red-tailed, Red-shouldered, or Rough-legged hawks. The crows like to raise a lot of noise around these hawks while they are perched but don't care much to bother the swift Cooper's hawk or the Goshawks. These can rip a crow to pieces in the wink of an eye. When the car slid to a stop behind a cut bank Henry stepped out and eased his ,22-250's muzzle through the honeysuckle that covered the fence at the top of the bank.

The crows were out about 150 yards and still doing a lot of cawing, diving and wheeling about while a few were in the top branches of the oaks. At the report of the .22-250 one of the crows plummeted to the ground. The rest really got busy now, diving down and swooping here and there, all the while filling the air with their cries. Henry had another cartridge in the chamber and when he got the cross hairs on a crow in the clear, the trigger was pressed. Another loud ''plop,'' another hit was marked on the score card. Before the crows left he had gotten three shots, all of them hits. Henry is a big stout fellow and his grin was just as big as he as he climbed back into the car. No wonder he said, ''Man, I'm really having fun today!'' We turned off this road and followed one along a small creek. There is a lot of swampy land along this stretch and it is nearly always sure of producing at least one hawk shot.

We had gone perhaps an eighth of a mile when a hawk was spotted eating something on the ground. Before Harman could get off the shot the hawk took off and lit in a tree along the next fence row and sat with his back towards us. We estimated the range as being close to 350 yards. Shooting from the prone position with sling, Harman held the Lee Dot about six inches above the hawk's head and pressed the set trigger. I was watching the hawk through my 12.5X Fecker and at the report of the Swift he just fell forward off the limb. Farther down this road we came to a long meadow with a creek flowing through. Bordering the creek was swampy ground and a good growth of swamp alders. Back of this was a woods with a number of tall poplars in it. These trees are convenient for the crows to perch in. When we came in sight, the meadow had about 100 crows scattered here and there feeding. As the car drew near they began leaving by twos and threes all through the area covered by the flock, until not a single one was left.

A number lit in the tall poplar trees and we judged the range to be about 200 yards. I slipped a cartridge into the chamber of the .219 Donaldson and resting against the bottom rail of the fence, placed the Lee Dot on the head of a crow in the clear. He fell at the shot, hit in the small of the back, as a later check-up showed. While the crows did some diving and cawing and flying around the fallen one, none alighted to afford another shot.

We had a most excellent bit of shooting that morning and it was now time to head for home as Harman likes to be at his taxidermist shop on Saturday afternoons because a number of his customers call for their finished work at that time. When a man is in private business he nearly always seems to have to work on holidays and Saturdays or whenever others can go somewhere and take in a shoot. So a man simply has to make the best of what exists and go shooting when he can.

On the way home from this trip we totaled the score card and found that we had fired 46 shots and had made kills on all but nine. In other words, we killed 37 crows and hawks, of which five were hawks. We do not do as well on all occasions, I can assure you, but you know that there are days when everything goes along just fine. Some shooters, no doubt, do even better but we consider this a very good morning's work. We take every safe shot that is offered up to 300 yards which is about the limit for hits on crows, at least by us. Most shots are taken at 125 to 250 yards, in average weather and with normal backgrounds.

On arriving at my place I got out at the end of the lane to get the mail and let the fellows go on. My boy and youngest girl came running down the lane to meet me with the news that there were five crows in the tree over the one I shot before leaving home that morning. Giving my shooting bag to the boy to hold and the mail to his sister, I put on my padded shooting glove and lying prone rested on a stone bordering the lane and knocked another crow out of the tree. This was a shot at approximately 175 yards. The others never let out a single squawk, just flew back into the woods out of sight.

A word about the glove: It is one formerly used when I shot small bore awhile back. It is made by the IO-X Manufacturing Company, and I added a good thick piece of lamb's wool on the inside where the wrist and back of the hand rests. This comes in very handy when using a 15- or 20-pound rifle and when resting across whatever is offered in the field be it rock, fence rail, etc. This prevents the objects from cutting into the bony structure of your hand which, by the way, is covered with more tender skin than is the palm of your hand which is toughened by work. The pain from the pressure on the back of your hand causes the rifle to tremble from the reflexes of the muscles in your hand and forearm and most times results in a flinch at the exact moment of shooting.

I killed some more crows late the afternoon of the day just described. I shot them at the edge of my woods and another one was bagged the next morning. I take the crows or whatever is left of them and tie a string about a foot long to the neck and attach a stick about 12 inches long and heave this up into a nearby tree. Whenever any other crows come along they come over these decoys and dive and swoop around the dead crows and if one gets tired and sits and voices its feelings for a moment, I usually get a shot. I've killed 19 with the .219 Donaldson in a few week ends right from my back door. Our house, possibly it should be explained, is a new one, sits by itself sort of dug onto the side of a hill which ground slopes down to the road and we are protected considerably from the force of the northwest winter winds by the hill and by the woods which is on top of the hill and strung along on its north side. I keep my registered beagles up in the protection of the woods, in their little kennels, and the range is located so that I fire into the hill. I have some protection there from wind drift, but not too much.

I feel that I have given this .219 Donaldson built by Bob Wallack a good tryout on chucks, and also on crows and hawks, and at the target and find that for me it is all one could desire. It has mild report for a powerful rifle — which is what it is. It has splendid killing power on all varmints in southeastern Pennsylvania, it has superb accuracy. The rifle itself is a consistent deadly varmint and bench-rest rifle. It is the outgrowth of my lifetime of experiment and field shooting during which I have tried many of the more efficient of the .22-caliber varmint rifles — all of them woodchuck rifles. I have explained in the forepart of this chapter what these were and what they have done.

While still sufficiently young to believe that I have most of my shooting life ahead of me, I am much more fortunate than many in the rifle game in that I have not been too severely handicapped in my younger days by inefficient and ineffective rifles or ammunition, and that from here on I can progress while being equipped with rifles, telescopes and ammunition such as those of one, two or three generations ahead of me never imagined could exist. Had we the varmints and the small game to shoot at which existed in the United States between 1850 and 1890, and had we our present rifles to use against them, and if we then had the time and the opportunity to hunt which was given to some in the opening of the west during the buffalo days, there would be no reason to adopt Horace Greeley's injunction to ''Go west, young man, go west''; except for the bison and the Indians, we'd have it all here, and an opportunity to enjoy it with the means of rapid transit supplied by the automobile and the paved highway.

While man can do nothing today but look back and dream, like many of my age and kind I can look forward to better shooting tomorrow and next week. The younger woodchuck hunter of today will live to see the sun come up warm and bright. The dew will be on the clover and the woodchucks will come out to feed in the pastures.

The Indian's Happy Hunting grounds will be with us, then.

1950 EXPERIENCES WITH THE .219 DONALDSON-WASP

During the late summer and early fall of 1950, Charles E. Travis, Jr., added considerably to his experience with his 15-pound .219 Donaldson-Wasp bench-rest rifle on woodchucks.

I went down to Bill Ryan's farm to continue the chuck season and met Bill driving the cows from the barn, the milking being finished. I had always been allowed to hunt there, but invariably make it a point to call on the landowners each season to see if everything is still favorable and the shooting would be convenient.

Leaving the car at the barn and taking my heavy .219 Donaldson, I headed for a hay meadow that had been cut and raked the week before. This field always provides an ideal set-up for shots to 250 yards. Shortly after settling myself, a large fat chuck came into view. On a stand such as this, I rarely shoot at one chuck at a time but wait until at least two are out in the field as then, frequently, both can be shot in a matter of seconds.

After a moment, sure enough there came another. I rolled over into a good solid prone position and put the Lee Dot on the face of the chuck peering from the den. When the set trigger was pressed, I heard a hard "blop." Working the bolt I threw out the empty case and picked up a fresh round which I always place on the ground about the same position as the cartridge block would be in target shooting. The second chuck sat up and looked around and I took him through the base of the skull. His tail came up and waved as I lay there watching through the Fecker. A young chuck began to whistle along the fence row where I was sitting and kept this up for half an hour. Nothing came into view in that time, so I decided to change my position so he would stop his whistle and then maybe I could get another shot. I slipped into the woods and circled the field. I had just taken up a stand when a chap came through a barway to my right. He said he lived over the hill and had heard the shots (this suggests the .219 Donaldson will be heard clearly at least over the top of a hill — something to bear in mind in certain districts).

At that moment I saw a movement in the mouth of a den at 225 yards. Putting the glasses on it showed a young chuck, about half grown, with its head just showing. While my newly found friend was using the glasses, I sighted a chuck coming from the fence row to feed out in the field. The distance was about 200 yards. This animal, no doubt, was the chuck that was causing me all the concern a while back by his whistle of anger that kept the other woodchucks under cover.

Jamming the sling keeper up tight I said I'd take the second chuck first. (I had put the sling back on the rifle and didn't use the chuck rest much this season because the ground proved too hard in most places to allow one to push in the point of the rest.) My friend never before having seen a real heavily barreled woodchuck rifle or target scope in action together remarked that these chucks couldn't be touched at that distance. To make a long story short, I slammed a bullet into the skull of the chuck selected, then moved myself around a bit, reloading at the same time, and looked for the second chuck. He was still peering from the den but had drawn his head back a little farther than when I first viewed him. I pressed the set trigger and the bullet was off on its way across the little valley. It hit with a pronounced "blop." Both of these shots had gone through the head from side to side. I like to make this type of shot land right under the chuck's ear if at all possible. They were run-of-the-mill shots for the Donaldson but my companion was amazed.

We went down and picked up the four chucks. All were shot

through the head and had been well chewed up. The Donaldson seems to kill as a result of great impact and the shredded area seems to be as large as with the .22-250 which I have used extensively, or with the .220 Swift which is used by my hunting companion. The load I was using on this occasion was the 55-grain Sisk Express bullet driven by 30.2 grains No. 4320 powder and the Winchester No. 115 primer. During the winter I had used the 55-grain Sierra semi-round nose bullet with fine results on crows, hawks and other varmints. At this time I was unable to buy them, possibly due to the Korean War and tightening of supplies and materials.

The next evening Harman and I went out to Harvey James' farm after being told tall tales about the place being "lousy with woodchucks." We were a little skeptical about this, having heard this kind of talk from other farmers before only to find they had very few chucks. But Harvey wasn't just talking. He really had the chucks. We saw nine all in view on our first visit to the clover field, a field hemmed in by woods on three sides. What a place! Shots were there at 300 yards or a little farther, and away back off the road and thus perhaps·unknown to the "road" type of chuck hunter who is too tired to get off the car seat. We killed two chucks apiece from this stand just inside the cart road. These were along the next fence and shots averaged 250 yards. The rest dove into their dens at this salute. We moved to a little knoll to obtain a better view of three sides of the field. One favorable thing was that these chucks weren't very scary for very soon three were out in sight again. They were all busy feeding, paying little or no attention to us.

See that one down in the far corner, along the edge, and right in the shadow of that hickory tree? There he's moving out into the field. The shooter's elbows are dug in, his legs are spread out, bolt shoved home and the trigger set. The last little bit of excess breath is let out as the Lee Dot finds its mark. Then the pleasant report of the .219, "blop!" comes back from away down near the hickory. The chuck never moved. Watch now to see his tail buzzing. That which follows is satisfaction, the first shot from a cold slightly oiled barrel landing right in there where it does the most good. Harman and I took five chucks apiece from that field before we left. Here in Pennsylvania the daily bag limit has been five chucks for some time, but the season take is unlimited. Some complain about the relatively small daily bag limit, feeling it does not give a man enough shooting if he has but a few days to hunt during the summer, or if he makes a long trip to a shooting grounds, but it is a good measure in one way. With the rifles that are available today for woodchuck shooting, a good rifleman can shoot himself right out of business in a couple of seasons if he doesn't carefully watch the ratio of the number shot to the breeding and den facilities of the district.

Harman and I hunt in the evenings after work, and usually only then, and are well satisfied with three to five shots per evening. The bulk of our hunting is confined to fields ten to fifteen minutes drive from home. So when we have good shooting so handy, why spoil it by overshooting? We rarely hunt the same farms two times in a week, we give them a rest, as it were, and spread the shooting over several fields.

When we got back in the car at dusk with ten chucks, Harvey came off the porch to look them over. "Fat as butter balls," was his comment. Then he added, "Just imagine the amount of clover they would eat in a season." As I backed the car around he called, "Come back any time," and we did.

Later in the season I was hunting alone down at Joe Brooks' old place. As I topped a knoll in a pasture bordering a fresh cut hay meadow, I saw a large chuck sit up. When he dropped down to eat again and started nibbling off the clover with his sharp teeth I eased over to the fence row and pulled the bushes apart. Counting the big one I had first seen, there were four chucks out. One away up along the far fence lying on a big rock; one sitting erect at the entrance of a den and two others rapidly filling themselves with alfalfa. I decided to fire at the one sitting on the burrow, for the first shot, as he would be the one most likely to get out of sight the quickest after the rifle fired. The muzzle of the .219 was carefully shoved through the weeds bordering the field and a few leaves were pulled off here and there to give a clear field for the scope. The sling was tightened, the trigger set and everything was ready to shoot. I looked through the scope and the big chuck was still there. He was facing me at 250 yards; not a muscle moved, even his eyes didn't blink. This was a sign he was intently sniffing or watching something. Most likely he was aware of some danger about but wasn't sure what.

It may be true that an ill wind never blows anyone any good, but it is dead certain that a breeze that carries the hunter-man scent means possible trouble for the woodchuck and he is well aware of it. Possibly he just sits up sensing that something out

of the ordinary is wrong, but is not sure what, or where lies the
danger. The chucks alive today are still there because they have
not been caught napping too frequently by foxes or man.

With a scope like the 1-1/2-inch 12.5X Fecker such as I use,
it is a pleasure to watch the game and to study it before the
trigger is pressed. The chuck turns his head sidewise and the
Lee Dot nestles just below his ear. How black and clear the dot
stands out! Many a time I've thanked "Tackhole" for that dot.
Finally the trigger is touched and the chuck is slammed over
backwards with all four feet sticking stiffly up into the air. The
two that were feeding quickly ran to their dens and went right in
but the one on the rock was still there. Apparently the report of
the Donaldson didn't alarm him. I held the Lee Dot right at the
base of his ear and touched the set trigger, there was a loud
"blop" and the chuck rolled down off the rock to the ground below — soon his tail came up and waved. This shot was at 250
yards. I waited for twenty minutes before entering the field but
nothing else came into view so I went over to pick up the two
chucks. Both bullets had expanded their energy inside the chucks
— no exit wounds being visible.

I have described earlier in this chapter the nature of the
wounds created by a rifle chambered for the .219 Donaldson so
it will be unnecessary to go into detail here. This has been my
26th season hunting chucks. With the exception of the World War
II years, and the summer we built our home, I have spent two to
six evenings per week in the field after the hay has been cut and
prone shots are to be had. I have ceased trying to run up a high
score. The satisfaction that follows making the long shots connect is better than killing hundreds under 100 yards.

I had a run at one time this past season of 50 woodchucks
killed with 52 shots fired. These were shot two to five an evening. I killed the first 12 of these with 12 shots, then missed the
13th and also the 15th, then killed the remainder up to 52, which
makes the last 37 straight. No sighting shots were fired after
taking the rifle from the rack, each time, and wiping out the
Hoppe's No. 9 from the bore by a patch pushed through the bore.
No shots were under 100 yards and several were at 300 yards.
Most of them from 225 to 250 yards.

I again weighed my outfit at Harman's and it weighs 15
pounds, 6 ounces. The Gregoire barrel is 26 inches long, which
is handier for chuck shooting than the 30- or 31-inch of the exclusively bench-rest rifles. The barrel is well bedded and the

rifle is quite stiff and rigid.

I do not mind the weight particularly, because I never hurry much while hunting. I hunt for the pure joy of being outdoors, Speaking of results in the field, I spoke to my barber, who is a shooter of sorts, about missing the first chuck. I couldn't give a reason; I had a good solid prone position and the chuck was but 125 yards. I told him I tried the rifle at the bench rest to check the scope's sighting after I came home, but everything was okay. He said, ''Do you mean to tell me that because you missed one chuck that you went and checked the sights on a target!'' I said, ''Well, Joe, I felt that the hold was perfect and the distance was relatively short, and I don't shoot just to hear the rifle go off. So I wanted to find out why I had missed.'' The next time I came to the same spot in the field, I found that there were some weed stalks sticking up about 12 feet from the muzzle but did not seem to be visible in the field of the scope. I shoot from a very low prone position, but four to six inches off the ground, so I must have fired right through the weeds and the bullet may have become deflected, or exploded.

I feel, that everything considered, I have had the best season on chucks this year I've ever had. I've used a number of most excellent calibers of woodchuck cartridges, and am most satisfied with the performance of the .219 Donaldson on woodchucks.

Next season I'll be shooting woodchucks, I hope with my own make of bullets. I have ordered from Fred T. Huntington of the R.C.B.S. Company a set of bullet swaging dies, a lead cutter, core swages, and core extruding die, also a Pacific Super Frame; and five thousand bullet jackets; also from the Rochester Lead Works, 50 pounds of 3/16-inch lead wire for cores. That should make me largely independent of bullet shortages or the existence of lots of commercial bullets which lack accuracy. When you make your own bullets you make them for use and you use every care possible. That spells accuracy, if you master the knack of swaging bullets.

A final word in closing: I try to do most of my field shooting with the sun at my back, and from a slightly elevated firing position. I use mosquito dope on my face, neck, ears and arms, if exposed, so that I am not bothered by insects and can lie quietly observing any chucks which may be out along fence rows, or feeding in alfalfa or clover. I follow fence lines rather than cross fields. These methods produce where chucks are educated and a bit wild. It pays to wait chucks out.

CHAPTER 8

Experiments by Eric Farr

M R. ERIC FARR, Packanack Lake, New Jersey, is a mechanical engineer with DuMont Laboratories, television manufacturers. His hobby is woodchuck shooting, varmint rifle development, cartridge loading and experimental ballistic work of
various kinds. This chapter contains many helpful mechanical
suggestions in rebuilding and fitting Winchester hi-side actions
which are so widely used for the rimmed type of woodchuck
cartridges. — The Author

My gun history is quite long and though at first frowned upon
by my non-shooting father, he has calmed down as time has
passed, seeing that my future was becoming more and more
obscured by gun smoke and realizing that sometimes the part of
wisdom is to bow gracefully to the inevitable. My first love was
handguns and I have been through the lot. My preference is for
the .44 Special in the Smith & Wesson Model 1926 Target. I
developed a bullet for it weighing 184 grains which I call the
Apache, and with it guarantee to do anything that any hand-gun
center fire cartridge will do, and do it better. This includes the
.357 S. & W. Magnum, which I have explored. I built a machine
rest for my .44 revolver and have fired 50-yard groups of under
2 inches and 100 yard groups of 4 inches and less.

I built a ballistic pendulum (now torn down) for checking my
experimental results and have driven my .44-caliber 184-grain
Apache bullet well over 1500 f.s. with apparently safe pressures. This is possibly due to the greater area of the base of the
.44 as compared to that of the .357.

I used the R-2 on the ballistic pendulum and was surprised
at the pessimism of the pendulum, as compared to advertised
and ballyhooed velocities claimed for this R-2 cartridge. I have
every reason to believe that the pendulum was correct.

When Meredith's article on his ballistic pendulum came out,
I nearly tore my buttons. His pendulum was much nicer in

150

appearance and maybe better put together, and obviously was a precise job. Mine was a piece of yellow pine, 8 inches by 8 inches by 6 feet. However, mathematics was definitely 1900, or fifty years back of present known mathematics, and he also fooled around with removing bullets and so forth.

The formulae used by one of my shooting partners, George V. Chapman, and me makes the use and knowledge of pendulum weight and change unnecessary. When using an organic pendulum such as I used, this is important. We used the acceleration of gravity for calibrating the instrument. As you wish the derivation and formulae, it will be supplied. The pendulum is not hard to make and use. It's better than the best guess and much easier and cheaper than a chronoscope.

SUGGESTIONS FOR AVOIDING ERRORS
IN USE OF BALLISTIC PENDULUM

In the use of every piece of scientific apparatus there are certain things to bear in mind so that you may obtain the most accurate results. This is particularly true in the use of the ballistic pendulum.

The following comments you will find helpful:

The length of suspension should be four feet or over.

The pendulum should weigh 100 pounds as a minimum.

Calibrator should weigh enough to produce at least 50 per cent of the displacement of the load to be tested.

Suspension wires should be of equal length.

Calibrator suspension point should be at front pendulum suspension point and its tether should be of string. It must fall straight with uniform release, point of impact and X_c.

X_c should agree to $\pm$ .005 inch from day to day and within .002 inch on the same day.

Measurements should be accurate to $\pm$ .001 inch.

Point of calibrator impact should be near lower pendulum support.

Pendulum must be at rest before X or X_c can be tested.

BALLISTIC PENDULUM FORMULA DERIVATION:

$$X^2 + (L - Y)^2 = L^2$$

$$X^2 + \cancel{L^2} - 2LY + Y^2 = \cancel{L^2}$$

$$X^2 - 2LY + Y^2 = 0$$

$$X^2 - Y(2L + Y) = 0$$

$$X^2 = Y(2L - Y)$$

$$X = \sqrt{Y(2L - Y)}$$

When Y is very small*

$$Y = \frac{X^2}{2L} \;\&\; Y \sim \frac{X^2}{L}$$

$$L - Y = \sqrt{L^2 - X^2}$$

$$Y = L - \sqrt{L^2 - X^2}$$

*When L = 48 inches and X = 1.5 inch

$$Y = \frac{2.25}{2302.25} = .0009 \text{ inch error}$$

However, when $X_c = X$, error is cancelled.

$$\text{Kinetic Energy} = 1/2MV^2$$

$$\text{``}\qquad\text{``}\quad = \frac{1/2W_p}{G*} V_p^2$$

$$\text{``}\qquad\text{``}\quad = W_p y_2$$

$$\frac{1/2\cancel{W}_p}{G} V_p^2 = \cancel{W}_p y$$

$$\frac{V_p^2}{2G} = y$$

$$V_p^2 = 2Gy$$

$$V_p = \sqrt{2Gy}$$

$$V_p = \sqrt{\cancel{2}G \frac{X^2}{\cancel{2}L}}$$

$$V_p = \sqrt{\frac{GX^2}{L}}$$

*G = acceleration of gravity

$$V_p = X \sqrt{\frac{G}{L}}$$

$$W_p \, V_p = W_b \, V_b$$

$$V_b = \frac{W_p}{W_b}(V_p)$$

$$V_b = \frac{W_p}{W_b} X \sqrt{\frac{G}{L}}$$

$$W_p \, V_{p_I} = W_c \, V_c$$

$$W_p = W_c \frac{V_c}{V_{p_I}}$$

$$V_c = \sqrt{2GH}$$

$$W_p = W_c \frac{\sqrt{2GH}}{X_c \sqrt{\frac{G}{L}}}$$

$$W_p = W_c \frac{\sqrt{2LH}}{X_c}$$

$$V_B = W_c \frac{\sqrt{2LH}}{X_c} \times \frac{X}{W_B} \sqrt{\frac{G}{L}}$$

$$V_B = \frac{W_c X}{W_B X_c} \sqrt{2GH}$$

$$V_B = \frac{W_c X}{W_B X_C} \sqrt{64.4 \, H}$$

$$V_B = 8.019 \frac{W_c X}{W_B X_c} \sqrt{H}$$

When W_c is in pounds

When W_B is in grains

When X is in inches

When X_c is in inches

When H is in inches

PENDULUM RESULTS

.22-3000 R-2 Lovell, 15-degree shoulder, 27-inch barrel.
WRA .25-20 S.S. Cases, R.A. 6-1/2 primers, .020-inch wads.

Bullet Weight	Propellant	Charge Weight	Velocity
54.5 grs.	4227	15.5 grs.	2,660 f.s.
45.0 "	4227	16.0 grs.	3,005 "
50.0 "	4227	16.0 grs.	2,955 "
40.0 "	4227	16.5 grs.	3,100 "
50.0 "	4198	17.0 grs.	2,620 "
.22 Hornet	1.27-46.		
46.0 grs.	Super-X factory load		2,570 "

Some years ago I made up my mind to have a super accurate varmint rifle on a hi-side action. Hartung made me one, chambering for the R-2 case with 15-degree shoulder slope which was the R. S. Risley version. The barrel was 27 x 1-3/16 x 1 inch, with a 14-inch twist. The barrel was bored by Buhmiller. This was to be his .22 Comet, but he was too busy to make all the dies at the time, so it came through as an R-2. The Comet was made from a reamer he made to chamber for the then .220 Donaldson-Wasp. He couldn't make any of the three rifles he chambered for it shoot to his satisfaction, so he lengthened the reamer by moving the stop back, and also making it smaller at the shoulder with 28-degree angle. These later Comet rifles all shot well, and I've heard of the results from several. It will not accept the .219 factory-loaded Zipper case, however, the reason being that the .219 Zipper case is too long to chamber.

When my R-2 arrived, it was short of what I desired. The rifle however, had a good chamber and the most gorgeous stock, very full and of most excellent design.

The breech block dropped 0.060 inch upon final closing. This will amount to over 0.003 inch opening. Fitting new pins helped but it still dropped 0.040 inch which gives 0.002 inch in opening. I fitted the lever to stop it from falling so far and fixed this dropping to be a safe minimum.

The firing pin was poorly fitted to the bushing and started to deface it. So I pulled out the bushing which was threaded in 0.20 inch deep, 3/8 x 24 inches. When I fitted in an aircraft stud same size, it cracked the block through the bottom of the pin bore. I magnifluxed it and found it cracked elsewhere, as indicated. This had been drilled for the torsional main spring action. The holes were too close to the rear of the block. The pin set screw hole was also cracked through at the rear. I welded it all up and recased it for spare.

The late Bert Foster of Maplewood, (then Sales Manager of Colt's gave me a spare from his .45-90 Schuetzen single shot. This I carefully fitted with a 1/2 inch 20 AMS 6310 chrome-nickel steel 35 R.C. aircraft engine stud-ground threads. This I fitted 0.150 inch deep to a square and spotted-in counterbore.

This was fitted very tight and faced. The torsional spring holes were drilled a good distance back from the edge. The unit was then magnifluxed. All being okay, I fitted a firing pin but after firing couldn't get one that wouldn't bend after 100 shots. I finally went to an eccentric one turned with a 0.0625 inch point turned concentric with the bore of the rifle. I forgot to mention previously, that the hole in the bushing was dead center with the bore — a very necessary consideration.

The pin has a reduced forward diameter and an 0.020-inch diameter spring around it. This pin assembly has stood up for over 1500 shots and shows no signs of wear or distortion. It is necessary to half-cock the hammer before dropping the lever to allow the pin to retract, but several friends have neglected to do so and no damage was done. Pin protrusion is 0.050 inch.

I believe it is a mistake to make the above spring strong enough to push back the hammer or to make the pin inertia type, especially with heavy loads in such intense numbers or high intensity cartridges like the R-2 which works best only at a very high pressure level. This present pin has withstood loads that blew out primers so hard as to cock the hammer. The shooter (myself) was unaware of any untoward event — this in the R-2.

The usual main cross pin through the lever is such that if it is closely fitted it is hard to assemble. I made one according to a sketch shown here. At any rate, the cross pin has a slight taper, is cut with a 6-32 thread, has a knurled knob on one end and a somewhat similar one, threaded to screw onto the smaller end of the taper pin. The taper indicated is less than .005 inch for its length and all parts are so reamed. This makes a tight pin and one easy to assemble. It too is of AMS No. 6310.

The fore-end is held on, as is the flat spring, by small bases screwed to the underside of the barrel as I did not favor the idea of slots.

I shot this rifle with all loads in the R-2 for 3700 shots and with good results on chucks. I killed 106 woodchucks with it in the year 1946 at distances from 100 to 300 yards. Two were shot at 300 yards and several at 260. I preferred a case level full of 4198 and 55-grain Sisk-Neidner bullet and a 0.020 inch colloidal wad of my own manufacture.

At the end of the 2700 rounds I could easily see rounding of the lands existed but the bore was still all shiny and with little or no apparent erosion. However, it wasn't a rifle that I could then trust at too great a range to center each shot. However, there was still nothing on which I could put my finger as being obviously materially below its original performance.

Hartung rechambered this barrel to his Hawker because of the good luck I have had with the Enfield.

ENFIELD HAWKER

I have this handsome Enfield Hawker which shoots exceptionally well and have my R-2 back from Hartung as a .22 Hawker. This later rifle is a 15-pound H.S.W., S.S. trigger job which cost me lots of time to build up. Using the loads given below, in my Enfield Hawker, I obtained the results given here. Shooting done April 20, 1947. All at 100 yards.

34.0 grains of DuPont No. 4064 — 49-grain Sisk Express — 0.58″.
34.0 grains of DuPont No. 4320 — 49-grain Sisk Express — 0.58″.
33.0 grains of DuPont No. 4320 — 49-grain Sisk Express — 0.48″.

I fired 15 shots, all X's, in three groups of five each, starting from a cold, clean barrel — no scope changes — I used my 20X Fecker, 1-5/8-inch scope. I have a difficult time shooting 10-shot groups, the psychological reaction affects me, I nearly always blow my tenth shot. This Enfield has had 416 shots through the barrel and despite the best efforts of my trained eye, I cannot see the slightest signs of rounding of the lands. At 400 rounds I could see this in my R-2, but not in the Hawker.

After the groups mentioned were fired the Sunday before writing this, I switched the 20X scope to the H.S.W. Winchester and started testing with 33.0 grains of 4320, 50-grain Sisk bullet, and the usual other components and details of loading. This shooting started out with fair results, but the group soon spread out to about 2 inches. I was all set to smash the rifle over the bench, when I found the scope loose. Having only five shots

Remarkable 5-shot target, measuring ¼″ center to center, made by Eric Farr with an R-2 Lovell rifle. Load was No. 1½ small pistol primers, 17.0 grains of DuPont 4198. Cases neck sized. 0.020 Ipco wad.

Four groups by Eric Farr.

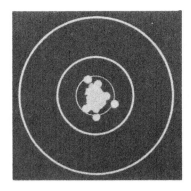

Fired at 100 yards with .22 Hawker test rifle and 20X Fecker 1⅝″ scope. Score is a 10X possible, measuring 0.98″ center to center. Load was R. A. #9½ primers, WRA case trimmed, reamed, and beveled, 49-grain Sisk Express .224″ bullets, 33.0 grains 4320 measured, 0.20″ wad.

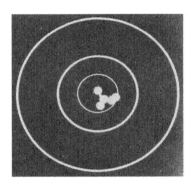

5-shot group at 100 yards, measuring 0.48″ with .22 Hawker Test rifle, 20X scope. Load was 49-grain Sisk Express bullets, 33.0 grains 4320, 0.20″ wad, and WRA cases reamed and with No. 115 primers.

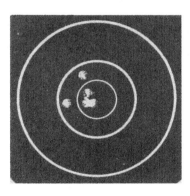

Cast bullet group fixed at 100 yards with .22 Farr Zipper Enfield #1, 2″ Unertl 24X scope. Cast bullets lubricated, 13.0 grains 4227. Temperature 44° F.

5X possible shot at 100 yards with .22 Farr Zipper Winchester Hi-side with one-piece Farr stock. Measures 0.73″. Load was Western No. 8½ primers, 31.0 grains 4320, .105″ wads, 49-grain Sisk Express bullets.

left, I fired them for group and they went into 0.69 inch at 100 yards.

Some of my friends do not care for the looks of either the Enfield bolt action nor of the Sharps-Borchardt hammerless, single shot action. Possibly this is due to the vagaries of what is good taste, or judgment between different men, as to what is handsome or made to good lines. Trying to determine what is good taste in contours of a weapon is like trying to solve differences which arise in international politics. A great many underlying facts contribute to any choice.

An honest evaluation of what I consider a good-looking rifle rather parallels the promulgations of the late Clyde Baker. That the Enfield is not handsome, I must agree. On the other hand, carefully and tastefully reworked, it can be quite presentable. I believe a principal objection to the looks of the 1917 Enfield rifle is the crooked bolt handle. Again taste enters and I must confess that I do like that bolt handle.

Of course, my rifle is minus the ears, the slot is filled, the contours resemble, to some extent, the Model 70.* Other alterations are conventional, such as the straightened floor plate, and reworked trigger guard and mechanism.

I had an awful time with the pull of this rifle, and while it is now a clean 2-1/3 pounds, military style, I believe I'll add a single-set trigger some day. When I had this rifle made into a Hawker, I fitted a new and tighter bolt. The bolt sleeve was welded up to be a closer fit in the action. All this was necessary to get a uniform pull. Mr. P. O. Ackley's article in your .22 Caliber Varmint Rifles about blowing up rifle actions intrigues me, more probably for what it does not say, than that which it mentions. He speaks of relative strengths, but doesn't say a word about:

1. Caliber used in each arm.
2. Type of chamber.
3. Headspace setting.
4. Bullet size and weight. Especially weight in proportion to caliber.
5. Were all rifles loaded to the same pressure? Each has a bearing on results.

The clue to the whole thing in blowing up the lovable old

---

*Author's Note: Also later on, the Models 721 and 722 Remington, which were not made at the time this was written.

Springfield is that he (Ackley) is favorably impressed with protection for the action's hood by machining ring or, an enclosed bolt head to protect from renegade gases, as demonstrated in the Arisaka.

I must assume that our Springfield and Enfields were standard jobs in the .30-1906 caliber. This (the .30-1906), is of course a rimless case and a large proportion of the brass sits right out in God's own air. If a rimmed case were properly set up and used, I'd bet the Springfield and the Enfield would show up better than the Mikado's Arisaka. For confirmation, please see Mr. Hercules' tests some years back on the pressure tests which were more scientific — all .30-1906 caliber, same barrel and headspace, etc. Results:

No. 1.	Enfield	120,000 p.s.i.
No. 2.	Springfield (nickel steel receiver)	110,000 p.s.i.
No. 3.	Mauser (good con.)	100,000 p.s.i.
No. 4.	Model 70	95,000 p.s.i. Quite springy too.

There are many things which enter into a rifle's ultimate strength that may not have been considered, or at least taken into account, in this series of tests.

I like the high side wall Winchester s.s. action very much, and believe it to be a strong action, relative to withstanding heavy and abusive loads.

But I do not consider a hi-side desirable for anyone except a crank who endeavors to understand it, and use it accordingly. For example, the hammer should not be snapped on an empty chamber reasons are obvious — the rifle was not designed to be so used.

In the just mentioned case, the pin may become damaged, or the bushing loosened. While it may not be so, I have had a harder time getting really fine accuracy and uniformly small groups from hi-side single shots than from corresponding bolt actions.*

*Author's Note: Definitely, this seems to be the general opinion and experience among chuck hunters. Especially well-stocked, well-bedded, stiff-actioned and heavy barreled hi-sides, with the flat spring mainsprings sometimes give almost as small groups as the best bolt actions, but they do not always average as small; especially with the more powerful cartridges. The trigger pull, however, may be shorter and better, and they are easier to fit with a good Schuetzen double-set trigger. The smoothness and especially the evenness of let off of the pull, has a great deal to do with whether a rifleman of experience and skill can deliver six or seven shots out of ten, as well delivered as they have been held, on the aver-

The superiority of the bolt action exists — I'm not quite certain but I believe it is in the symmetrical layout of the action, compared to the more specific concentricity of the bolt and striker, plus the even abutting action of the lugs. There should be some grounds, too, for the claims of two-piece stock lack of accuracy. This also is probably greater with the higher intensity cartridges and those giving the more recoil and thrust against the bolt face.

The hi-side Winchester single shot action, I think, occupies much the same general station among older varmint actions and rifles, as the Colt single action occupies among revolvers.*

RIMMED VS. RIMLESS CARTRIDGES

The comments of the late J. George Schnerring, the rifleman who, as Proof House Foreman at Frankford Arsenal, had supervised the testing of more accurate .30-1906 ammunition than any other person, made relative to the 20 per cent reduction in strength due to making a case rimless, are very apt. In the face of this, and the fact that nearly all varmint rifles for rimmed cartridges are single shots, possibly it might be argued why do rifle cranks use rimless cartridges in their bolt actions and then argue about minute academic and imaginary weaknesses of action? My Enfield Hawker uses the .219 Zipper brass quite readily and easily. Reworking of the bolt face is simple.

age, before giving that final bit of pressure, or whether he can get off the whole ten shots almost perfectly. This makes a tremendous difference in the total group size, and especially in the figure of merit of the group. That part of it is a combination of stock fit, rifle balance, and trigger pull. Rifle design in general, has little to do with it. In these particulars, especially that of trigger pull, the single shot may be definitely superior to the average good bolt action rifle. It is something like the fit of a well-made suit of tailored clothes. The gunsmith and the tailor occupy corresponding positions in the final result.

*Author's Note: It is a splendid old gun, but the Winchester was the Model 1887, as generally found, and that was over 60 years ago. Possibly some of the features represent a challenge to firearms designers even now. It was not often that a man challenged the reliability of the Colt single action .45, the Winchester hi-side single shot rifle, the Sharps Buffalo rifle the Winchester Model 1886, .45-70 or .45-90, or a bit later, the Winchester Model 1897 repeating shotgun. No other arms in near-modern history had such reputations unless it be the 7 m. m. Spanish Mauser and the 7.92 m: m. pre-World War I, Mausers. It is only just therefore that the hi-side Winchesters are still the favorite s.s. action among chuck hunters.

Of course this makes that bolt unusable in the future with rimless cases, but what of it? Bolts are readily obtained, inexpensive, and easy to fit and headspace. I shy clear of rimless cases wherever possible.

I have frequently asked questions of recognized authorities and almost never do I receive a straight forward reply. For example: Given two identical rifles, with supposedly identical barrels, loaded to the same velocities and using ammunition with identical bullets that one uses the .220 Swift cartridge case and the other uses the .22-3000 R-2 Lovell — which, if fired side by side, would wear out first?

None of the authorities would answer definitely, nor stick their necks out. My personal belief is that the R-2 would wear out first because I feel the critical erosive level of temperature reached by the barrel at the critical point is not only of longer duration in the R-2, but actually the temperature is probably much higher. The R-2 and the .22 K-Hornet are hot little numbers and derive their fine results from outlandishly high pressures. Pressures in a rifle also mean high temperatures at the time of firing and for the duration of the time the bullet is going up the barrel, especially the lower 30 per cent of it.

It is like a large engine in a motor car compared with a small engine in another, but corresponding car. The big engine is working perhaps at 59 per cent rated H.P. at 50 M.P.H., whereas the small one may be working at 90 per cent. The engine life is directly proportional to the power taken out of it! A fact, isn't it?

ARGUMENTS FOR GRAPHITE WADS IN WOODCHUCK RIFLES

Mr. Eric Farr was, previous to 1948 or 1949, a very enthusiastic exponent and champion of the use of graphite or other lubricated wads in .22-caliber varmint rifles of high intensity and the upper level of rifle barrel temperatures at the time of firing. He was sincere in this belief. So are thousands of others, including many of the most widely known varmint rifle shooters. His letters previous to 1949, written to me, are reproduced here with his permission because they express so clearly and forcibly the arguments most often given in favor of the use of such wads. It should be understood by every reader, however, that Mr. Farr, after continued use of and experiments with such wads, has now concluded, as of 1950, that the bother and annoyance of loading such wads, the fouling and probably also extra barrel wear they produce, especially in cooler or in colder weather, result in lack of accuracy and too much barrel wear, and that as a result he is not today using such wads and does not recommend their use.

So as to reproduce both sides of this argument regarding the very important matter of using lubricated wads between powder charge and bullet, Mr. Farr's arguments are presented for the use of such wads, and then following, in the same chapter, his later conclusions that today the use of the slower burning, larger granulation IMR powders without wads is the wiser policy.

Some years ago there was quite a how-to-do about graphite wads, colloidal graphite wads, and so forth. A well-known author whose writings, I like quite well, gave the graphite wads quite a black eye in his article concerning the .250 O'Neil Magnum. The truth of the matter was that this author used Donaldson's formula which at that time contained rosin. Most riflemen would sense what temperatures of 2500° F to 3500° F and 50,000 p.s.i. would do to rosin. I was blithely overlooked! *

*Author's Note: This author did mention that to know much about the melting point or the flash point of rosin, or the various resins, a man would almost need to be a technical expert experienced with the manufacture or use of such products. The experimental rifleman lacking such contacts, has few if any opportunities to obtain the data he could use to advantage except perhaps by previous training.

As a matter of information to readers, a rosin is a resin, but all resins are not rosin. This is a bit like mentioning that a tiger is a cat, but all cats are not tigers. It does infer, however, that rosins are just one groups of resins. Rosin is a particular type of resin which most often comes from the sap, or by steam distillation from the stump wood of the long leaf southern yellow pine tree. Synthetic resins, of which there are many, are produced from a condensation of phenol and formaldehyde, or a condensation of urea and formaldehyde. The melting point of rosin is about 180° F. The flash point is approximately 390° F. Very few organic chemicals will stand a temperature of 1000° F, without carbonizing. Both resin and rosin are organic materials. This rosin and resin data has been checked with a chemist who is a rosin expert associated with the largest manufacturer of wood rosin in the United States. One of the things which chemists, rifle experimenters, and physicists are baffled by is to see and to tell just what goes on in a confined, very small volume of a rifle chamber, when the cartridge is subjected to very high pressure and also to shortly-sustained but also excessive temperature. The observer can analyze the product both before and after the firing of the cartridge. He has opportunity, many times, to vary the size of the sample, the degree of heat and pressure developed, and the length of time to which each sample is exposed to both heat and pressure. The two of course, go together. After a few weeks, during which he may have made a hun-

I'm not claiming that colloidal graphite wads, or even wads is the answer to the problem of barrel wear and of erosion, but I'm fairly sure that nonsolid forming lubricants in the form of a base wad is a definite step in the right direction.

To not supply any insulation or lubrication to the barrel and the projectile, to my mind is not helping the situation. A certain amount and rate of wear and erosion is to be expected and it probably depends upon: 1. Temperature; 2. Duration of maintainance of this temperature.*

dred determinations, he arrives at a point where he can anticipate what the product might be expected to do. But the layman and the average rifleman, including also most experimental riflemen, lack the chemical and physical education and the laboratory equipment, including very high temperature recording thermometers. How for instance, would you record a temperature of 2000° to 3500° within a rifle chamber? If you bore a hole in the side of the chamber, your barrel ceases to be a rifle barrel. It is then only a chamber pressure rifle or a test tube. If you put the thermometer inside the barrel, the shot destroys the thermometer. The barrel never becomes as hot on the outside as in the chamber, because the flame is not there long to heat the steel clear through, like it heats the inside surface of the barrel.

Merton Robinson, formerly, and for most of his lifetime, ballistic engineer of Winchester, and by common consent the most experienced ballistic engineer in North America, once told me that their experiences failed to show much if any decrease in erosion due to the use of graphite and similar wads in rifle cartridges. They were a bother to load and gave some fouling, as well as some lubrication. Fouling may give a grinding action between bullet jacket and barrel steel. That would increase, not decrease the wear on the lands and grooves. There is also the quality of insulation or partial insulation of the base and sides of the bullet from some of the heat, by the way, and this is independent of the lubricating value of the wad. Another application of the same principle is the use of an asbestos pad under a stewing pot on a cook stove or a gas range.

When a cartridge is fired in the chamber of a rifle, solids are converted into gases and vapors and into ash or carbons. The molecules of super-heated gas are whirling and ricocheting around in the chamber like billiard balls, off the walls and also off each other. Machinery's Handbook, 11th Edition, gives the melting point of steel as 2500° F.; of brass, of which the cartridge case is made, as 1700° to 1850° F.; and the melting point of copper, the main constituent of the bullet's jacket, as 1981° F. An alloy of one part tin, nine parts lead, melts at 577°, pure tin, 450°. The melting point of pure lead is 619° F. Various alloys have different melting points, some higher, some lower than the pure metal which is the principal constituent of the alloy.

We could do very little shooting with any rifle barrel if the maximum heat of discharge of high intensity "hot" loads, were continued for a minute or so, or even a few seconds. The lands and throat would soon be gone — then the remainder.

*Author's Note: For some years, Winchester supplied .30-1906 target ammunition at the National Matches at Camp Perry, the bullets of which were coated with carnauba wax which was then claimed to be a lubricant to the bullet, also useful in wind estimation because it left a slight smoke trail as the bullet trav-

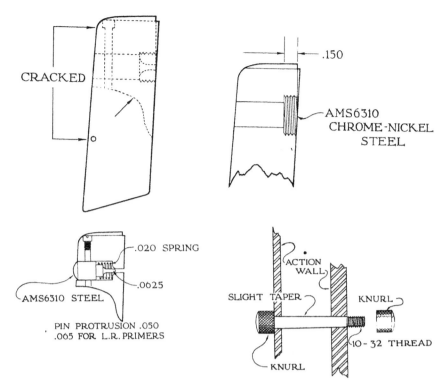

How to strengthen Winchester single shot actions for woodchuck rifles.

Eric Farr's Farr Zipper, R. A. Enfield action, Buhmiller 20″ preturned chrome-moly 14″ twist medium-weight barrel, Mannlicher style stock.

George Ohlmann's Farr Zipper, Springfield action, Buhmiller 24″ preturned chrome-moly target-weight 14″ twist barrel, issue "C" stock, 10X Lyman Junior scope.

Eric Farr Zipper, Eddystone Enfield action with Farr set triggers, Pfeifer 27" bullweight 14" twist barrel, Chapman-Farr maple stock with Schuetzen butt plate, 24X 2" Unertl scope.

Arnold Osterlund's Farr Zipper, Gustlof Werke 1943 Mauser action, Buhmiller 26" preturned chrome-moly 14" twist medium-weight barrel, walnut target style stock, 20X 1⅜" Fecker scope.

Frank Uhrich's Farr Zipper, Spandeau 1915 Mauser action, Buhmiller 26" preturned chrome-moly target-weight 14" twist barrel, 20X Lyman Super scope.

Donald K. Tag's Farr Zipper, Winchester Hi-wall, Buhmiller 23" preturned carbon-mang. target-weight 14" twist barrel, one-piece Farr stock (cherry wood with ebony fittings), Weaver K-6 scope.

Left to Right: Loaded Farr Zipper, .22 Hornet, Original L-17 .22-3000 Lovell, .22-3000 2-R, .219 Donaldson Wasp, .22 Savage Hi-Power, .219 Zipper, Griffin & Howe Improved Zipper, Farr Zipper, Hartung Zipper, Hawker, Marciante Zipper, Marciante Blue Streak, .22 Gebby Varminter, Wilson Arrow, .220 Swift, .250-3000 Savage (Blue Pill), .275 H & H Magnum, .30-40, .30-'06, .348, and .300 H & H Magnum.

To erode a barrel made of carbon-manganese steel (steel containing a certain percentage each, of carbon and manganese), requires that it be heated to a certain critical temperature for a certain period of time. If a certain load has a very high peak pressure for a relatively long period of time, we might expect considerable erosion. If the length of time of exposure is less, the barrel will last longer.

We may imagine that the .22 Hornet cartridge gives us a peak pressure of a figure bordering into the erosion level, but of a duration short enough in most loads, to obviate much of, or maybe even all of its importance. Frictional barrel wear is then about the only factor which is really important. The use of a soft, colloidal graphite wad would likely both insulate from the heat and lubricate against friction. Wads thicker than .020 inch in such a small capacity case fail to completely melt or flash and consume, and thus foul up the bore. This is quite noticeable in cool or cold weather, less so in hot weather. In very hot weather almost any thickness can be used — according to my experience. One reason for the unsuccessful use of wads in small stuff is the fact that these wads are not commercially available thinner than .033 inch. The foregoing has been reasonably well established by firing 2700 shots through my R-2 Lovell and some 3000 through a Sedgley Springfield .22 Hornet.

One week end in 1947, on Saturday, I took my H. S. W. Hawker up in the brush after ground hogs. There was a 7 o'clock, 30 M.P.H. wind during the sighting in at 175 yards. It was sufficient to blow the bullets 2 inches at that distance. I did get five whistle pigs, or woodchucks, one of which was at 281 long steps. I was using the 49-grain Sisk Express and 33.0 grains of 4320, and an .035 inch wad. It appears that the wad is too thick as there was evidence of fouling — it was a cool day.

Sunday I went to the 100 yards range for an accuracy check of this H.S.W. and did not get what might be called gilt-edged results. A careful investigation revealed some streaks in the grooves at the throat. Some W.R.A. Crystal Cleaner and elbow grease took it out but whether the deposit was metal or wad, carbon or ash, was not determined by an analysis. It may be that this rifle won't use wads to advantage.

There is a little heard of type of bullet lubrication that Frank Virginia used to use in the .220 Swift. He used to dis-

eled from muzzle to target and you could see approximately about how far the shot drifted to right or left, in traveling say 600 or 1000 yards, to the target.

solve a small amount of Japan wax in CCl4 and dip his loaded rounds into it, bullet first, case mouth deep. I have used it before in various calibers and with some success in my Apache loads in the .44 Special. I suppose I will resurrect the process for my Hawker.

When I was investigating the .22 Hornet in my Sedgley Springfield, I was having quite a time getting accuracy with it. It was apparently quite throat-worn and I had difficulty in engraving bullets on the throat.

BASE WADS

For base wads, I use a semi-solid mixture of castor dag and Japan wax, both vegetable and no rosin or resins. Carnauba wax comes from the leaves of a Brazilian palm tree and is exceedingly hard. It is similar to Japan wax whereas the melting points differ. That of Japan wax is 118° F. to 127° F. and carnauba wax is 183° F. to 186° F.

Nearly everyone I mention wads to says, "How can a wad possibly lubricate a bullet when it is behind the bullet?" The facts are that it can lubricate a bullet and what's even more important, it insulates that portion of the bore from the heat, which section normally burns away first.

When a cartridge is fired, what is it that comes out of the muzzle first? The bullet? No, it is gas which drives out of the bore and emerges in some volume from the muzzle before the bullet, as ultra-high speed photography has shown. If a wad is used, part of the gaseous mixture is wax and grease vapor.

My .22 Hawker now has exactly 900 shots fired through it and shows no visible erosion at all, and no streaks. However, it does show slight rounding of the lands — not actual reduction but a polish which no one but a crank like myself can see. The cartridge cases do not get greasy on the outside, nor are there signs of undue pressure. In my 1650 f.s. hand loads in the .44 Special, with a grooveless bullet, I neatly subdue lead with wads. I feel that the function of wads is two-fold; namely, that of heat insulation as well as barrel lubrication. Practically, it is proved by a glance at the rifle's muzzle after a long string. The very thin film of lubricant can be seen. Theoretically it is proved by imagining that as gas precedes the bullet up the bore, part of this gas is vaporized wad material from the edge of the wad.

The principal objection to wads that I have is the fouling of the bore in cold weather. This is worse in crow shooting season than when out for woodchucks. It is produced by excessively thick wads in cases of the .22 Hornet and .25-20 type of cartridges. Thinner wads help or eliminate.

Previously I failed to mention an additional operation I perform in bullet lubrication. In a quantity of carbon tetrachloride, I dissolve as much Japan wax as possible and then bottle it up tightly. I then dip my loaded rounds, bullet down, into the dissolved Japan wax poured into a shallow pan, pushing the bullets down into the wax, case-mouth deep. In other words, I dip the exposed portion of the bullet, but keep the outside of the cartridge out of the wax. This prevents wax solidifying on the outside of the cartridge neck where it would, of course, increase the neck diameter just twice the depth of the wax film. The cartridge might then be difficult to seat in very closely chambered rifles, and when fired, the wax would melt and lubricate the outside of the cartridge case and the inside of the chamber. This would greatly increase the thrust upon the bolt face, similar to that which occurred and broke bolts and wrecked actions in Krags and Springfields when Mobilubricant was used on metal cased bullets in the .30-40 and .30-1906 calibers. This occurred mostly back in the 1920's. These rifle actions were then accused of a good deal that was really largely the fault of using Mobilubricant. Most high intensity varmint rifles are high pressure jobs, especially when designed with very sharp shoulders and loaded to capacity.

After the CCl_4 dries, a very thin film of Japan wax is deposited uniformly upon the bullet. This provides a good lubricant as the bullet seats into the throat against the rifling. Japan wax is an excellent metal drawing die lubricant, consequently should be good as a metal-cased bullet lubricant. The situations are comparable, although not identical.

No matter how long a string I shoot, nor how many times I fire at woodchucks in the field, between morning and night, I never have any of the lubricant go farther back onto the outside of the case than the case neck and very little runs back onto that. It is possible of course, that the thickness of the film of wax deposited upon the bullet might have something to do with this, but such film would be determined largely by the temperature of the liquid wax in the pan and the time the bullet in the inverted cartridge was permitted to remain in the wax as it was dipped.

Much material has been written on the merits of one particular case or shape but probably there is no one item quite so important as capacity. This matter of cartridge capacity will determine in large measure, with the caliber as another important item, what type and thickness of wads and which powders and the granulation of same, will perform best. No consideration is given seriously by me to any rimless case except the .30-1906. For example, the .22 Hornet and its derivations will handle only powders that are on the fast side of the scale — because of the very limited capacity of this small cartridge. It will handle these small charges quite well but one should not attempt to make a .218 Bee or a .219 Donaldson out of it by obvious overloading.

The .220 Swift, on the other hand, handles the slow powders quite well but will not handle reduced loads too well, with but few exceptions. It is thus not a good all-around cartridge, being too difficult to reload successfully with a wide variety of charges. In addition, when using full charges, the cartridge cases lengthen materially and then after a number of shots, the front end of the neck must be trimmed off before reloading again or the loaded cartridge will not then fully go into the chamber so that the bolt can be closed and locked without difficulty.

Cartridge cases of in-between capacity will in most instances, handle a variety of loads to better advantage. For example, the .219 Donaldson will most times, shoot well with reduced loads in the vicinity of the .22 Hornet factory charges and of the velocity also of the R-2, or of the Super-Lovell or expanded R-2, known by Lovell as the .22 Maximum Lovell and by Kilbourn as the .22 Kilbourn K-Lovell.

CASE CAPACITY VARIATION OF .22 HORNET CARTRIDGES

In desperation, I measured the case capacity of 50 W.R.A. cases with a burette and found a twelve per cent variation. Selecting twelve that were within two per cent, I used 11.2 grains of 2400 (Hercules), with W.R.A. 116 primer and the 50-grain W. M. 8-S bullet. I fired a 0.70 inch 100-yard 10-shot group with it. This is mentioned because I had never heard of parallel tests although that doesn't preclude such having been consummated.

Again to the throat in my H.S.W. Hawker and the streaks. I preclude the likelihood of erosion because it is a new throat, having been chambered out from a R-2 after 2700 rounds as an R-2 and only 141 as a Hawker. There were no such streaks as an R-2, and my other Hawker has 416 rounds through it, no streaks or visible wear in the slightest.

DESCRIPTION — THE .22 HAWKER CARTRIDGE

The .22 Hawker is an Improved .219 Zipper resembling Lovell's No. 7 cartridge. The Hawker will accept factory ammunition in that caliber and of any make. The .22 Hawker is a product of the brains and resourcefulness of Albert L. Hartung, R. D. #3, Pomeroy, Ohio. It is the result of several years of experimenting. I know of no failures and have shot five of them personally. I am enclosing a sketch of the .22 Hawker chamber. Since I discovered or became acquainted with Hartung several years ago, he has made up about ten rifles for my friends and myself. I have never met Hartung personally but know he is over 60 and that suggests experience.

A GOOD LOAD DUPLICATING THE .22 HORNET

WITH THE .22 HAWKER

As a matter of fact, 18.3 grains of 4227 behind the 45-grain Sisk Hornet bullet duplicates the factory Hornet loads and shoots one inch below my regular hunting load at 100 yards. So, I usually carry and use both loads in the .22 Hawker when it is sighted at 100 yards, one inch high with the regular load. All shots under 150 yards are then taken with the lighter load. It makes less noise, and it shoots right on the point of aim at 100 yards. This makes it very convenient as no sight change or holding allowance is necessary. I'll admit that my 14-inch twist only shoots this 45-grain bullet into 1.12 to 1.25 inches at 100 yards but greater accuracy is not necessary up to 150 yards in woodchuck hunting. Should it ever be required, I'd simply switch to the 45-grain 8-S bullet which shoots in this load to perfection.

In one of your .22 books, under an unannounced heading on scopes, I noted that you seemed to prefer and recommend that scopes around 6 power be used. I'm sure that on the basis of your recommendation, many folks will procure scopes not to exceed this magnification.*

*Author's Note: Readers may stop to consider here that while the power of a scope is a matter of personal opinion and whether the shooter can hold a very

For a few years, I've been using a 10X 1-1/8-inch Lyman Targetspot which I still believe has excellent optics. This scope saw service on my R-2, my 52's and later upon my .22 Hawker. Under no condition that chucks could be seen through the scope and shot at, except that of distances under 25 feet, where they would be out of focus and the lenses appear foggy, have I felt handicapped by the higher magnifying power of the 10X scope.

Thanksgiving time of 1946, I purchased a new 1-5/8-inch 20X Fecker target glass. After trying it out, I sent it back to Fecker with comments. I felt it could be improved. About February 1, 1947 they sent me a replacement scope that was a honey. I used it for chuck shooting on my Hawker. For use in the field I set the parallax adjustment at 200 yards and took in everything from 25 yards to 350 yards with the same setting. It is true that at ranges of less than 100 yards, things were a bit out of focus, but not seriously except when shooting closer than eight or ten yards. For the long shots the 20X was really helpful because of its greater magnification of the small details of chuck and surroundings. Despite predictions that the 20X would have too small a field, be too dark, impossible to hold steadily so that one could fire with consistent accuracy, and so forth and so forth, none of these seemed so in my case.*

high power scope steadily enough to get off shots uniformly, it is a matter of fact that scope manufacturers practically all recommend scopes of 6 to 8 power, with 7X as a preferred selection with Fecker, and 6X or 8X with Unertl, 6X by Lyman, 5X or 6X by Weaver.

*Author's Note: A well-known experimenter and chuck hunter, now of advanced years, claims the same thing. He says it is impossible to hit in the field, what you cannot see, and that the 20X enables him to kill chucks offhand up to 200 yards. He gave the impression that he felt he could do this regularly. Others, both good offhand shots, with much shooting experience on chucks, are skeptical. Especially are they doubtful of the ability of those far up in years, of a more nervous temperament, and with less strength than younger men, to do this.

Of course this might introduce the question of what is consistent offhand shooting on woodchucks at 200 yards. Also, if all are inclined to recall misses and cripples which drag in, as readily as kills. To me, six to nine kills in each ten chances offhand would be regarded as consistent killing, but many doubt that even a very good offhand shot of younger years would kill so many, even with his faster mental and physical responses. Even these, it is believed, would usually have great difficulty killing more than three or four woodchucks above ground, at average accurately estimated ranges between about 160 and 240 yards. Especially would this be likely in irregular, very hilly, woodchuck country, where winds, light conditions, and horizontal distances are quite often difficult to estimate and to calculate mentally, to a small error.

It is one thing to kill a chuck instantly, on a 200-yard shot, in a field in which you have killed many chucks and in which you have paced off the differ-

Left: G. V. Chapman's spotting scope and Krag Hawker. *Right:* Eric Farr's Winchester Hi-side .22 Hawker.

The men, *L to R:* Arnold Osterlund, James Scott, Warren Comfort, and Eric Farr. The rifles, *L to R:* .257 Remington 30-S; Hartung stocked Springfield .30-1906; maple stocked Enfield .22 Hawker **by** Farr with Hartung barrel; Hartung rebuilt Model 52 Winchester, owned by Farr; Hi-side Winchester, Hartung job, owned by Farr.

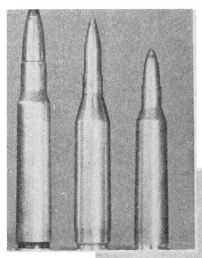

Left to Right: .30-1906; 5.6 x 61 M.M. with 78-grain Sisk bullet; .220 Swift. CREDIT: JAMES M. SMITH.

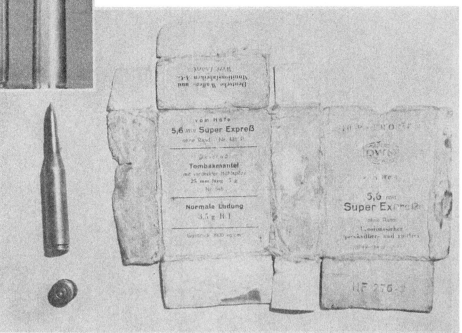

Original 5.6 M.M. cartridge and DWM box; base of cartridge at lower left showing headstamp. CREDIT: JAMES M. SMITH.

Left to Right: .22 Varminter (.22-250); 5.6 x 61 M.M. Vom Hofe Super Express (as made from .30-1906 brass), with 70-grain Western S.P. bullet; .30-1906; .22 P.M.V.F.; .25 Magnum on the .30 Newton case; 5.6 x 61 M.M. 78-grain Sisk bullet; .220 Swift; .219 Donaldson Wasp. CREDIT: JAMES M. SMITH.

I do find it more difficult to shoot with good vision, quite as late in the evening as the other lads, although often I do so anyhow, even though my scope seems darker when looked through than the average good scope of lower magnifying power. My friends have the 1-5/8-inch Feckers but of 12.5X and 16X; none but mine, locally, are of as high as 20X.

When the vertical cross wire in this 20X Fecker of mine failed, I sent the scope back and used my Lyman 10X again, both for testing and for field shooting. I cannot tell you how handicapped I felt with it until the 20X came back again.

There is always a resistance to new ideas and to new equipment. Although high power scopes have been used for many years, nevertheless, the large tube, high grade, modern lens rifle scopes are relatively new in the powers over 15X. I vote for the 20X scope for my own use.

Regarding the .22 Hawker, I have used loads recommended by Hervey Lovell for his No. 7 Improved Zipper. These included a case level full of No. 4064, a 0.070-inch wad and the 49-grain Sisk Express bullet. I personally have found 4320 to be better for this cartridge and bullet and use 33.0 grains of 4320 in it as the regular load. This gives me around 3600 f.s. f.p.s. with very mild pressures. Some of my cases have been loaded over fifteen times with no failures aside from those on the initial fire-forming operation, or on swaging down. Regarding the forming loss, I have had roughly, 10 per cent failures no matter how I load them, factory loads or not. Remington Arms Company factory loads fail rather consistently and regularly, so I restrict my Hawker to the use of Winchester cases which appear to be made of better brass or brass which is annealed to the best degree for such work. They also appear to be made of thicker brass, which makes them stronger and better able to resist the sudden stresses of fire-forming and swaging up or down.

ent dens from a common convenient firing stand. But it is an entirely different proposition to be driving along in an area not too well known to you, and suddenly you have to take the shot as it is, immediately, or drive on. Maybe one instant the chuck is in the sun and the next moment he is in deep shadow. Or, the last time you were along that lane, the chuck was out in a 115° in-the-sun temperature, and now it is 65 degrees and you haven't fired your rifle for three weeks and the bore is still a bit oily and cold. Also, you have just had five days of rain, high humidity and the stock has absorbed moisture. How much has the rifle's zero changed and where to? Many different results can be obtained by adding X to Z to A, when all four vary. Also, how steady are his nerves and is he seeing what he looks at, where it is, after having driven 225 miles.

The following is my woodchuck kill since 1945.

WOODCHUCK RECORD — ERIC FARR

Year	Shot at	Killed	Rifle	Scope	Load
1945	42	16 chucks 6 crows – 2 at 300 yds.	.22-3000 2-R Lovell H.S.W.	10X Lyman Targetspot	42-gr. Sisk wartime 16.5 gr. 4227 0.026″ wad West 1-1/2 primers
1946	200 plus	119 chucks 6 crows 1 hawk 1 cat	above	above	17.0 gr. 4198 50-gr. Sisk Lovell same as above
	15	10 chucks	Enfield 30.1906 Chapman maple stock	Lyman Alaskan	2 with Rem Corlokt 8 with 45 gr. 4198 110-gr. Rem. bullet
1947	41	39 chucks 1 fox	Enfield- Hawker .224″ tar- get wt. bbl. Buhmiller. Chapman- Farr maple stock	Fecker 20X 1-5/8″	49-gr. Sisk Express 0.36″ wad 33.0 gr. 4320 45-gr. Sisk Hornet 18.3 gr. 4227 0.035″ wad
1948	203	165	Enfield Farr Zip- per .224″ Pfeifer bbl. with 14″ twist. Heavy bbl. No. 17 gun. Chapman- Farr maple stock	Fecker 20X 1-5/8″	55-gr. Sisk Express 0.035″ wad 31.0 gr. 4320 45-gr. Sisk 16.0 gr. 4227
1949	40 plus	35 kills	Hi-side Farr Zip- per .224″ target wt. Buhmiller bbl. One piece stock by Farr	Fecker 20X 1-5/8″	55-gr. Sisk Express 0.035″ wad 31.0 gr. 4320
1950		Not complete at time of writing.			

THE SEASON IN NEW JERSEY

Prior to 1947, woodchuck shooting in New Jersey was a clandestine affair, akin to hip flasks and necking in rumble seats. In addition to rifles, we armed ourselves with vermin permits, hunting licenses, farmer's permission, visited remote districts and farms and peered out from the cover of trees, before firing. Having developed the proper amount of poise and courage we shot chucks, but cautiously, when we found them out, from March to October.

Suddenly, we obtained a new hunting law. This permitted holders of special permits to shoot woodchucks with a rifle. This also gave us a season, July 1, to September 31, inclusive. When this law was in force the wardens put the pressure on and held us to it.

We were soon knee-deep in groundhogs. The farmers had lodged a great big fat gripe and rumor has it that the season will open eventually on May 1.

SNIPER'S MATCHES IN NEW JERSEY

Up here at Packanack Lake we have a nice bunch of woodchuck hunters and other types of rifle shooters. They take well to chuck hunting but like an accuracy match now and then. Our men like hand-loading and group shooting. So we started a shooting match program. Since the war this program has come along well. We had heard of the Sniper's Congress in the State of Washington and decided the idea had merit. So, in 1947 we put on two matches designed to bring out the center fire high velocity rifles without catering particularly to the 15- to 20-pound bench-rest rifles.

Our matches were called the Senior Snipers' Match and The Any Rifle Match. At first these matches were annual affairs but later developed into semi-annual matches.

The Senior Snipers' Match is an exciting affair. It is a rest match with any rifle, any sights permitted. The course of fire is ten shots on one target in a single group. The ten-shot groups in our opinion are a more comprehensive test of rifle, shooter and load, then five-shot groups could be.

Twenty minutes was permitted for the shooting. Foulers and warmers were allowed. Re-entry was permitted, for a re-entry fee but no series of groups could be fired for a single fee. You indicate your record group on the record target before you begin to shoot.

Many will not believe it, but it wasn't until the 1949 fall matches that anyone shot a ten-shot group under one inch, center to center. I believe that if the Bench Rest Shooters Association boys came up under these conditions, their 15-to 25-pound rifles would not fare any better, if as well. However, they were firing sitting, which is more comfortable, often suited also to better seeing and smaller groups, and their rifles mostly ran to 5 or 10 pounds greater weight. Their stocks also were, in instances, more massive through receiver and at the grip. This produces greater rigidity and less spring, but does not contribute to handiness and ease of handling in a woodchuck rifle.

The Any Rifle Match was developed a bit later and was programmed to permit center fire rifles in our prone contests. The rules are the usual NRA except the course of fire is ten shots prone in twenty minutes for score on the standard yard prone target.

The Packanack Lake Gun Club had suffered in numbers during the war, as had most others, so, when the day of the first Snipers' Match arrived, November 9, 1947, our attendance was encouraging but moderate, weather considered. It was a typical November day, cold, raw and windy. We lacked nothing but snow or rain to make it more uncomfortable. But it was a test of woodchuck rifles, woodchuck loads, and woodchuck shooters.

SNIPERS' MATCH RESULTS, NOVEMBER 1947

The records kept are complete except the size of the groups, which for that match are unavailable.

Winner: Warren Comfort. Rifle: Winchester Hi-side S.S. .22 Hawker, by Hartung, rifle previously owned by E. Farr. Arm had 27-inch heavy 14-twist barrel by Buhmiller. Was of carbon-manganese steel. Scope Fecker 16X, 1 5/8 inches. Load: 33.0 grains 4320, 0.035-inch wad, W.R.A. Zipper brass. 55-grain Sisk bullet.

Second place: E. Farr, shooting above rifle, but with 20X 1 5/8-inch Fecker scope. Load, 22.0 grains 4759, 0.035-inch wad. 45-grain R.A. S.P. Hornet bullet. Loaded ammunition by Comfort.

Third place: Ed. Knoblock. Rifle .220 Swift, heavy barrel Model 70. 20X Lyman Super Targetspot. Load, 33.0 grains of 3031, 55-grain Wotkyns-Morse S-8 bullet.

During the early months of 1948, greater activity developed. I had conceived the Farr Zipper and had gotten some very fine results with it. Don Tag had the Hawker barrel on his high side changed and replaced by one chambered for the Farr Zipper. Warren Comfort had one made up for his Springfield which his father uses. My next door neighbor, Arnold Osterlund, had one made up on a Gustlov Werke Mauser. And another friend, Frank Uhrich, who recently caught fire as a shooter, had one built up on a fine 1915 Spandau Mauser. So, by the time the next fall match rolled around, a good many of the men were primed for it. I had tried to be of assistance in helping them to load good ammunition, and supplied a complete set of loads. Eventually, the day dawned. Better still, it was clear and warm. Results follow:

SNIPERS' MATCH RESULTS, NOVEMBER, 1948

Winner: Eric Farr. Farr Zipper, Enfield action, Pfeifer barrel, 27 x 1-3/16 x 1, 14-inch twist, 17-pound outfit. 20X x 1-5/8-inch Fecker scope. Hartung's work in assembly. Load, 55-grain Wotkyns-Morse 8-S bullet. 0.035-inch wad. W.R.A. .30-30 brass reformed. 31.0 grains of 4320, Western 8-1/2 primers. Group size, 1.16 inches center-to-center, 10 shots.

Second place: Frank Uhrich. Farr Zipper, 1915 Spandau Mauser, Buhmiller 26 x 1-1/4 x 7/8 inch barrel, 14-inch twist. chrome-molybdenum steel. Hartung's work. 10X Lyman Target-spot Junior. Load, 55-grain Sisk Express, 0.035-inch wad, W.R.A. Zipper brass. 31.0 grains of 4320, R.A. 9-1/2 primer. Group size, 1.31 inches for 10 shots.

Third place: Warren Comfort, .22 Hawker——same rifle as used in match of November 11, 1947. Group size, 1.49 inches 10 shots.

The boys all decided that a whole year didn't give them enough shooting, so they arranged a semiannual program with a match in the spring and one in the fall. In the meantime, George Ohlmann, an old Camp Perry shooter, had his Springfield rebarreled and chambered for the Farr Zipper.

Possibly readers may have the idea by this time that only Farr Zippers and Hawkers were allowed to compete or were available. Not so; all sorts of calibers and outfits have competed, some of which were reputed to be super-super.

Our program was a tough pair of matches to fire. The ten-

shot group was making minute-of-angle groups look very difficult. It has in fact, made most of us look askance at anything
but ten-shot groups.

So, the next Senior Sniper's Match was scheduled for May
15, 1949. This date dawned clear and with plenty of mirage.
Results follow:

SNIPERS' MATCH RESULTS, MAY, 1949

Winner: Frank Uhrich. Farr Zipper. 10X Lyman Targetspot.
Load, 55-grain W.M. S-8 bullet and 20.0 grains of 4759. W.R.A.
Zipper brass, 0.035-inch wad. R.A. 9-1/2 primers. Group size,
10 shots, 1.16 inches.

Tie for second: E. Farr and George Ohlmann, group 1.31
inches for 10 shots each. George Ohlmann used the Farr Zipper, on high number Springfield action, fitted with 24-inch Buhmiller heavy, preturned 14-inch twist, chrome-molybdenum
barrel and issue stock. Hartung's work. 10X Lyman Targetspot
Junior. Load, 55-grain Sisk Express. 0.035-inch wad, 31.0 grains
4320. WRA Zipper brass R;A. 9-1/2 primers.

E. Farr: Farr Zipper on light Mannlicher style Enfield action .22-inch Buhmiller medium weight preturned 14-inch twist,
chrome-molybdenum barrel. Hartung's work. 20X 1-5/8 inch
Fecker. Load: 49 grain Sisk Express. 0.035-inch wad. W.R.A.
Zipper brass. 30.0 grains 4320. Western 8-1/2 primers.

Having by this time discovered about what they could expect
in the way of accuracy from their pet woodchuck rifles, loads
and scopes, in practice shooting and in their Snipers' Matches,
the boys went heavily into woodchuck shooting. I unfortunately,
missed some of the chuck expeditions.

Investigations conducted by myself indicated that the quality of the commercial bullets had deteriorated to such an extent
that no real headway could be made unless the quality improved
or we made our own. At that time none of us had tried the Sierra
bullets.

In the fall matches, some of the boys started to inspect
quality of commercial bullets. A friend supplied me with some
home-made bullets which let me shoot a nice tight, 1.58-inch
group.

The fall matches were held October 16, 1949, a clear, warm
day with light mirage.

SNIPERS' MATCH RESULTS, OCTOBER, 1949

Winner: R. Depuy, using George Ohlmann's Farr Zipper, same load and rifle used in matches May 15, 1949. His group size was 0.87 inch, for 10 shots. Center to center, measurement.

Second place: George Ohlmann. Same outfit, group size 0.88 inch.

Third place: Frank Hopper using Warren Comfort's new Hartung Zipper, Springfield action with Canjar single set trigger. 26-inch medium weight preturned Buhmiller chrome-moly barrel with 14-inch twist. Hartung's work. Load unknown to me. Group size, for the 10 shots, 1.25 inches.

So that's the story of the Senior Snipers' Matches held with woodchuck rifles up to the spring of 1950. The inch was finally broken, but not without real effort and development of rifles and loads. Incidentally, these matches are all shot prone, with rests. We do not have bench rest facilities for firing from the sitting position, which to some is more comfortable and permits shooting strings with a bit less eye-strain.

These have been interesting matches. We have not barred rim-fires but as yet none have placed. I have shot in them with the .22 rim-fire and have ended up with 1-3/4-inch groups. Conditions during the firing of these matches, year after year, have never been really good and some years have been very tough and rugged.

Just prior to the last set of matches, there has appeared to be more secrecy in the matter of shooters keeping load details to themselves, and there seems to be no logical reason unless it be that competitors are beginning to feel that to win they must have a definite "edge" of some sort on the others.

ALBERT HARTUNG'S GUNSMITHING

I would like to mention a few things about Albert Hartung, who has had much to do with the accuracy we have obtained. Now in his sixties, he has been a shooting enthusiast since boyhood and is a full-time gunsmith. He is a Browning representative. His average workmanship as it leaves his shop, equals that which I have examined from the most celebrated. That includes work from Griffin & Howe, Ackley, Marciante, Sabyan, Papernek, C. C. Johnson, Hervey Lovell, W. R. Douglas, J. R. Buhmiller, Neidner, Pope and some others.

Hartung does not have an engineering, educational or similar field background, but he knows his dimensions and can do things few gunsmiths will attempt. On his average workmanship, I'll select Hartung as tops with any of them. I have seen about twenty top quality G & H jobs owned by a friend of mine, and all are splendid, but G & H also turn out other qualities of work at lower prices.

THE REBUILDING AND RESTOCKING — WITH A ONE-PIECE STOCK, OF A HI-SIDE WINCHESTER

I promised to include copy which is in effect, the saga of a Winchester High-side which failed miserably to perform for a while. This rifle is owned by Don Tag and is a very honorable thin-wall which was originally a take-down .22 long rifle.

When it went to Hartung to be rebarreled into a Farr Zipper, Hartung fitted a new breech block of tool steel and did a fine job. The barrel fitted came off my very accurate Enfield Hawker. Two inches were cut off the breech and another inch off the muzzle. Hartung fitted a buttstock, unfinished on the outside — as ordered — and made it with a thru-bolt and fitted the fore-end on a base beneath the barrel, which base was held on by two 6-48 screws. A center 10-32 hole provided for the fore-end attaching screw. The rear end of the block was squared off to provide a recoil shoulder for the fore-end. The barrel was fitted tightly to the action and the takedown feature was not retained, nor was the detachable front section retained which makes this feature possible.

This had been done some time back when the action was originally converted from .22 long rifle to .22-3000 R-2 Lovell. After R-2, it had been a .22 Hawker. It was a very accurate rifle as an R-2.

Don Tag finished up the stock and in his own words, "loused it up a bit." It made its debut at one of the Senior Snipers' Matches and shot a group there having a 4-inch vertical. This set Don off on a stock-bedding endeavor which failed to help. Occasionally it shot a fair to good group but always failed to produce when on demonstration.

Finally, probably in desperation, Don left the rifle with me to see what, if anything, I could do to make it shoot. I tried the rifle out from sandbag rest with loads that could usually be depended upon. It shot into about 3 inches.

All the mechanical details necessary to a high-side which would group were checked. These included bore condition, firing pin protrusion, tight tang screws, etc., and all found to be okay. It looked as though the stock was at fault. When pressure was put on the through bolt to make the joint rigid, the sides of the stock began to spread. Seventy-five shots were fired trying to discover what was wrong. It did its best shooting when just the iron parts were used, the barrel and metal action, when firing from sandbag rest. I finally split the butchered stock trying to make it tight.

Then of course it was decided that nothing but a new stock would be satisfactory. Research indicated that, considering the design of the hi-side action, a wood which would resist cleavage was required. Cherry was such a wood. Also, it has a nice color when finished.

A close friend of mine, Steve Sebeck who knows more about woods than a woodsman or a woodpecker, said that cherry was the ticket. He also told me that cherry was very stable, would take a high polish, and was easy to work. Better still, he provided a very fine piece of cherry.

With caution and foresight I laid it out and Steve band-sawed it and bored the thru-bolt hole. I gradually let the action in maintaining 100 per cent contact at the recoil shoulders. The thru-bolt was periodically tightened to test the rigidity of the assembly. There was a tiny bit of play but it was felt that when it was completely let in, this would disappear. However, when all was full depth and snug as could be, there was still some play. Tightening the thru-bolt only failed to hold, but split the wood tangs inward. What to do!

A long time back I had thought about a one-piece stock for a hi-side and now decided to try one. An examination of the iron suggested that the only thing preventing the whole action being dropped into a one-piece stock was the long, lower tang which could be lopped off. Recoil shoulder and attaching screw could well be the fore-end attaching screw and base.

So, I laid out in the cherry blank, a one-piece stock and let the action in it as we planned. There were no hitches and it worked along quite well. I left the flanges on the action as I was not sure it would be successful and I might have to make one of the conventional type if this one was a failure.

The pictures in this chapter show the details of the inletting and general details of the rifle. The action proper is just clear of the stock in every respect. However the barrel itself is 100 per cent in contact. It acts as though it is in a machine rest.

Testing the rifle in the one-piece stock was a pleasure. Right from the start it has been docile and dependable. It shoots with superb gilt-edge accuracy and holds its zero without change from day to day. Mr. Donald Tag who owns the rifle, will attest to this. I will supply test groups fired with the others.

I recommend this one-piece stock for a Winchester hi-side s.s. rifle to all owners of such rifles and enthusiasts as the only sure way to get bolt action reliability in accuracy and daily uniformity of center of impact of groups.

A hi-side so stocked is indistinguishable from a bolt action performance-wise. It looses none of its advantages as a high-side but it does look rather unusual. In this prototype it is a bit thick through the action, but as pointed out, unnecessarily so.*

Good friends who have shot this rifle have commented that they have never seen a hi-side perform as well or remain so reliable as to daily group variation. As a matter of fact, today I wouldn't own a hi-side unless it was fitted with such a stock because I know it won't be reliable until it is so stocked.

It is generally unfair and in fact warped judgment, to condemn a whole line or rifle model. Because of certain characteristics one rifle of the same model produced more desirable results generally, because its stock design was different, or as in this case there was such a complete turn-about that the writer is of the opinion that most of the drawbacks of the hi-side Winchester single shot, and of the low-side s.s. as well, have been due to that unfortunate two-piece stock.

We all know that we can influence the point of impact of a rifle by the way in which recoil is absorbed by the shooter, although this is less pronounced in the case of very heavy weapons shooting light loads. In such instance the recoil is very light.†

---

*Author's Note: This thickness of wood through from side to side opposite the receiver, does more to increase the accuracy of the rifle than anything else. This is the exact spot where most rifles are weakest although many shooters think it is through the grip. I just about doubled the accuracy of a 52 Winchester by having it restocked with a blank thick through at the receiver. It now cannot spring there like it used to. I also have a .22-250 Springfield spotter so stocked.

†Author's Note: It might be mentioned here that very few .22-caliber high velocity rifles develop more than 4 or 4-1/2 foot pounds of free recoil, even in

If the stock comes to rest in respect to the irons differently oriented from shot to shot, the point of impact will vary from shot to shot. It is here felt that to suppose that the loose joint of the conventional hi-side stock will not vary the zero and/or point of impact, is to ignore the plain facts. Likewise it may be possible for a more skillful stockmaker than I to make the joint right. However, I do not feel that, all things being equal, a two-piece stocked hi-side rifle performs in the same class as a one-piece stocked one, which is of the target bolt action class. Had more effort through the years been put on cleaning up this angle of the single shot rifle design, they might today be figuring much more prominently in the center fire varmint rifle picture and also in the small bore target shooting competitions. As it is, the day of the hi-side with two-piece stock is rapidly sinking into oblivion as its sun goes down in the west.*

standard weight barrels and stocks. The .22 rim-fires, of course, have quite a negligible recoil, yet the Winchester single shot action either in the .22 long or the .22 short calibers never gave the accuracy the Model 52 bolt action has given ever since the latter has been rather heavily stocked. In one instance, a professional small bore rifle shot employed then by Winchester had a Winchester single shot barrel in .22 long rifle caliber installed on a Model 44-1/2 Stevens single shot action, and stock; thereafter it shot better on the Stevens action that it had previously on the Winchester action. Much of the improvement to the rocker action of the Stevens 44-1/2 was credited to seating the cartridge in the chamber. I think that the Winchester single shot action has delivered better accuracy, speaking relatively, with .22 center fire varmint cartridges than it ever did with the .22 long rifle cartridge. I had a heavy hi-side .22 Hornet Sedgley rifle for years, which I used to shoot side by side, at 100 yards, with my Model 54 Winchester bolt action .22 Hornet. Regardless of the make of ammunition used, the 54 always gave the finer accuracy. The Sedgley-Winchester was fitted with a Model 52 barrel, at that. It had been rechambered for the .22 Hornet cartridge, by Sedgley's firm. Incidentally Mr. Sedgley told me repeatedly that the .22 Hornet shot better from a Springfield bolt action than it did from the hi-side.
*Author's Note: The Winchester hi-side has had a life of sixty years or more. In its earlier days it was used extensively in the large .38, .40, .44, .45 and .50 calibers on bison, antelope, elk, grizzly bear and both white-tail and black-tail deer; on moose, caribou, sheep, goats and even Kodiaks. Tens of thousands of them made history in the opening up and settling of the prairie states and the West. But the Winchester and other repeating rifles took their place. Only in the hands of the woodchuck hunters and the other varmint hunters has the popularity of the Winchester hi-side S.S. been retained. It has been a long and an honorable life. Its place in the history of the settlement of North America, on both sides of the boundary between the United States and Canada, will never be forgotten. Today, among the woodchuck hunters of southern Ontario it is still the standard and most popular rifle action.
Possible the one-piece stock, built ruggedly and more for results than ap-

DIMENSIONS OF STOCK AND RIFLE — WINCHESTER S.S.
HI-SIDE AS RESTOCKED WITH ONE-PIECE STOCK
BY ERIC FARR

Weight of rifle, less scope, with 23-inch target weight barrel, no sling:	9.0 lbs.
Length of pull from trigger to center of buttplate: Stock came out longer than expected due to use of rather thick ebony buttplate.	14.0″
Length of fore-end from trigger:	15-3/4″
Drop from top of scope blocks: At comb	1-3/16″
At heel	2-1/8″
Pitch (down):	5-3/4″
Cast-off (to right):	1/8″
Thickness through action:	2″
Thickness at fore-end tip:section of fore-end semi-beavertail:	1-13/16″
Buttplate dimensions:	6-3/4″ x 1-3/4″

pearance, will again restore much of its former popularity. Mr. Farr should be thanked most gratefully for his unselfish effort to put the rugged hi-side Winchester single shot woodchuck rifle back in the gun rack of the varmint hunters of North America.

CHAPTER 9

Chuck Shooting in New Jersey
with James M. Smith

IN THE locality of Bound Brook, Lebanon, and North Plain-
field, New Jersey, is a group of rifle experimenters and woodchuck hunters which has included Lawrence Ramsey, Al Marciante, the late Robert Bley, James M. Smith, Jr., and half a
dozen others who make the rifle and chronograph range at
Lawrence Ramsey's Clear View Farm, near Lebanon, their
headquarters. I have enjoyed the companionship and hospitality
of this group on the Ramsey farm. We have shot together, and
it is with pleasure therefore that I include this account of New
Jersey woodchuck shooting, and the development of cartridge
cases and loads for this very powerful and long-ranged German
Mauser .228 Express. It should be especially interesting to
readers of this book, not only because the rifle and cartridge
are generally unknown to American sportsmen, but for the added reason that most woodchuck hunters do not know that fairly
good chuck shooting is today obtainable in the hilly and rather
mountainous area in two counties of New Jersey. Dr. Smith, a
chemist by profession, has done extensive work in the development of this rifle and cartridge.

The 5.6 x 61 m.m. Vom Hofe Super Express is a development of Ernst-August Vom Hofe, a former associate of Walter
Brenneke, whose Brenneke Mauser rifles, cartridges and bullets, are so well and favorably known to many admirers and
users of bolt action rifles.

The 5.6 x 61 was made in both rimless and rimmed bottle-
necked cases, and used a 77-grain sharp pointed bullet 25 m.m.
long. According to Vom Hofe, as reported in American Rifleman,* the powder charge was 54 grains of Rottweil N. C. leaf

*June, 1949, page 46.

181

powder while the muzzle velocity was given as 3707 f.p.s.; muzzle energy 2351 ft. lbs; at 300 yards the remaining velocity was 3808 f.p.s., and the striking energy at 300 yards, 2351 ft. lbs. The chamber pressure was 57,000 lbs. per square inch.

The cartridge was loaded commercially by Deutsche Waffen-und Munitions fabriken A.-G. (D.W.M.) for a short time, at least. In a letter to Mr. J. Murray Leyde, dated October 2, 1939, they gave the following data:

1. Without rim, powder charge 3.5 grams RI, gas pressure maximum, 3900 KG/CM^2, velocity VO=1100 M/S.
2. With rim, powder charge 3.3 grams RI, gas pressure maximum, 3300 KG/CM^2, velocity VO=1000 M/S.

Converted to more familiar units for American readers, the values are:

1. Rimless—54.0 grains RI, chamber pressure 55,469 lbs./sq. in., muzzle velocity 3608 f.p.s.
2. Rimmed—50.9 grains RI, chamber pressure 46,935 lbs./sq. in., muzzle velocity 3280 f.p.s.

The bullet weight was given as 5 grams or 77 grains. There is, as you must realize, a very great difference between the muzzle velocity given to a 45-, 50-, or 55-grain bullet of .224-inch diameter, and that which can be imparted to a 77-grain bullet of .228-inch diameter. The 77-grain German bullet had a Tombak jacket, and was made with a hollow point, protected by an aluminum cap.

The 5.6 x 61 m.m. is therefore a cartridge with excellent ballistics, at least on paper. The D.W.M. outfit recommended it for red deer hunting and on this side it should prove to be a real long range outfit for our larger varmints. In my state, (New Jersey), only the woodchuck or groundhog may be shot (legally) with a rifle, and it is on this game that I and others have actually used this rifle. The cartridge really has too much powder capacity, at least in my opinion. The Ackley .228 Magnum will probably do most anything that the 5.6 m.m. will do. However, in the hope that the readers will find it interesting, the following is the story of how a 5.6 x 61 m.m. Vom Hofe Super Express Rimless Mauser came to the U. S. A. and found a good home among sportsmen.

The discussion which follows is intended for the woodchuck shooters and the experimenters who are interested in developing new cartridges — the type of experimental rifleman who produced the .22 Hornet and the .257 Roberts in recent years, and much earlier the .22 Savage H.P. and the .250-3000 Savage, all of which have become standard factory cartridges of wide popularity. Among others which are widely known as wildcats are the .219 Donaldson, the .22-250 or .22 Varminter, the .22 Marciante Blue Streak, and a host of others of considerable merit and, in some instances, of outstanding performance.

The 5.6 x 61 m.m. was developed by a different group, in another country, under different conditions, and possibly with another purpose in mind. The fact that the measurements are given by the metric system has not a thing to do with the splendid ballistics developed by the cartridge. To designate any of the well-known American .22 wildcat cartridges in millimeters and to add the length of the case in millimeters, to the common designation of the wildcat in its public description, would in no case detract from nor would it add to ballistic performance of the cartridge or its work on woodchucks.

The universal aim seems to be to produce small bore high velocity cartridges of improved ballistics and deadliness. The 5.6 x 61 m.m. is a fairly recent development and is a cartridge with intriguing possibilities. It is a large cartridge, decidedly out of the ordinary, and it is because of this unusualness that the data on this cartridge has been collected and coordinated for presentation here. Starting with a rifle chambered for an unknown cartridge, American components were adapted to it, and the rifle and ammunition were tested ballistically and used successfully in the field. It shows what can be done by careful work. You may be sure that the development and testing of this cartridge, both on the range and on woodchucks, nearby, was enjoyed by each of those concerned.

But to go back to the obtainment of this rifle: One day a friend called up in great excitement to tell me that he had a 5.6 x 61 m.m. Mauser. To put it briefly, he felt that he had a small bore high velocity arm that would throw some excitement into the rather prosaic lives of the local rifle experimental group. Weeks of experiment on the range and on woodchucks with a supersmall caliber rifle of this type should prove highly interesting. It was!

A rapid check of Stoeger's catalogue failed to show any such cartridge listed, and the local cartridge collectors had never heard of it. Therefore the owner's identification was somewhat discounted and the consensus of opinion was that it must be a 6.5 x 61 m.m. which was listed in the gun and rifle material we had available. Nevertheless examination of the rifle proved that the caliber was indeed 5.6 x 61 m.m. A soft lead slug was pushed through the bore and miked 0.228 inch; this immediately suggested, that the .22 Savage H.P. bullets could be used. The bolt head and chamber in the barrel looked as if the .30-1906 case might be suitable for reforming. A rough trial confirmed this. Since it was fairly certain that readily available American components could be used to make up loads, a price was quoted and I became the proud owner of a new woodchuck rifle.

Before purchasing the outfit, I had paid a visit to my good friend, the late Robert F. Bley and presented the problem to him. He was an experienced hand-loader and shooter who was interested in experimenting with new cartridges and could be relied upon to rise to the challenge of getting loads for this rifle. Bob Bley was probably less well-known than some of his associates in experimental shooting, such as Al Marciante, Vaughan Cail, Sam Clark, and George Schnerring (now also deceased), but he had a wealth of material at his finger tips and was always ready to tackle a new problem. He went to work on this one.

A few cases were soon produced from .30-1906 cartridge cases by necking down the case, first in a .250-3000 die, then in a .22-250 die, and cutting off the neck to give a case of 61 m.m. length. You will recall that all the common German Mauser cartridges are designated as to case length, in m.m. A few 70- and 63-grain bullets of 0.2275-inch diameter were obtained. Two firings, at least, with 20.0 grains of DuPont 4759 powder were necessary to expand the case to full chamber size. The shoulder was particularly difficult to form, probably due to the thickened brass produced in reducing the neck size to hold a 0.2275-inch bullet. In the blowing-out or case-expanding process, the overall length of the case was shortened somewhat, so that the cases after forming and in use were not quite a full 61 m.m. in length. As can be seen from the illustration, the 5.6 x 61 m.m. Mauser case is a very large case with a powder capacity almost as great as the .30-1906. The base of the bullet is slightly smaller in diameter so that when fired in the 5.6 x 61 m.m. chamber, the head bulged perceptibly about 1/16 or 0.0625 inch ahead of the rim.

At about this stage in the experiments, John Brookes attended a meeting of the Ohio Gun Collectors and there saw the original 5.6 x 61 m.m. Vom Hofe Super Express Rimless cartridges. A search was begun for more cartridges and for information and data applicable to this caliber.

The case as made from the .30-1906 empties holds 55 grains of DuPont No. 4064 powder or 54.6 grains of 4350 powder, when such extends up to the base of the neck. Since we had no information on the German loading, various powder charges for the Swift, the Varminter, .22 Newton, etc., were discussed at great length. The conclusions reached were that 35.0 grains of No. 4064 should develop approximately 3000 f.p.s. with the 63-grain bullet and slightly less with the 70-grain bullet; that the pressures should be within reasonable limits and also safe. Obviously, the .30-1906 case was too small at the head, and this discrepancy gave warning to go slowly until more was known by us about this cartridge.

In sighting in the first day on the range, eighteen loads were made up with this powder charge, ten with the 63-grain Sisk and eight with the 70-grain Western soft point. With this somewhat limited supply of ammunition we set out to see what the rifle would do. There was a very little difference in the 100-yard sight setting for the 63- and the 70-grain bullets. With the 70-grain bullets a five-shot 2 1/4-inch group was obtained at 100 yards, one inch above a point of aim. Two shots at 200 yards indicated that the load was dead on at that range. The high-mounted scope was concluded to be the cause of this rather than any really unusual ballistics. It was a lovely day in July, and Lawrence Ramsey's range is a particularly delightful place to shoot. A large bench rest with a comfortable seat, makes it possible to test rifles and ammunition in maximum comfort. The range extends northwest up a wide ravine, with alfalfa on the hillside to the left, a pasture in the center with a grove of large oaks beyond, and a steep bank to the right, with a rail fence and an old orchard above. Woodchucks are sometimes apparently rather dumb brutes; they insist upon occupying dens in the alfalfa, in the woods, and on the steep banks below the orchard.

Bley has shot as many as five chucks in an afternoon with the .22 Hornet, firing directly from the bench rest. On the particular afternoon in question, an especially stupid and unfortunate chuck crawled out from under a stump back in the woods, 225 yards away. At the time we were relaxing in the grass, casually scanning the surroundings with the binoculars. One cartridge with the 70-grain Western soft point bullet, and 35.0 grains of 4064 remained, and the pointed picket post of the scope was carefully placed high on the chuck's shoulder. The set trigger was carefully touched and the resounding, unmistakable ''plop'' indicated a hit. The chuck merely raised up a bit when the bullet hit him, then dropped back and lay still. We had a chuck rifle. This was very gratifying — the first shot at game had gone home.

No more group shooting was done that summer. We had eighteen cases and very limited supplies of primers and bullets. Primers were selling for thirty dollars a thousand at that time, when you could get them. Most times you could not obtain as many as 100 at any price.

But the woodchucks in Somerset and Hunterdon Counties, New Jersey lived hard. The performance of the 5.6 x 61 m.m. was excellent, using the above-mentioned load with 70-grain bullet. This relatively heavy bullet is a much better windbucker than any of the .224-inch bullets weighing around 45 to 55 grains. The weight is so much greater in proportion to the caliber, one does not need to hold over into the wind so far on long shots.

However, even with the 70-grain bullet some dismal misses resulted at first, due possibly, (I like to think), to the unfamiliar reticule. However, as the chuck season continued, the record of shooting improved. The performance of the Western 70-grain bullet left very little to be desired. One day, after an inglorious miss at 150 yards at a chuck that, surprised some distance from his den was running through a clover field, stopping at intervals to sit up and look at us, a good hit was made at 175 yards. Then a short time later a huge chuck was discovered sitting at the top of a clay bank; the shot was taken from the sitting position; the chuck rolled down the bank and disappeared. The distance proved to be 250 yards when we stepped it off. The chuck was just inside the hole at the base of the bank, was in head-first, and obviously instantly killed. A short time later a shot was taken at 410 yards, same sight setting, with the post on the top of the head of a standing chuck. It was a hit, but regrettably the chuck made it to his den, dragging one hind leg. This was the only one which made it to the hole when hit, out of twenty-five or so shot that summer with the 5.6 x 61 m.m. Mauser. On the last hunt of the season, late in September, four shots resulted in three kills at 135, 195 and 250 yards. The last was across a deep wooded gulley at a chuck in a high alfalfa field. A standing rule on our hunts is that whenever possible the hunter pace off the shot, and the boys insisted that I step off this one. The estimate of 250 yards is conservative since pacing through thick brush is uncertain. When I emerged on the other side and got to where I thought the chuck should be, the boys waved me on. Two holes were passed, and finally, beyond where it seemed reasonable for him to be, the chuck was found on his mound, a 70-grain bullet through his shoulder.

DESCRIPTION OF THE 5.6 x 61 M. M. MAUSER RIFLE

Perhaps a description of the rifle itself is in order now. It is a fine specimen of the German custom-built sporter. The Mauser action has double-set triggers, a push-button side safety, in addition to the regular Mauser safety, and a hinged magazine floor plate. The action is beautifully engraved. The receiver is marked "5.6 x 61" on the left side, together with the serial number. The 25-inch medium weight barrel is engraved on top Nimrod Gewehrfabrik. Suhl. Underneath are various proof marks and the trade-mark of a hunter, with gun at shoulder level and "Nimrod" in a semicircle below. The twist of the rifling is one turn in 9.2 inches. Most important, probably, of all, is that the barrel has a perfect 6-groove bore. The stock is of dark walnut with forearm tip, pistol grip cap, and butt plate of horn. It is somewhat the worse for wear but is well designed and very graceful with a high comb, full cheekpiece and comfortable pistol grip.

One of the most interesting things about the outfit is the telescope sight of 4 or 5 power, which is mounted in Mauser-type quick detachable bridge mounts. It is adjustable for both windage and elevation by means of large knurled knobs on the top and the left side. The scope is very clear of field, with a wide field of vision and an objective lens 1-1/8 inches in diameter. The reticule is the pointed picket post with horizontal post found in so many continental-made scopes. There is no maker's name on the scope, only the markings "1939" and No. 6-37890. On the rear leg of the mounts are the words Waffen-Schmidt. Suhl in small, inconspicuous letters. I believe this scope is in all probability a Russian sniper's scope mounted on a German custom sporter! The identification is reasonably certain from published photographs of authentic specimens in two American sporting magazines.

In addition to the scope sight, nonadjustable open sights are provided which can be used with the scope in position. The mounts are simple and sturdy, a marvel of precision fitting, and removal and replacement of the scope does not change the zero of the rifle. Mounting the scope with line of sight two inches above the center of the bore is a rather high position; however, it gives some advantage in increasing the distance of the apparent point blank range of the rifle.

This Mauser weighs 7-3/4 pounds, the scope 1-3/4 pounds, and with the braided leather carrying sling, the outfit comes to 9-1/2 pounds. Possibly plenty of rifle and scope to carry around on a hot day, but it has the rigidity and stiffness necessary to making consistent long range shots.

LOADING THE MAUSER RIFLE

Later in the same fall more time was available for work on the loading problem. The first load tried, 35.0 grains of DuPont No. 4064, had worked so well that no changes had been attempted on the theory that there is no sense in breaking up a winning combination. However, more cases were reformed and eventually about seventy were available. During one case-forming session, using 20.0 grains of No. 4759 powder and the 63-grain Sisk soft point, just for fun a "group" was fired on a piece of two-inch pipe driven in the ground at 100 yards. Four of the five shots hit the pipe and penetrated both sides; the vertical spread was 1.5 inches. Another time, using 25.0 grains of No. 4759 and junk bullets from Bley's discards, diameters mixed of .223 inch, .224 inch, a few .227 inch, and in unknown weights from 40 to 55 grains, we killed three chucks at 150 yards (from that same bench rest at Ramseys) in six or seven shots.

Then, getting down to business, the Lewis-type chronograph was set up in front of the bench rest and a series of loads was checked for velocity. The chronograph consists of a high-speed electric motor of 3535 r.p.m. which spins two discs, 16 inches in diameter, 42 inches apart on the shaft. When a bullet is fired through these two rotating discs about one inch from the edges, with the rifle bore lined up parallel to the shaft, the velocity can be calculated from the angular distance between the two bullet holes in the paper discs. Results are tabulated below. All are for 70-grain Western S.P. bullet and Western 8-1/2 primer.

Powder Charge	Velocity at 35 ft.	Max. Variation from Average Velocity
1. 35.0 grs. 4064	2856 f. s.	54 f. s.
2. 40.0 grs. 4350	2751 f. s.	54 "
3. 45.0 grs. 4350	3046 f. s.	47 "
4. 50.0 grs. 4350	3374 f. s.	0 "

Remember, this is with the 70-grain bullet.

Runs No. 1 and 2, are average of 5 shots; runs No. 3 and 4, average of 4 shots.

Therefore it may be seen that my favorite woodchuck load had but a velocity of 2856 f.p.s.; but it was imparted to a heavy 70-grain bullet that definitely laid out a chuck, largely regardless of the range at which he was shot. The load using 50.0 grains of 4350 looked very promising as it seemed to be burning uniformly, and was kept in mind for future varmint shooting. The bullet shortage was acute at that time, so when some 70-grain Remington Core-Lokt bullets turned up they were tried at once. Groups proved disappointing, however. They were perceptibly larger than those obtained with Western 70-grain or Sisk 63-grain. The Remington bullets did not spin true in a Wesnitzer bullet spinner, while the others did. Maybe that had something to do with it. The center of gravity would not be coincident with the center of form. We tried some 78-grain Sisk bullets in 0.226-inch diameter, made of copper tubing over lead cores, for the Ackley .228 Magnum, with 50.0 grains of 4350. The first five shots made a reasonable group, somewhat less than three inches at 100 yards,—the sixth shot at a chuck at 300 yards was a little low, shots number 7 and 8 did not reach the target, and the bullets apparently disintegrated in midair.

The bolt was very hard to open, and signs of excessive pressure were unmistakable so no more were tried. A brief trial of Sisk 55-grain, .226-inch bullets with 20.0 grains of No. 4759 and Remington No. 9-1/2 primers indicated good accuracy (five-shot groups of 1-1/2 inches at 100 yards), and so we resolved to stick to the heavier bullets for woodchuck shooting.

The next July when the chuck season opened again, and with the best load we had developed; i.e., 50 grains of 4350 and the 70-grain Western soft point, I was all set to slay chucks again, even at 300 yards or more. On July 4, a hot, sunny day, an enthusiastic young farmer took me out to a recently cut hayfield, where we found five chucks playing around like puppies. One shot at 250 yards sounded like a hit, but we couldn't find the chuck. Then with three chucks out around one hole, I lay down in the sun, at 300 yards, to really do some damage. After four shots the chucks were not much disturbed. Those bullets were kicking up the dust about forty yards in front of the muzzle— and I finally caught on and switched to the 63-grain Sisk and 35.0 grains of 4064, and got one chuck. Very much disgusted, I packed up and went home, much to the amusement of the young farmer, who had been hopefully looking for a slaughter. My only explanation is that the loads tested in cold December weather were just too fast for those bullets when pushed through a barrel heated by a hot July sun. Also, the powder would develop higher pressures with every rise in temperature. Bullet jackets designed for a given velocity and a certain working pressure and temperature rarely can stand the gaff when fired through a quick-twist barrel by a hotter and stronger charge.

I returned to the old favorite, 35.0 grains 4064, and things began to click again. On another day Bob and Bill Bley and myself, after driving all around the country with very little success, finally looked at a back field of alfalfa and found it fresh cut. That was a day! In less than an hour we had eleven chucks from that field. Bill and I took five from one stand, without moving. The ranges were moderate, 75 to 185 yards. Bob Bley picked off four with the .22 Hornet. Bill killed four with the Krag using the frangible bullet and 35.0 grains of HiVel No. 2.

On another notable day, my young son, age 5-1/2 years at the time, accompanied me on a chuck hunt, his first. On this day, five shots resulted in five kills. The first was offhand at 110 yards; another, also offhand, at 65 yards; one from sitting at 65 yards; one prone at 325 yards; and the last offhand at 55 yards. The last one was in his hole, showing the top of his head. At the shot he dropped out of sight, then kicked completely out of his hole and his tail wagged its last outside the den mouth. Hugh Stewart, the same day, got three with the .22-3000, a heavy barreled job on the Remington-Hepburn action. A week later, at the same farm, after some bad misses, I slipped through a hedgerow and found three chucks sitting up, one down the field and two up to the left. Firing from the prone position, as rapidly as the rifle could be loaded, three shots nailed all three chucks; distances were 210, 188, and 190 yards. Bob Bley, in the meantime, stayed at the bench rest, and got three for six with the Model 70 Hornet. When I returned triumphantly, and was in the midst of telling him about it, a big chuck suddenly (it seemed to me), appeared across the way. Bob said it was my shot, so I touched off carefully, saw hair fly, and then scored another hit. Something seemed odd though. The position of that woodchuck appeared lacking somehow in naturalness and poise, and a number of sly grins from Bley and Ramsey called for questions. It seems that Bob had killed that chuck some time before, and then had set it natural and propped it up. Did this, so he said, for C. H. Bean (the engineer), who was another member of the party. It was just a case of first come, first served, I suppose.

Still on the trail of some heavy bullets that could be driven at 3500 f.p.s. satisfactorily in the quick-twist barrel, some 75-grain Speer bullets were obtained. These were .2285 inch in diameter and looked bad from the beginning of their testing. With 50.0 grains of 4350, they keyholed and spread all over, some missing the two-foot square target at 100 yards. Varying the powder charge had no effect. George Schnerring suggested that this was caused by not having enough neck clearance (there was none in this instance due to the large diameter bullets and the thick case necks), and reported a similar experience at Frankford Arsenal in some experiments on the .30-1906. However, reaming the case necks did not help a great deal. Bob Bley made up some cases with flash tubes, these extending to the base of the shoulder and carrying the primer flame up to the head of the charge instead of only to its base, as in the usual loading. These flash tubes gave variable pressures with this cartridge. One load, with 50.0 grains of 4350, blew out the primer and enlarged the primer pocket tremendously. The bullets did not reach the targets.

Some heavy jacket caps for .220 Swift bullets have been obtained, and these were formed, with lead cores, in R.C.B.S. swedges to give a bullet of 70 grains weight which closely approximates the shape of the 70-grain Western soft-point. It is hoped that here we will have a satisfactory high velocity bullet. This will have to be proved. As insulation we plan to try dipping the bullet cores into cellulose acetate (Duco cement) as described publicly for type-metal bullets recently.

Fortunately, the reloading problem was solved quite easily. Bley fitted an ordinary bolt to the Pacific .45-70 bullet seating die in place of the regular bullet seater. In one end, a hole .260 inch in diameter was drilled for neck sizing. This reduces the neck to .227 inches inside and makes a nice snug fit for the bullet. No expansion is necessary, and this saves wear on the case necks. After two years use, either the cases are getting thin, or the die is wearing, or both, because .2275-inch bullets fit more loosely than they used to. The opposite end of the bolt was drilled to form a pointed cavity for bullet seating. The bolt is simply reversed in the die for this operation. A small punch is used for depriming and then the regular .30-1906 case holder and priming arm are used for seating the new primer in the Pacific tool. The cases have never been full-length resized.

The long sloping shoulder of the 5.6 x 61 m.m. is very different from the shoulders of the latest American and Canadian wildcats, with their abrupt 28- to 40-degree shoulders. It is more like those on the earlier experiments, such as the Dubiel and O'Neil Magnums. The question of barrel erosion as influenced by this shoulder shape is one which will probably have to remain unanswered here. It is not likely the rifle will be shot enough on either chucks or at the target to burn it out any time soon. We lack cases and the chuck supply is limited by the hilly area and the number of dens to harbor breeding pairs.

Through an advertisement asking for information the 5.6, contact was made with several other proud owners of 5.6 rifles, all of them looking for ammunition. Later an article in the Rifleman brought more contacts. These fellow enthusiasts have been very helpful and most informative. Lawrence Ramsey suggested that P. O. Ackley at Trinidad, Colorado, might have some experience with the 5.6 Mr. Ackley was long-suffering in answering my letters. He has had several of these rifles in his shop for rebarreling — "has beens" he calls them. He pulled the bullet from one of the original German 5.6 cartridges and seated a 70-grain bullet which he then chronographed. The velocity obtained was 3400 f.p.s.

L. S. Huffman has a rifle in perfect condition. With the help of R. B. Sisk, some interesting loads were developed. Forty-six grains of 4064 and a 70-grain bullet, and 55 grains of 4064 and a 55-grain bullet. Samples which Mr. Huffman sent to me had bullets of 0.225-inch diameter. A fired case showed no signs of excessive pressure.

Some of the correspondents gave details of their outfits. These are summarized below.

1. Mauser action; barrel by Carl Bock has full length matted rib, action and metal parts (case hardened?) in color, and highly engraved. Floor plate is marked "Ong Fabrikat Vom Hofe 5.6 m.m. Super-Exp. No. 1344"; on left side of the receiver is Ohr. Friedr. Friebel-Suhl 8649. Barrel has groove diameter of 0.229, land diameter 0.229, land diameter 0.221 inch. Twist, one turn in 8.65 inches.

2. Mauser action, engraved; double-set triggers, Circassian walnut stock and telescope mount similar to the Jaeger. The

twist is one turn in 9 inches.

3. Mauser, 6X Carl Zeiss scope, Receiver marked "K.M.S., N 51. gr. Barrel marked "39 - 5.6 M.M. 61-140-28."

4. (L. S. Huffman). Mauser action, Mannlicher type bolt handle, 25-inch Krupp barrel, 4X Dr. Walter Gerard, Charlottenburg scope "G.DRGM" in quick detachable Mauser mounts. Barrel mikes 0.228 inches, No. 1768, K.M.G.-N 51 gr. proof marks, and the name "J. G. Auchotz." Twist of rifling, is one turn in 9.2 inches.

5. (F. Murray Leyde). Shotgun type action Frederich Friebel, Suhl, barrel and stock by Franz Kopka of Muelhausen, Thuringia. Bore is 0.228 inch with 3-groove rifling, and a twist of one turn in 15 inches. This is chambered for the rimmed version of the 5.6 m.m. Mr. Leyde has used .40-85 Ballard cases for reforming to rimmed 5.6 x 61 m.m. Mauser.

6. Shotgun type action by J. P. Sauer and Sons, with Carl Zeiss scope. The owner sent samples of cases made by cutting off .30-1906 brass and pressing over .30-40 cases cut off to about one inch. He did not say he had fired the cases, however.

One enterprising correspondent had picked up a 5.6 x 61 barrel off the floor at a well-known gunsmith's shop. The barrel is 24 inches long, heavy breech tapering down to exactly the size of the head of a .30-1906 cartridge case. It is marked 5.6 x 61, has Suhl proof marks, and is stamped "E. H.," which may stand for Ernst Vom Hofe. The barrel was fitted to a Czech Mauser action. He blew his cases with 25.0 grains of 4198 and 63-grain Sisk bullets, 0.226 inch in diameter; and used a proof load of 50.0 grains of 4198 and the same bullets. This blew brass into the extractor out of the bolt, the head spread, and the primer pocket enlarged.

Some original German ammunition would be very interesting, provided of course we had enough to play around with, and determine velocity and its accuracy. The Rottweil No. 1 powder is an interesting item. It is used in a wide variety of German cartridges, from 6.5 x 52 m.m. to the 8 x 75 m.m., and usually with heavy bullets. Mr. F. Murray Leyde, in a very informative letter, mentions a book, The Modern Rifle,* with which I am unfamiliar. The book is a small, red cloth-bound volume of very practical ballistic data and formulas.

I had expressed the hope of obtaining 3650 f.p.s. with a suitable 70-grain bullet and 54.0 grains of 4350 powder. I quote

*Vol. I, "Practical Exterior Ballistics," Bevis & Donovan.

from Mr. Leyde's letter. ". . .these authors offer several formulas together with examples, which, if correct, can be worked by a person of average intelligence and technical learning, to figure out various interesting results. Referring to your load of 50.0 grains of 4350 and the 70-grain bullet, at a velocity of 3400 f.p.s., the calculated mid-range trajectory over 300 yards range should be slightly less than 3 inches, this bettering the .220 Swift loads over the same range and with a materially flatter trajectory between 200 and 300 yards and with considerable added energy due to the heavier 70-grain bullet. . . . . referring to your hope of obtaining 3650 f.p.s. with 77-grain bullet and 54.0 grains of 4350: using their formula for necessary increase of powder it figures out to require an additional 5.8 plus grains of propellent to gain the additional 250 f.p.s. above the present 3400 f.p.s. and this with the present 70-grain bullet. This of course, is not considering the rapid increase in pressures, which is inevitable."

So, while we are working on the bullet problem, accurate and effective loads are available for use at ordinary long ranges on woodchucks, and amid the varied conditions as we find them in the Middle Atlantic States.

TABLE I

Measurements of 5.6 x 61 m.m. Vom Hofe Super Express

Original	Rim	Base Ahead of Rim	Shoulder	Neck Base	Mouth	Length Neck	Length Shoulder	O.A. Length
1. Rimless								
	0.478"	0.477"	0.456"	0.260"	0.257"	0.325"	0.332"	2.395"
From 30-1906 case	0.4707"	0.4795"	0.459"		0.262"			2.352"
Chamber Cast		0.482"	0.459"		0.267"			
2. Rimmed								
From .40-85 Ballard case	0.541"	0.480"	0.461"			0.275"	0.266"	2.399"

TABLE II

Loads for the 5.6 x 61 m.m. Vom Hofe Super Express

Powder	Charge	Bullet	Velocity	Remarks
R.I	54.0 gr.	77-gr.	3,600 (3,700?)	D.W.M. (Rimless)
R I	50.9 gr.	77-gr.	3,280 f.p.s.	D.W.M. (Rimmed)
4064	35.0 gr.	70 Western	2,856	Accurate load
4350	40.0 gr.	70 Western	2,751	
4350	45.0 gr.	70 Western	3,046	
4350	50.0 gr.	70 Western	3,374	Cold weather load
4064	35.0 gr.	63 Sisk		Accurate load
4759	20.0 gr.	63 Sisk		Accurate load
3031	35.0 gr.	55 Sisk		Not accurate
4065	35.0 gr.	65 R.C.B.S.		Accurate load
4064	35.0 gr.	75 Speer		No good
4064	40.0 gr.	75 Speer		"
4350	50.0 gr.	75 Speer		"
4350	50.0 gr.	78 Sisk		"

WOODCHUCK SHOOTING DURING 1948 AND 1949

Two woodchuck seasons have passed since the first portion of this manuscript was written. There have been many pleasant days spent in the chuck fields and on the target range in the meantime.

My first woodchuck was shot near Bound Brook, New Jersey with an old Remington slide action .22 rim-fire, and ordinary .22 long rifle cartridge. The rear sight on this weapon was loose and could be moved back and forth at least an inch, so that it was necessary to bracket the chuck to right and left, as he sat up seemingly almost as big as a bear. He sat there until the third shot caught him squarely in the center of the chest and he ran a good 50 steps before collapsing. My second chuck was shot with a .32 Special and from there I progressed to the Savage Model 219 Hornet and a Lyman 5-A scope. This was the outfit I used some five or six years ago, with another hunter who was using a .25-35 Krag Special, firing 29.5 grains of 3031 and the 100-grain Western openpoint bullet. As recollected now, we bagged about nine chucks apiece that day, and most of the shots were at 60 to 125 yards, firing from the offhand or sitting position.

The .25-35 was a revelation to me. It was a very deadly rifle up to 250 yards; beyond that, at unknown ranges, the trajectory was too high to insure certain kills. It had the 1898 Krag action and it also had a 26-inch Winchester barrel fitted and chambered by R. F. Sedgley, using a reamer made by J. G. Schnerring. The case was somewhat larger than the regular .25-35, and had a sharp shoulder with an almost straight-sided body. Herman Treptow of Milltown, New Jersey did the stockwork.

With a Lyman Junior Targetspot of 10X it weighed 10 pounds, 11 ounces, according to the old notebook now here before me. During the season of 1943, the only one of which complete records were kept, 143 chucks were taken with this outfit and 90 shots missed, an excellent record for almost any hunter. The average distance was about 125 yards. Its owner thought very highly of this rifle until he was placed in a position where chucks were in view around an arc of perhaps 275°, but they were all at ranges between 300 to 500 yards. The .25-35 was completely outclassed that day, and in 14 shots, all the cartridges he carried in the belt, only two chucks were killed. One, it must be admitted was at 430 yards, but it was the fourth shot at the woodchuck. The others had been observed with the glasses and sight correction made accordingly. The .25-35 was just outclassed under those conditions. The .25 Remington shone that day, using 100-grain Barnes bullets, and bagged three or four at ranges of 300 yards. The .25 Remington is an excellent little cartridge, vastly underrated by the big-boom boys.

Mr. C. H. Bean is the dean of the chuck hunters in this vicinity. He used to fire in the Schuetzen matches in the Middle West at the turn of the century, and is still a tireless and inveterate chuck hunter. One of his favorite rifles is a Winchester hi-side, originally bought about 1905 in .22 short, later rebored to .25 by Hubalek, and then chambered for the .25-20 single shot cartridge, with which he did much damage on groundhogs. It finally wound up as a .25-35 and with its worn-out barrel and 16-inch pitch of rifling, it still did a lot of fine shooting. As I remember, Mr. Bean used the 60-grain .25-caliber bullet and in excess of 30.0 grains of 3031. He speaks highly of a .32-20 Merwin & Hulbert falling block rifle, and has a .22-3000 R-2 Lovell in the Model 54 Winchester which works very nicely too.

The Savage 219 .22 Hornet worked out fairly well, although some disdained it at first. One shot in particular showed con-

vincingly that it had possibilities. This occurred one afternoon when chucks were not showing, and a black and white animal, the species that yells ''Meow'' appeared in an alfalfa field
half a mile from any house obviously hunting small game or
birds. The shot was squeezed off from the sitting position, and
was a hit at a distance of 219 yards when paced later. It failed
to anchor chucks at longer distances, and was used only until
something better could be had.

Shortly after this I obtained a .25-35 Winchester single shot
in new condition from the late Albert Foster, of Colts. Although
it was the take-down style, with the 117-grain factory ammunition, this proved to be a very accurate rifle, using a Fecker
10X scope. One day we obtained three successive kills at 300
yards. Usually however, that high-arching trajectory caused
trouble and the danger from ricochets was always present. Some
reformed 87-grain soft points in reloads worked very well, and
certainly laid out the chucks.

As new rifles came out after the war, the Winchester Model
70-caliber .250-3000 in the standard barrel, Marksman stock
type was tried and it was soon demonstrated that this is very
nearly an ideal chuck rifle. A few 87-grain original Newton bullets turned up. This is one of the most perfectly designed bullets
ever made. In the Weschnitzer bullet spinner no trace of wobble
appeared. With a fairly heavy load of 3031, the performance was
amazing. Apparently Barnes bullets, pre-war, were modeled
on similar lines, and eventually Huntington made an R.C.B.S.
die for producing this type of bullet. In 80-grain weight it became a high class varmint bullet, and in 90-and 100-grain
weights a target bullet of phenomenal accuracy. In a .250-3000
Bull Gun, with Sukalle barrel, chambered by Marciante, this
bullet (80 grs. wt.) was tried in the fall of 1949. The first five-
shot group from the new rifle fired at 100 yards, was 3/4 inch
center to center, and the second was 5/8 inch center to center.

While we are on the subject of bench-rest shooting, the .219
Donaldson cannot be overlooked. One of the original ''guaranteed'' outfits by Morgan and Cail was given a trial and the
groups that rifle would shoot were unbelievable. It was a heavy
piece, ''Old Rupture'' being the best term for it. In the first
700 shots, including blowing out of cases by fire-forming, the
average of the ten shop groups was well under an inch in diameter, all fired at 100 yards from bench rest. The first time I
fired the gun, the group was 11/16 inch center to center (ten

shots). In another demonstration, one shooter fired five shots and then another fired five shots, and the total group of ten shots was less than 3/4 inch center to center. The arm was too heavy to use conveniently as a chuck rifle, but from a stand where a lot of territory could be covered without moving, it was superb.

My experiences with the 5.6 x 61 m.m. have been detailed at considerable length, possibly because the data was kept and experiments documented better.

The .220 Swift now appears on the scene in the form of a rifle which we tried out a few years back. I witnessed a shot on a half-grown chuck through the head at 225 yards, from the off-hand position, and several other spectacular shots which were made that indicated at least some of the things said about it were true. With a load of 36.0 grains of 4320 and a 55-grain R.C.B.S. bullet it performed very well. For most of one season I carried along the Swift and the 5.6 x 61 m.m. in the car, but when obtaining good bullets for the latter became a problem, the Swift was used more and more. With the 15X Lyman Super Targetspot it makes an outfit that can hold its own in the chuck field, and when compared with the .30-1906, .257, .250-3000, .22 Varminter and such, the chap with the Swift does not need to feel undergunned. A lot of remarks have been made about the difficulty of loading for the Swift, but I have never experienced these troubles as long as ordinary precautions were observed.

A recent article on reloading for this caliber states the case very well, and comes to the same conclusion I did, —the Swift is a fine cartridge. Using standard factory cartridges has its advantages from a financial and convenience angle, and this is no exception.

Early in the summer, after the first crop of hay is cut, the chucks are naive and don't know what the crack of a bullet means. That is the time for those hunts where the party as a group reports 15 to 20 kills and an unspecified number of miss-es. They are vague on distances, too. After a week or two of heavy shooting, the little animals which are left get wise and take cover more quickly. Perhaps the hot weather may have something to do with it too, as they appear less frequently. This midsummer hunting is the time to select a spot under a tree or hedgerow, in the shade, with a jug of ice water and just relax. The binoculars come in handy then; these 8 x 56 and 6 x 30 Army and 7 x 50 Navy war surplus items are very useful. One man snoozes while the other watches lazily. As the sun goes down the chucks come out a little more frequently, with the best hunting in the hour before dusk. The average hunt, in my area, will afford ten or twelve shots in an afternoon.

In September, the chucks that have survived are fat and smart and then offer good sport. Stalking plays its part now, as a sudden move can send the fat rascals waddling home, with the sun glistening and glinting on the fur over the ripples of fat. For a time we used to weigh all the kills after stepping off the distance. The largest may run 14 to 18 pounds in New Jersey, but the average is more like 6 to 8 pounds. There is an unverified report of one that weighed 24 pounds, taken last year, but this is the exception. The best hunts of the year come late in August and September when after a few days rain, the sun comes out, the weather is neither too warm nor too cool,——maybe a bit on the cool side——and every chuck in the countryside comes up for a last meal of clover or alfalfa before settling down for the long winter sleep.

It was on such a day that the last hunt of the past season occurred. It was a memorable hunt. We went to a farm which one fellow insisted was shot out because he and others had worked it over thoroughly a few days earlier and had found nothing. Incidentally, earlier in the year I had taken twelve from one field there myself. However, it seemed unlikely that the farm had been ''shot out'' since to my knowledge two or three hunters had taken 25 to 50 chucks apiece there each season for several years past.

So, over some protestations, we went on. From the barnyard, on glancing around with the 8 x 56 binoculars, five chucks could be seen out feeding. I started the day right by missing the first shot at 250 yards, and one companion missed a chuck at 180 yards. Another hunter then knocked one over at 90 yards. I was using the .220 Swift, the others .250-3000's. We moved to the river-bottom field, and counted four or five chucks feeding. It would be boring to recount every shot because we obtained thirteen shots apiece, or 39 in all, that day.

My kills were at ranges of 150 yards to 425 yards, and three were more than 300 yards distant. One fellow got two that were over 400 yards, both by the range finder and by pacing. The range finder was the ''Wild,'' Swiss-made, and a useful, lightweight gadget with an accuracy approximating plus or minus 5 per cent. The wind was blowing a gale and most of the shots were across the wind. At 400 yards the Swift was off about 5 inches, the .250 about 3 inches. But that made little difference once the amount of "Kentucky" windage had been determined. One chuck bore a charmed life. In every locality there are one or two that do. At 375 yards this one kept coming out to get that alfalfa, and the next shot would send him scampering and diving for his hole. He must have had five or six shots fired at him, and to the best of my knowledge is still alive, well fed and happy, and probably looking around for someone else to come out and defy. Of course this is like teasing the neighbor's dog or the lion at Ringling's. The thing is eventually tried once too often!

The load used was 39.0 grains of 4064 and the 55-grain Sisk Express while the two other hunters were using 80-grain .25-caliber bullets and 38.0 grains of 3031. One shot in particular tickled me immensely. One of the other fellows usually got 70 to 80 per cent of his shots; but on this day he had forgotten to clean the oil out of the rifle before he left home. As we had no cleaning rod in the car, there was no choice but to shoot it out. He missed his first four or five shots clean. On one of these, an easy shot at about 300 yards, he fired and the bullet kicked up dust in the plowed field beyond. A short time later the chuck stood up again and I took the shot. There was no puff of dust beyond but both boys in the gallery assured me it was a miss. At the end of the hunt we walked down and found a nice chuck, with a bullet through his chest. So I made the shot after all. This was one of the few times I was able to best that fellow at this game. It was a crisp cold day, and every chuck on the place must have been out. Total for the day, five for each of the others, six for me.

My Swift rifle is unnecessarily heavy and for those hot days when a lot of walking is in prospect, I have a .257 Roberts on a Springfield action; it is short and light, with a Weaver K-6 scope. This is a neat outfit, and with 40.0 grains of 4064 and an 87-grain bullet, works very well. There is another Sukalie .257 Springfield in the club that is highly regarded, and some acquaintances use .257 Winchester Model 70 Target rifles successfully. The long range load there is the 117-grain bullet and 49.0 grains of 4350. My rifle is limited to 100-grain bullets as a maximum because it is bored with a 14-inch pitch of rifling.

Just for the record it does not pay to disregard the old timers, shooters or rifles. One lucky boy was presented with a Krag military rifle in perfect condition, and when fitted with a Lyman Junior Targetspot 10X, and charged with a 110-grain spirepoint Speer bullet ahead of 42.0 grains of 3031, it is a very accurate and deadly outfit. The owner is an excellent field shot, particularly from offhand or kneeling positions and when that old cannon roars it sure does lay out the chucks.

There is no reason why the .30-1906 should not work as well, and with many D.C.M. Springfields around, the trial will surely be made. These .30-calibers are not much more noisy than the .220, .257, or 250-3000 so it seems to some: on the other hand the .30-1906 burns up to 15 to 17 grains more of powder per charge than some of the other larger-case cartridges of smaller caliber many of which use 28 to 35 grains. This of course definitely produces a greater volume of sound but not always of as high pitch. The big difficulty with the .30-1906 sporters on chucks is that most of the 150-and 180-grain hunting bullets for this caliber have been designed to expand on game animals weighing 130 to 800 pounds, and in some instances, 50 per cent more than that; they cannot therefore, be expected to expand immediately on a 5 to 12 pound woodchuck. The .30-1906 must use a higher velocity, softer jacket, softer core, and softer point bullet than the big game bullets, when used extensively for woodchucks.

In closing, I'd like to say just a word of explanation about the eastern preoccupation with chuck hunting which occasionally draws some whistling and wise-cracks from our western friends. Over most of the East the big game is pretty well shot off, regardless of all the ballyhoo by game departments and their officials to the contrary.

The sport of chuck hunting has an advantage in that it is more leisurely. It is a more scientific type of rifle shooting than most big game hunting, for instance, and it requires more skill and a higher degree of precision of man and rifle. It occupies the off season when the weather is more reasonable and also, most times, more comfortable and the season lasts for months, not ten days or two weeks.

Also, at the time, the hunting grounds are less crowded with trigger-happy nomads from the urban districts who in some cases seem to be out for the day with a grim determination to kill something. Sometimes the first thing that moves. Apparently some fire with little regard to proper identification of their targets.

I hope woodchuck shooting stays as it is, a sport for the technical man and the rifle specialist. In New Jersey the ground-hog is the only game which can be taken legally with a rifle, and reader, you don't realize how much real pleasure it is to be allowed to use a rifle in the field, even on varmints, until you have lived under such restrictions. I was brought up in a state where there was more freedom permitted a rifleman and in Jersey only the chuck hunter has it.

CHAPTER 10

Phil Wismer Discusses Cartridges and Loads

M R. PHILIP WISMER, SR., of Jordan Station, Ontario, with whom I have hunted on a number of occasions, is one of the most experienced and successful chuck hunters in Canada.

Well up from the apple, peach, vineyard and tobacco regions of Ontario, the Wismer car is a familiar and welcome sight to dozens and dozens of farmers whose hay fields have been plagued and sometimes even made unprofitable to farm by the presence of considerable colonies of Marmota Monax. There are often 20 to 30 dens within a small area which have been scattered throughout these farms for generations.

Phil is one of those generous souls who thinks nothing of driving 150 to 200 miles to pick up a friend and take both him and his host for chucks; as they drive along they may stop for another rifleman or two. Phil has a great preference for driving on back roads, which parallel the main King's highways which are numbered on the road signs and from which you cannot legally shoot at woodchucks. Also, as they drive along, Phil's enthusiasm soon reaches the boiling point; everyone is busy talking; all are too busy propounding this theory or that one, as it concerns woodchuck rifles, cartridges, loads or shooting procedure, to listen too much to each other, and it is a fact that Phil drives FAST, in earnest, and is determined to arrive as soon as possible at that happy hunting ground in which he promises the visitors with much earnestness, that they will be shown at least 100 shots that day. Of course he does not have time, as he buzzes along, to stop to let the visitors shoot at any one, two or three chucks which may be seen now and then feeding out in a pasture 50 to 150 yards from the highway. No sir, the woodchuck hunters are on their way to the REAL hunting grounds for woodchucks, and anyone who becomes impatient and indignant and demands the opportunity to get out and stretch his legs and let off a shot or two, receives no more definite consideration than a chap about to be hanged. After all, the ride is merely something to be gotten over in the shortest possible time, and if the chap who is to be hanged, or the man who is going woodchuck hunting becomes impatient and insists upon having his say, he is talked down by people who have more important things to discuss, such as getting "100 shots in a day."

If you think this, in a sense of humor, a bit overdone, you ought to go on one of those woodchuck excursions with Phil Wismer. You will soon discover that the most important matter before the house is covering space to the extent of about 150 or 200 miles, with your enthusiasm for chuck shooting at fever heat at the exact moment you arrive on the edge of the long promised hunting grounds where woodchucks are supposed to be thicker than flies at a bartenders' picnic.

If you don't get shots at 100 woodchucks —— or more that day, well, it was just one of those things and the profuse explanations and apologies are such that you are soon convinced that at least Phil believes that 100 shots are to be had at chucks in a day —— weather, season, grass, temperature, rain and whatnot, all being favorable. If not, then you may obtain good chances at ten, twenty or thirty woodchucks, which to you will seem like a chuck hunter's dream of heaven, but which to Phil will be announced as a most disappointing day indeed and something which will have to be explained and apologized for during most of the drive home. Consequently, on both the drive north and the trip back there is rarely a dull moment and certainly not a silent one.

An orchardist, who has half a dozen or a dozen men to oversee, and tens of thousands of bushels of apples, peaches, pears and plums to market during the season, has a few other things to do besides pound a typewriter or wear out a ball-point pen, and consequently Mr. Wismer has condensed into a few pages, the results of thousands of shots and the "whizzing" of more than ten thousand chuck tails. The recommendations he has given below are based on extensive experience covering a territory which is much larger than the one in which many do most of their woodchuck shooting.

Probably no one in Canada is more experienced in shooting woodchucks at really long range. He is not particularly saving of ammunition and he uses a 12-pound rifle. Very definitely Phil Wismer LIVES to shoot woodchucks. All other matters are relative and, while on a chuck hunt, comparatively unimportant.

One hundred shots in a day and no fooling. The wide open spaces of Canada are before you. It is May, the grass is still short, you can SEE a chuck at an ungodly distance and he is usually out feeding with little attention or thought to death or taxes. You haven't seen a cop in fifty miles, and not over four or five farmers. The land is not posted, and when you climb up on a fence rail to rest, you look down, and there are twenty or twenty-five dens within fifty yards, and ten or twenty within thirty feet.

Of course, things are not quite perfect. Your tail feathers have been ruffled and your back acre bruised by 100 miles of fast driving on water-bound macadam, and your middle feels like nine hours since breakfast, because whatever had been there, four hours before, has been well shaken down. Maybe you have a bit of a headache and are just a trifle dizzy. You wonder how loud your rifle will crack in that distance and how soon it will be until you obtain your first shot — meantime you think it was all a crazy idea that you drove past ten or fifteen or twenty easy shots on the way up. So we will let you sit there and mull it all over, while brother Wismer gives us a few of his conclusions.

Phil's idea of the matter is about 125 shots over the next few hours with a rifle that will group rather consistently within less than 1-1/2 inches at 200 yards. He has it sighted for 350! Chucks are commonplace to Mr. Wismer and he likes to make the shooting difficult.

PHILIP WISMER'S PERSONAL COMMENTS

I have now had the .22-303 a sufficient length of time to enable me to form an opinion of its merits in comparison with other woodchuck rifles I have used.

Although I have killed many thousands of chucks with the Hornet and K-Hornet, I was never completely satisfied with their performance. Even with peak loads, neither was a humane killer at much over 150 yards, and there were too many ricochets both on misses and head shots.

I finally settled on a load of 12.8 grains 2400 behind the Remington 46-grain h.p. bullet and confined myself to chest shots. This load was accurate and killed quickly up to between 175 and 200 yards. This rifle as a Hornet and then a K-Hornet killed 4500 chucks and many crows and jack rabbits during the ten years I used it (I averaged about 700 chucks per season for many years).

I used the R-2 Lovell in a good C. C. Johnson barrel for one season, but could not see enough improvement over the K-Hornet to warrant the many undesirable features I found on it. Its sure killing range was hardly more than 25 yards over the K-Hornet. If I had my choice of the two, I would take the K-Hornet, although the R-2 is slightly more accurate.

I have killed 500 chucks with the .22-303 Varmint-R, ninety per cent being taken over 200 yards, two over 500 yards, the average being 250 to 350 yards (the chuck sat up as I fired), the other, a head shot at about 175 yards, took the nose off from the eyes forward. These two died in a few seconds. Shots on chucks up to 250 yards are ridiculously easy. In some districts the shots over this range have to be taken from a slight elevation or prone through one or two wide fences, and most land-owners don't thank you when you happen to cut a wire on their brand new fence. Also, I am not too sure about the ricochet question on shots at the extreme ranges.

THE .22-303 ON CROWS

This rifle has been phenomenal in the number of hits on crows at the longer ranges. Two hundred and twenty-five yards down the road and 140 paces to the right, in the bush, plus the angular distance to the top of a tall beech tree, is a dead limb from which I have taken eleven consecutive crows. When you take into consideration the fact of the first shot from a cold clean barrel spread over ten months, April to January, it speaks well for the part I am most interested in — the first shot.

During the past season, I had a life-sized image of a crow set up 225 yards from my house. I always fired one shot at this target for checking before going on a crow shoot.

During the season of 1947, I fired 23 shots, some prone, some from a slight elevation with rest, all shots were in a group of 3-1/4 inches, 22 being in 2-3/4 inches.

PRONE SIGHTING FOR CROWS

I always sight my rifle so that I can hold on, or nearly on, at the longer ranges at which I intend to take my shots. This makes the point of impact quite high at 100 yards but does not worry me as I proved to myself long ago that I can estimate range and hold under more accurately at the shorter distances and, with exception of crows, I very seldom take a shot under 200 yards.

Not being a competitive target shooter, I do all my practice shooting at life-size images of crow and chuck. With my present loading of 36 grains 4320, and 49-grain Sisk express, also 50-grain Speer bullet, which is not quite as accurate, but opens up slightly better on chucks at ranges over 300 yards, I have my rifle sighted to hit just above the 3/4 minute dot at 200 yards and just below the dot at 300 yards.

Thus, if the reticule covers approximately one third of a crow, the range is 200 yards, and the bullet will strike just above; if the dot covers one half of crow, the range is 300 yards, and the bullet will strike just below the dot.

Constant practice at images cut out of black or dark brown cardboard will give you a mental picture of the reticule in relation to life-sized targets at the various ranges which I will guarantee will make one an extremely deadly long-range varmint shot.

Of course, other things enter into the picture, i.e. wind-drift, different kinds of rests taken in the field, all of which can be tried out at home and memorized. Some days, under certain light conditions, chucks stand out very clearly, seemingly much larger through the scope. Unless the ranges are checked very carefully, i.e., known width of fields, fence panels, etc., ranges will be greatly underestimated.

In summing up, I would say cartridges having 3500 to 3700 f.s. muzzle velocity in an accurate rifle make short range chuck shooting so easy as to spoil the sporting part of it.

THE .170 FOR CROWS

The .170 may be the answer to many of our problems. It should be good out to 250 or 300 yards, makes much less noise, which noise, I believe, is going to get us varmint shooters in trouble in southern Ontario.

While I am well satisfied with my present rifle, the .22-303, I am having Charles Parkinson of London, Ontario, make up his version of the .170 for me, using the 30-grain Sisk bullet or the 35-grain if Sisk decides to manufacture it. The .170 might possibly take the place of the K-Hornet, R-2, etc., eliminating the few faults of those good cartridges.

There has been considerable agitation to the Department of

Lands and Forests to have the center fire rifles barred in southern Ontario. I do not think this is coming from the farmer. Last fall I spent a day in my hunting territory and the only complaint I received was "You don't come around as often as you used to." This would be sad, leaving only the .22 rim-fire, which is probably the worst offender in the matter of ricochets, especially when in the hands of irresponsbile persons, which it usually is.

Readers might be interested in some of the five-shot 200 yard groups I have been working up for the bench-rest shooting coming up this summer (1948). Western 8-1/2 primers are used in all loads, 34 grains 3031 49-grain Sisk Express 1-1/2 inch, 4 shots in each group in 1 inch.

33-1/2 grs. — 3031, — 55-gr. Sisk Express 1-1/8 inches, 1-3/4 inches, 1-1/2 inches, 27/32 inch.

34 grs. — 3031, — 55-gr. Sisk Express 1-1/2 inches, 1-5/8 inches, 1-3/8 inches, open center gr.

34 grs. — 3031, — 50-gr. W.M.8S 1-1/2 inches, 1-7/16 inches - four shots in this group touching.

34 grs. — 4320 — 50-gr. W.M.8S 2-1/2 inches, some vertical stringing.

34 grs. — 4320 — 55-gr. Sisk E. 1-3/4 inches, 1-7/8 inches three in one hole.

33-1/2 grs. — 3031 — 49 Sisk E 1-5/8 inches, 1-3/8 inches.

3031 is more accurate if charges are weighed and if you don't exceed 34 grains.

35-36 grains 4320 makes an excellent field load and when thrown through an Ideal powder measure, it will give very close to a 2-inch average accuracy at 200 yards.

WOODCHUCK RIFLES AND SIGHTING

The comments in this section were made in a letter to Mr. D. P. Noel, of Philadelphia, Pennsylvania:

I want to thank you for the primers and bullets — I had just finished the 50-grain Sisk bullets on Saturday, August 19, as I was then hunting with my brother in the area where you, Landis and I went on the last day we were together in 1947.

About 5:30 p.m. on August 19, I made 26 shots in the two fields without moving from one shooting position. I made 24 hits in the 26 shots, at ranges of 150 to 300 yards. I was using my .303 heavy single shot Winchester hi-side necked to .22-303 Crandall Varmint-R by G. B. Crandall of Woodstock, Ontario, the rifle you shot some the first of the last week you were up here.

My brother took the shots closer than 150 yards, using his K-Hornet, making 23 kills in the same two fields. We then moved on to the hills — you will recall where you took a long shot at a chuck in the mouth of its den using your target weight Swift.

On this recent trip I parked myself on a light ridge and took 19 shots over a lower ridge having a lesser elevation, and shot onto a third ridge which was higher than the intermediate rise of ground. I hope you understand this.

The sun was behind me, the chucks stuck out on that hillside like a sore thumb. I estimated the range at 350- to 375 yards and proceeded to miss them nearly every shot. When the war was over, I had 7 kills lying on that hillside. My brother and I then did a little stepping off and found the approximate range to be at least 400- to 475 yards. Now you tell me how I hit seven with a three hundred and fifty yard hold.*

1948 TESTS OF THE .170 WOODSMAN CARTRIDGE

IN A WINCHESTER H. S. SINGLE SHOT RIFLE

I am listing herewith all of the loads tried at my rifle range here at home, and am making comments concerning each of them. All groups were made at 200 yards. I was using Winchester No. 116 primers. The Donaldson primers seat very tightly in the Griffin & Howe R-2 necked down cases.

Loads Tested:

25 grains Sisk soft point bullet: These are used in all loads mentioned until the 30-grain bullets which are listed farther along in the tests.

12.0 grains of DuPont 4227: Groups at 200 yards strung up and down into 6-inch verticals.

---

*Author's Note: The low shots, the low bad pulls are usually out between 5 and 7 o'clock, for a right handed shooter, also, the size in a vertical direction of a large chuck sitting up, permits hits at other than the exact distance — in fact permits hits when firing with an astonishing error of sighting. About the last of August, 1947, I shot a 9-3/4 pound woodchuck which was abnormally squat and fat in appearance when dead, but which stretched up to an apparent height of three to four feet, and a width of only four to six inches, when viewed through a dense poison ivy tangle. This chuck was shot offhand, directly through the heart, at a range of but 30 or 40 yards. It was impossible to see it at a greater distance, and I could not have backed away anyhow without it immediately going into the burrow in front of which it was sitting watching.

12.5 grains of 4227: Vertical stringing and cases show some pressure.

16.0 grains of DuPont No. 3031: This is a very good load. Average groups at 200 yards are 2-1/2 to 2-3/4 inches.

16.5 grains of No. 3031: This is the best load with this powder, but it is a charge which is very tedious to load as the powder has to be tapped into each case, even with the long drop tube. Load shows some pressure.

15.5 grains of 4320: Gives some slight traces of vertical stringing. Average groups with this load are 3-1/2 to 4 inches at 200 yards.

16.0 grains of DuPont No. 4320: Shoots better than previous charge. Not as good as 3031. Average groups are 3-1/4 to 3-1/2 inches at 200 yards.

13.8 grains of 4198: High pressures developed. Bullets go to pieces on hair on shoulder shots on woodchucks. Kills well on shots over 150 yards or if the bullet is placed behind the shoulder. Case life short. Average accuracy is 2-1/2 inches to 2-1/4 inches at 200 yards.

13.5 grains of DuPont No. 4198: Bullets break up badly and still show pressures. Average group is 2-3/4 inches. Case life short.*

13.0 grains of 4198: This makes a very good-killing load. Average group at 200 yards was 3 to 3-1/2 inches. Moderate pressures shown.

11.5 — 12.0 grains of English Kynoch powder: This English leaf powder is very good (and is commonly imported into and sold in Canada). This charge kills well on woodchucks up to 200 yards if the bullet points are filed slightly. Average accuracy is 2-1/2 to 3 inches at 200 yards.

LOADS WITH 30-GRAIN SISK BULLETS

16.0 grains of 3031: Very good load. Kills well on woodchucks. Average accuracy at 200 yards is 2-3/4- to 3-inch groups. Some signs of pressures.

*Author's Note: In my opinion the velocity got up to the point with this relatively fine grain powder, that the bullet was breaking up too quickly when it struck the woodchuck over a bony or hard portion of its body. The higher pressure would make more heat and tend to soften the core of the bullet to a greater degree, hence cause it to break up or spread more easily, and more quickly nearer the surface or on the surface of the animal. I have never had this happen so far, when shooting woodchucks with the .170.

16.5 grains of 3031: Good long range loading for woodchucks. Average accuracy is 2-3/4 to 3 inch groups at 200 yards. Pressures shown. Case life is short. Loading of this charge is tedious.

15.8 grains of 3031: This is a good load. Probably the best but still tedious loading. Average accuracy is 2-3/4 inches at 200 yards.

15.5 grains of 3031: A fair load. Begins to show signs of vertical stringing. This powder has to be compressed for best results in this small cartridge.

16.0 grains of 4320: Very good accuracy and killing power. Cases show some pressure. Groups are 2-3/4 to 3 inches at 200 yards. Thirty-grain .170 bullets are not as accurate as 25-grain bullets. Workmanship on the 30-grain bullets was not as satisfactory.

15.5 grains of DuPont No. 4320: This is the best loading with this powder and with this bullet. Average accuracy 2-3/4 inches at 200 yards. This is the load that I would use for the longer shots on woodchucks.

13.5 grains of DuPont No. 4198: A very hot load. Pressures indicated.

13.0 grains of 4198: A very good-killing load. Accuracy is good. Shows some evidences of pressure. Case life rather short.

11.5 grains of British Kynoch: This is the load I am now using, and the accuracy is very nearly as good, 2-1/2 to 2-3/4 inches at 200 yards, as with 3031 or 4320. Point of impact at 200 yards is one inch lower. Pressures are mild. Kills very satisfactorily up to 200 yards. I have not tried 12.0 grains of Kynoch with the 30-grain bullet but feel certain it would be satisfactory.

15.5 grains of U.S.G. 4895: Good accuracy. Have not tried it in the field. Point of impact same as with 4320 and 3031.

In my opinion, the .170 Woodsman is not a long range, humane chuck caliber. What makes one inclined to take shots at too great a distance with it, is the ease with which you can hit on the long shots.

Strange to say, I have had better results with 25-grain bullets at extreme ranges; have made kills up to 400 yards on facing shots, which is all I take with it, at the longer ranges. I now try to refuse all shots over 200 yards when using the .170 Woodsman with the Kynoch loading. On the last trip I had 34 hits in 37 shots, — only two chucks moved after being hit.

I had my .22-303 Crandall Varmint-R along but only fired seven shots with it. This is the only time I have taken it along, so you can see I have fallen in love with the little Woodsman.

The brass in the majority of cases put out by G. & H. (and made up for them by Winchester) seems very soft and I don't believe any loads tried are in the dangerous bracket, even if they do show pressure indications in some cases. I have used several cases ten or more times with the loss of only two cases, which cracked but did not separate above the web. Only a few of the frequently fired cases accept the Dominion No. 1-1/2 primers. Those which did accept the Dominion primers of No. 1-1/2 size, were those fired with 13.8 grains of 4198.

If you file the points of the 25-grain bullets, they kill very satisfactorily with the milder loads, with about the same accuracy. I hollow-pointed several with a very fine drill; these were deadly on chucks and exploded crows in a cloud of feathers.

While the .170 may be a bit light on woodchucks, especially at very long range, it sure is one grand crow rifle, even though accuracy today, with present bullets, is not quite all one would desire. I feel sure this is due to the bullets.

I still seem to make long runs of hits on crows and on chucks, and you don't get too close to the black devils, not in my section, at least.

It — the .170 Woodsman — never fails to kill cleanly on jackrabbits and skunks. I also have taken several large hawks and one owl. I do not condone too much shooting of hawks and owls, — the types we have here — but just tried the .170 in the interests of science. With reduced loads and the 25-grain bullet, the rifle should also make a very nice squirrel rifle.

AUTHOR'S NOTE: The .170 Woodsman — R-2 cartridge necked down — was designed not as a long range woodchuck cartridge, but as a medium cartridge of no ricochets and very low report for settled district shooting. One which could be used safely almost anywhere, because it would not supposedly kick up enough fuss to have the rifleman chased out.

For Philip Wismer's long range Ontario shooting, which the author shared with him in 1946, 1947 and 1948, a .170 cartridge made by necking down the .219 Zipper, the .22 Savage Hi-Power, or the .25-35 case, would produce much greater power and longer range, probably 100 to 150 yards longer effective range for hi-side single shot Winchester, and similar actions. For the Mauser, Springfield and Enfield actions, the .22-250 or

.250-3000 Savage cases are the ones to neck down. A charge about the same as that used for the .219 Donaldson or the Lovell, No. 7 cartridge, should work splendidly. Charges therefore of 29 to 33 grains of 3031 or 4320, would be the ones to try. It is assumed that Sisk's .170 bullets made with soft points in 25- and 30-grain weights, would stand the pressures and velocities developed.

If not, or if the bullets were found too quick in expanding at the higher velocities, then either the jacket material would have to be thicker — which would reduce the sectional density and specific gravity of the bullet (a thicker jacket would necessitate a lead core of smaller diameter), or the bullet core would need to be made of a harder alloy. In other words, it would need to contain a higher proportion of antimony, which is of much lower specific gravity than lead — it weighs less for the same bulk.

However, there is no real reason why harder and tougher bullets could not be produced commercially which would be accurate if they are really needed.

The .219 Donaldson cartridge necked down to .170 with a good long neck to prevent the hot powder gases from striking the walls of the barrel just opposite where they originate in the case, would make a fine .170 cartridge, for it is about the right length and capacity, but it looks a little too much bottle necked to me, which would probably result in very high pressures when necked down still further from .22 caliber to .170 caliber. It would have a suitable powder capacity when so necked down and cut off. However, they have quite a few operations on this case in shortening it to 1-1/4 inches as it is in .22 caliber and to reduce it still more would make two or three additional operations. Consequently, a case like the .219 Zipper or the .25-35 might be better to start with.

Probable high pressures due to having a case built like a barrel at the breech and a darning needle at the muzzle, is one problem in designing a .170-caliber rifle, and another is that of excessive barrel wear at the breech if the pressures get too excessive or the powder charge too large. Still another is the difficulty of making such a very small bullet — only 60 per cent the weight of the .22 long rifle rim-fire bullet.

Add all these together and you will see why it is most desirable to design a .170 which has a gradual taper to the case so that the .170 cartridge can be formed to chamber size without too much reworking, too many operations and too much laborious work.

In spite of everything, we have a fine cartridge in the R-2 .170 and anyone who likes a light fly rod for his fishing, who is a dry fly or a wet fly man, or who is essentially a "small bore" rifleman of the Nth power, that chap is going to fall for the .170 like a ton of bricks. It will kill woodchucks. Wismer, Parkinson, Wood and myself, have all proved this. I think you will like it if you don't expect the impossible.

PHILIP WISMER'S RESUME OF THE WORK

OF WOODCHUCK RIFLES AND CARTRIDGES
(As of the Close of 1948 and Beginning of 1949)

We had a very unusual season, dry and cool. The fruit and agricultural seasons started late, and then all jammed together, leaving me very little time to shoot as compared to some other years.

I loaded up 150 rounds for the .22-303 Varmint-R this Spring: fifty with 36 grains of 4320 and the 49-grain Sisk Express bullet; fifty with 23 grains of DuPont 4759 and the 50-grain Speer bullet — a medium range charge; and fifty cartridges with 33.5 grains of 3031 and 49-and 55-grain Sisk Express, my bench-rest load. I still have more than half of them left. You can see that I did very little shooting with that rifle.

Bill (Elliott) was out to my range last week end and I fired a group at 200 yards, the first since August. The 5-shot group measures .270 inches I offered to put the other 5 shots in the group for a dollar, but no takers. I think Bill was foolish, because the putting of another 5 shots in a very small group, which group center has already been established, is a horse of another breed and color from putting 5 shots in any old group.

I have now fired between 3100 and 3200 rounds through this .22-303 Crandall Varmint-R, and have a suspicion it is beginning to slip a bit. The groups are not so much larger but are more open and I get the odd flier without its having been called. It always makes me feel sad to see a good barrel go.

I used the .170 Winchester S.S. Parkinson rifle to the tune of 600 and some odd shots. After my "fiasco" this Spring, I found it to be a pretty fair chuck gun if the 25-or 30-grain bullet be placed right. I had very good results with the 25-grain bullet (Sisk) and 11.5 grains of Kynoch smokeless powder. I filed the points slightly for better expansion. I am now using 12.5 grains of Kynoch and same 25-grain Sisk bullets. The points of these are filed. The cases seem to last well and the point of impact is the same as with 16.0 grains of 3031. This was a good load but being a case full of powder, was rather tedious loading. It also gave high fliers. I blamed these on crushed powder. The groups, discounting the odd high shot, were much smaller than with any other loading with the possible exception of that hot 4198 load I used this last Spring. I believe there is something a bit out of balance with this case and caliber. On the other hand, I never had good accuracy with the 2-R except when that was overloaded.

I had my son along on most trips, and put the K.H. job in the car for him to use and strange to say, I found myself using it more than sonny. My old load of 12.8 grains of 2400 is away too hot for my new barrel, so I used 12 grains of 4198 and the 45-grain Speer .224-inch bullets. This was a very accurate load. I am now using 11 grains of Kynoch and same bullets. (Just in case you are interested, the 4198 load was a case full of powder.) I am enclosing a group fired at 50 yards, put that beside that group fired by your son and shown in .22-Caliber Varmint Rifles. If I hadn't looked I might have put them all in one hole. Anyway, the first four were in one hole.

Getting back to the .170, if I can get the 200-yard group size down a bit, it is going to make a grand crow rifle. I recall one trip to my favorite crow shooting ground where I killed over 50 crows, making 23 straight kills. Most of these shots were within 150 yards. The trajectory is about the same as that of the .22-303 Varmint-R (.303 British case), and if I could get 2 to 2-1/2-inch groups at 200 yards, it should give hits up to 250 to 350 yards. Using the same 200 yard point of impact as for the .22-303 job, and the 3-dot Fecker scope, I managed to make a pretty fair average number of killing hits on chucks up to 350 to 400 yards with the .170 Woodsman—the R-2 necked down, holding the same as with the .22-303, I mean.

On one trip I killed five in six shots at distances of at least 350 to 375 yards. I did not go over to check the hit but could see blood on the throat of one through my 20X spotting scope. None of these chucks moved after being hit. However, I do not recommend this caliber over 250 yards. I tried one fox (I only had the 25-grain loading with me), the shot being at around 200 yards. The first shot—in the chest, put him down but not out, and another in the same place, made him a very sick fox indeed, but he had to be finished off. I had three other chances at foxes during the season but by-passed them. The .170 is not a fox rifle.

CHAPTER 11

Ramsey Cartridge—Sisk Express Bullet—Johnson Rifle

A MODERN type of .22 Maximum Lovell woodchuck cartridge was developed and chronographed by Lawrence Ramsey of Lebanon, New Jersey. He has been described to me by his fellows as "The No. 1 Rifle Crank of New Jersey." I know Mr. Ramsey personally, have shot on his range and have also observed his privately-owned chronograph in action. He is a dairyman with a large farm and a considerable herd of dairy cattle which keeps him quite busy, but he also has a bent for experimental work and has a very fine and complete machine shop where he can make chambering reamers and chamber rifles for himself when he feels like it.

The .22-357 Ramsey cartridge is made from the Western Super-X .357 Magnum revolver cartridge. The cases are put through three dies in the resizing process and some of the cases have to be annealed if they are too hard, as is sometimes true of pistol or revolver cases as well as rifle cases.

Mr. Ramsey's rifle is a .30-1906 Springfield action fitted with M-1, .22-caliber barrel with 16-inch twist. It is of .218-inch bore and .2235-inch groove diameter. The barrel is chambered for a modified 8-S type of bullet of 50 grains or less.

The following loads gave good results when tested at 100 to 300 yards on Mr. Ramsey's range:

Charge	Powder	Bullet	M.V. in F.S.
18.5 grs.	4198	46-gr. 8-S R.C.B.S.	3125 f.s.
19.0 grs.	4198	45-gr. bullet	3350 f.s.
20.0 grs.	2400	46-gr. R.C.B.S.	3375 f.s.
17.0 grs.	2400	46-gr. R.C.B.S.	3450 f.s.
19.0 grs.	HiVel No. 3	46-gr. R.C.B.S.	3225 f.s.
17.0 grs.	4227 DuPont	46-gr. R.C.B.S.	3300 f.s.
17.5 grs.	4227 "	45-gr. bullet	3450 f.s.

The case is reported to be very flexible as to powders and bullets. He has used all weights of bullets in this rifle, from 35 to 50 grains, both inclusive.

Ramsey and the late Bob Bley ran a test with a Maximum Lovell Kilbourn rifle using 18.0 grains of 4198 and the 50-grain bullet and the best they obtained was 3000x f.s. The case is much longer and rather straight.

Ramsey reports killing woodchucks with this .22-357 up to 300 yards and killing the first five straight he shot at.

THE .22-1906 EXPRESS

Mr. Ramsey has another cartridge he designed, and a rifle for it, called the .30-1906 Express. He uses this for the longer range shots. It uses a 65-grain bullet and with this he has killed chucks up to 500 yards. He used a 5-power telescope for this shooting. The case is a nice looking case, very similar to many other .30-1906 cases necked down to .22. Three sizing dies were used for sizing down from .20 to .22. Ramsey thinks this cartridge would be better in a .236-inch bore than in a .224.

For target work, 43.0 grains of 4064 and the 55-grain 8-S type bullets gave him groups under 1 inch at 100 yards. That load shot well up to 500 yards but at greater ranges or at 500 yards, he preferred the 65-grain bullet. It was a better windbucker.

Ramsey's .22-06 case was made from the .30-1906 case by shortening the neck about 1/8 inch, and giving the body of the case a taper of 1/2 inch per foot.

Neck slope of the .22-357 was 28 degrees and of the .22-06 about the same. The large case will handle bullets from 40 to 65 grains, all of which have been used in it. This .22-357 case can be packed more readily in boxes of 50; it would be a cheaper case to manufacture in quantity. should give better accuracy; be lighter and easier to carry in the pocket; be cheaper to load and should sell at a lower price. It could readily be made in a rimless shape as well as in the present rimmed case especially adapted to the single shot actions, although Ramsey had his on a Springfield bolt action. It has the modern sharp shoulder which in the Bench Rest Rifle Association matches has consistently outshot the gentle slope cartridges for accuracy and also does better out in the field at longer ranges. The Ramsey .30-1906 case was made up on a Mauser action with a heavy .220

Swift blank and used a .224-inch barrel. I believe both of these Ramsey cartridges are worth further attention, especially the .22-357 Ramsey.

THE .234 SISK EXPRESS

R. B. Sisk, the well-known custom bullet manufacturer of Iowa Park, Texas, rather recently developed a small bore, high velocity, varmint cartridge known as the .234 Sisk Express.

About January 1, 1949, I received a letter from Mr. Sisk in which he made the following comments regarding this cartridge and its work in the game fields. It is well to recall in this matter, that Mr. Sisk does not live in a woodchuck district, but on those numerous occasions when he goes up to Trinidad, Colorado, to experiment with P. O. Ackley, he does often get some shooting at those high altitude marmots found in the upper valleys of the Rocky Mountains in Colorado.

Wrote Mr. Sisk, "I have just had a little deer hunt in South Texas, with my .234-caliber rifle. I fired four shots, and got four head of game, —— one coyote, one javelina, and two bucks. One of the deer weighed 137 pounds, which is getting up close to the top for Texas bucks.

"This cartridge case has the same shape as Hervey Lovell's .230 Thunderbolt, but the groove diameter of the barrel is about five thousandths larger, making it a true .23 caliber.

"My hunting load is 59.0 grains of DuPont No. 4350 behind a 70-grain bullet. My wife and I each have rifles in this caliber. She got one buck in South Texas. We each shot an antelope in Wyoming in September. Also, two small bears were shot with these rifles in New Mexico, however we didn't do the shooting. One shot each has dropped every one of these animals. Of course I am not trying to suggest to anyone that these rifles are more powerful than .300 Magnums or similar calibers, but we surely do like their ballistics and killing power.

"In regard to your inquiry regarding better bullets for the .22-250 and the .22 Varminter calibers of rifles, the only 55-grain bullet we make is the 55-grain Sisk Express. This bullet is used quite frequently in the various .22-250 rifles, however, in general I believe the 49-grain Express gives slightly better accuracy in the .22 Varminter and the .22-250's. More shooters report a high degree of accuracy with the 49-grain bullet."

The .234 Sisk is much like the .228 Ackley in ballistics, except that it is about a 12 or 13 grain greater capacity case. It handles the long, heavy 70-grain bullets splendidly. It is definitely a big game rifle, or a very long-ranged woodchuck, coyote, wolf and antelope rifle. Ackley reported most excellent results on deer, antelope and elk with his medium and Magnum .228 Ackley cartridges. Ackley suggested his .228's were not woodchuck cartridges in the ordinary sense of the word, because they were more powerful than was necessary for most woodchuck shooting although they were extremely effective on very long range shots on woodchucks. On those chances where shots at 350 to 500 yards must be taken.

Any small caliber cartridge firing 59 grains of powder as coarse as DuPont No. 4350, will have a very sharp report and an annoying muzzle blast. The muzzle blast will not be so annoying to the shooter but it may be ear-splitting to any other person within 15 or 20 feet of the rifle's muzzle, or to anyone slightly in front of the muzzle as well as to one side of it. Such cartridge should never be fired past the ears of anyone within 30 feet or so almost directly ahead of the muzzle.

The .234 Sisk is one of the ''whammiest'' small calibers extant and is definitely a 250 to 500 yard proposition, with good accuracy to be expected at 600 yards, when not too much wind is blowing, and for long—very long range work on coyotes, wolves and woodchucks.

As a comparison of case capacities, the .220 Swift with 55-grain bullet and 38.0 grains of DuPont No. 4064 powder gives 3605 f.s. muzzle velocity; the .228 Ackley case, the largest capacity of the three .228 Ackley rimless cases, develops 3700 f.s. muzzle velocity with 46.0 grains of DuPont No. 4350, and a 70-grain Sisk bullet. Along comes the .234 Sisk with 70-grain bullet shoved along by 59.0 grains of 4350. A great load for bumping off that woodchuck that dives in every time he sees you climb out of a car stopped 400 to 500 yards off, little more afraid of a man armed with a .22 Hornet or an R-2 than if he were a Kodiak bear. However, even such wily old chucks, battle scarred and wise from years and years of knowing when to dodge and duck and when to hole up in time, can be shot with a .234.

ELLWOOD EPPS' LOADS FOR THE .22-25-35

C. C. JOHNSON RIFLE

Mr. Ellwood Epps, of Clinton, Ontario, a sporting goods dealer with a clientele covering Canada, owns a Charles C. Johnson .22-caliber Marciante Blue Streak heavy barrel rifle using the .25-35 case necked down, with which he did exceptionally accurate long range woodchuck shooting in the spring of 1948, while the two of us hunted together in southern Ontario, over a very wide area. On that hunt Epps killed a great many chucks which were paced or estimated as being 250 to 350 yards from the rifle when killed, and a few which were probably around 400 yards from the rifle.

Epps has a shop and loading room at the back of his sporting goods store in which are a considerable number of loading tools, powder measures, etc., and he has access, through his stock, to many different powders, bullets, and primers.

At the end of the year, 1948, Mr. Epps listed the following as the most accurate and successful loads which he had tried in his .22-25-35 rifle made up for another rifleman, by Charles C. Johnson, of Thackery, Ohio.

The loads follow: His best load is the 55-grain Sisk Express bullet and 34.0 grains of DuPont No. 4064 powder. He targets his scope sighted rifle to shoot 1 inch high at 100 yards with this load, and it then shoots 1 inch low at 300 yards with the same sighting. This makes aim at the top line of the back, or the top of the head, or just above the head, as the best sighting for 300 yard shooting, with this charge.

55-Gr. Sisk bullet, 34.0 grains of DuPont No. 4320
55-Gr. Sisk Express, 33.0 grains of DuPont No. 3031
50-Gr. Sisk bullet, 35.0 grains of DuPont No. 4320
50-Gr. Sisk bullet, 32.5 grains of DuPont No. 3031
50-Gr. Sisk bullet, 35.0 grains of DuPont No. 4064. The latter charge is with the case full of powder and tamped in.

CHAPTER 12

.170 Caliber Woodchuck Cartridges
and Rifles

THE past fifty years have seen almost revolutionary changes in the density of population paralleling the New York City to Washington, D. C. highway, in the southern portion of California, and in many other sections of the country: in fact, all over the nation.

The modern automobile and its general public use; the relatively high-speed commuting trains; the wide, four-lane paved highways linking the larger cities; concrete or black-top surfaced two-lane roads linking almost all centers of population have all combined to create concentrations of population located from five or ten to one hundred twenty-five miles from the major cities and employment centers. Fifty years ago, this condition did not exist. This situation has brought about a change in the public's attitude toward hunting with rifles and has been mainly responsible for the passing of most of the laws about shooting from the edge of, or from a public highway — most times the safest place in the locality from which to shoot provided you do not stop your car in the middle of the highway, nor fire across the highway at car level.

It is obvious that the .22-caliber woodchuck rifle, with its multiplicity of standard factory and wildcat cartridges has been exploited and developed until it would seem almost impossible to make most of them better ballistically without new and more uniform propellents, still more accurate bullets, or silent means of projectile propulsion.

Consequently some riflemen have turned to the .25-caliber rifles to try to produce better bullets, more accurate medium size cases, and better wind-bucking qualities when that is required.

Others of us have turned to the smaller bore .170-caliber cartridges primarily for one or both of two purposes: To eliminate report of sufficient volume or pitch to carry to consider-

221

able distances. To as nearly as that be physically possible, eliminate ricochets or glancing bullet fragments. The normal weights of .17-caliber bullets are 20, 25, and 30 grains. You cannot have a ricochet with mass (bullet metal) which does not exist.

Today there are tens of thousands of riflemen who must obtain most of their woodchuck shooting within 10 to 100 miles of where they live, and where they live is not always where they want to live, but where they must reside for the sake of convenience.

Consequently all such persons, or at least most of them, require a woodchuck cartridge of low report, which can be shot extensively without alarming the landowners and the traveling public, one which rarely, if ever, produces a whining ricochet, or a deflected whole bullet.

THE DESIGN OF .17-CALIBER WOODCHUCK CARTRIDGES

For the past five years or so, I have devoted considerable time to the design, development, rifle production, and the collection of data about the results obtained with, and the loads used in various .17- or .170-caliber cartridges. Quite a bit of that will be given in this book because relatively few know of these results. I have done more long distance traveling to test .170-caliber, small-cartridge rifles on woodchucks than probably anyone else, and I have been partly responsible for the use and purchase of these small-cartridge .170's in Ontario and the Middle Atlantic States in considerable numbers within a relatively short time. This is not a personal matter with me but born from an interest in finding a good, workable model to use in my favorite sport — woodchuck hunting.

As compared to the best of the smaller .22 wildcats, the .170's have and probably can have, but four advantages. These are: about 300 f.s. higher relative muzzle velocity; much less report; practically no ricochets; a flatter trajectory over 150 to 250 yards than cartridges like the .22 Hornet and the R-2. The larger .170's will have, of course, sharper reports than the .170 Woodsman, either with 15-degree or 28-degree shoulder, but then their killing power will be much greater, and they will have very flat trajectories over muzzle to 350 or more yards. Many chucks are killed as if by electrocution, by each of these .170's. We will discuss the design of larger .170's first, and then the smaller ones most suitable for thickly settled areas.

THE .170-250-4500 LANDIS DESIGN

The .170-250-4500 came into existence because of the suggestion of a draftsman acquaintance of mine that I design a .170-caliber high-velocity woodchuck cartridge using the .250-3000 Savage case as a base. This large case was designed by me in August, 1946, and a rifle and cases of that design were made up and tested by P. O. Ackley, of Trinidad, Colorado, as soon as he was given the dimensions.

Shortly after the design of this cartridge was sent to Mr. Ackley, he wrote as follows: "I believe the .170-350-4500 will be the most useful and satisfactory of all the .170 designs." Parker Ackley's reasons for this deduction were that the new cartridge has a head diameter and a body size, that it will fit all of the standard size and short bolt actions now on the market. This would include the short Mausers and the Model 722 A Remington.

It seems logical that it could also be adapted without difficulty to the .30-1906 Springfield, the 1917 Enfield, the Models 30-S and various other Remington bolt actions, the Mauser 1898 and its modifications, the Savage Models 20 and 40, the Winchester Models 54 and 70. I am quite convinced the very small and light Model 43 Winchester action would not stand the pressures which could be developed by full charges.

It could also be adapted to the imported custom British-Mausers put out by Holland and Holland, Westley Richards, Rigby, Jeffrey, and other British custom rifle makers. It would give too high pressures, in full loads, for the Model 1899 Savage lever action, therefore a barrel of this caliber should not be fitted to that action.

It could also, most likely, be adapted to a host of Martinis and German Schuetzen rifle actions of various type brought or sent home from Germany.

Unfortunately Mr. Ackley used six to eight grains more powder than I had anticipated for the .170-250-4500 and of course ran up his pressures. As he was testing the rifle on a completely enclosed, small, indoor range, the sharp high-pitched, and piercing report was painful to the ears. He did, however, get 4935 f.s. muzzle velocity to the 25-grain Sisk bullet on his chronograph. Such a cartridge would shoot very much flatter over

200 yards or so than the .220 Swift. Even with a normal load it would. And when you wanted to use a reduced load of course you could do so.

LIMITING FACTORS IN CARTRIDGE DESIGN,

The drawing board is the workshop of the designer. Any cartridge or any rifle chamber can be laid out on drawing paper, magnified in size, three times, five times, ten times, or even more, as desired, and every small but important detail studied on this enlarged scale drawing.

No cartridge should be designed without a careful study of the cartridge length to shoulder; the diameter of the case at the shoulder; the degree of shoulder slope as measured with the center line of the cartridge, or lines parallel to this; the neck length; cartridge wall thickness; and all other physical features of the cartridge including the ignition which is extremely important.

In the design of any small bore wildcat rifle cartridge, the length of the case, diameter of the cartridge head, thickness of head, type of rim, and allowable breech pressure, are all limited by the type, strength, width, height, and length of the rifle action used. If we have sufficient size, metal thickness, good material, and strength of design, then top working pressures and very high velocities are allowable but not always too desirable, and a smaller charge than the absolute maximum you can drop and tap into the case is generally far more accurate and gives a much longer barrel life. One thing of extreme importance in the design of all .170-caliber rifles is that the bullet is light in comparison to its length. It has also but little mass. Its specific gravity is less than that of .22-and .25-caliber cartridges of comparable size because the lead core is smaller in volume as compared to the jacket. Hence you need a longer neck so as to grip the bullet securely than you do relatively, in either .22- or .25-caliber rifles. Don't forget this.

In this regard, also it is advisable to obtain, measure, and carefully study and set down in a table so they can be compared dimensionwise, the .22-caliber cartridges of greatest accuracy and efficiency, or the ones which seem best suited to your shooting. Then compare your .170 design with these. I'll do that here.

A cartridge should burn its powder efficiently and completely. It should be ballistically practical, not just a new design.

TABLE SHOWING A FEW .170 AND .22 WILDCAT CARTRIDGES

Cartridge	Shoulder Slope	Shoulder Diameter	Length to Shoulder	Length Case	O. A. Loaded	Neck Length
Factory						
.250-3000 Sav.	26°30′	.4137″	1.52″	1.90″	2.50″	0.25″
		.415-.418″	1.54″			
.170-250-4500	30°	.416″	1.48″	1.90″	2.40″	0.33″
.170-250-4000	30°	.417″	1.30″	1.72″	2.22″	0.33″
.170 Landis	28°	.295″	1.25″	1.64″	2.02″	0.30″
Woodsman		.299″			2.04″	
.22-250	28°	.420″	1.50″	1.92″	2.38″	0.25″
.219 Donaldson	30°	.407″	1.30″	1.75″	2.25″	0.325″

It will be seen from this that the .170-250-4500 has much the same dimensions up to the neck, and in over-all case length, as the .22-250 or the .22 Varminter, but is slightly smaller at the shoulder, and has a longer neck so as to hold the smaller bullet securely.

I believe one of my later designs will give probably better all-around results in the necked down .250-3000 Savage case, and that I call the .170-250-4000, although it will likely give 4300 to 4500 or 4600 f.s. muzzle velocity with 25-grain bullets, if fully charged with 3031.

THE .170-250-4000 LANDIS

This case is a moderate size one, has the same length to the shoulder as the .219 Donaldson, a slightly shorter case length, because it is necked down farther at the shoulder. It has a greater diameter at the shoulder than the .219 Donaldson. Possibly slimming it down to the shoulder diameter of the .219 would help things but it would make more work in forming the cases. This I wished to avoid, as many do not care to spend all their spare time preparing ammunition. The more operations, the more work to do. You may have three to six swaging operations.

THE .250-3000 SAVAGE CASE AND ITS DESCENDANTS

The standard factory .250-3000 Savage cases are made with a rim or head diameter of .473 inch as a maximum. In actual production in the ammunition factories, cartridge cases with a greater head diameter are normally rejected, but cartridges with smaller head diameter are accepted and loaded. The average rim of the .250-3000 Savage cases will be found within .465 to .470 inch diameter as I have measured them. Few cartridges are perfectly round, either on the rim of the cartridge head, or the body of the cartridge at the shoulder. This will come as a great surprise to many riflemen, who for years have fussed with weighing cartridge cases, filling one and then another with water, to find out how much they varied from the average in water content, and therefore in powder capacity. The plants, however, measure the cartridge case on head and shoulder by revolving it in the fingers and measuring it carefully at different points on the circumference with a very accurate outside micrometer.

It may be that the inaccuracy of your shooting is due in part to the fact that you are shooting elliptical cartridges in a round chamber and are centering a supposedly round chamber mouth with an elliptical cartridge head. Don't take my word for it; get out your micrometer and measure them for yourself.

What makes the .250-3000 Savage case, incidentally the most accurate factory .25 caliber cartridge of them all, and .250-3000 caliber bolt action rifles break in much more accurately than a lot of .257 Roberts barrels? As a Gun Editor, I've had plenty of kicks on the .257 Roberts barrels not shooting well for the first 200 to 500 rounds. In addition, the case is too large anyhow, in powder room, for a 25-caliber cartridge of maximum efficiency. But it is a good heavy case, heavier and stronger than the .250-3000 Savage case, which should now be made heavier. If it then holds a bit less powder, what of it?

The 7 m.m. Mauser case, the .257 Roberts and the 250-3000 each have the same maximum head diameter, .473 inch, and so has the .22-4000 Schnerring cartridge which Sedgley once made rifles for until it was discovered that the .220 Swift cartridge could be exploded in this chamber with about one shot in three causing quite a disturbance. The .22-4000 case was then discontinued.

The .25 Remington rimless cartridge makes up into a very fine .22 wildcat, or a .170 medium size wildcat — I designed a good case for that caliber from the .25 rimless about four years ago. P. O. Ackley had designed an equally fine one from the rimmed .219 Zipper case. The .25 Remington rimless has an outside head diameter of only .422 inch maximum, and this is 0.051 inch less than the diameter of the head of the following woodchuck cartridges: .257 Roberts, 7 m.m., .22-4000 Schner-

Bench rest and chronograph at Ramseys with one of group firing.

Veteran chuck hunter C. H. Bean, of Lebanon, N. J., in his favorite shooting outfit.

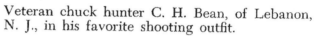

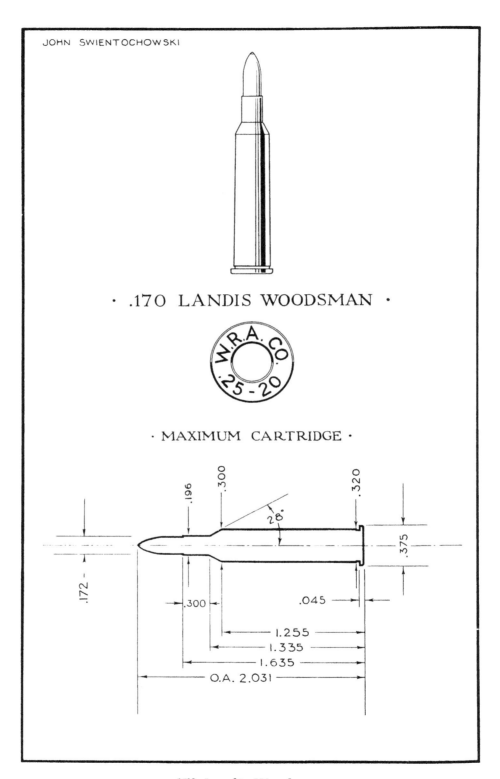

· .170 LANDIS WOODSMAN ·

· MAXIMUM CARTRIDGE ·

.170 Landis Woodsman.

ring, .22-250, .170-250-4500. This much smaller head definitely insures two things at least, that the wildcat cartridge made from it will hold far less powder and that it can only be fitted to the bolt of any of the bolt action rifles handling cases of the head size of the .30-1906, 7.92 m.m., .257 Roberts, 7 m.m., .250-3000 and the like, after considerable work is done in fitting the bolt face to handle the smaller case. Then at no time in the future can you readily convert that bolt back again to handling the larger cases.

So here we find ourselves with an offshoot of the late Charles Newton's designing ability which many, many years later just fills the ticket for a .170-caliber varmint case which actually hurled a bullet through space at 4935 f.s. muzzle velocity. This is close to 65 per cent higher velocity than developed when put out by his .250-3000 Savage rifle. It had a 26-inch barrel, too.

Newton was generally credited with having been ten to twenty years ahead of his time as a rifle cartridge designer, although not as a production man, a factory manager, a sales manager, or as a chap who could get rifles rolling out the side door in a steady stream. But a good designer has done his day's work if he has turned out a design which is still tops among .25 calibers a generation later.

One of the most interesting things any rifle crank can do is to compare the case shapes and the shoulder slopes of about 50 of our factory cartridges (of factory design, incidentally), one with another, and see the diversity of case shapes and shoulder slopes used, and consider also that a very high percentage of them have turned out to be "clucks." Then compare the whole bunch with the .250-3000 Savage, the .22 Varminter and the .219 Donaldson and you can see without looking twice, why so many of them were clucks.

It used to be and still is, in some towns in New England, a good winter sport to take a repeating rifle designed forty to sixty years ago, and then try to design and produce a modern cartridge which will fit in, be handled by, and can be shot in a barrel on that action, without wrecking the action.

The way to build a modern, efficient, high velocity, small caliber woodchuck or other rifle, is to first design a modern cartridge, without too much regard to any existing rifle, except maybe the short Mauser, and then design a rifle action and, of course, the complete rifle to handle that cartridge. Then you'd have something worth while, modern from comb to muzzle.

Of course this would cost a few thousand dollars. It would not cost so much if they'd supply the proper people to do it, and some of these could be lassoed with a net at any meeting of the Bench Rest Rifle Shooters Association. After one man has designed a cartridge, and another a bullet, a third a barrel-boring system, still another a chambering system; then you had a set of Red Elliott's chambering reamers, and still another fellow to design and do the stocking of the rifle, you'd finally get a rifle that would now and then shoot a 1/4 to 4/10-inch 5-shot group at 100 yards. And sometimes you'd have three or four such on one frame of targets. When a factory designs a cartridge and rifle, they turn out a combination which may, if luck is with them, make groups four to eight times as large. This thing of haughtily ignoring what any reasonably smart grammar-school boy could pick up at a meeting of rifle cranks, shows a spirit of individuality, and a rugged independence, of thought which probably meets with acclaim among that company's directors, but it does not meet with acclaim among the woodchuck hunters who would much prefer a rifle and cartridge which might reasonably be expected to hit something.

RIMMED CARTRIDGE CASES FOR HI-SIDE

SINGLE SHOT RIFLES

It should be understood quite definitely and clearly by the reader that we have been talking almost altogether about rimless cartridges, to be used in bolt action rifles. Now we come to the rimmed or outside rim cartridges, which are the only really satisfactory cases to use in single shot rifles like the Winchester hi-side, the Stevens 44-1/2 — including in the higher grades Nos. 45 to 54, but that action; the Sharps-Borchardt, Farquharson, Martini, Remington Hepburn, and the German falling block actions of appropriate strength. The type of extractor used in such actions does not fit or handle the rimless cases to good advantage. For such actions the .170's made from the .219 Zipper, and the R-2 are much better.

The .303 British service cartridge case, especially those made for anti-aircraft machine gun use, when cut off and then swaged down, made a very fine case for hi-side actions of about the general power level of the .22-250 Varminter. Cutting off and necking down this case took a number of operations, and one could work up a sweat doing this. But the .22-303 Varmint-

R is a very effective cartridge on woodchucks up to 450 yards or so, and if cut off still more, and necked down still more to .170 caliber, it could be made into a .170-303-4500 or a .170-303-4000 case for single shot rifles. This should only be undertaken on a large scale by a chap who regards swaging down, cutting off, chambering and cartridge loading as something to which he has devoted his life.

THE PREDECESSOR OF THE .170 LANDIS WOODSMAN

THE .170 PARKINSON WOODSMAN

Years back Parker Ackley developed a number of .170 Pee-Wees and Super PeeWees, and he learned through his barrel man how to bore .17-caliber barrels, still stay solvent, sell them for about $30 per barrel blank which is a little more than twice what good .22 barrel blanks cost gunsmiths.

Ray Weeks and Phil Wismer and his brother, and half a dozen others had been shooting a lot of crows and woodchucks around southern Ontario.

No gent living in a settled district in which two to six woodchucks in a week are considered a great many woodchucks can conceive of a situation in which half a dozen farms adjacent one to another would produce 50 to 200 or maybe even 300 woodchucks of all assorted ages and beliefs gamboling around on the short grass and eating their way straight across field after field. Like the grasshoppers in Kansas, they had woodchucks in southern Ontario twenty to thirty years ago. They have them now in many districts.

Consequently, an experienced and successful woodchuck hunter has about as much chance of being unknown and unobserved for long by the dirt farmers with too many woodchucks on their hands, as had Babe Ruth of being unobserved at a baseball game.

Here in the States, a man going out for ten days of woodchuck hunting, with a little shooting thrown in for good measure now and then, can expect to find 90 per cent of the farms posted and the rallying cry of the country gentlemen is not "Hey Rube," but "Hey You — GETTOHELL OFF MYFARM!"

In Ontario, on the other hand, about 1945-1947, you seldom saw even one no-trespass notice in a day's hunting by automobile. It was to be expected that in a day's shooting actually in heavily chuck infested areas, at least 25 to 33 per cent of the farmers would come out to the road and insist you come in and shoot their woodchucks because otherwise you "might get arrested on the road."

Not always did this include a hot dinner, but on one occasion Stan Adams and I did mange to wangle two sandwiches each and a fairly generous slab of pie. Definitely it did include woodchucks.

However, the use rather generally of .22-303 Varmint-R's and other rifles of similar power, report and range, did eventually in some areas, stir up the farmers to a certain amount of alarm and protest and the hope that somehow the riflemen could shoot the woodchucks with less noise, fewer and softer ricochets, and yet with equal success.

Charles Parkinson produced a .17-caliber cartridge by necking down the R-2 case with a 15-degree shoulder slope, which gives, incidentally, a rather long and gentle shoulder slope when carried down to a .17-caliber neck. He hoped to keep township politicians and authorities from putting bans on woodchuck hunting in summer by producing a rifle they wouldn't hear and from which they would also not have to dodge ricochets. The problem then was; did it have enough killing power to regularly and consistently kill woodchucks? After all, the primary purpose of a chuck rifle is to kill woodchucks. It may make good in every other way, but if it doesn't kill woodchucks so that they stay "dead," and "dead 'em" up to ten, twenty and thirty straight tail whizzings, it lacks something as a woodchuck rifle.

Parkinson is a graduate pupil of the Ray Weeks school of rifle shooting. Weeks considers chuck shooting as not especially exciting — probably because his local chuck shooting is only mediocre by southern Ontario standards — but he explains that crow shooting takes much more ability. Gradually Parkinson shot enough chucks and crows with his little .170 so that he arranged to have me give it a public trial in company with other expert local riflemen as shooting companions, also probably as rather skeptical onlookers to see maybe a bit more of what it really would do.

That day we drove out together, and after I had shot two or three woodchucks with my .22 Hornet, he handed me his settrigger hi-side action fitted with a 24-inch .170 barrel, and an 8-power Fecker scope which was rather foggy and had a lump of thread or something wound tightly around the crosshair intersection. I had never shot the rifle, had no opportunity whatever to sight it in, had to use Parkinson's sighting, and was not familiar with the settrigger, trigger pull. That can be disconcerting too, until you become accustomed to it. Some are set much too light for field shooting.

Parkinson had fired at a couple of chucks with it without much evident effect, and then centered and just blasted a crow which lingered too long on top of a fence post to cuss and jeer. Then I found myself holding the rifle and cartridges with a chance to use it.

I'd much rather try a new rifle and cartridge for a few days by myself, to become accustomed to the trigger pull, report, trajectory, uniformity of delivery of a shot from a cold barrel, grouping, killing power on shots placed in different vital areas, the point of impact of the normal group from the rifle, the peculiarities of the scope and its mounts, and such things each of which has a definite bearing on what you are likely to do when firing this rifle in the company of some of the best rifle shots in Canada. However, I had to shoot this rifle from scratch.

Parkinson's sighting proved to be 100 per cent perfect for me that day, although we resemble each other but little, physically, and there is enough difference in our ages that a scope set for one could scarcely be expected to suit the other without refocusing.

The first eight chucks were each killed instantly as if electrocuted. They did not kick, each one just sank down and was motionless. The cartridge had chronographed around 3200 to 3300 f.s. with the 25-grain bullet and 4320. The most peculiar thing was that all one heard was a peculiar "plop" when the rifle fired, the chuck went down before you sensed you had shot. You had no opportunity to flinch because the chuck was dead before you fully realized you had released the trigger. Seven of the eight, had been shot cleanly through the brain, and the other, in the neck just below the butt of the ear. Sometimes brain shot chucks, or brain shot anything else, kick around a little, but these didn't. They seemed to be stone dead instantly. Even the muscles and nerves were paralyzed. A jack rabbit shot up a furrow and suffered a similar fate. Then after I had killed two instantly at well over 200 yards, one shot was fired at a chuck away across a long, shallow ravine and we don't know what that struck because a .170 Woodsman bullet striking dirt does not throw up a splash of dirt (in grass, it also does not mark its strike). There were so many chuck dens there when I finally got across the hollow, I never could tell which one had housed the chuck I had fired at. Then a few more were killed instantly and finally one was shot in the head and fell off his mound on the rear side, and I could not see him. The fence proved difficult, so a companion killed him from a distance down the field from a point where he could be seen, paralyzed and possibly blinded, turning slowly in a circle, unable to go underground and unable to escape. I still couldn't see the chuck from my position.

THE LANDIS WOODSMAN

Parkinson later asked me to redesign the cartridge my way, to give it a sharper neck, and somewhat greater powder room. This was done, the Landis Woodsman being given a 28-degree shoulder slope, a longer neck, and slightly over one grain more powder capacity. Altogether this added more report (but not a loud report), gave considerably more striking power and a velocity of 3300 to 3500 f.s.m.v. In 1948 I killed 16 chucks a day for 11 days with it in Ontario, as described earlier in this book. The kill was 2 chucks with a .219 Donaldson and 173 with the .170 Landis Woodsman.

Seven barrels at $30 each were ordered in the first group chambered for the .170 Landis Woodsman. Ackley has made many others since, and Parkinson has chambered a high percentage of them.

Oddly enough each of us has today a wish for at least two of the more pronounced characteristics of the other man's cartridge to be a part of his own design. The .170 Woodsman is considerably more powerful and a better killer when the cartridge contains its full expanded case charge of 3031, 4320, or 4895. Attached is a condensed load table. See the 1948 trip and Harold Wood's chapter for additional data.

A Condensation of the best loads to date, for the .170 Landis Woodsman Cartridge collected from various sources. Most of these will develop between 3200 and 3550 f.s. M.V.

Powder Charge			Bullet
14.5 grs. DuPont 4227			30-gr. Sisk S.P.
17.4 "	"	4320	30-gr. Sisk. 3/4" group at 115 yds.
16.5 "	"	3031	25-gr. Sisk S.P.
17.0 "	"	4320	25-gr. Sisk S.P.
12.5 "	"	4227	25-gr. Sisk S.P.
17.0 "	"	3031	25-gr. Sisk S.P.
16.0 "	"	3031	25-gr. Sisk S.P. This load gave 2-1/2" to 2-3/4" groups at 200 yds.
16.5 "	"	3031	25-gr. Sisk S.P. This load must be tapped in shell with long drop tube. Quite accurate.
15.5 "	"	3031	25-gr. Sisk. Makes 3-1/2" to 4" groups at 200 yds.
16.0 "	"	3031	25-gr. Sisk. This test of the load gave 3-1/4 to 3-1/2" groups at 200 yds.
11.5 "	"	Kynoch	A very satisfactory and accurate load. Powder used extensively in Ontario.
15.5 "	"	4895	The author shot many chucks in Ontario in 1948, with 4895. It seemed to be both accurate and powerful in the .170.

In 1948 on one hunt Phil Wismer killed 32 chucks out of 34 hit, while shooting at 37 woodchucks, with the .170. He was using 11.5 grains Kynoch and the 25-grain Sisk bullet. This is an abnormally high percentage of both hits and kills for any cartridge or load anywhere. His rifle has 24-inch medium weight Ackley barrel chambered by Parkinson, and the rifle weighs about 8-1/2 pounds.

Up to the first half of 1950, there has been far more demand for the small .170 Marksman case than for either the medium size or the two larger size .170-250 cases. Shooters seem to feel that lack of report was the most important single consideration. Many used the .170 Marksman for short and medium range shooting, and for shots past 250 yards used their longest ranged .22 wildcat carrying two rifles in the car at one time. Time and again men have reported killing far more chucks with the little .170 than with rifles as powerful as the .220 Rocket and using the .170 for much longer shots than they had anticipated.

CHARLES PARKINSON'S COMMENTS ON THE .170 CALIBER WOODCHUCK RIFLES AND CARTRIDGES

The following comments were selected from correspondence from Charles Parkinson, of London, Ontario, custom gunsmith, who has had probably the most experience of anyone to date in the making up of .170-caliber rifles, the testing of different .170 cartridges and types of shoulder, and in the extended testing of the .170-caliber in the field over a considerable period of time.

These comments are not always connected, because they were received over a period of two or more years, and were taken from letters written on numerous subjects. Nevertheless, they are most interesting as they throw light on many things with which Parkinson has experimented, and has developed with the .170 woodchuck and crow rifles.

Under date of January 3, 1948: ''I have delayed answering your letter until I could give you some idea as to how your .170 rifle was coming along. As you know, I had a set of three new chambering reamers made up by the H. & M. Tool Company of Detroit. I changed the dimensions somewhat. So I now have the barrel set back a half inch on my own rifle and rechambered with the new and latest chamber which has a 28-degree neck and a longer neck. I also had a new throating reamer made. The new case has a neck 9/32nd inch (0.28") long, and the neck of the chamber has been increased .002 inch in diameter to get away from reaming the case necks; also the s.s. neck thickness is not too uniform.

''The chamber cuts 1/32nd inch (.03125") longer than the case length which allows for somewhat uneven case lengths. The throat is slightly free-bored for about .010 inch and this reduces breech pressures very much.

''I find now that I can use 14.5 grains of 4227 DuPont and the case falls out of the chamber after firing. No signs of pressure at all. I have not been able to make many extensive accuracy tests with the old rifle since rechambering it, due to the weather (December and January), however today I put a 15X Super Targetspot on the rifle and with the load of 17-1/2 grains of 4320 DuPont I shot a 3/4 inch group at 115 yards. I would say this is by far the best group I have had with the 30-grain bullets. The pressure was very low, the primer showing no signs of pressure, and the case fell out of the rifle when the breech was opened. So it would seem that the enlarging of the neck and the slight lengthening of the chamber neck, has reduced the pressures somewhat and has improved the accuracy.

"Now, what about dies for case forming? We need three dies to neck the G & H R-2 cases down to .170. You will require the case-forming dies only to form cases, and if you had 200 formed cases, you would then likely have enough cases with which to wear out a barrel. A Pacific Tool or a B & M tool can be used with the dies. I can make you a straight line, hand-type bullet seater and a full-length sizing die, an expander, and also a bullet seater, and that would be all that is required to reload the cases. However, if you have a B. & M. No. 28 Appl. for the Lovell R-2, I could make you a neck sizing die and also an expander, and a bullet seater for the B & M tool. This is what I use, and it works out fine. I can supply whatever you want as outlined."

Mr. Parkinson supplied a set of the three reloading attachments for $10 and these were used in putting up most of the ammunition for the 1948 hunt in Ontario, which netted 173 woodchucks and two crows for the .170 rifle.

Mr. Parkinson wrote further under date of February 19, 1948:

"I have been getting best results with 16.5 grains of No. 3031 powder but 17.0 grains of 4320 also gave good results. However 3031 seems to be the more accurate in the .170, and also gives the highest velocity.

"It will take about two firings or case-forming operations to completely blow out the case to full chamber size, after which it will take the full maximum loading for the .170 Woodsman. Then you can use 17.0 grains of 3031. You could also use 12.5 grains of 4227.

"I would not be interested in the .170 Hornet case, as it will not hold enough powder to give over 2700 f.s. muzzle velocity.

"I just had a letter from Vernor Gipson and he is discarding the .170 made up from the .218 Bee case for the same reason. The .170 is at its best with slow burning powders, and the Hornet and the Bee will not hold enough powder to drive the bullets very much over .22 Hornet velocity, unless pressures are very high. Charles Parkinson."

JULY 1949 COMMENTS FROM PARKINSON

"Dear Charley,

"Glad to hear from you. I have done relatively little shooting this year, so far, but expect to take a trip out to British Columbia next month and will try and get in some shooting there.

"I did shoot a few woodchucks with the .170 Woodsman last April and May. Our friend from Detroit came over and we went up north to the old grounds and the Detroit man got 37 woodchucks (he was using a .219 Donaldson with very heavy barrel, at last accounts), and I killed 16 crows. It was a cold, windy day.

"Another afternoon we went up to a different locality and shot about 40 woodchucks. I have shot around 35 crows this year. One day I had to do some game protective work. A group of foxes were destroying a flock of 200 pheasants domiciled in a swamp. They were certainly having a time with those pheasants. I shot nine of the foxes.

"I have not done anything in the making up of .170 rifles with the larger and longer .250-3000 cartridge cases necked down as suggested. I made up a few more .170 rifles this past year, using the necked down R-2 cases to make up the Woodsman .170's.

"We took in the bench-rest matches at Bradford, Pennsylvania, July 3, 4 and 5, 1949. Frank Bacon from here — you will recall meeting him when you were here last time — averaged .678 inch for 50 shots, using his hi-wall .219 Improved Zipper I made up for him. This average did not win any matches, but it was very good for a hunting type rifle. Ray Weeks was there but averaged over 1 inch and dropped out after five matches. Both Bacon and myself won a couple of matches on Monday, at the 200 yard competitions.

"We inquired about the Banta bullet dies, while at Bradford, but none of the bench-rest shooters there seemed to use them. They mostly use the R. C. B. S. dies by Huntingdon. The Banta dies are okay for hunting bullets but some feel that the R.C.B.S. have an edge for target bullets.

"All the boys at the bench-rest matches that do not use hand-swaged bullets seem to prefer the Sierra bullets. Both of the winners used them at Bradford, and they seemed very accurate. We used the Sierra bullets while shooting at Bradford.

"The Pfeifer barrels are tight in the bore for my reamer pilots which are .218 inch, while a lot of his barrels run .217 inch. I do not like to use barrels which are too tight in the bore. But they are nice, smooth barrels. Maurice Atkinson, whom you met at Ray Weeks' last year, made up three bench-rest rifles for the .219 Donaldson. He used two Pfeifer and one Buhmiller barrel for these. The Buhmiller barrel shot much the best of the three, but that may not mean anything, as barrels by any maker vary as to accuracy, particularly when using a given bullet or a certain load, which may have been determined for another barrel of different groove and bore specifications and different throating. Regards, Charles Parkinson."

CHAPTER 13

Experiments of Harold C. Wood

M R. HAROLD C. WOOD, Deputy Collector of Internal Revenue, for the United States Government, living in Allentown, Pennsylvania, is also a woodchuck hunter of note for most of his life-time. During the years 1946, 1947, and 1948 he and his brother Millard M. Wood (who discusses various topics associated with chuck rifles elsewhere in this book) engaged in extensive woodchuck hunting in New York State. He used the .170 Landis Woodsman, the long ranged .220 Weatherby Rocket, and the .219 Donaldson, each in a heavy varmint rifle.

Both of the brothers Wood are experienced small caliber varmint rifle shots. Mr. H. C. Wood has a very good battery of rifles, which I have examined while in his home in Allentown. He is an expert loader of varmint rifle ammunition, and has even made up some polished and highly finished cases for me. The Wood brothers hunt in good woodchuck country. Both men are reloaders. The younger Mr. Wood is also an expert tool maker who chambered his own rifle for a special sharper-shoulder version of the .170 Woodsman. Due to piling up of his work in the spring of 1950, following an illness, Mr. H. C. Wood was not able to write the following material as a chapter of the book. I have therefore, taken portions of his comments from the numerous letters which have passed between us since 1946.

I will mention here that the brothers Wood killed between 2100 and 2200 woodchucks, according to their tally, in the years 1946, 1947 and 1948, with the three cartridges described, the .170, the .220 Rocket and the .219 Donaldson. Each man has used two of the rifles mentioned extensively and over considerable periods so that accurate deductions of their worth could be given.

The .219 Donaldson was a 15-pound bench-rest rifle, stocked very similarly to the heavy barreled Winchester Model 70, with Marksman stock, and was very accurate although not a bumble bee rifle to the degree that is sometimes found in an occasional rifle. The decision made during some of the shooting as done by the younger Mr. Wood, to use the lighter .170 in place of the 15-pound 219 is significant. Also it is in order to bring out here, that due to the very small mass of metal removed in boring and chambering a .170 Woodsman, a .170 with 24-inch barrel but 3/4 inch in diameter at the muzzle, weighs 9-1/2 to 10-1/2 pounds with scope, and feels fairly heavy in the barrel, while the .219 Donaldson in his possession topped this by 4-1/2 or 5 pounds and was so stocked that it felt clumsy to carry in the field. The 70 Marksman stock is certainly neither a neat nor a sporting stock. The .170 uses but 50 to 55 per cent as much powder as the .219 Donaldson, shoots nearly as flat over 250 yards, the report and blast are far less, and ammunition weight and expense are lower.

The reader might well consider here, that in the three years under discussion, these two hunters killed more woodchucks than will the average rifleman and his companions in a lifetime. They had more opportunities therefore to observe the relative range, ease of hitting, the killing power and worth of these three popular cartridges, than will most people on this earth. Also, Mr. Wood may help to allay the suspicion in the minds of some who may read this book, that "There just aren't that many woodchucks." In the proper areas, at least there were that many.

The first letter from Mr. H. C. Wood of special interest here, was written as of April 11, 1948. Said he:

"Received your most recent letter and glad to hear from you again. I took the new .170 out yesterday and although conditions were anything but favorable, I shot some fairly good groups, so good in fact that I am satisfied the rifle will shoot.

"I do not know what is wrong with the chucks around here this spring. I drove through some of the best chuck country we have here, over two week ends, and I did not see a chuck. I got the rifle set and shot a few groups. I then started to drive through the country looking for woodchucks. In one field alone you can sit by the fence and count fifty chuck holes in a two-acre patch, some of them over 200 yards from the point of observation. The weather was sunny and I sat down in a ravine where the wind did not hit and I watched those holes for over an hour, in early April, and believe it or not, I did not see a single chuck. I saw but one chuck all afternoon and saw him as I was watching a bunch of holes. I took a pot shot at him about 125 yards distant. When the .170 "popped" he just sort of wilted down and made not a move of any kind for about a minute and then his tail went up and down just twice and that was the end. There would have been a lot of mud and trouble getting over to where he was, so I left him there. There was a deep ravine and a stream at the bottom of it.

"My brother wrote me to come up next week end, and to bring the .170 along as he is anxious to see it.

"So far as I can see now, there will not be any difficulty in making the trip to Canada, with you, on the 15th of May.

"If something intervenes, we can take a trip up through Potter County and on over into New York State. If I go up to my brother's place next week I will pick up a license in New York, as I will be going up there several times this summer. As soon as the chucks are out up here, I would like you to come up and we will give them a whirl. Sincerely, H. C. Wood."

Allentown, Penna.
July 25, 1948

"Dear Mr. Landis,

"My brother has his .170 built on a Winchester Model 70 action and reports very good results. He has killed about 150 woodchucks with it so far and says it is okay. I expect to go up the end of the coming week to hunt with him for a week, and will then have more to tell you. He sent me one target he shot with his .170 Model 70 that was very good.

"I believe we will eventually have to discard all of the Winchester hi-walls if we want to secure the very best accuracy, day after day, much as we like this action. I always did like the hi-wall. But it has been amply demonstrated that the bolt actions have it on the hi-walls when it comes to nail-driving accuracy. The trouble is the hi-walls are temperamental. They go along okay for a while and then all of a sudden they are off standard in accuracy, or uniformity of grouping. There was a time, fifteen to thirty years ago when we could not consistently shoot small groups with any rifle and the hi-wall was then as good as any. But things have changed in both barrel making and in ammunition components until now we have rifles which will perform consistently for long strings, day in and day out. In fact it is nothing short of miraculous how some rifles now perform. The old hi-wall has not kept up with this progress. Its standard of grouping is that of its day of design, plus of course the improvement in ammunition components and in telescopes.

"I have as nice a hi-wall action as you will find in many a day's travel and it works splendidly. The rifle complete is a swell little rifle, but it still can't quite make the grade with a first class bolt action. A lot of people argue that this doesn't make so much difference because the hi-wall will shoot closer than any man can hold in the field. No doubt this is the truth, and for woodchuck shooting they are probably right. But when you go out and try it out from a bench-rest and try to get really small groups consistently, competing against men who have the best-built bolt actions that are properly and heavily stocked, you are licked before you start. You may get an occasional very fine group but the law of averages and the capabilities sneak up on you and throw you down.

"So I will probably have to try out a lot of loads in my rifle until I finally hit upon one that will give the best results and then stick with it. Personally I do not believe the very finest results can be had with No. 4895 powder in that small case, (the .170 Woodsman), but as they say, the proof of the pudding is in the eating. If it works, and apparently it does, from the group that Mr. Noel shot, it would solve the problem of inexpensive powder and lessen the cost of loaded ammunition, although the cost of the powder is a very small item in hand-loading such a small cartridge which is essentially a 16-grain case. No. 4895 was never designed for such small cases, but from all reports it does appear to work, at least reasonably well in most every case in which it has been tried. I believe that 4198 is the powder for the .170 and is the powder with which I am going to experiment.*

"I'll write you again when I get back from my week's hunt the first week in August. Will be able then to give you the results of a comparison of my hi-wall and my brother's No. 70 bolt in the .170. There is as mentioned previously, a design used in which both have the same general dimensions, but it has a slightly sharper shoulder and has a sharper angle to the neck where the shoulder and neck come together.†

---

*Author's Note: Later results showed that while 4198 shot well in the .170, 4320 and 3031 as well as Kynoch, seemed to give better accuracy in more rifles.
†Author's Note: I saw this cartridge of the younger Mr. Wood. His angles of two meeting surfaces are quite sharp and not slightly rounded as in our designs. We felt the flow of the powder gases would be less disturbed with rounded corners, and also there should be less difficulty with cracked cases.

"His case will chamber in the breech of my rifle, but he says mine won't go into the chamber of his rifle. I do not believe there is sufficient difference in the design of the two cases to make appreciable difference in the shooting in the field. Harold C. Wood."

Allentown, Penna.
April 20, 1948

"Dear Mr. Landis,

"I went up to New York State on Friday and came back Monday. Your letters were here when I returned. We hunted two days. The weather turned cold and very windy and it was not good weather at all for chuck hunting. Nevertheless we did well enough, considering conditions. We killed 16 on Friday and 26 Saturday and one crow. Then, on the way down on Monday I shot two more. I saw four on the way up, early Friday, but did not get a shot. Three of them I saw crossing the road and by the time I had the car stopped and the rifle loaded, they had gone in."

THE .170 ON CHUCKS

"I killed about six chucks with the new .170 and it really lays them out. I had two rifles with me, and my brother had his heavy, target-type Morgan & Cail .219 Donaldson. So, instead of trying out any of the longer shots with the Woodsman we only used it on the shorter and medium range chances. On Saturday morning we drove back into an old field and both of us got out and made a trip across the field and back again. The sun was quite warm, although the wind was sharp and felt cold. We sat on the side hill for a while and watched across the hollow to the other side. I spied one sitting out of his hole and told my brother to take him as it was too far for the little .170 in the wind. 'Why don't you try him with that pea-shooter of yours and see what it will do?' asked he. 'You might as well find out now as some time in the future.' So I thought, as I had nothing to lose, I might as well shoot at it. It is difficult to say just how far it was, but I feel that it was at least 150 yards across the valley and when the rifle cracked, old Mr. Chuck never moved. He stayed anchored right on the spot, and I had held right on it. My brother exclaimed, 'Well I'll be darned!'

He said he never thought the bullet would carry over there,

nor lay out the chuck so instantly, if it did! I only had a 5-A Lyman on the .170 and did not bother changing as it was too windy to do much sighting-in anyway. My Lyman Super Targetspot was up there and he wanted to put it on but I remarked that I had the 5-A sighted in and did not want to bother sighting in another scope, even though better. We wanted to spend all our time hunting during the two days available. I have the Super Targetspot on the .170 now and will get it sighted in this week and see if it makes any difference in results. The 5-A is okay for certain purposes but after you are accustomed to the 10- or 12-power scope and go back to a 5 power, it makes quite a difference.''

A COAL BLACK WOODCHUCK

''You mentioned you wished to obtain a coal black woodchuck in the letter to the Minister in Canada. Why didn't you also tell me you wanted a coal black chuck hide? The last chuck I shot the evening of the second day out on this last trip was a pure, coal black chuck and I mean it was black. I have been shooting chucks all my life and that is the first all black chuck I ever saw in the country. My brother went down and brought it back and we took it to the car and he mentioned that it would be a nice one to mount if anyone wanted it, but neither of us cared to keep it mounted, so we threw away the carcass, hide and all. My brother said that he had seen some chucks which were partly black, but never before one that was as completely black all over as this woodchuck.

''I shot one chuck on my way down on Monday, with the .170 and I must have held a little high, and scalped the whole back of the skull, off his shoulders. The hair flew at least ten feet high. It went up in a cloud like when you hit a pillow of feathers with a baseball bat and the feathers fly all over everything. I never saw the fur and hair fly so high off anything before, as it did from that woodchuck.* It was late and I did not tarry long after shooting this chuck as I wanted to get home, and so did not go over to examine the carcass. I do not therefore know what the bullet really did to the little animal.''

LOADS FOR THE .170 WOODSMAN

''I had a short note from Mr. Parkinson. He asked me to let him know if I had done any further testing with the .170. He said

*Author's Note: Phil Wismer has recounted the same thing when using his .170 and sometimes the skin around the bullet entrance was completely devoid of fur.

he had shot four chucks and four crows in one day, using his 10X scope. I am really sorry now that I did not put my 12-power scope on the .170 and take more shots at chucks while I was up in New York State. We saw quite a lot of chucks and it was not so long between shots up there so if you do miss one it is no great loss as you should soon see another. Parkinson wrote that he was having the best luck with 16.0 grains of 3031 powder and the 25-grain Sisk bullets. When he wrote me last winter he said he was using 30-grain bullets. I was anxious to find out whether the 30-grain or the 25-grain bullet seems to be giving the better results. I only have the 25-grain bullets, but so far as I can see and as far as I have tested it out, I believe it would be difficult to improve upon the results I have been getting with the 25-grain Sisk bullets.''

FIRST SIZING AND EXPANDED CASES COMPARED

''I can only get 15.0 grains of powder in the cases before they have been fired in the .170 Marksman chamber, but I can crowd 16.0 grains in after firing and expanding or ''blowing out'' the case to chamber dimensions. My brother and I loaded some up at his place and with most of them 16.0 grains of 3031 filled the cartridge case level full. I have not tried any of the cases we loaded there for accuracy. All the cases I fired previous to this loading were really forming cases and contained 15.0 grains of powder so that it may be that more powder will tighten the group and again it may be too much, for best accuracy, and not as good therefore as the lighter load. It often happens that a fellow will obtain tighter groups by not loading the maximum charge, so that the only way I can really find out is by trying them out. I have always been partial to 4320 powder and I want to try it in the .170.*

''I am going to do most of my experimenting from now on, for a time, on the .170 and if it will be found to reach out and perform reasonably well at medium ranges, I may take only one rifle along when I go with you to Canada. I would like to take the .170 and the .220 Rocket, but it makes an unhandy number of rifles in the car. If you have but one rifle you can take care of it, to hold it between your legs and by the barrel, when not driving, but if you have three or four rifles in the car someone is

*Author's Note: The eight instantaneous kills I made on woodchucks, and another on a jack rabbit, when first trying Parkinson's .170 rifle with the original chambering, was the work of 4320.

tramping over them or they bounce up and down when stowed in the rumble seat or up on the ledge above the back seat, or bounce back and forth when hung on the back of the front seat, and if one has a two-day drive, both car and rifle will or at least may show scuffing, even when the rifles are wrapped in old comforts or blankets.''

NEW STOCK FOR THE .220 ROCKET

''I have a stock on my .220 Rocket that could only be classed as 'fair'. It is modeled after Winchester's Model 70 Marksman stock, as I believe I told you previously, and this stock is rather clubby and clumsy, but it is far ahead of the stock I previously had on the rifle. The rifle weighs an even 15 pounds with scope, so it is a real load to lug around, especially if the land is hilly and the day warm. Or either! I will keep you and Parkinson both informed of my progress with the .170. Sincerely, Harold C. Wood.''

Allentown, Penna.
June 3, 1948

''Dear Mr. Landis,

''I received your letter from Tillsonburg, Ontario, and was very glad to hear that your trip was turning out well.

''I have spent another week with my brother in New York State. We hunted seven days and the two of us killed 267 chucks during that time. But I am sorry to say that I did not learn too much about the .170 hi-side during that time. I had it along every day but we hunted for blood. My brother is a hard hunter and he never seems to know when to quit. We started early and we hunted until dusk every day. We used two rifles. My brother was all sighted in with one load, and he has had plenty of experience as to where it groups. He hunts quite a few evenings nearly every week in season. He uses 31.0 grains of 4320 in the .219 Donaldson and the 55-grain soft point express bullet which he makes himself with bullet swages he got from Fred Huntington. He hit chucks like clockwork, although he did have a few unaccountable misses the last couple of days. We killed 11 crows and 1 hawk in addition to the chucks I mentioned.

''My brother has 323 chucks so far this year (1948) to his credit. Last year he killed 489 for the season. If nothing happens this year he should go away beyond the 500 mark, as he is more than 100 ahead of his 1947 record on this date. The crows were very shy, and we had trouble getting them to sit long enough for us to take a shot. As soon as the car stops they are gone, in fact they often fly as you start to slow down the car, even on back roads and lanes. We had some luck in an old barn; we lay on something soft and shot out the back door. After we killed the first crow the remainder became excited and would set up quite a racket and caw around and alight on an old tree and we shot six at the one place. We could have gotten many more shots, but we passed them up as the crows were sitting in trees with no background and the country is rather thickly settled, also, a lot of fishermen are along the streams and in the bushes. We shot at only those crows on the ground or against a hill for a background.

"The grass around there was much too high for woodchuck shooting in most places unless you were hunting in a cow pasture. Of course where chucks stood up, their heads were visible but as soon as they got down they were entirely invisible. The first several days were very bad, rain every day and cold and windy and then the last few days were ideal, but the grass had grown too high for best results. The shooting will not be good now until the hay is cut. I imagine the grass in Ontario would be much shorter because of the later spring the farther north you go.

"I suppose I killed as many chucks as you, in Canada, and probably traveled fewer miles. I drove my car all the time and made about 1500 miles in all, but I am still very much disappointed in not being able to make the trip with you. It is something I have talked about and thought over for a long time. I always hoped to make such trip, sometime."

TWENTY-FIVE- AND THIRTY-GRAIN BULLETS IN THE .170

"I would appreciate it if you could find time to write me the results of your trip in full and what you think of the .170 by this time. I have some 30-grain bullets now and will load up some cases and give them a try. I only had the 25-grain soft point bullets before, as I mentioned. My brother got some 30-grain bullets from Sisk and they seemed to be good. My brother is figuring on having a .170 built on a Model 70 Winchester action and will try it out. He has rather soured on the hi-wall actions although he used to swear by them. He has his reamers made and is going to change the case some and see how that works. He figures on making the neck about 1/16 inch shorter and increasing body length that amount, making the case hold a grain or a grain and a half more powder, with the same shoulder slope. Whether that will be an advantage or not, remains to be seen. Parkinson writes that the case as he has it now is a big improvment over what he first had. Mr. Wismer wrote me that he had trouble with bullets going to pieces and not penetrating enough to do enough laceration and mutilation of flesh to make clean kills at short ranges, which would indicate too much speed now for the bullet jacket supplied on the Sisk bullets. If he gets more boiler room in the case, he may not have much success until we get bullets with heavier jackets, then they may not open up enough and he'd have trouble the other way. In the development of a small-caliber, high-velocity bullet used on game of different resistance, there are often many things to balance, one against the other, until a desired medium result is obtained. Sincerely, H. C. Wood.''

"I once made cases for the .224 Donaldson Krag, and believe me that is some job. The case was drawn down to quite a taper. Donaldson told me he did this purposely in order to burn the powder he had to use when he designed the case. The Varmint-R that Mr. Crandall makes out of the .303 British case is a later and better design as the case is left fatter and should be much easier to make. In fact I think it should be a mighty efficient case to use.

"I was out for chucks, last evening, for a few hours, after a farmer invited me who is an ardent chuck hunter. He assured me we would get plenty but we did not kill any chucks at all. Not exactly the chucks' fault. I missed one offhand at about 75 yards, and two more shots prone at 300 yards. I then wished for my .220 Rocket. I took a new rifle I have, a K-Lovell. We finally came to a field where the hay was cut, and two chucks were out about 400 yards off. We crawled up to a knoll, still about 300 yards distant and I tried the first one. The bullet hit 20 feet short. I soon discovered the K-Lovell is not the .220 Rocket. He had a Krag fitted with scope and he blazed away with no more success. We both scared the chucks, but that was all. We came back to the same field about 45 minutes later and did the same thing over again. Still no tail! Then I saw one eating down over the edge of a knoll, it was either offhand or not at all, so after waving around for about two minutes, I finally pulled on the zig instead of the zag and the chuck ran in.

"You exceeded my chuck kill on your Canadian trip by 15 chucks. My own kill was an even 160. I shot 159 in New York State and one on my way home. You shot 175. I was up in New York in April and got 23 myself, which makes 183 for the two trips, and I may have killed 17 around here, which would make me about 200 all told for the season, to date. They do not count up so fast around here. Of course I don't hunt here like I do up in New York, here I go out in the evenings and in my spare time; up there we hunted from daylight to dark every day I was there. Will have to close for this time. Sincerely, Harold C. Wood."

A LATE SEASON TRYOUT OF THE .170 WOODSMAN
AND THE .220 ROCKET IN NEW YORK STATE. (1948)

Allentown, Penna.
August 11, 1948

"Dear Mr. Landis,

"Will drop you a few lines this evening and tell you the results of one week's woodchuck hunt that I told you I intended to take in New York. We hunted eight days in all, and as usual we hunted hard. However, this time we did not return home in the evenings. We stayed out in the field so we could get an earlier start and not have to drive so far night and morning. We hunted some new territory farther afield than the district in which we had hunted mostly before. It would have been almost impossible for us to have driven back each evening. We centered our activities about 100 miles north and east of our former haunts. Some of the new territory was productive and some was only fair. We killed a total of 263 chucks, 11 crows and one hawk, not to mention two red squirrels which annoyed us so much that we finally shot both of them.

"I took my .170 and my .220 Rocket with me, but I did not use my .170 at all, in fact I left it at my brother's house. I think I told you before that he used the barrel I got from Ackley and had a .170 built on a Model 70 Winchester action. He had an Unertl one inch 6X scope mounted on it and believe me this bolt action .170 is a hard combination to beat at anything like decent ranges. He took only his .170 and I took my .220 Rocket. This meant the .219 Donaldson of his and my .170 remained at his home during the hunt.

"Two men and two rifles is plenty to go in one car for the best results and to take the proper care of both car and rifles. We used his .170 almost exclusively for shots up to 200 yards. and I used the Rocket for longer shots. He rode in the back seat and could shoot from either side or fence line and I did all the driving and could shoot from either side of either fence or field, as conditions and requirements dictated. We tried to divide up the shooting as best we could, but of course the man on the back seat gets the most shooting. That is inevitable, even in pasture or deserted fields. Of the 263 chucks, I killed 123 and my brother killed 140. I also killed but one crow for the same reasons. We had to take the crows quickly before they sensed what was up and left the locality in nothing flat."

THE .170'S WORK COMPARED

TO THAT OF THE .22 HORNET

"Before going on this trip, somehow or other, I had very little confidence in the .170 rifle for the reason that I had not given it a really fair trial. I was almost convinced that it would do little or nothing the Hornet would not do, and the Hornet might do it better than the .170. In times gone by, I have had much in the way of favorable Hornet anchors on chucks, on the spot too, day in and day out with far more regularity than many larger calibers and without all their fuss and fury. When you shoot a .22 Hornet you shoot something standard all the way through. But when you get a .170 to use afield, you have to buy everything new from a cleaning rod, which must be made special, to the neck sizing dies, bullets, cases and everything. I was beginning to think, why go to all the bother if the .170 is little or no better than the .22 Hornet—a good Hornet?

"Since seeing what a .170 will do on a real tryout and on a good bolt action, I am fully convinced the .170 has it all over the Hornet, and if made up in one of the larger cases as you suggested, it would of course have a still greater margin of effectiveness. It is better than the Hornet particularly out beyond 100 yards. I still think that closer than 100 or possibly 125 yards, the little Hornet is as good as any, but it is amazing what that little .170 will do out at 200 yards and even over that distance.

We used both the 25-grain and the 30-grain bullets, and while the 30-grain bullets are poorly made, relative to the 25-grain bullets, they seem to shoot well and give fine results on chucks.

"Mr. Wismer said the 25-grain bullets he has gotten from Sisk, at various times, were well made and accurate; but the 30-grain bullets have never been as well formed at the base, nor as accurate. The same has been true in my case and that of my brother. The first 25-grain bullets I got from Sisk were very well made, but they were almost entirely copper covered, no lead showing at the point at all. Then my brother ordered 1,000 25-grain bullets and the last ones were somewhat different from the first ones. The last lot had quite a bit of lead exposed and appeared to give more expansion on game than the first ones purchased. The 30-grain bullets, while less accurate, at least in the twist we used, all expanded fine on all kinds of game and varmints. It is almost unbelievable what that little soft point bullet will do. On the other hand, it is also almost unbelievable how a woodchuck can be damaged and yet in a few minutes pick himself up and take the elevator down into his burrow.

"With the .170 especially, we tried to place our shots as much as possible in the head, neck or shoulders. When hit in these parts the chuck stayed anchored to the spot, but on a long, 200-yard shot, especially in the wind, you shoot for the chuck. While you may aim for the head, at that distance you may gut-shoot a chuck unintentionally, and the majority of those hit in the entrails will make it to their den, and down they will go. This is especially so if they are sitting on top of the den, or very close by. They make the den and slide down backwards if they cannot make it otherwise. A chuck which doesn't seem to be hit very hard will dive right down the den, but one which appears to be largely paralyzed in the body, will roll or slide down, usually tail first. Most of these will die. But not always immediately.

"Numerous chucks which fall in or slide into a den mouth can be reached and hooked and pulled out if you are equipped with a wire hook, and sufficiently interested in looking at the results of the shot to go into the matter of subway recovery.

"My brother had his .170 bolt action sighted in when I got there, and it seemed to do the work as well as anything I have ever shot. He has a fine cross hair reticule with a fine dot as made by Unertl, and while I do not think the .170 Marksman is a 300- to 400-yard rifle — there are larger designs of .170's for that sort of shooting, yet a man would have to be very hard to please if he asked for anything better inside of about 250 yards or so. My brother said he had killed chucks all the way up to 275 yards with this rifle in calm weather, and you don't get many shots that you really expect to score beyond that distance. In fact, my brother likes it so well that he is thinking of selling his .219 Donaldson and his other rifles and keeping only the .170. So far, at this writing, he has killed 288 chucks with it, about 20 crows and a few hawks. I think he might be wise to sell his other rifles and stick to the .170 as he is doing so well with it. And it is really a quiet rifle, as compared to most others.*

"With the .170 caliber using the small Marksman cases, you cannot always take the extremely long range shots, particularly if you have a 25- or 30-mile 9 or 3 o'clock wind. But often you can Indian up closer and then fire. One day we drove along a road and saw eight chucks in one field, all out at one time, and all at ranges of 300 to 500 yards.

"Ordinarily I would have tried the closer shots with the .220 Rocket, as I have killed plenty of chucks at ranges longer than some of these, but the wind was blowing very strong, and being a week-end day when travel is normally rather dense, I did not know how the natives would take it. These chucks were, at the moment, all across on the far side of a ravine. If we shot from close to the edge of the highway, considering that the .220 Rocket makes a sharp, high-pitched and rather voluminous report, it might stir up someone to making a complaint simply out of annoyance from the sound. So, I did not fire at any of them.

"My brother decided to put on my boots and wade across the stream in the ravine and try a shot or two from 200 yards closer, using his .170. He waded the stream and shot four of the woodchucks in less than a half-hour and would probably have gotten more if he had stayed longer. He had scored four brushes due to skillful stalking. No reason why he should not!

"One thing that bothers my brother is the idea of how many

*Author's Note: One thing to bear in mind when designing a .170-caliber bolt action rifle, particularly if a full length standard size bolt action is used, is this: The .170 caliber, which has a .168-inch land and a .172-inch groove diameter, and has only a relatively small chamber cut out at the rear, loses so very little metal in the boring, that even the choice of a 26-inch barrel on a bolt action will give you the problem of keeping the muzzle size down and the size of outside of barrel four inches or more ahead of the face of the breech bolt. The chap who thinks he simply cannot hunt with a woodchuck rifle having a barrel less than 1-1/4-inches in diameter at the breech and 7/8 to 1 inch at the muzzle, and 30 inches long, had better not order a .170 built to those dimensions or he will have to import his own personal gun bearer from darkest Africa.

shots the .170 Woodsman barrels will stand before serious ero-sion sets in. Apparently no one having a .170 seems to have shot it out, so we do not know. Also, no one has so far reported observable burning or wear just forward of, or in the throat.

"So far this year my brother has killed 664 chucks, last year 489 and the year before that almost 400, or nearly 1500 chucks in three years. So far this year I have killed 325, which has been my best year for a long time. Of course I have spent more time this year hunting chucks, than in former years, and he has had many evenings in the chuck fields. This is my third trip to New York State to go hunting this year. Last year I was up but twice. The number of times you are out and the ground you cover has much to do with your success. To shoot many chucks, you must be where the chucks are, at the right time of day, in the right season, when weather is favorable and they have something like clover to feed upon. The year before, as I recall, I was up three times, but made a shorter trip each time. I don't have the exact figures for the other years, but suppose I have killed between 600 and 650 chucks in the last three years, and most of them in New York State. This together with my brother's 1500 will make a total of between 2100 and 2200 wood-chucks bagged by us in three years. This is quite a lot of chucks in any man's country and the supply is beginning to feel the ef-fects of it. While the farmers give us a vote of thanks, for they really would like to see the supply dwindle, I can't say that I appreciate that the supply is gradually dwindling.

"In some places there seem to be as many woodchucks as ever, but in many other fields in which we used to shoot chucks extensively, one is rarely seen today. Of course, it may be largely due to causes other than shooting. Many farmers have engaged in gas poisoning campaigns. However, I am fair enough to say that I feel that possibly our shooting has had some effect upon the ultimate supply in the areas shot over most extensive-ly. In other years, other riflemen probably followed the same or similar procedure. A man usually obtains his maximum field shooting experience within relatively a few years, — when he has the health, the opportunity and the best firearms and telescopes, and of course, a suitable car in which to get around over the different thickly populated chuck areas. No one, of course, can today expect to cover all these on foot and get as many wood-chucks because the automobile covers so much more ground within a few hours, and the hunter must lose much less time reaching and returning from his hunting grounds. The major influence in enabling a man to hunt, shoot and kill more chucks in a day, a week or a season, is not so much improvement in the skill of the hunter, better rifles and scopes, or even better roads and more of them; it is the automobile, which enables a man to cover 50 to 400 miles in a day, when forty or fifty years ago he usually had to hunt within an 8 to 20 mile radius of his home or stopping place. Sincerely, H. C. Wood.''

GENERAL COMMENTS ABOUT VARMINT RIFLES

Allentown, Penna.
August 17, 1950

''Dear Mr. Landis,

''Received your two letters and also one from Mr. Wismer all of which I have perused with a great deal of interest. I have no doubt that his data is very accurate according to results achieved with his own particular rifle, however they do not agree entirely with the results which my brother and I have had with our rifles. This small difference seems to be common between different shooters and different arms of the same caliber.

''After P. O. Ackley shipped my barrel to Allentown, in error, Mr. Parkinson said he would fit my action with one of his barrels and I could send him any barrel sometime. But my brother became interested in the .170 and I asked Parkinson if I might let him have the barrel I had here, to which he agreed. My brother intended to send the barrel to Parkinson to have him chamber and fit to the action, but he had come to the conclusion that a bolt action is more dependable than a hi-wall, and he did not know whether Mr. Parkinson was equipped to chamber other actions than the hi-wall, since it takes a much longer shank on the chambering reamers when chambering for a long bolt action than when chambering for a hi-wall. The upshot of it all was that he took the dimensions from my case and had reamers ground and had his .170 barrel fitted to a Winchester Model 70 action and it has made up into a mighty fine and quiet woodchuck rifle.

''My brother and I were raised in Clearfield County, Pennsylvania, which is a grouse, bear and deer, also a turkey country; but he has been in New York State for the past ten years, working mostly around Endicott, Binghamton and Cortland. He has been hunting chucks for over twenty years, although still relatively a young man, but never went into it as extensively as he has during the past four or five years. He only had fair chuck hunting equipment until he got to hunting with me in 1943 and 1944. He used to hunt chucks with a .30-40 Krag, a .35 Remington, or any rifle which he happened to have for deer, although he did have a standard .220 Swift the first year we hunted together, but it was equipped with a 29-S Weaver scope. He hit a lot of chucks but missed a lot too. He thought he had a good outfit until I showed him that his scope was no good for that kind of rifle, so he purchased a 10X Targetspot and got it properly adjusted and then he began to really go places, but then he had no time for a bolt action rifle.

"I had a couple of swell rifles built on hi-wall actions with set triggers and he fell in love with that type action. At that time I had a .219 Zipper and a .224 Donaldson Lightning with 10X and 12X Super Targetspots, both swell outfits, and he kept after me to let him have one, which I eventually did. He then got a nice hi-wall action and took it up to Risley and ordered him to build a .224 Lightning with a heavy barrel. In the meantime I was getting the dope on the .219 Donaldson and sent a copy to my brother, so he had Risley build him a .219 Donaldson on a hi-wall action instead of the .224 Lightning. I had an order in with Morgan & Cail for a .219 Donaldson to be built on a Model 70 action and waited for it about nine months, so that my brother received his .219 several months before mine arrived, and his rifle worked so well that he turned a deaf ear to all insinuations that a bolt action was any better than a hi-wall. However, after I got my .219 on the Model 70 bolt action, he began to weaken and when I later sold it to him, he admitted that the bolt action had something on the hi-wall and that is why he wanted the .170 on a bolt action.

"His case is practically the same as mine, a wee bit shorter, or so he said. As mentioned previously, his case will chamber in my rifle but my case will not chamber on his. Also, I have two .219 Donaldsons which do not have the same depth of chamber and one will accept the other's ammunition but not vice versa.

"My brother has only tried one load so far and it has worked so well that he has not bothered to experiment further. He has been loading 14.0 grains of 4198 for both his 25-grain and his 30-grain bullets and strange to say it doesn't seem to matter which weight bullet he uses, he seems to get top results. I did feel that the 30-grain bullets were blowing up better and giving more instantaneous and uniform kills, although we both knew the 25-grain size was the more accurate in the twist we were using——one turn in twelve inches. This does not agree altogether with the data supplied by Mr. Phil Wismer who claimed that 13.8 grains of 4198 and the 30-grain bullet is too hot and shows too much pressure.*

"As I said before, it may come from the difference in chambers,† but I have not seen any evidence of excessive pressures with any of the cartridges shot in my brother's rifle, my loading or his. They do however, seem to get down to the chuck in an awful hurry. §

"Also I don't see why Mr. Wismer has trouble getting 16.0 grains of 3031 in his Woodsman cases. I have been loading 16.0 grains of 3031 right along in my .170 and it does not fill the case up level, in fact most of them have at least 1/8 or .125 inch above the powder to the top of the neck. I have been loading this charge of 16.0 grains of 3031 right along for my rifle, so that it could therefore be due to a difference in the chamber size of our respective rifles."

CASE LIFE WITH THE .170 WOODSMAN

"As far as case life is concerned, neither myself nor my brother has any idea how long the average case will last as I have over 300 cases formed and my brother has 500. He ordered 500 cases from Griffin & Howe in New York City and he ran them all through my forming dies and then I loaded them all up. He now has all of them fired at least once and a few of them fired a second time, so you can see it will be a long time, probably, before we know very much about average case life in the instance of the .170. I don't recall that I have had any failures so far and I have fired some of my cases three or four times, but I still do not have all of my cases fire-formed. I have not loaded any cases with 4198 powder as yet but intend to try it as soon

*Author's Note: He probably used Dominion primers which might be stronger than the ones the younger Wood was using, also they almost invariably fit tighter in the cartridge case.
†Author's Note: Or also if Mr. Wismer's scale weights or his powder measure was throwing heavier charges.
§Author's Note: That is characteristic of the .170 rifles——they normally develop 250 to 350 f.s. more velocity than comparable .22-caliber cartridges, for instance, the R-2 and the Super Lovell in that case.

as I have a little time. It may be that it is the ideal powder for the case, and it may be that it will work well in some rifles and not in others. One of my difficulties is that I do not have the facilities to test out rifles properly at bench-rest shooting on a good range. I would like to have a really suitable range to try the .170 at its best distances. I could also test my .220 Rocket at 300 and at 400 yards. I have been talking with a dealer here who has a farm near Allentown on which he says we can get almost any distance we want, so now that the grain is cut I expect to get out two of my rifles and try them properly on his farm. Then I'll know what they will do.''

CARE NEEDED IN FIRING AT WOODCHUCKS

''Both my brother and I are extremely careful where we shoot. We have passed up many a good shot at chucks this last summer which were located along a hedgerow. We could not see over it and not what was beyond that growth. In New York State there are hundreds of dairy cattle pasturing all over the country-side and many times some are lying down in the shade, back of a hedgerow and can not be seen from the side on which the hunter is gunning. A bullet, if it went a bit high, and overshot a standing chuck might go right on through and kill or wound a fine milk cow.''

RIFLE TESTING ON STEEL PLATES

''My brother had a piece of new, cold-rolled steel, a half-inch thick, on which we tried his .219 Donaldson made by Morgan & Cail, and loaded to the gills. I tried the .170, and we also tried the .30-1906 with metal cased bullets and none of them would penetrate the plate. Some did cause a bulge on the other side. I tried it with my .220 Rocket and it went through slick as a whistle. Of course penetration in steel is not, after all, a sure sign of the best in a woodchuck rifle or bullet. I do not at the moment recall whether we ever tried the .22 Hornet on this steel plate, but anyone interested could make a similar test.

''A lot of the people I have talked to about the .170 ask me what it will do that the .22 Hornet will not do. I did think that maybe it did not have much on the Hornet until we made this last hunting trip. I am thoroughly convinced it has the Hornet outclassed when it comes to ranges longer than 100 to 125 yards.

I have always had a great respect for the Hornet, as I have mentioned previously, but within the range of the Hornet which I put at not over 125 yards for certain results. It will kill at greater ranges occasionally and might make kills up to 200 yards and beyond but you and I both know it is not a dependable 200-yard chuck rifle. Mr. Wismer says he has killed chucks at 400 yards with the .170 Woodsman. I don't see how he did it. Possibly it was a freak shot or two. Four hundred yards is a long ways to hit a chuck, even if you have a rifle which has enough wallop left to kill a chuck at that range. Then we must, of course, consider the drop of the bullet over 400 yards, which we both know is considerable. If he knew just exactly how far away his chuck happened to be, he might make an occasional hit, provided there was no side wind and a dozen other things which we both know would interfere with the flight of a bullet. The fact of the matter is that I often wonder how any of us are able to shoot as well as we do, everything considered. Sincerely, H. C. Wood."

THE .250 DONALDSON

Allentown, Penna.
January 10, 1950

"Dear Mr. Landis,

"I had Bob Wallack build me one of the .250 Donaldson's since you were up here. I just received it December 22, 1949 and have only fired it about two boxes of cartridges so far. It is made regularly on the .257 Roberts case with the shoulder pushed back a little, the case blown out larger at the shoulder, and given a 30-degree taper. It will hold about the same quantity of powder as the regular .257 case but it is shorter and fatter. In my first 20 shots fired out of the rifle in fire-forming cases it did so well I wrote Wallack about it.

"I just had 20 cases loaded and I stuck the scope on here at the house and bore-sighted it out of the kitchen window, so I did not have it exactly where I wanted it on the target. I expended seven shots in sighting it in. Then the next five shots at 100 yards could easily be covered with a dime and nothing showing. That left me eight more shots to go, so I moved over on another target. Six of the eight are all cutting into one ragged hole which a dime will barely cover, the other two are cutting into each other, making a hole about one and a half times bullet diameter but directly to the right of the other group about three-quarters of an inch from the center of the other group. As to what caused this change of grouping, I can only hazard a guess. What I think caused it was that I made the cases before I received the rifle and being a rimless case, I was afraid of getting the cartridge cases too short and thus automatically making the head space too great, so I left the cases as long as possible. Some of them turned out to be a few thousandths too long, and it was with difficulty that I was able to force the bolt closed on those. In that instance, you have too little head spacing.

"Anyway, I believe this .25-caliber rifle has definite possibilities. I know I was so well pleased with the results right off the bat, that I really think the thing will shoot once I get a stock made for it. At present I only have the old military stock cut off and grooved out to take a larger diameter barrel. I got one of Wallack's heavy bench-rest barrels 1-1/4 inches at the breech and tapered to 1-1/8 inches at the muzzle, 20 inches long, built on a high numbered Springfield action. Wallack seemed to have done a good job on it and I believe it will make a nice outfit when I get it all rigged up. It would sure make a honey to shoot chucks from a car, or from a substantial rest of size, or a portable woodchuck rest from the prone position, but it is much too heavy to tote around if you really are going to walk in the fields.

"I believe the .25-caliber is better ballistically for the longer ranges when it is windy. However, it also cracks louder. Wallack says he feels certain he can obtain 3300 f.s.m.v. with the 100-grain bullet if the case is loaded to the maximum. That is making it step right along. He also says that he can get that without the excessive erosion and barrel burning that you get with a couple of the .25-caliber magnums now on the market.*

"Roy Weatherby claims he can get close to 4000 f.s. with his .25-caliber magnum, but how many rounds will it be good for? Some think about 300 rounds and few can stand the expense of a barrel wearing out with that small amount of shooting. I had one of his .220 Rockets and after 600 rounds it was shot out. I only loaded this new .250 medium velocity as I figure I can get better accuracy and the shooting will be easier on the barrel. My loads for the groups above mentioned were 36.0 grains of 3895, lot unknown, 100-grain Sierra bullet and Winchester No. 120 primers. Wallack told me that he got his smallest group

*Author's Note: A .250 Donaldson with 100-grain Sierra, 45 grains 4350 and 120 primer was recently chronographed at Remington Arms Company — average velocity 3307 f.p.s.

with this .250 Donaldson with 41-1/2 grains of 4350 powder behind the 100-grain Sierra bullet. He claims he obtained one group that measured a quarter inch from center to center of the 5-shot group, which is considerably better than my groups. I don't know whether it pays a chap to fool with this 4895 powder. I have been getting a pound here and a couple of pounds there, and that doesn't seem to be good policy because I understand there are a lot of different lot numbers and they vary widely in results. I got myself a supply of it and after I use up the remainder of the last cannister of a former lot, then I should be set to obtain more uniform results. If you do not have any cases of the new Donaldson .250, let me know and I will send you samples. I think it makes a nice looking case and I really believe it will deliver the goods. But they won't all go in one hole and we shouldn't let ourselves be kidded by that idea, regardless of the opinions of some riflemen. Sincerely, H. C. Wood.''

WOOD'S EARLY SUMMER COMMENTS — 1950

Allentown, Penna.
June 25, 1950

''Dear Mr. Landis,

"I have not done much shooting this year so far. The weather was not fit a lot of the time and I was too busy to go out when a decent day would come along. I took six days off over Memorial Day and went chuck hunting in New York State with my brother. We had a lot of fun but still did not do as well as we have on many other trips we have taken. The Spring has been so wet and the grass grew so fast that by the last of May it was so high you could not see a chuck unless he stood up. We tried to hunt in pasture fields where the cattle had it eaten down and you could see them better. But believe it or not, the chuck population is not what it used to be, especially in the parts where we hunted. I used to tell my brother that it would not last forever. He used to say they will come from the hills and as fast as you clean them out, others will come to take their places, but now he is ready to admit that is not so. In territory where we used to make large kills now you drive around a whole day and are lucky if you get five or six shots in a day. They have been having a scourge of rabies up through a lot of those counties and it has affected the foxes and various other animals and my brother believes it may have gotten into the woodchucks.

Whether that is so or not we have no way of knowing. He told me of a wild fox that came right into a yard in a small community and attacked a young boy. It bit him quite severely and then escaped into the brush. The next day it was back and attacked a little girl. She tried to get away and it tore most of her clothes off before she got away from it. So if the foxes are running over the country with rabies, the chucks may also have it in some of these areas.

"We got 112 chucks in five days hunting which is below our usual average, but we still did pretty well considering everything. As I told you in some of my previous letters, my brother keeps an accurate record of all the chucks he has shot, with day and date and number shot during the last five years. We were checking over his books this time when I was up and for the years 1946-1949 and so far in 1950 he lacked at that time, six chucks of having killed 2000, but he is over the 2000 now as he wrote me he was out the following Saturday afternoon and got five, so by now he probably has ten or twelve over the 2000 mark, which is a lot of chucks in any man's country. It would be interesting to know how much on an average each of those chucks cost him in money spent for guns, scopes, ammunition and gasoline and car expense, not counting his time, meals, lodging, etc., during those five years. He never drives less than 100 miles in a day as he has to drive at least 50 miles before he gets to chuck country and then the driving only begins. It is usually a couple of hundred miles a day, so if you figure that up, it is no small item. I drove over 1000 miles on our hunt on Memorial Day, but it is good sport and I like it. You can't go in for any kind of sport nowadays unless it costs you money.

"A lot of fellows go up in Canada and spend three or four hundred dollars trying to get a shot at a moose and maybe then never get a shot. At least we got some shooting. I shot nine shots at one before I got it. It was a very long shot, at least 400 yards and possibly quite a bit more. It was across a deep ravine. The ravine was possibly 300 or 400 feet deep and on the opposite side, the land sloped away for possibly a quarter of a mile. We spied this chuck out nosing around and my brother egged me on to try it. The first shot he said I was about a foot to the right and several feet short, as he could see the dirt fly through the 20X spotter. The chuck ran in but was back out in about 15 seconds, so I held higher and more left windage and shot the second shot. He said I was nearer but still quite a bit short and to the right. The chuck ran in again but right back out. I kept on shooting like that until I had shot eight shots. The old chuck was getting a little leery as he ran on up the hill about 50 yards into another hole but came back out as usual, so on the ninth shot I decided to give him plenty of both elevation and left windage, even if I did overshoot. By golly when she cracked that time the old chuck just seemed to wilt and his old tail waved a few times and he did not go in any more. It was one of the longest shots I ever made. My brother said I did not hit him. He said the old chuck just naturally fell over from exhaustion from dodging all of that lead and gave himself up as dead. Anyway it was a good shot and worth the price of the entire trip. We both used .219's on this trip and he used his 20X two-inch bench-rest scope. Good Luck and I will drop you a line from Erie if anything new turns up. Sincerely, H. C. Wood.''

CHAPTER 14

Cartridge Comparisons by
Millard M. Wood

M R. MILLARD M. WOOD, woodchuck hunter of southern New York State, resident of Endicott, New York, is an expert mechanic, tool and die maker and machinist. His discussions are from a mechanical standpoint. He brings in many things which bear directly upon rifle accuracy which men lacking his skill in these trades may not think of.

I have been a chuck hunter for the past 25 years and have used everything from a pick and shovel in my boyhood days, to the .170 Woodsman. I have had a great many pet chuck rifles in my time in all calibers from the .30-40 Krag down to my present special .170 Woodsman which I am now using exclusively.

THE .220 SWIFT

In years gone by I thought the .220 Swift was the only real chuck rifle but since then I have experimented with a number of various calibers and special cases. Please let it be understood before we go any further that I do not wish to imply that the .220 Swift is not a good chuck or varmint rifle. It uses a very good cartridge but has a very short barrel life. For various reasons there are other rifles that are better for woodchuck shooting in areas similar to mine.

THE .220 ROCKET

I have had experience with one version of the improved .220 Swift called the .220 Rocket — put out by Roy E. Weatherby. I cannot say that I feel that it is an improvement over the standard .220 Swift. From what I have seen, one rifle of this caliber proved to be rather undependable as you could not rely upon it from one shot to another.* The .220 Rocket did not do well for us when using anything close to maximum loads.

A number of different loads and bullets had been tried in this .220 Rocket and none proved entirely satisfactory. I did not own this rifle, but would have liked to have owned it — to have experimented until I had found out why it would not shoot as close groups as one might expect. My theory in regard to this cartridge is that there is excessive boiler room as compared to the very light weight of the bullet. That with normal .220 Swift type bullets, the cartridge is not balanced between bullet size and weight and cartridge volume. It develops too much push for such light bullets. Twist of the barrel of course largely determines the weight and length of bullet which may be used in it successfully.

A CUSTOM .219 ZIPPER

I own a custom .219 Zipper, barrel chambered for the Winchester factory. I have done quite a lot of hunting with this particular cartridge and I have found that the .219 Zipper factory ammunition is not nearly as dependable in the same rifle as handloads. Good handloads make all the difference in the world in the shooting of the standard Zipper cartridge.

I have also observed numerous versions of the Improved .219 Zipper. The one that I am most familiar with is the K-Zipper put out by Lysle S. Kilbourn, Whitesboro, New York. I have shot this version of the Improved Zipper and it will really shoot 100-yard groups. I also have witnessed many groups shot by it and have chronograph test sheets on it in my files that showed the bullet speeds up to 4305 ft. per second with 33.5 grains of No. 3031 powder. For further information on this .22 K-Zipper contact Lysle D. Kilbourn at Wood Road in Whitesboro.

THE .219 DONALDSON

Another of my pet chuck rifles was a .219 Donaldson built on a Winchester hi-wall action by M. S. Risley, Hubbardsville, New York, and chambered by Bob Keel, of Albany. I received

---

*Author's Note: I have seen the same thing happen with the target weight factory .220 Swift which had to be shot-in extensively before it would give uniform elevations. After it was settled into the stock and the barrel had worn a bit, it shot much more uniformly and held its elevations from day to day far better.

this rifle the first of April, 1945. At the time components were very hard to obtain and very high in price. I made all of my cases for it from new .25-35 ammunition. This was the only source of cases available at that time. Primers and bullets were so scarce and difficult to obtain that I made an oil hydraulic die to blow out my cases so that I could obtain a full size case more readily and load a full charge the first time, as the case was then full size of the chamber. This saved on primers and bullets, both nearly unobtainable. In fact, primers were "gold" in the possession of the hand-loaders at that time.

THE DONALDSON CHAMBER

The chamber of this Donaldson was of the latest design. There had been a half-dozen or more earlier versions but then it came to the final decision and was called the "latest design." It was 1/16 inch longer on the length of the neck. By making cases as stated above in the oil hydraulic die, using full loads for the first firing, I obtained very good results. I used 30.0 grains of DuPont No. 4320 with .045-inch graphite wads and 55-grain bullet and Winchester No. 115 primers. This load gave best results of any load I tried. This load was capable of shooting 5/8 inch or less, 5-shot groups at 100 yards. I have also shot chucks with this same load up to 483 yards using a Unertl scope with 2-inch objective in 10X power. I used a variety of weights and makes of bullets and found that the Sisk Express bullet in 55-grain weight gave the best results. I then obtained a set of dies and material from Fred Huntington (the R.C.B.S. dies of California) and started making my own bullets in 55-grain weight. These dies are used in the Pacific tool.

I obtained one of the new Pacific Super Tools for doing this job of bullet making. As for the new cast steel frame that they are putting out called the Super Tool; it has a very strong and sturdy frame but before I had completed making my first hundred bullets, I had to rebuild the Pacific Tool as it comes with standard toggle joint and pin just like the old Pacific Tool. This toggle joint pin is 3/8 inch in diameter which did not stand the pressure for making bullets. I made a new pin to replace it.

THE NEW 5/8-INCH PIN FOR THE PACIFIC TOOL

The new pin that I turned out was 5/8 inch in diameter ground and hardened; by doing this I had to make a new toggle link in order to take the larger pin. I made this out of 3115 steel hardened and I also made a new handle from 3/4-inch drill rod.

All that had to be altered on the Pacific frame was to ream out the toggle joint pin holes to 5/8 inch diameter which action does not weaken the frame. After doing this I had a good stout and sturdy tool with which to turn out bullets.

PRECISION BULLET MAKING BY HAND

Precision bullet making by hand is a man's job. Speed or production in quantity does not enter in, as you must take your time in making bullets if you want precision made and, therefore uniform bullets.

Anyone can make bullets if he has a good strong back and a good strong arm and along with it, the right kind of equipment and material. He must have all of these and with them he must use good judgment. He can then turn out from 75 to 100 precision-made, uniform bullets per hour.

Later, I obtained a bullet-core swage from Huntington and swaged all my cores in the jackets before forming the bullet. By doing this I obtain more uniform and better bullets.

Jackets of pure copper may be obtained from Huntington and in different lengths to provide bullets of 35 grains to 70 grains in weight. He can also supply lead wire, dies, core swage, wire cutter, Pacific tool, Super tool and all necessary components for making precision bullets; also, a variety of different bullet shapes can also be purchased from the same source.

I have made and used both recessed and flat-base bullets and cannot say that I can see any difference in the performance of the different types. Base design is optional with the rifleman.

Since I obtained these dies back in the fall of 1945, I have made approximately 6000 bullets and the dies do not show any visible wear. I ordered dies to mike .2236 inch as nearly as possible for use in a .224-inch groove diameter barrel. Thus I allowed four ten-thousandths wear in the dies before the bullet would be up to groove diameter. In ordering dies I would suggest that die diameter should not exceed .223 inch for a .224-inch groove diameter. In my experience, a little smaller bullet will give better accuracy than a bullet up to bore diameter. Pressure will expand the smaller diameter bullet to fit the bore and much better accuracy is the result.

I have made all of my own .22-caliber bullets for the past

three years and a few for my close friends. I do not try to make bullets on a production basis but during the winter months try to get enough made ahead to carry me through the target shooting season and also through the woodchuck seasons.

In July 1947, I bought a Morgan & Cail .219 Donaldson. This rifle is built on a Winchester Model 70 action, heavy barrel Marksman stock. It weighs, with Unertl 2-inch scope, 15 pounds 4 ounces. I made all new cases for this rifle from .32 Winchester Special brass as ammunition from previous .219 described would not interchange due to .005 inch difference in chamber length.

I loaded all ammunition with 31.0 grains of DuPont No. 4320 — 55-grain own make bullet and Winchester No. 115 primers.

By making cases from .32 Special brass, the case fits the chamber before firing except at shoulder angle but would take full load of 31.0 grains No. 4320 for first firing. Accuracy between first load or first firing of new cases and formed cases shows but very little difference. The average five-shot group prone, at 100 yards, with sand-bag rest under forearm, is 3/8 to 1/2 inch. I have shot chucks up to 487 yards with this rifle using the chuck rest prone.

THE .170 CALIBER WOODSMAN, MODEL 70

In June 1948, I had a .170 Woodsman built on a Winchester Model 70 action. I made my own chambering reamers and changed the shoulder angle to 30 degree sharp-corner angle instead of approximately a 22-degree radius angle as the sample which I had obtained. I had Lysle S. Kilbourn fit the barrel and chamber with my supervision as to the way I wanted it done. I am using Griffin & Howe .22-3000 or R-2 cases. When miking up these new cases for over-all length, I found quite a variation in length of the cartridge case. I decided to shorten the chamber and trim all brass to one length that would fit this chamber very snugly. On doing this, I also made reamers .002 inch smaller than the sample case on body diameter next to head.

Before spending any more money on this rifle for a new stock, I was determined to find out what it would do in the way of grouping and on chucks. Using the Winchester sporter stock, I inletted the forearm larger in order to take the new barrel and made it a full floating barrel rifle. On Saturday evening, June 12, 1948, I finished this rifle complete and made up 50 cases loaded with 14.0 grains of DuPont No. 4198 using Sisk bullets. I loaded one half with 25-grain bullets and one half with 30-grain bullets, using, in both cases, Winchester No. 116 primers.

On June 13, I took this new rifle out for its first test. Not having a range available, I selected a stone quarry where I could get a full 100 yards. Shooting prone with sand-bag rest, this rifle was capable of shooting half inch or less 5-shot groups using a Unertl 6X scope with medium cross hairs. I was amazed at the performance of this new arm as to what it would do on paper (at the target) and was very anxious then to try it out on old Mr. Marmota Monax. I could see no difference to speak of between the 25- and 30-grain bullets, using the same powder charge of 14.0 grains of 4198 behind both weights for target shooting. I then started out to find a chuck!

My first woodchuck, fired on at 135 yards, was hit. The bullet went in the back just below the shoulder, and knocked the chuck over. He lay there for possibly one and a half to two minutes. When I arrived at the hole, the chuck was in, out of sight. I could not get him out. There was a pool of blood from the lungs, about 3 inches in diameter, where the chuck had lain on the turf. The second chuck which I shot with the little .170 was struck at 128 yards. The 25-grain bullet entered the chuck's right side, in back of the shoulder, and went through the lungs. The chuck never moved for possibly a minute and a half and then slid into the hole. I could not get him out. I then began to realize that I was not shooting a rifle of the energy of the Donaldson. With the .219 Donaldson my favorite spot is back of the shoulder, through the heart and the lungs. I then began to place my shots with the .170 through the head or through the front of the shoulder. The next three chucks I shot at ranges of 150 to 175 yards. Bullets entered either head or shoulder; the chuck lay where shot and never moved. On the number six chuck shot the first day with the .170 Woodsman, I tried another back-of-shoulder shot to convince myself that the chuck must either be hit in the head or the shoulder or neck to get tails for count. That concluded my first day's experience with the .170 Woodsman.

Since I have obtained this rifle, I have hunted twenty-three different times and have used it exclusively with the exception of two hunting trips when I also carried the Model 70 Winchester. Fortunately it happened that I had two very good days' hunts. I ran out of ammunition for the .170 Woodsman and had to use the .219 to finish the day's shooting.

I was in doubt, when having the .170 rifle built, whether it would be an improvement over my Winchester Model 70 .22 Hornet rifle, I shot this .170 and used it exclusively on my recent hunting trips and have shot chucks with it when it was raining quite hard. I have given it almost all the tests that a varmint hunter could ask a rifle to stand for all shots up to 300 yards.

For a comparison between the .170 Woodsman and the standard .22 Hornet, I would say the Hornet will no ways near reach out as far nor bag a number of chucks or crows as the .170 Woodsman.

As to the ballistics of the .170 Woodsman, I have been told that it was capable of 5000 feet per second but that I do not believe. A much larger capacity .170 case is required to obtain such velocities. I do not have a chronographed test for this little .170 Woodsman but the impression one obtains from field shooting is that it is producing possibly 3800 to 4000 f.s. muzzle velocity.*

All chucks that I have shot with this rifle have been hit with either the 25- or 30-grain bullet. The bullets went through the chuck with the exception of one. When using the 25-grain bullets it is often very difficult to find the hole where the bullet entered. In the greater percentage of shots there will be a hole about the size of a half-dollar or a little larger, where the bullet comes out.

One very strange thing happened on one chuck. Where the bullet entered, the hair was entirely gone and the skin was bare about an inch around the bullet hole. The hair was not burned off. I cannot explain it. The hair was simply no longer there. I have been told, or have heard from others that have used the Woodsman, that it would burn the hair off around the hole where the bullet enters, due to bullet speed. I hope that I am not sufficiently dense to believe such a theory. I have had plenty of experience with ''wild cats'' in high speed and have shot many a chuck and I still have to see my first chuck where the bullet burned off the hair. This chuck which I mentioned did not have the hair burned off. But the hair was gone just the same!

I have shot a number of chucks in one of my favorite fields where I hunt in the evenings. The field runs up hill about possibly a 15 degree angle and the shooter is looking west towards the sun. Sometimes it is very difficult to shoot with aim, unless

*Author's Note; It gives that impression, but chronographed tests so far give 3500-3600 f.s.

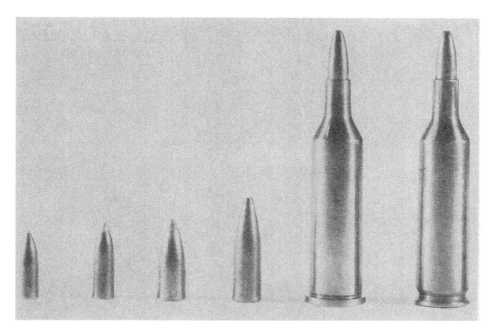

Left to Right: 25- and 30-grain caliber Sisk bullets: two .22 bullets; .170 cartridge made by P. O. Ackley; .170 cartridge designed by the author.

Three small size woodchuck cartridges. *L to R:* .170 Landis Woodsman; .222 Remington; .22-357 Ramsey.

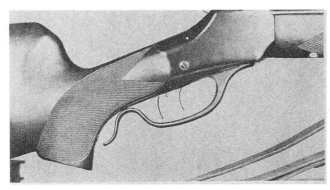

Close-up of a Winchester Hi-side action, high-comb scope stock, Winchester Scheutzen double set triggers. CREDIT: D. M. FELLOWS.

The late J. Bushnell Smith firing from his portable woodchuck rest. CREDIT: D. M. FELLOWS.

Frank M. Riddle, showing how to use a Mauser action with special stock. Gun can be aimed with the left eye and fired from the right shoulder.

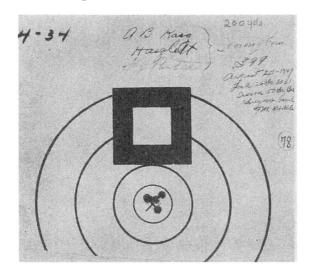

Two groups by Frank M. Riddle.

you shade the objective lens of the scope. By shooting in the direction of the sun, you can see large clouds of hair rise and float in the air when the chuck is shot. It is, in my opinion and personal experience, all in the way the bullet strikes the chuck that loosens the hair and makes a bare spot. Where the bullet enters, I have yet to see any smoke coming from the chuck where the hair has been burned off.

In regard to the work of the 30-grain bullet on chucks, the hole where the bullet enters is practically the same as the hole from the 25-grain but the hole where the bullet leaves the chuck is as large as your hand and sometimes larger. The skin is slit in several instances for approximately three to four inches from the bullet's exit, as if it had been slit with a razor blade. This shows that the impact of the bullet is great enough to cause a bursting and shattering effect upon the animal tissue and upon the skin which contains it. The reason for 30-grain bullets making larger hole of exit is due to a soft lead point on the 30-grain bullets. The 25-grain bullet is practically all covered on the point by the jacket and no lead to amount to anything is showing.

Crows, when shot with the .170 Woodsman, just seem to pulverize into small pieces and to disappear. All that is left of them are the wings, head, and feet—the body is entirely gone.

I am going to have the .170 chronographed to see what I am getting in the matter of muzzle velocity. The shooting of the rifle gives the impression that one is getting as much muzzle velocity as in the case of the Donaldson although some seem to feel differently. The above-mentioned load shows absolutely no indication of excessive pressure.

Up until now, September 1, 1948, I have shot 560 rounds through this .170 rifle. The barrel does not show any wear at all. As for cases, I bought 500 new .22-3000 or R-2 cases from Griffin & Howe. When necking these cases down to .17 caliber, I only lost one case out of 500. It was my fault, due to trying to form it in two operations.

FORMING CASES

These cases are the easiest made, of any cases I have ever tried to swage into shape. They do not require any pressure at all. They are so easily made that one could make them with one finger, this showing how much or rather how little pressure is required to form them.

I have fired all cases once. My loss in brass when first fired was only one case out of 499. This case split on the shoulder angle. I do not know the cause. Perhaps it was a defective case.

RELOADING TOOLS USED

I like Belding & Mull tools for loading and use them exclusively. This includes neck sizing, decapping and repriming. For bullet seating I use straight line hand bullet seaters of my own make and I have a small arbor press for seating the bullet instead of rubber or wooden mallet.

I like the Belding & Mull reloading tool best of all as you can see every operation. I am very particular about my reloading. Everything must be done correctly to produce uniform loads; 99 per cent of your accuracy is in the loading of the ammunition. If you have good ammunition and know that it is loaded correctly, then you have confidence in it.

I own and use Henry Troemner Laboratory Balance Scales. They are accurate to one hundredth of a grain. When weighing powder charges, I balance the scale within one kernel of powder so that every load is uniform.

Everyone should take great care in loading his ammunition to make every load uniform in all ways as to seating primers, seating bullets, powder charge and neck sizing. His cases should be segregated as to make. Different makes of cases have quite a variation in thickness of brass. This makes a lot of difference in the boiler room of them. One make of case may not give as good results as another using the same powder charge.

Use caution when loading ammunition. Never load maximum loads at the start, either with a new rifle, or at the beginning of your reloading experience. Always be a trifle cautious and develop your heavier charges gradually. You could have a rifle with a very tight chamber, a very short or abrupt throat, or all three of these plus too much headspace. I do not load maximum charges. Better accuracy is almost always obtained, and fewer fliers, with a milder load than the absolute maximum. Also, the slightly-below-top charges are definitely safer.

I have owned and used a good many different actions. I had been under the impression, for a time, that I could not shoot well except with the aid of a set trigger. Those days are gone. Never let yourself think that you must have a set trigger. A crisp, uniform, and rather light trigger pull is normally better in the field than many set triggers, although not always better than all of them. It is generally much safer.

My choice of actions for this day and age is the prewar Model 70 Winchester. Notice that I said, prewar. The prewar Model 70 seems to have almost everything. I have owned a couple of post-war Model 70's and I do not cotton to them nearly as well as the prewar Model 70's.

I have owned, in past years, a number of Winchester hi-wall actions in many different calibers. I own two of these at the present time and find both of them very good shooting rifles.

The Mauser action is a good strong action but it does not appeal to me. For one thing, the average Mauser trigger pull could be better.

The Enfield action is one of the strongest actions available. In my opinion it has several disadvantages when being remodeled into a .22-or .17-caliber Wildcat.

The Springfield action is my second choice as a good bolt action for building into one or the other of numerous wildcats.

ANNUAL KILLS OF WOODCHUCKS AND CROWS

In the last three years previous to this writing, and up to September 1948, I have kept account of the number of chucks, crows and other varmints that I have killed. I have hunted 123 different times, but not all full days of hunting. Sometimes it has been a few hours after work in the early evening.

1946 SHOOTING

In 1946 I hunted 47 different times which included parts of days. I shot 368 woodchucks but I did not keep an account of the number of crows killed.

1947 SHOOTING

In 1947 I hunted 39 different times, including part days or evenings, or whenever I had a few hours of spare time. My total kills for that season follow:

Woodchucks 489
Crows 47
Red Foxes 5

1948 SHOOTING

Up to September 1, 1948, I hunted 37 different times. My kills for the 1948 season to September 1, were:

Woodchucks 651
Crows 22

To December 31, 1948:

Woodchucks 707
Crows 24

This shows 218 more woodchucks bagged than in any other recent year and most of these were killed with the little .170 Woodsman. Crows, however, either were not so plentiful as in the previous season, or I devoted less time to hunting them.

From my records for the past three years, my total is 1508 woodchucks and 69 crows. My best day's hunting in 1946 was May 30 when I bagged 30 woodchucks. In 1947 my best day was August 1 when I bagged 33 woodchucks. In 1948, the high two days were July 17 and July 18 when I bagged 86 woodchucks and two crows. On the 17th of July, 1948, I shot an all red chuck which was definitely a fireman except for a few black hairs in the tip of his tail. I have seen and have shot quite a number of all black woodchucks in my hunting, but have seen only the one all red woodchuck. I have been on the look-out for a freak white chuck, but up until this time I am still waiting to find it.

When hunting, I do not pace the distance of every shot as my time is limited. Since I go for the pleasure of hunting woodchucks, I do not take the time to step them off, with the exception of the occasional very long shots.

The majority, or possibly I should say 75 per cent of my chuck shooting, is at ranges of 250 to 375 yards, or possibly a little farther. As long as the woodchuck is visible and lays where shot, I do not take the time to go and look at it as I have found numberless times that the chuck is then there to stay. Attracting additional attention to yourself serves no useful purpose.

USE OF THE CHUCK REST

I use a chuck rest for field shooting as it serves a number of different purposes. One is as a rifle rest. Another is as a spear. It carries a hook inside it for the chucks which slide into the holes and may be hooked out. It also serves as a cane. I find the chuck rest a necessity while engaged in long range chuck shooting.

My equipment also includes a "Sport-Scope" in 9 x 50 size for spotting. It is much more convenient than a rifle scope. It is much lighter and easier to carry in the field than a pair of binoculars of equal power.

From June 13 until September 1 there had been 333 kills made with my new Woodsman .170. There were 319 chucks and 14 crows at ranges of 100 yards to 300 yards as previously mentioned. It is an excellent rifle for hunting in closely inhabited districts as the muzzle blast is not any more than a good healthy "pop." When hunting in "civilized" areas with the .219 Donaldson or other case of similar or larger size, the muzzle blast is terrific in comparison. It is very noticeable to everyone including all those whom you would rather would not notice it. The local inhabitants seem to think one is blasting stumps. Cartridge holding 30 grains or more of powder always crack sharply.

Once when shooting the .220 Swift in a populated area, I shot a chuck about 200 yards from a house. The lady came out and asked me if someone had dropped a bomb!

I do my woodchuck hunting alone except when hunting with my brother Harold C. Wood. We made an eight-day hunting trip this last season using the .170 Woodsman exclusively. Out of the kills made with this rifle, I made about 250. I witnessed the balance made by my brother.

WOODCHUCK RIFLES AND WOODCHUCK SHOOTING

BY FRANK M. RIDDLE

Mr. Frank M. Riddle, of Oil City, Pennsylvania, is a gunsmith, one of the outstanding Bench Rest Rifle Association match shooters, and a woodchuck hunter of many years of experience. His skill in rifle stocking and in the making up of bench-rest and woodchuck rifles is well known. His skill in shooting woodchucks is probably less advertised, one reason being that not many know that he lives in a fine woodchuck district and has friends in others in his home state. Since his experience should be of interest to others, I asked Mr. Riddle to contribute the comment upon chuck rifles and their use in the field, which follows below.

Having read a number of your books on .22-caliber rifles and their use, I feel honored by having the opportunity to contribute to your most recent book, that on woodchuck rifles and woodchuck shooting. If it is only one half as instructive and interesting as your other books it will tell the woodchuck hunter about all he will have to know to be a past master at woodchuck hunting and shooting.

Having hunted woodchucks and crows all my life, I believe I have killed more chucks than any other person in this section of the country. There has always been really good chuck and crow shooting near my home here. Before the State Game Commission put a season and a daily bag limit on chucks it was not unusual to kill twenty chucks on a day's hunt. The last shooting I did in the year 1948, which was the last year that there was no limit on the number you could kill legally, the hunting was in Potter County, Pennsylvania. A friend of mine, Mr. L. E. Ferringer, and myself killed 104 chucks and 22 crows on a two-day hunt. On the last of this shoot I was so fortunate as to have an average of 100 per cent kills. I have only had a few days with no misses and never before with that much shooting.

My friend, Mr. Ferringer, and I have never thought it very sporting to shoot at and strike a chuck any place other than the head, and that means the vital portions of the head. That limitation usually keeps our shooting within 300 yards. We do not go in for short range shooting or for stalking unless the chuck is over that range. When a chuck is beyond 300 yards it is beyond the certain accuracy of any of the ultra high speed, super-accurate woodchuck rifles when you are firing at the head only.

The chucks we kill are all used for one purpose or another. We never leave them in the field to spoil. There are too many people who enjoy the meat of woodchucks and we do not find it too much trouble, therefore, to bring the carcasses home. You would be surprised at the numbers of people who look forward to being supplied with a mess of chucks once they learn the ones you have for them are not all shot up. There is nothing that will turn a person against eating chucks as having some given to them that are all shot up with the flesh torn and blasted full of particles of bullet, hair and bone. So we are careful in our shooting and it makes everyone happy. There is nothing in the shooting game that makes a chuck hunter more elated than to overhear someone say, ''I saw that lot of chucks that Bill Daley was given the other day, and every one had been shot cleanly through the skull.''

I don't carry my 22-pound .219 Donaldson in the hunting field so I seldom shoot my crows through the head purposely. Just any vital place will do on crows for we do not have a demand or a market for crows. They do not look as if they would make a tasty potpie after you see twenty feet of dust, "smoke" and flesh spurt from the other side of Mr. Crow.

My first woodchuck shooting began when I was about twelve years old. I worked and sweat on a water-carrying job for about thirty to fifty road workers most of whom seemed to be thirsty from morning until night. I carried water until I had accumulated $11.65 with which I purchased a brand new Model 4 Remington .22-caliber single shot rolling block rifle. This rifle has a 24-inch octagon barrel. With reasonable luck a person could fire all the shots from it into a group one could cover with a dime at 25 yards, which was really good accuracy in those days. This little Remington accounted for a lot of chucks in the next couple of years. Then came a Krag which shook the countryside and also the shooter (who was a bit light) each time he pulled the trigger, but with it I could reach out a lot farther. The danger of shooting it in settled areas soon put a stop to using it for chucks. From then on I think I covered them all from the .25-20 right on up using both hand loads and the factory cartridges. It was a good many years before a first class chuck rifle found a home in my gun rack, and I suppose that is true of most of those of about my age and length of chuck shooting experience. We just didn't have the chuck rifles in those days that we have today.

Then came the .22 Hornet. I bought one of the first that were made by the Savage Arms Corporation. With hand loads you could stay in a group the size of a silver dollar. With this rifle I could head-shoot chucks up to a range of about 175 yards. I killed more woodchucks with this rifle than any other gun I ever owned, the principal reason for this being that I used it for chuck hunting over a longer period of time.

When rifle cranks started to rework Hornet cases and add a few more such as the Lovells and the other, and later sharp shoulder hot jobs, the chuck shooting stayed about the same — not too much improvement over the regular Hornet. Then came the real high velocity hot jobs such as the .220 Swift, the .22-250, the .219 Donaldson and so forth. I have done much chuck shooting with nearly all of the wildcats as they came out and have found the .220 Swift to be one of the best all-around varmint rifles even today. When a man says he has a wildcat that can outshoot a Swift on chucks I feel that he has never had a hot

Swift or ammunition that would really group in a Swift without blowing up the bullets when fired from a cold barrel in the field. I know that it has its drawbacks, that it is noisy and that the cartridge has a habit of eating out the barrel at the breech enough to ruin accuracy in the first couple of thousand rounds. But that is a lot of chuck shooting and if you figure a .220 Swift barrel in dollars and cents, it doesn't amount to much when you consider all the other costs involved in real honest-to-goodness woodchuck shooting on a considerable scale. I find that the average farmer in my area, which is rather extensive and contains much rolling farming and oil country, seldom objects to the noise too much, if you go to him and tell him frankly what you are shooting and explain that the soft point bullets at such extreme velocity seldom ricochet or bounce and are quite unlikely to tear a chunk out of his favorite cow or his best breeder bull. As one might paraphrase it, ''A little bull here and there helps to soothe the worry about the more valuable bull over in the woodchuck pasture.''

The .22-250 or .22 Varminter is in much the same class as the Swift; generally most of the loads are somewhat softer in report, and the blast is not quite so high-pitched and painful, yet the .22-250 is no parlor rifle. It burns a good charge and it drives the bullet out to the chuck quite quickly. It will cover about the same ranges and the same type of country as the Swift and give much the same killing power and report insofar as that is heard from a distance. Practically all of the 3750 to 4000 f.s. cartridge cases, and those giving still higher velocities have about the same faults and the same general characteristics. It is not the name of the cartridge but its capacity, charge and design which give certain results in the field or on the target range.

Were I to pick a chuck rifle, there are only a couple of cartridges that I would consider. My first choice would be a rifle chambered for the .220 Swift. If the places in which I had to do my hunting were too thickly settled, or were settled by a class of people too exclusive and unneighborly or too snobbish to permit any trespassing for chuck shooting generally, then I would go to the .170 Landis Woodsman which was designed to permit a man to obtain a reasonable amount of shooting without arousing a neighborhood. In many areas rifle shooting is taken in its stride as something almost every man does, at least in season. But I realize that in some other areas a rifleman is a rarity as compared to golfers or fox hunters on horses, and in such localities a man must hunt silently or he cannot hunt at all.

As a general and all-embracing proposition, it may be well to set down that there are a lot of things more important in the average chuck rifle than the exact cartridge it uses, or even its caliber. Any of the well-designed and perfected wildcats and a lot of the commercial cartridges are plenty accurate and sufficiently efficient for most woodchuck shooting. The specifications and qualifications for a good woodchuck rifle should be about as follows:

1. The cartridge should have sufficient velocity to cause the bullet to break up upon impact as soon as it penetrates the woodchuck. It should not promptly produce a whining ricochet to bounce around and whistle across the country after it strikes something fairly solid. The cartridge should be designed for the range shot over, and the bullet to expand in an animal the size and toughness of the average woodchuck.

2. It should be sufficiently accurate to shoot one minute-of-angle groups over all ranges at which it will be used.

3. The rifle should not exceed twelve pounds in weight, including the scope.

4. It should be equipped with a first class target-type telescope sight of not less than six power and in my opinion, nor more than ten power.

5. The barrel length should not exceed twenty-six inches unless the rifle is to be made up in one of the bull pup designs.

6. The stock should be made up to handle well in offhand, sitting, kneeling or prone positions.

7. The rifle action should be of the bolt action type to assure the highest degree of accuracy and to provide safety to the shooter.

In selecting the material for a good chuck rifle, barrel, action, stock and scope are all quite important, and most important of all is a good gunsmith to assemble the combination. For the chuck rifle there are a number of good actions to consider. My choice is from the following: Springfield, Enfield, Mauser or the Winchester Model 70. The scope should be one of the target type, my choice being a Unertl, Lyman, or Fecker. Unertl builds a very fine varmint scope that is just about tops for a wood-chuck rifle.

As for rifle stocks, the stock must be as good as the re-mainder of the equipment or you will wind up with a poor shoot-ing job. The stock has a few musts. The most important part of the stock-making job is the inside fitting. This should be done by a good stock maker who can speak from his past stock work, not his intended future.

There has been a great deal of information put out on rifle stock making and fitting but really nothing that is basic and es-sential. As I see it, there is not a stock maker that can actually guarantee a rifle to shoot its best after he stocks it, unless he has the opportunity to shoot it before shipment, or to see it shot and then to do the final fitting. There are a lot of would-be gun-smiths around the country, and a few really good ones. Many say they can make Old Betsy shoot them all into one hole with the wood from any old stock blank, or words to that general ef-fect, but I just don't believe them. I have had twenty-five years of experience in these lines and the following method of stocking gets the highest quality results for me:

I bed the barrel and action full length of the stock to the very best of my ability, making all points fit as close as possible in my target and varmint rifle stocks. I then test fire the rifle. After this is done I remove the barrel and action placing paper shims at places where I think pressure should be applied. After this I do more test shooting and more shimming until I think I have received the maximum in accuracy of which the barrel is capable. At this point I note the points where pressure was ap-plied to get the best results and then do my final fitting by shap-ing the stock to apply pressure at these two points without using the shims. One thing I know is that no two rifles require the same pressure at the same points to obtain the very best accu-racy. Wood for the stock is very important; it must be thorough-ly seasoned and straightgrained, at least in the fore-end and magazine area. If you must have a burl or other fancy grain to satisfy your love of beauty in the rifle, be sure to confine it to the butt stock only.

We now need some good hand-loaded cartridges for the rifle to finish the job completely. For chuck loads I recommend some of the good jacketed bullets with thin enough jackets to open up well upon impact. I do not care for the gas-check bullets for they cannot be driven fast enough to warrant good kills at long ranges. The hard cast bullets of the Kirksite type can be driven fast enough but they are too hard to break up as soon as they penetrate the head of the woodchuck. They only punch a hole in the game, not breaking up and mushrooming sufficiently to make clean kills. As for the use of grease wads in varmint rifles, I do not suggest them as I contend that they ruin accuracy. There is plenty of good loading dope in the pages of the hand-loading books published today for any of the cartridges that make good chuck rifles. Most important in the hand-loading is the use of uniform and accurate bullets, and the uniformity of loading of the various components so as to make each complete cartridge as nearly as possible exactly like each other complete cartridge in that lot. Then comes the selection of the exact load that works best in your rifle.

When you have a good barrel and action, properly assembled, then have it stocked with a blank of proper selection, fitted as above described, and shot in, and with this you have a lot of ammunition which has proven best by accuracy test in that rifle, then, reader, you have a woodchuck rifle. Until then you have never really done your best shooting.

STOCKING WOODCHUCK RIFLES

The finest barrel and action is of little value to the varmint hunter unless it is stocked with precision and care. Previously I mentioned the details as to stocking that are not apparent to the eye, but did not discuss the outward appearance.

Eye appeal, while not essential to accuracy, is very important and rates very high in my opinion. Many cumbersome, ill-shaped and poorly designed stocks are prettied up with an overabundance of checkering and fancy inlays, which only detracts the attention of the admirer from the things for which he should look.

To create the proper eye appeal, a stock should be laid out with the proper dimensions and design to assure the shooter the ultimate in shooting pleasure. The fore-end should be sufficiently large, not too round, not too flat, but pleasingly shaped to feel comfortable to the hand, and sufficiently long to accomodate the requirements of a properly bedded barrel, remembering, of course, that the gun is going to be fired offhand without sling and prone with a tight sling. Stiffness is essential.

The butt stock, or that portion of the stock from the trigger to the butt plate, is the bugaboo of most stock designers. Here is where ingenuity and foresight pay off. For instance, a pistol grip without symmetrical curves is certainly a far cry from one of beauty. It should flow gracefully from the trigger guard and have a shape that is comfortable to the hand — neither too large nor too small.

The cheek piece is a monstrosity in some instances. It is placed on the stock for utility value and not as an ornament. A cheek piece that does not support the face in a normal shooting stance, be it offhand, sitting or prone, is just so much extra bulk to haul around. It should be well forward on the comb of the stock and sufficiently thick to support the face in such a position that the shooting eye is naturally centered in the eye piece of the sighting instrument.

The stock maker should blend the cheek piece to the butt stock very carefully, with graceful and uniform radius. Above all eliminate the hump back so many employ in the Monte Carlo design. It is unsightly, unnecessary and ruins the appearance of a stock.

The comb should be of maximum height. By maximum height I mean a comb just as high as possible, still permitting the removal of the bolt from the action and allowing the cleaning of the bore from the breech. Certainly we realize many intricate and neatly sculptured designs are employed but, generally speaking, the utility value is destroyed or impaired when so used.

The butt stock is likewise important. It should emerge from the rest of the graceful and streamlined design into a trim and well-proportioned butt, neither too large nor too small, and be capped off with the shooter's choice of metal or rubber.

This discussion, of course, leaves much to the shooter's imagination, but show me the man who can put into words the feeling obtained from a correctly proportioned and designed gun stock. One must actually handle and feel to appreciate his desires. He cannot tell you what he wants, because he doesn't know, but let him pick up the gun, place it to his shoulder and immediately he is figuring out ways and means to finagle the "little woman" out of sufficient money to provide a new and handsome custom rifle stock.

If you were going to place an order with your custom stocker and used the following general dimensions, altering to suit your own physique, you could not be far wrong:

CARTRIDGE COMPARISONS

STOCK DIMENSIONS FOR A CHUCK RIFLE

Length of fore-end for a 26 inch barrel — 12 inches measuring from the front edge of the receiver. One inch should be added or deducted for each 2 inch change in barrel length.

Length of butt stock — 13-1/2 inches from center of trigger.

Length of pistol grip from center of trigger to bottom edge of grip — 3-1/2 inches.

Length of comb forward from top edge of butt plate — 9 inches.

Depth of fore-end from center of bore at a point one inch from forward end — 1-3/8 inches.

Depth of fore-end from center of bore at front action screw using Mauser action — 1-7/8 inches.

Depth of pistol grip at forward edge measuring from center of bore — 4-1/2 inches.

Pistol grip cap — 1-3/4 x 2 inches.

Thinnest part of grip — 1-1/2 inches thick.

Circumference of grip at smallest part — 5 inches.

Width of fore-end one inch from forward edge — 2-1/8 inches.

Width of stock just ahead of bolt handle — 2-1/4 inches.

Drop of butt stock measuring from center of bore — 1/2 inches.

Drop of comb at forward edge — 3/8 inch measuring from center of bore.

Butt plate — 5-1/8 x 1-5/8 inches.

Cheek piece should be approximately 9/16 inches high at bottom edge.

Butt plate should be fitted so it will be square with bore.

STOCK DIMENSIONS FOR A BENCH-REST RIFLE

Length of fore-end for a 30 inch barrel — 14-1/2 inches measuring from the front edge of the action.

Length of butt stock measuring from the center of trigger to center of butt — 13-1/2 inches.

Length of pistol grip, from center of trigger to forward, bottom edge of grip — 3-1/2 inches.

Length of comb from butt plate — 9 inches.

Depth of fore-end from center of bore — 2-3/8 inches.

Depth of fore-end at front guard screw on Mauser action — 2-3/8 inches.

Depth of pistol grip at forward, bottom edge of grip — 4-11/16 inches.

Pistol grip cap — 2-1/4 x 2 inches.

Thinnest part of grip — 1-5/8 inches thick.
Circumference of grip at smallest place — 5-1/2 inches.
Width of fore-end all the way back to the bolt handle — 3 inches.
Drop at butt from center of bore — 1/2 inch.
Drop of comb at forward edge — 3/8 inch from center of bore.
Butt plate — 5-1/4 x 2 inches.
Cheek piece should be approximately 9/16 inches high at bottom
    edge.
Butt plate should be fitted so it will be square with bore, in
    other words no pitch up or down of muzzle.

MR. FRANK M. RIDDLE'S 1949 BENCH-REST
SHOOTER'S ASSOCIATION RECORDS

One 5-shot group at 100 yards measuring 0.142 inches center to center of widest shots. Fired at Johnstown, N. Y., September 4, 1949.

(R) Eight consecutive 5-shot groups at 100 yards. Aggregate average 0.412 inches, center to center of widest shots. Fired at Johnstown, N. Y., September 4, 1949.

(R) Ten consecutive 5-shot groups at 100 yards. Aggregate average 0.429 inch center to center of widest shots. Fired at Johnstown, N. Y., September 3 & 4, 1949.

(R) One 5-shot group at 200 yards measuring 0.399 inch center to center of widest shots. Fired at Oil City, Penna., August 20, 1949.

(R) Five consecutive 5-shot groups at 200 yards. Aggregate average 0.889 inch center to center. Fired at Oil City, Penna., July 24, 1949.

(R) Ten consecutive 5-shot groups at 200 yards. Aggregate average 1.019 inch center to center. Fired at Oil City, Penna., July 24, 1949.

The above scores were fired in competition in Bench Rest Association Tournaments and were governed by the bench-rest shooting rules used by Johnstown, Dubois, Oil City and Bradford bench-rest groups.

They will give the woodchuck hunter an idea of what is possible these days with very accurate woodchuck cartridges using match grade ammunition of most accurate loadings in heavy rifles. The scope, of course, had to be on a par with rifle, ammunition and rifleman.

D. M. FELLOWS ON THE R-Z FOR WOODCHUCKS

March 26, 1950

"Dear Mr. Landis:

"Thank you very much for your letter of March 14th regarding the .170-caliber cartridge. You asked for some of my thoughts on chucks, etc., so here goes but I am afraid that it will not be anything too interesting.

"Upon reaching the age of 12 years I was finally allowed to use, after much persuasion on my part and a word from a kindly uncle, my late father's heavy Stevens .22-caliber target rifle. This was the Walnut Hill model with peep sights, palm rest and a long-pronged Schuetzen butt. It was chambered for the .22 short cartridge and must have weighed close to 12 pounds. Red squirrels were plentiful among the nut trees in the Mohawk Trail region of Massachusetts and I sharpened my shooting eye on these, always shooting offhand although my stance must have been terrible.

"I will never forget the first chuck that fell to my wandering aim. One day, while hunting alone just over the brow of a high hill, a chuck startled me by running for his den. He stopped short and sat up scarcely more than 50 feet away. Even though I was trembling with "buck fever" and every other variety of stage fright known to strike a chill into the heart of the stoutest hunter, somehow I managed to put the sights on him and he went down like a poled ox. Examination proved that a .22 short had penetrated his brain. No mighty African safari hunter was ever prouder of a kill and I lugged him all the way home to show off.

"Many summers have passed since that event but today I still get a thrill from hunting chucks. One of my favorite spots is on the brow of a hill from which one can command a view of about 15 chuck dens at varying distances from 100 to 300 yards. What more can anyone ask than to lie there on a lazy afternoon soaking up the warm sunshine in your bones, with binoculars and a high speed .22-caliber, scope-sighted rifle by your side? But wait—there's something moving down there by that rock. Quickly the binoculars are put on the spot—sure enough it's a chuck. Bringing the rifle into position you spot him again but this time through the 10X rifle scope. What a monster! His grizzled old whiskers show plainly as he clambers towards his lookout. The same familiar thrill runs down your spine as you watch his every move through the glass. It looks about 160 yards away. He snips a bit of clover here and there as he continues his meandering climb toward a knoll. While all this has been going on you've shoved a cartridge home in the chamber, closed the action and are ready for business. Finally he stops and seems about to sit up. With a faint "snick" your set triggers are cocked. Sure enough, up he comes on his haunches. Now's the time! With the dot of your scope steadied on him you squeeze off the shot. C-r-a-a-ck! Simultaneously you see Mr. Chuck collapse and another chuck that you hadn't noticed before in the grass leaps like a startled deer for its den which it gains with ease before you can reload your single shot rifle. The late Mr. Chuck's tail rises slowly in the air — up, up, it comes and then descends slowly, a sure sign that he's a goner. Keeping a watch on him through the glass you see that he lies motionless. Later you'll go down and heft him for size. Chalk up another for old Betsy! Now with your binoculars again you search the surrounding countryside for any relatives of his that might be abroad. With a rifle of not too loud report that can easily happen within a reasonable distance. And so it goes — but don't shoot too many, leave some for other days and also for next year!"

CHUCK DENS UNDER RAILROAD TRACKS

"In certain localities in the East, chucks seem fond of making their dens beside and under railroad tracks. I know of many such burrows that are shaken and rocked every day by the thundering trains but it never seems to bother the chucks in the least. If they are out feeding when a train approaches they will sometimes dive for their dens and other times just crouch low where they are and let the train pass. At times I have had a shot spoiled by an approaching train and at other times have been aided by them in locating a chuck that otherwise was unnoticed. Chucks are certainly curious creatures and sometimes, if they live under an old tumbled-down stone wall and see you before you spot them, they will lie flat on a slanting stone with just their heads showing, watching every move you make. Even so if you are careful and move slowly you can get into position and get off a prone shot if the distance warrants it. I have seen but one albino chuck.

"There's no question about it — chucks are tough and you've got to sock them to put them down for good. Quite a few years ago the late Major Ned Roberts introduced me to the 2R-Lovell cartridge and I've stuck with it ever since for chuck, crow and fox hunting, also hawks. Here in the East it really is an ideal caliber. The mighty Swift and its relatives are a bit too noisy to suit me. The late J. Bushnell Smith once told me, while we were hunting crows, "If I could have but one rifle it would be the 2R-Lovell." I agree with that one hundred per cent. The absence of appreciative recoil and metal fouling is a big factor in its favor. Its light report and economy of loading makes it a "sweet" rifle to shoot. It is true that as a rule the 2R is not as accurate as the Donaldson, Swift, Varminter, Arrow, etc., or similar cartridges, but it seems to be accurate enough for the purpose. I have never had a 2R bullet ricochet and I have deliberately tried to make them do so (in safe places) by shooting at ricochet-producing angles, at hard flat ground, rocks, water, etc. I have also seen a 2R that would shoot 5-shot groups as big as a dime (the outside edges of all shot holes inside the dime circle) as long as the shooter did his part. This was a hot load of No. 2400 powder and is NOT recommended to anyone. This rifle had a Diller relined barrel and was chambered and fitted by Jerry Gabby. The average 2R probably will shoot 1-1/4-inch groups at 100 yards. Many of them will shoot 1-inch groups and an occasional rare one, 1/2 inch at 100 yards. My standard load is 15 grains 4227 behind a 45-grain Sisk, W.M. or Sierra bullet.

"My favorite rifle consists of a Winchester thick-wall hi-side S.S. action with Schuetzen double-set triggers. This has a No. 3 barrel and a very high-comb stock. Mounted on the barrel is a 10X scope with a Lee dot installed. At least twice a year I soak the inside of the fore-end with linseed oil and of course frequently rub the outside well with it as well as the whole stock.

"While it seems to be true that on the average a bolt action rifle in a one-piece stock will beat a lever action single-shot rifle in a two-piece stock for tack-hole accuracy day in and day out, nevertheless many of us love the old Winchester S.S. actions too much to cast them aside. I always file or grind the half-cock notch off my hammers so that there cannot possibly be any interference with a fly or the notch itself when the hammer falls. When hunting, the lever of the action is thrown way down with the action wide open. A glance shows always whether or not there is anything in the chamber if the question arises. It is really one of the safest actions that one could possibly have to hunt with. Regards, D. M. Fellows, South Sudbury, Mass."

CHAPTER 15

Woodchuck Hunting Across America
with Parker O. Ackley

Mr. P. O. ACKLEY, the well-known custom gunsmith of Trinidad, Colorado, was brought up in the northeastern section of the state of New York. While there, he hunted woodchucks extensively in New York and Vermont. His early chuck shooting therefore was at our eastern woodchucks.

As mentioned, he went West in the late thirties and has hunted the Rocky Mountain and Sierra varieties of marmots known generally as Rock Chucks and as Whistling Marmots, ever since. He is an enthusiastic hunter and rifleman, and in this account gives you both types of chuck shooting, but devotes considerable space to the hunting of chucks at very long range and at quite high altitudes in remote areas of the western mountain country. He also gives advice for those hunting above timber who carry a minimum amount of hair on top of the head. Specifically, he suggests among other things, that while hunting the Rocky Mountain marmot you keep your hat on. For two reasons.

I was born in one of the best woodchuck hunting areas of the East, Washington County, New York. This small county is also surrounded with fine chuck hunting territory in New York and Vermont. When a boy, my favorite pastime was hunting chucks with a .22 rim-fire single shot rifle. Later on, I was to gain considerable experience in other parts of the country, such as the Middle West, then Colorado, Idaho, Oregon and California. I prefer the Rocky Mountain area, but it is a much more costly pastime here than in the East or Midwest. More equipment is needed and higher power, longer range rifles are necessary.

When seven or eight years old I tried out my first rifle which happened to be an old Stevens Maynard tip up single shot, but a short time later I was granted the use of a brand new Stevens Favorite. This was a pretty accurate little gun, even judged by present day standards, and my first chucks were killed with this rifle, many of them with black powder shorts. Before getting to high school age I had, along with some of the neighborhood boys, become very proficient at stalking, or to put it more bluntly, sneaking up on our game. We became able to place our shots very accurately, and I don't suppose there will be a gun in my life which will account for so many chucks as the lowly .22 R.F. As .22 ammunition became improved, so did our score on chucks. We became so proficient, in fact, that we could kill chucks fairly often up to 150 yards or so. If one becomes familiar enough with a rifle it becomes second nature to take a bead on the sky somewhere and drop one on the target quite often without the aid of fancy sights, or a sling.

Finally, along came high school and with it the desire to try out a bigger gun which took the form of an old .38-56 1886 Winchester with 26-inch octagon barrel. This old cannon should have had wheels, but it shot like heck, and being so heavy, the recoil was mild and didn't bother. This old cannon threw 255 grains of lead, and was little better than the .22 LR in the way of trajectory, but when it landed it had a wallop. Not many chucks "walked away" from that when it connected. About this time I also tried out the old 12 Ga. double. But wore too much hide off the elbows crawling up to them to make it much fun. We sometimes "rolled our own" for the old scatter gun, and often loaded the shells with rather coarse shot; then before crimping the shot charge was poured full of tallow. The idea was to hold the charge together. I never knew for sure how the idea worked, but whenever a direct hit was made at close range the damage was terrific at both ends.

All of this was before or during World War I, and right after the war a great deal was written about the .30-06, which later developed into a fad among riflemen to build up Springfield sporters. It became the ambition of many chuck hunters to own a fine Springfield, and several in our area built up fine chuck rifles using both Springfields and Krags as foundations. A few went so far as to install scopes. We found rifles of this class extremely effective on chucks, but the noise was terrific, and the ricochets had everything from jet propulsion to technicolor. When that old 190-grain .303 Savage bullet, which we found about the best for chucks in the '06, struck one of the big flat slate rocks on which chucks so often sun themselves in that area, it sounded like a buzz bomb, especially if you were on the receiving end. One example of a ricochet I well remember. One of our neighbors used to hunt chucks for food, although this was not a common practice in New York and New England, and he used an old Model 86 .45-90. New York and New England have countless stone wall fences which are favorite places for chucks to sit and sun themselves, or from which to observe their surroundings. I was raking hay with a one-horse rake in an orchard and I heard this individual bombarding chucks down over a hill several hundred yards away. He finally took a shot at one on a stone wall and that old .45-90 slug sounded like a silver dollar coming end over end. It struck in the branches of the apple tree under which I was passing at that instant. Such carelessness can easily prove fatal, and this particular individual finally did kill a man while hunting chucks. He and his son-in-law were hunting in a meadow through which ran a shallow ditch. They spotted a chuck at the lower end of this ditch, and the son-in-law elected to crawl down this ditch to get a closer shot. After some time had elapsed, the boy stuck his head up out of the ditch, not far from where the chuck had been. The old man cut loose with the old .45-90 and made a direct hit. Such occurances taught us to look before we shot, and we often resisted taking shots at chucks because of a remote possibility of a ricochet, even with .22 rimfires which can be plenty dangerous with either the standard velocity or the modern high speed ammunition.

Due to the dangerous characteristics of the big guns, and a growing desire to become more scientific, and also due to some rather startling developments in the way of new cartridges and rifles, my attention gradually turned toward high velocity light bullets which had a tendency to blow up upon impact. The Hornet was the first of these, and it developed into one of the finest little chuck rifles that any eastern chuck hunter could desire. We were able to make astonishing kills at relatively long ranges. I have killed many chucks with this little cartridge up to 200 yards. This introduced me to high velocity which started something which has not yet been finished. It simply started the desire for more and more speed and as soon as the .220 Swift came along I couldn't rest until I had one. Outside of the noise, this cartridge was just the ticket. It was apparently less susceptible to ricochets than anything previously developed, and it was not necessary to hit the chuck in the head or heart to prevent him from getting into his hole. It is unbelievable how much lead a chuck can carry away. When hunting with the old .38-56 I blew chucks practically in two, and still they would drag themselves into their holes. The Swift cured that trouble in a hurry.

I have even seen chucks killed at short ranges by a Swift bullet which barely grazed them.

The accuracy of the Swift left little to be desired, and its range was more than adequate for any part of the Northeast. The Swift still remains one of the best woodchuck cartridges for east or west, although some of our newer wildcat cartridges are better for the Rocky Mountains and far west. My long and intimate association with the .220 Swift cartridge leaves me with nothing but respect and admiration for it both as a varmint cartridge and a big game cartridge. It can hold its own in pretty fast company on the target range. It has made as many one shot kills on big game as any big game cartridge, and more than most especially on game such as antelope and deer. I would not recommend it as a big game cartridge for everyone, but many who so enthusiastically condemn it have probably never given it a fair or unbiased trial. I am afraid that high velocity cartridges are here to stay, regardless of what some old timers and some so-called authorities say to the contrary, just as the automobile is here to stay. The trend is toward higher velocities and lighter bullets, and better bullets. It is now possible to produce a bullet which will open up at low or medium velocities, yet have no tendency to blow up even as fast as 5000 f.s. Such developments enable the hunter to make use of all of the advantages of high velocity, and yet be assured of deep penetration. They bring to the varmint and big game hunter alike, real shooting pleasure due to reduced recoil, the elimination of guess work such as leading, holding over, etc. They enable the shooter to take advantage of the fine optical sights now on the market and enable him to make shots never before dreamed of. This is especially true for the Rocky Mountain country where visibility is unlimited and where there is little danger from glancing bullets and little objection to loud report.

Along about 1936 I decided to leave the East and try my luck in the West, and to take up gunsmithing full time. On the way west I saw thousands of prairie dogs, also woodchucks, which I learned later were called marmots in the Rockies, and about a million jack rabbits. Naturally, I started laying plans to try out new ideas in what to me at that time was a new country. For a while things sort of repeated themselves. The .22 LR was used on the ground or "digger" squirrels of California, Oregon and Washington, but the old speed bug was still there, so I tried out the R-2 Lovell.

The accuracy of this R-2 Lovell little cartridge was hard to beat, and still is. I built up a very fine heavy barreled Lovell. on a Winchester hi-side, using one of the first barrels which I produced myself. I had a 6X Malcolm scope which seemed adequate for the rugged Oregon country. Up to 200 yards it murdered the squirrels. I used loads ranging from 15 to 16-1/2 grains 4198 behind the Winchester 45-grain round-nose Hornet bullet. The western ground squirrel is about the size of the New England gray squirrel and could be mistaken for such by eastern tourists. He makes a very small target beyond 100 yards. He is extremely lively and nervous, and is reluctant to present a still target. He also becomes "educated" very rapidly, and presents a tricky target for the varmint hunter. I have seen hundreds of these squirrels on a mountain side which had been slashed and sometimes not even get one shot. The instant a car stops every squirrel promptly melts out of sight when every old log, rock and stump, had a squirrel on it before the automobile came to a stop.

THE MAXIMUM LOVELL

Due to the difficulty of getting enough powder into the R-2 case, I conceived the idea of "improving" it. I was not alone in this. "Maximum" Lovells started to spring up like mushrooms, all of them being about the same. My own idea was to blow the case out so that it would take 16-1/2 grains 4198 by simply dumping it in. However, as soon as the gun nuts and the handloading speed merchants got hold of it they even rigged up oscillating machines to shake the powder down so as to get 20 grains into that small case. I still regard the Maximum Lovell as one of the best varmint cartridges for some parts of the country, particularly if regular R-2 loads are used in it. Its accuracy is tops, the report is mild, and it has sufficient velocity to disintegrate most bullets at reasonable ranges, thereby minimizing the danger of the bullets breaking someone's window a mile or so over the hill.

THE .22-250'S

Along about this time the Varminter and a whole host of ".22-250's" made their appearance, so the Lovell went into the corner. I had to make a .22-250, which I proceeded to do. To make the project more fun, I decided to shorten a Model 1898 Mauser action to make it exactly the right length for the .22-250 cartridge. I decided to simply neck the .250-3000 Savage cartridge down, but changed the shoulder angle from 26-1/2 degrees to 28 degrees. This little gun was made in sporter weight and equipped with a six power German hunting scope. It was stocked with a piece of fancy walnut from southern California and made a very neat little piece weighing around 8-1/2 pounds with scope. This barrel, which was made from an old truck axle, would not accept maximum loads, and I finally settled on 33 grains of 4320 behind the 45-grain Hornet bullet, or the 50-grain Sisk. These loads gave 50-yard machine rest groups in this light rifle of the size of a dime. I finally wore the barrel out after killing hundreds of digger squirrels, jack rabbits, and woodchucks. It was also used on deer with complete success. I used it two seasons in southeastern Oregon along the California-Nevada border, which is a very fine area in which to hunt mule deer. It is one of the best areas I have ever hunted. This cartridge also has proven effective on antelope up to reasonably long ranges.

THE WESTERN ROCK CHUCK

The first woodchuck hunting that I was able to do in the far west was in the lava beds of Oregon and California. The chucks in this area are usually called "rock chucks," but appear to be almost exactly like the Midwest groundhog or New England woodchucks, although I can recall none quite as large as the eastern type. Rock chucks are found around the rimrock in the western states, in the lava beds and in other parts of the high country. I cannot recall ever seeing a rock chuck at a very low elevation. All of them in my experience have been from 2500 feet up to some of the lava beds occurring well up toward the tops of the Cascade and Sierra Nevada ranges. Rock chucks, like their eastern relatives, are often found in meadows or grain fields, but usually near rocky formations. One of their favorite lookouts is to climb up in the rimrock and find a spire or point upon which to perch and from which a wide area can be seen. Sometimes a chuck can be seen silhouetted against the incredibly clear western sky. Such a shot is the woodchuck hunter's dream. In these high dry atmospheres, distance is very deceiving, and an easterner is apt to underestimate the range by half. I found this out in a hurry. I also found that a chuck silhouetted against the sky is one heck of a hard target. There seems to be an excess of room on all sides of him. Usually the bullet cannot be spotted unless it strikes the rock under the chuck and unless you are a good range guesser, you are apt to run low on ammunition before doing any damage. Such shots would not be safe in the East, but in the West most such shots are perfectly safe. Many times such chuck hunting areas can be found close to towns and cities, and in such areas woodchuck hunting rapidly becomes a science. The old boy who was seen on the spire exposes only the very top of his head and can be spotted only by careful observation of the rimrock and other likely spots with a high power target scope or a high grade pair of binoculars. When the chuck is finally spotted, he offers a very limited target. Through experience he has found that that old profile of his is apt to get him into trouble if he exposes it unnecessarily, so he is rather conservative. Also, in these areas there is often some wind which complicates matters.

My first hunt for rock chucks convinced me of the inadequacy of the Lovell. This rifle which had been doing so well on the squirrels of the western valleys suddenly became weak and inadequate. The .22-250 even seemed to lack something. To this end, I started to dream up a new cartridge. I knew that it must have everything from jet propulsion to technicolor, and the first attempt resulted in the original .228 Ackley Magnum. The case was the .257 Roberts necked to take .22 high power bullets. This cartridge at least partially filled the needs, but later was changed, and, through a process of evolution, the present .228 Magnum cartridge emerged. This one uses a special bullet, .2265 inches in diameter as designed and manufactured by R. B. Sisk and other custom bullet makers. It was made in 60, 70, and 80 grains with the 70-grain being best. Lately we have developed our new Ackley controlled expansion bullet in this caliber. The 70-grain bullet gave much better results on the rock chucks than the lighter Swift class of bullets. It bucked wind better, and sustained its velocity better. It had one of the same faults of the Swift, namely, limited barrel life. However, if medium loads were used, reasonable barrel life could be expected along with adequate power and range. The owners of the original .228 Magnums were not slow in trying their new pets out on deer and other types of big game. It was soon found that it was extremely deadly on all species of big game and it is still one of the best

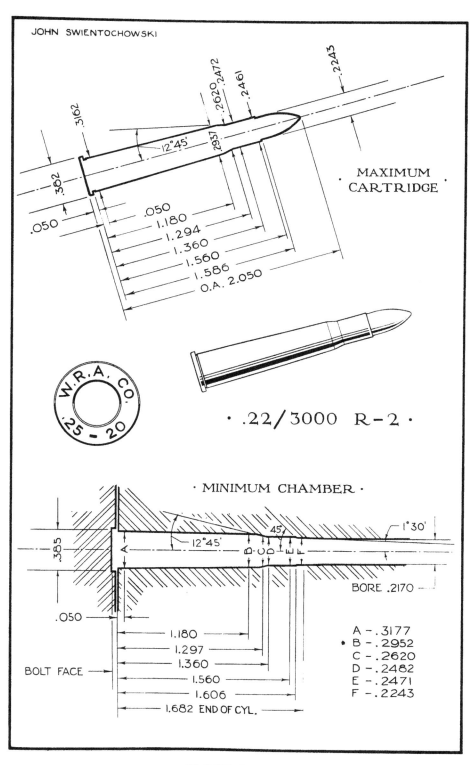

JOHN SWIENTOCHOWSKI

MAXIMUM CARTRIDGE

.3162

.2620 .2472

.2461

.2243

12°45'

.2957

.362

.050

.050

1.180

1.294

1.360

1.560

1.586

O.A. 2.050

W.R.A. CO.

.25 - 20

· .22/3000 R-2 ·

· MINIMUM CHAMBER ·

.385

12°45'

45°

1°30'

A

B C D

E F

BORE .2170

.050

BOLT FACE

1.180

1.297

1.360

1.560

1.606

1.682 END OF CYL.

A - .3177
· B - .2952
C - .2620
D - .2482
E - .2471
F - .2243

.22/3000 R-2.

F. Caporetta, A. F. Kapelk, and P. O. Ackley with eight rock chucks at 11,000 feet elevation near Telluride, Colo. CREDIT: P. O. ACKLEY.

Parker Ackley displaying a pair of rock chucks shot near Ouray, Colo.

combination varmint and big game rifles. Even though this cartridge combined most of the qualities needed for chuck shooting, such as wind-bucking ability, extremely flat trajectory, good accuracy and light recoil, the quest for something better continued, and it was not long before the .250 Magnums began to appear in the hands of chuck hunters.

Cartridges of the .257 Roberts class lack some of the things necessary to cope with some of the conditions in the western states, but many felt that the .25 caliber was the logical size bullet, but with a velocity comparable to the Swift. Almost every conceivable type of cartridge appeared in an endless parade, based on all sorts of cases, from the Roberts to the .300 H & H necked down and blown up for the very maximum powder capacity. Only a few have survived such as the .250 Ackley Magnum, .25 Weatherby Magnum, .250 Gipson Magnum, and a few others based on the belted H & H case, in either full length or shortened versions, one or two of the crop of .25-06's and the improved .257. Most of these cartridges did fairly well, exhibiting most of the characteristics of the Swift in an enlarged version. Of the whole batch of .25's, the improved .257 seems destined to go farther than most of the others. It is a very well-balanced cartridge of unquestioned accuracy and flexibility. It develops a very satisfactory velocity and reasonably flat trajectory. It gives satisfactory barrel life, and has proven itself both as a varmint and big game cartridge. It handles all of the extensive line of .25-caliber bullets, and last but not least, the improved chamber still handles factory cartridges. Cases are made by firing factory loads in the improved chamber and thereafter loaded to higher velocities. The 100-grain bullet can be driven up to about 3300 f.s. in the average rifle, and the lighter bullets considerably faster. Bullets lighter than 87 grains are not recommended because of decreased barrel life, which always results when the weight of the bullet decreases and powder charge increases. As the weight of the powder charge approaches that of the bullet, barrel life drops off very rapidly, and when a point is reached where the powder charge exceeds the weight of the bullet by as much as 20 per cent the barrel life drops to less than 500 shots, and sometimes a barrel is worn out before a good load can be developed for it because such unbalanced cartridges are very critical. Results seem to indicate that after the ratio of one grain of powder to one and one half grains of bullet weight, more is lost than gained, and for best results the ratio should be somewhat wider. Applying this theory, we find the following cartridges approximately meet the requirements: Improved Zipper, 50-grain bullet; .228 Magnum, 70-grain bullet; .250 Ackley, Gipson or short Mashburn Magnum (belted case) Magnum, 100-grain to 120-grain bullet; and the Weatherby or Mashburn long .270 Magnum with 120- to 130-grain bullets.

Hunting chucks in the Rocky Mountain area surpasses all others in thrills for the hunter with its opportunities for shots from ten feet to a mile. Usually, there is little danger in using rifles of unlimited power, so the hunter is largely relieved of the responsibility of first carefully figuring out where the bullet will go in case of a miss or ricochet. Here is the area in which all of the gadgets known to the game come into play. Often a Rocky Mountain chuck hunter's outfit will consist of cameras of all sorts with which to record some of the world's finest and most spectacular scenery, a high quality pair of binoculars, the longest range, hottest high-powered rifle with scope possible to obtain, about a bushel of ammunition, and numerous other pieces of equipment, all loaded into a jeep or station wagon. Most of the best chuck hunting can best be reached by jeep or horseback. All of this sounds rather expensive, and it is. A lot of fun can also be had in this area with just the ordinary outfit, but the very nature of this type of terrain and the variety of shots which can be had all at one sitting, makes the shooter want to apply all that science and ballistics have to offer. This results in a tremendous amount of experimenting with new cartridges, components, and new ideas.

One of the greatest hunts in which I have ever participated took place during the week end of July 4, 1946. Four of us left Trinidad on July 3rd for Durango, via Route 160 which runs through La Veta Pass in the Sangre de Christo range, and over Wolf Creek Pass in the San Juan range. Although we had not planned to do any shooting until the next day north of Durango, we ran into numerous prairie dog towns while crossing the San Luis Valley and spent an hour or two shooting at them with .22 pistols. These little animals offer great sport for the pistol shooter. At that time there were millions of prairie dogs in this one valley, but now one can criss cross it for days and sight only now and then a lonely pup. After crossing this valley, the road crosses the upper Rio Grande River and follows the South Fork up toward Wolf Creek Pass. At the foot of the pass it again forks and the road follows a small tributary up to the divide. One can see a small spring almost at the exact top of the divide where this small tributary of the Rio Grande rises. A hundred yards west of this small spring, one can find other small springs which are barely on the west side of the divide which constitute some of the headwaters of the San Juan River. If one were to follow a drop of water from the spring on the west side he would eventually wind up at the Gulf of California, while the water from the spring on the east side finally ends up in the Gulf of Mexico at Brownsville, Texas. Both of these great rivers are very beautiful, picturesque mountain streams similar to those found in New England throughout their courses through the state of Colorado, but as the Rio Grande passes through New Mexico and Texas it becomes very muddy and sluggish. The San Juan also becomes full of silt during its course through the desert on its way to join the Colorado river near Lees Ferry. If one were to follow the San Juan from its source to its junction with the Colorado, and then on down through the Grand Canyon to Lake Meade, one would see some of the most spectacular scenery in North America.

As you travel over Wolf Creek Pass, if a sharp lookout is maintained, it is not uncommon to see quite a number of chucks along the rimrocks. The chucks here are actually the hoary marmot. They appear rangier than the eastern or far western chucks, and have somewhat longer tails. They are quite similar to the eastern variety in weight. They are apt to raise the tail in a vertical position and swing it around and around like a propellor. Sometimes they give their position away by such actions the quick movement being visible for long distances. Wolf Creek Pass has a high elevation and is a long pull for a car, but most modern cars easily negotiate it in high, although in the summer they may have a tendency to boil a little. On this particular trip we encountered a blizzard on the third day of July. The pass itself, not being paved, turned to mud and we were lucky to make it at all. Passing on down the western slope we went through some of the most beautiful parts of the Rockies, and finally reached Durango where we immediately hunted up Fred Barnes, Bill Crawley, and Paul Crawford. The women, in Barnes' words, had planned "the gol darndest picnic I ever heard of" and they lived up to it. They must have killed half of the chickens in La-Plata County. The next morning we started north from Durango on the million dollar highway headed for Silverton. As I remember, there were some sixteen of us with various types of shootin' irons, plus a gang of women and kids. We had practically a convoy of cars once we were on the road. It would be hard to describe the trip from Durango to Silverton and do it justice. About half-way to Silverton someone in the leading car spotted a chuck on a high rim near Lime Creek. We all came to a sudden halt and everyone piled out with rifles and started blasting away. We were shooting up at a very acute angle, as can be seen in the accompanying photograph, and the range was probably over 800 yards. We laid down a veritable barrage and shot that mountain all to heck. That is probably the reason that rim appears lower than some of the others in the vicinity. So far as I know that chuck is still in good health, even though numerous slugs from .22's to .300's were flying past him. We had better luck with some other chucks who appeared at other points. They probably thought the war had broken out again on this side of the pond. Big guns, such as were firing up at that mountain side echoed and the echoes and re-echoes bounced from one side of the Animas River canyon to the other until one wondered if they would ever die out. We killed several chucks before reaching Silverton, where we stopped to look at some of the mining projects and other things of interest. Silverton is one of the real old hell-roaring mining towns of the past. In the old days it was the center of the mining activities in that area, being surrounded by large mines and other mining towns. It is very much the same today as in the old days, except things are a bit quieter. Leaving Silverton we proceeded on up to Eureka, an old mining town where a large mine is still operating, and then practically straight up the Animas toward the old ghost town of Animas Forks. The hills are honeycombed with old mine tunnels and shafts, and countless mine dumps. The ore in this area is complex, usually containing gold, silver, lead and zinc, and lately uranium has been discovered. Many of the old mine buildings still stand, and the old mills, cabins, etc., are favorite haunts of these mountain chucks. Eureka is around 10,000 feet altitude and from there the road rises rapidly until a point over 13,000 feet is reached, unless your car quits before that.

The higher the better for chuck hunting. They seemed to increase in numbers as we approached the higher altitudes, with the greatest numbers at or above timber line. We finally began seeing numerous chucks, so found a good place for the aforementioned picnic and unloaded so the women could get things started. Meantime, we spent a few minutes taking a look at each other's artillery.

THE .228 ACKLEY, .256 NEWTON IMP.

AND A 6.5 M. M. GIPSON MAGNUM

I had my favorite .228 featherweight with 4X scope. I was using Sisk 70-grain hollow point bullets ahead of 38 grains of 3031. This is not a high velocity load, but seemed to be sufficiently flat for all of the shooting I got during the day. Barnes had what might be called an improved .256 Newton bull gun with 4X scope. Bill Crawley had a 6.5 Gipson Magnum, also with a 4X scope. Other rifles which I recall were a standard Hornet on a low-side Winchester action, a .270 Winchester, a Krag, and numerous others of about the same class. Some of the kids had .22 rim-fires. We finally located a whole bunch of chucks on the side of a mountain, well above timber line where there were still patches of snow. These marmots make the finest target in the world when they get out in the middle of a large snow patch and sit up to take stock of things. Sometimes one can be seen taking off across one of these snow fields at a tremendous pace, waving his tail like a prop on a B-29. I suppose we were shooting at these particular chucks at around 700 yards, and I am telling you that they are hard to hit at that range. Some stories we read in sporting magazines lead us to believe that hits are made very regularly at such ranges, but among our party that day we had some of the best woodchuck shots in the U. S. A. who knew every inch of this country, and the misses greatly outnumbered the hits. There was one old boy who lived under a large rock up toward the top of the mountain. We first spotted him sitting on top of his rock watching the proceedings. The range was estimated at around 1000 yards. We all lined up in sort of a skirmish line, tied up in slings, with everything scientific. Everyone started blasting away and I soon found that my .228 was reaching out there with the best of them, but also found it more interesting to watch developments through the scope. Bullets were striking all around that chuck some 10 or 15 feet from him. Now and then one came fairly close enough to make him dig for his hole under the rock. Usually, when he made one of these dives, someone would yell "I gottim," whereupon the whole line would direct its fire at other targets. Pretty soon the old chuck would be seen on top of the rock again, and the whole performance would be repeated. I have often wondered how many shots were fired at that one animal, and so far as I know he was never hit. I often wondered exactly how far that chuck actually was, and two years later I happened to be at the same spot on another hunt and took time out to step it off as best I could. I had to go down through a small canyon and up the side of the mountain, and at that altitude one's wind is not so good, but I finally arrived at the spot, but with only about 700 steps. Due to the rugged terrain and the steep slope, I would judge the range to be considerably less than 700 yards. This will serve to give an idea of the difficulty of connecting consistently at such ranges, even when they are considerably less than originally estimated. Of course, tricky air currents are present for many shots. When all of the above shooting was done we were firing up at a very acute angle, across a rushing stream, which was being fed by melting snow fields higher up. The air currents are very tricky in these narrow mountain valleys over these streams. Also, the high altitude makes objects appear closer than they actually are, at least for a Yankee from New York. Before the day was over I concluded that the three rifles which were doing the best job were the .256, 6.5 and the .228. The three of us were apparently equally good shots, and we all accounted for about the same number of chucks. I was probably somewhat prejudiced, but I concluded that I preferred the lighter rifle because of its lighter recoil and flatter trajectory over the average ranges encountered. They were using 160-grain bullets in the other two guns, which may have been a little flatter way out, but the sighting equipment which we were using was not adequate for ranges over 400, or at the most 500 yards. We shot at a great many chucks that day which could not be seen at all with the naked eye. Such targets were spotted through the scopes. Since that I have been using a hunting scope with an 8X attachment with small Lee dot and a 10X target scope. I believe I prefer hunting with the 8X attachment with 1-1/2 minute dot to all others so far tried. I have used these attachments on the Alaskan, K 2.5 Weaver, and Leopold Stevens with equal success. Many times I take three or four rifles with only one of these scopes, all equipped with our quick detachable mount. This mount, being adjustable for windage and elevation, allows the same scope to be used on all of the rifles interchangeably.

We returned to Durango that night. I have forgotten how many kills we made that day, but probably more than 100 with the three rifles doing the greater part. We were able to get a few more shots on the way over Wolf Creek Pass, which were taken with the Hornet and a .22 USRA pistol.

During the week end of July 4, 1949, Dr. Kapelke, Francis Caporatta, Mrs. Ackley, and myself loaded our car down with ammunition, guns, cameras, binoculars, and other items like food, cooking utensils, etc., and headed over the very same Wolf Creek Pass to Durango, over the Million Dollar Highway, through Ouray and on around the mountain to Telluride where we had a date with my old friend Homer Reid, mayor of Telluride and a photographer of note.

We arrived in Telluride well after dark Saturday night but we located Mr. Reid, who had already made reservations at Telluride's one and only tourist camp. Telluride is one of the most picturesque towns of the old West. Like Silverton, it is a mining town and fairly active at present since the uranium boom has been on. In this area some of the largest gold mines in the country can be found. A few of them still are working, but most of them are only ghosts of the past. The town itself is at the very end of a tremendous canyon. You can't go any farther except with a jeep or helicopter. The fourth of July celebration is the big event in Telluride's yearly existence. The old gambling halls open up just as in the old days and everything roars for one day and night. One of the main events is the annual rodeo on the afternoon of the fourth. Mr. Reid, being mayor, had taken care of the preliminaries the day before so he could spend the day with us hunting chucks.

The morning of the fourth, we got up early and had breakfast with Mr. and Mrs. Reid and took time to check all of the equipment over and get it loaded into Mr. Reid's new jeep. With all of the guns, ammunition, cameras, binoculars, food for the day, and five people, that little jeep had a load. Leaving Telluride, we practically stood the jeep on end and started up. We gained 2500 feet in elevation in about four miles. Traveling up that mountain is an experience that will remain with all of us for a long time. The road is an old mining road over which tremendous quantities of mining equipment were once carried. The heavy machines were carried piece by piece up to the 13,000 to 14,000 foot levels on mule back and assembled at the mines. Mine buildings appear to be stuck to the sides of sheer walls thousands of feet high, with no visible means of approach. Traveling up this old trail which is carved out of the sides of the canyon, and largely composed of switchbacks, you can look straight down hundreds of feet into the river below. Even if we hadn't seen a chuck on the entire trip we would have had enough thrills to last for a long time.

The jeep would buck and jump over rocks and through washouts; it would get on top of smooth rocks and paw around for a footing, and go through all sorts of antics while we were wondering how long it would take the bottom of the canyon to come up to meet us if the vehicle decided to leave the road and take to the air. From this point we could see some of the most rugged country in the world. The city of Telluride could be seen directly below us, but so far down that it appeared in miniature; snow capped peaks were on every hand, and these peaks average close to 14,000 feet. At this point we found the first chucks of the day. I killed three with as many shots, with the .228 at about 100 yards firing over the windshield. On this trip I had one featherweight .228 built on a G 33-40 action with Mannlicher stock, set triggers and Leopold-Stevens scope with 8X attachment. The second rifle which I brought was a bull gun chambered for the .228 belted Express cartridge, which we have been experimenting with lately. The third rifle was a .17 caliber based on a 6.5 Jap action, and chambered for the Swift case necked to .17 caliber. The two extra rifles had our Snap-In-Mount, enabling me to use the same scope on all three rifles without sighting in.

Doc had his pet Improved .257 built on a Mauser 98 action with sporting weight barrel with K-4 Weaver scope, and Cap had my Improved Zipper based on the Remington Hepburn action. This rifle has only a 22-inch barrel, very light in weight, fitted with a very fine myrtle wood stock, originally built for a car gun. The short barrel and side lever action make a very fine gun, and it has proved to be exceedingly accurate. This rifle was equipped with a 10X target scope. Mr. Reid confined his artillery to a camera and pair of Zeiss 7 x 50 binoculars. For loads, the .228 was loaded with 46 grains of 4350 behind our new controlled expansion 70-grain bullet, and the Sisk 70-grain. The .228 belted express was loaded with 44 grains of 4350 and the Sisk 70-grain bullet. The Improved Zipper was loaded with the 48-grain Sisk bullet ahead of 32 grains of 3031. I don't know what the .257 was loaded with, except for the 100-grain bullet. No exceptionally long shots were made that day. The longest one was around 300 yards. Of course, this was by actual measurement, and about the same as the estimated 700 to 1000 yard shots that we read about.

We were able to connect with about 30 chucks that day between showers. At these extremely high elevations, the weather is very temperamental, so we were continually ducking into the jeep, which afforded only a little protection, or into some of the old mine buildings if one happened to be handy. Between showers the sun came out bright, although it felt rather chilly up among the snow fields.

CAUTIONS FOR A BALD-HEADED WOODCHUCK HUNTER

Let me say right here, that if you are bald-headed, be sure to cover that barrel bean up with a hat. I seldom wear a hat, and by two o'clock my knob looked like a broiled lobster and felt twice as hot. That sunburn kept me busy for a couple of weeks, and kept me constantly reminded of that woodchuck hunt. The .228 accounted for the largest number of chucks, but I had more close shots. The Improved Zipper behaved like a thoroughbred, and Cap stated afterwards that he never missed a shot which he could blame the rifle for. It made clean kills with a maximum amount of damage. The .257 also did very well, but did not have flat enough trajectory for the purpose, so Doc later sold it and had a .228 built before the big game season started. We will probably use mostly .228's and experimental 6 m.m.'s this coming season.

THE 70-GRAIN BULLET IN THE .228 ACKLEY

On this trip the 70-grain Sisk once again gave a fine account of itself in both .228's. It did not blow up when it struck a chuck, and therefore did not show the tremendous destruction that the Improved Zipper did, but it made instant kills every time. The .228 required no holding over at any range encountered during the day, and again proved itself to be one of the best for chucks in the mountain country. The large case .17 turned out to be a fizzle because of bullet failure. The thin jacket Sisk bullets would not stand the tremendous velocity that the Swift case gave them, and almost every bullet blew up before reaching the target. This one will be tried out again with the new controlled expansion bullet. This type of bullet will stand any velocity, and I am betting this cartridge will get the job done once the right bullets are developed. The Sisk 25- and 30-grain bullets have proven to be very good on prairie dogs when traveling at a velocity of no more than 4000 f.s. The most successful .17 cartridges are based on the Hornet, Bee and R-2 Lovell cases.

After a hard day, during which we had reached the 13,000 foot mark, we returned to Telluride and started out on the return trip to Trinidad the next morning. Not desiring to backtrack, we drove north a few miles to Montrose, where we took Highway 50. This route goes over Blue Mesa to Gunnison, and we were able to get a few shots at chucks on top of the Mesa, but didn't have much luck because they were mostly extremely long range shots and the chucks were reluctant to show. themselves. We arrived back in Trinidad about dark having completed a circle of some 850 miles. This may sound like a long trip for a woodchuck hunt, but out here we think very little of distance. Deer hunters think nothing of making a 3000 mile round trip each fall.

BINOCULARS AND CAMERAS FOR CHUCK HUNTERS

On these woodchuck hunting trips we have found that binoculars, cameras, etc., are almost as important as the rifles themselves. Last year we used a 7 x 50 Zeiss binocular which proved to be the best we have tried to date. Common 8X binoculars work fairly well, but do not compare to the larger type for this purpose. We have found that the smaller, more compact binoculars are more satisfactory for big game. The light weight 6 x 30 type seem to be fine for this purpose, but they lack what it takes to pick out a chuck on a talus slope 700 to 800 yards away. The 7 x 50's fairly reach into the shadows and pull the chucks into view. High-power target scopes do not compare to the binoculars, and are only a poor substitute for spotting the animals. Once they are spotted, then the scope picks them up clearly enough for a shot.

After doing some experimental work on the controlled expansion bullet, I took a short trip one Sunday late in the fall of 1949 hoping to get a few shots to see how the bullet would perform. I elected to take the trip up the north fork of the Rio Grande, and the trip turned out to be around 500 miles before getting back to Trinidad. Naturally, I had little time to get out and beat the brush, but was lucky enough to locate three chucks, two of which I killed at around 100 yards.

Near the top of Spring Creek Pass (elevation 11,025) I spotted a chuck sunning himself on a large rock about a hundred yards from the road. I looked at him through the scope, and then passed the scope along over some other rocks and located two more on other rocks. They were about 50 yards apart, but all about the same distance from the road. The first shot was a direct hit, as was the second. The third was a clean miss. I was using my short-barreled Mannlicher type .228 Magnum featherweight. Upon retrieving the chucks, they were found to be badly shot up. One was nearly severed completely through the midsection; the other had one side of the head missing. The load was 46 grains of 4350 behind the 70-grain controlled expansion bullet, probably giving a velocity of around 3600 f.s. in the 21-inch barrel. The destructive qualities of the bullet seemed to be almost equal to thin jacket types, indicating good expansion on light game. Subsequent trials of the bullet has shown that although it opens very easily on any game, it never disintegrates and therefore it passes on through the largest animal found in this area. Several elk were killed with this bullet with the load mentioned above for the .228, and some of the bullets passed completely through the animals endwise. The same results have been obtained on a recent African safari. In Africa the little 70-grain controlled expansion bullet really did itself proud on all kinds of medium sized African game, such as gerenuk, zebra, etc. It was also tried on lion, etc., but I have not yet received a full report.

Continuing the trip over Spring Creek Pass we finally reached Slumgullion Pass, which is 11,361 feet elevation. I saw some of the finest kind of chuck country, but the weather turned bad just at the time we reached the top, so nothing appeared to shoot at. I hope to try this area again next summer when the weather may be better.

Knowing that readers of woodchuck stories are more interested in the rifles actually used, and direct comparisons between various calibers, I will try to make a list of the rifles which we have actually tried in the Rockies. This list has been compiled upon the assumption that rifles for chuck hunting in the East have been covered in other chapters. Of course, all calibers have been used, and are still being used, in the mountain country on chucks, but the following are the cartridges with which I have personally had either direct or indirect experience:

.17 Pee Wee	.228 Magnum	.30-06
.17 Swift	.257 Roberts	.25-06
.22 Hornet	.257 Imp. Roberts	.300 Magnum
.22 K-Hornet	.250 Magnum	.308 Magnum

.22 Imp. Zipper	.270 Winchester	.35 Newton
.22 Standard Zipper	.270 Magnum	.22-250
Lovell R-2	.256 Newton	.218 Bee
.220 Swift	.256 Magnum	.219 Donaldson
.220 Imp. Swift	7 m.m. Mauser	

The larger case 17's are yet an unknown quantity, but when we have bullets which will stand 5000 f.s. they may prove to be adequate. If a bullet such as the Ackley controlled expansion or Nosler ever becomes available for this series of cartridges things may happen yet unheard of. Of course, we will have the problem of barrel life to worry about, but this may also be solved in time. The .22 Hornet, Bee or Lovell in any of the various versions are definitely inadequate in this area. They lack the range and power for these long shots. The smallest cartridges which have proven satisfactory are the .219 Donaldson, various Zippers, the Swift in all of its versions, such as the Ackley Imp., Weatherby Rocket, Wilson Arrow, etc., and the Varminter and various versions of the .22-250. I personally prefer the Imp. Zipper for the single shot actions, and the .22-250 or Varminter for bolt actions in this class. They seem to do almost anything that the larger cartridges of the sup .22 family do. They are flexible to load and the cases are easy to make.

The one group could be listed as follows: .228 Ackley Magnum, .250 Ackley, or Gipson Magnum .25-06. There would be little choice in this group judging by results on chucks. The range, trajectory, and killing power of each is entirely adequate. However, for me and others who hunt for the fun of it and don't like to be beaten to death, the .228 will be found more pleasant to carry and shoot than the larger calibers. The next class, which I personally feel is the largest cartridge practical to use here in the mountains on chucks, could be as follows: 6.5 or .256 Magnum, .270 Winchester and the various .270 Magnums, with the preference going to the smaller versions, like the .270 Ackley Magnum, .270 Gipson and short .270 Mashburn Magnums. The large blown out full length .270 Magnum cases show a rather short barrel life and one could easily wear such a barrel out on one hunt. On one of these hunts, such as have been described previously in this chapter, one may fire several hundred rounds at various types of targets. I have never seen it fail that whenever things begin to lag some member of the party will pick out a spot on the opposite canyon wall or some similar target and cut down on it. When this happens everyone in the crowd joins in. There are other kinds of targets too, such as coyotes, jack rabbits, and eagles.

In the last group, we can place the remaining cartridges on the list, namely, the .30 calibers and larger ones. In order to get the flat trajectory out of these large bores and the sustained velocity so essential to this type of hunting it is necessary to soup them up to the last notch. In order for the average man to be able to take the beating of a large number of shots in one day, it is necessary to have an exceedingly heavy rifle, and even then the medium-sized cartridges in groups two and three usually badly outshoot these cannon sized pieces.

THE 6.5 M. M. BARNES

There is one cartridge in the list which needs further description and that is one of the 6.5 m.m. Magnums with which Fred Barnes has been experimenting. This is based on the .275 Magnum case, or perhaps we should say the .250 Gipson case, and uses a 200-grain 6.5 m.m. bullet. The cartridge is loaded with a compressed charge of .50-caliber machine gun powder, and it is proving fine for the extremely long shots. Due to the scarcity of components and the highly specialized character of this cartridge it could not yet be classed as practical for the rank and file shooter. Barnes is now developing a .228 cartridge using a 120-grain bullet. This is a .2265-inch bullet nearly 1-1/2 inches long. I am now making the barrels for it and they have a 5.5-inch twist. The case being tried out first is the .250-3000 necked to .2265. It, of course, is intended for extremely long range chuck shooting only. More will probably be heard about this latest development shortly.

Our 1950 hunt will take place during the first week in July somewhere along the western slope of the Sawatch Mountains, just west of the Divide along the Taylor River. We plan to do this one on horses.

CHAPTER 16

Vernor Gipson Products

VERNOR GIPSON, of North Salem, Indiana, but who for years was located at Palos Park, Illinois, has been recognized as one of the most expert manufacturers of highly accurate, small caliber, woodchuck and other varmint rifles.

In his early days, Mr. Gipson did not always receive full credit for many of his developments, nor for his skill in rifle chambering, barrel fitting and rifle manufacture in general. He appears to have been the actual producer and manufacturer of the .219 Donaldson Wasp. The cartridge received its name, so it seems, largely from the very effective manner in which this cartridge, in its numerous variations, was advertised and presented to the public by Harvey Donaldson, Samuel Clark Jr., and other riflemen. Gipson, at one time, was co-owner and president, of the old Niedner Rifle Corporation at Dowagiac, Michigan.

In his manufacturing endeavors during the past five or six years, Gipson has been assisted by Byron E. Cottrell, of Galeton, Pennsylvania, a well-known and experienced writer for the sporting magazines, who handled most of the correspondence.

THE .236 GIPSON

One of the more powerful small-caliber Gipson cartridges is the .236 Gipson which is made up from the .220 Swift case. The rifles made for it by Vernor Gipson are chambered so that they will head-space correctly with the factory .220 Swift cases that are merely opened at the neck to take .244 bullets. When fired, these cartridges expand to larger diameter at the shoulder and the expansion produces a sharper shoulder angle.

The late J. Bushnell Smith chronographed the .236-220 a short time before his death in July, 1948. The velocities and loads are as follows:

.236-220 GIPSON

75-grain Barnes bullet and 42.0 grains of DuPont 4895 — 3755 f.s. m.v.
75-grain W-M 8S bullet and 42.0 grains of   "   4895 — 3790 "   "
90-grain Barnes bullet and 42.0 grains of   "   4064 — 3535 "   "
65-grain W-M 8S bullet and 45.0 grains of   "   4895 — 3998 "   "
90-grain Barnes bullet and 46.5 grains of   "   4350 — 3640 "   "
60-grain W-M 8S bullet and 46.0 grains of   "   4895 — 4113 "   "

J. Bushnell Smith tried out the 60- and 65-grain bullets and obtained a bit better than 4000 f.s.m.v. but we do not have that data. Gipson and Smith had intended to make up additional bullets and work out this caliber for a bench-rest cartridge and rifle, but as so often occurs at the interesting period of a man's career, death intervened. This .236 Gipson job was a Buhmiller barrel of .243 diameter and 26-inch barrel length, with six grooves. It shot numerous one-inch groups at 100 yards and some smaller. The bench-rest shoot at which this cartridge was first to be entered was that held at DuBois, Pennsylvania in the summer of 1948. The rifle was fitted only with a sporter barrel, but it was so accurate that Smith had intended to use it for serious competitive shooting, however, at the time he did not have enough bullets of that diameter, or of the proper weight or of first grade workmanship.

THE .236-256 GIPSON (ORIGINAL CARTRIDGE)

This cartridge was made up from the .256 Newton case necked to .236 caliber. Gipson made the tools and the first barrel for this while at the old Niedner Rifle Corporation plant. Rather shortly after it came out, the .256 Newton cases were no longer available. The cartridge cases were next made from the .30-1906 cartridge, which of course were plentiful. The brass of the .30-1906 case is usually a little thicker and the charges given below should be reduced a bit when using .30-1906 brass. The charges will go into the brass case but the breech pressures will increase, hence the need for reducing the amount of powder thrown when loading .30-1906 varmint-cartridge brass.

The following charges were chronographed in necked down .256 Newton brass, barrel was 28 inches long, cut with 12-inch twist, and bored and rifled by Vernor Gipson.

.236 GIPSON BALLISTICS

75-grain Barnes bullet, 50.0 grs. of 4064, M.V. 3,895 f.s.
75-grain Barnes bullet, 52.0 grs. of 4064, M.V. 4,027 f.s.
90-grain Barnes bullet, 45.0 grs. of 4064, M.V. 3,600 f.s.
90-grain Barnes bullet, 50.0 grs. of 4350, M.V. 3,611 f.s.
105-grain Barnes bullet, 48.0 grs. of 4350, M.V. 3,362 f.s.

The .236 Gipson with the Newton case is reputed to be a very accurate cartridge, suitable for very long range woodchuck shooting, and is just as effective for coyotes on the plains if the wind is not too strong at the time. It is a good wind-bucker but of course can be excelled in this by a larger caliber, long bullet. The rifle for the .236 Gipson should be cut with a 10-inch twist for all bullets heavier than 90 grains.

THE .220-257 GIPSON

This is a case of which both Gipson and Cottrell have spoken well in past years, but later and more extensive experiments proved it to be less satisfactory than when using the .22-250-3000 cases. Gipson no longer wishes to chamber rifles for the .22-257, however, the data is given as it did have some vogue. The .25-30-1906 varmint cartridges never proved to be as ballistically efficient as when smaller capacity cases were used.

The .220-257 is made by necking down the .257 Remington or .257 Winchester Roberts cases. The present-day .257 Roberts case has a different shape from the original .257 Roberts cartridge designed by the late N. H. Roberts.

The characteristics of this cartridge are a good heavy, solid head, strong side walls, as compared to the .250-3000 Savage case, but unfortunately it has too much powder room for highest efficiency in .22 caliber. Many of my correspondents have shown me that the average .257 Roberts caliber rifle has not shot as accurately, especially when having fired less than 250 to 500 rounds, as the average .250-3000 Savage caliber of rifle of similar mechanical design. In .22 caliber, the .220-257 case, while stronger and better suited to extensive reloading than the .22-250, and the .219 Wasp cartridges, will probably never prove as super accurate, on the average, as either of the others mentioned, particularly with very short, light bullets due to the great case capacity of the .257.

When loaded with very long, heavy bullets of 70 to 90 grains, this cartridge greatly resembles the .22 Newton in general outline.

The field for this cartridge, if used, is for long range woodchuck shooting, for use on hawks, crows, coyotes, wolves, open-country deer and antelope shooting, and with the longer and heavier bullets, for elk. It can be used for sheep and goats, but in any case, for elk, sheep and goats, it should be less effective than a good .270 W.C.F. With Gipson, the .220-257 is obsolete. He has abandoned it for cartridges cases of less capacity.

THE .220-250

Gipson has also made up numerous rifles for the .220-250 cartridge. Charles F. Miller, at this writing, Chief Building Inspector of the city of Reading, Pennsylvania has done most excellent shooting with the .220-250. Miller has been an expert and well-known long range, military rifle shot since about 1911. In 1947 Miller killed five woodchucks in six shots at ranges given as "between 400 and 500 yards"—this occuring in the presence of Byron Cottrell. Shooting was in Potter County, Pennsylvania, where the hills are in many cases both high and very bare. Miller used a .220-250 rifle made by Gipson.

Cottrell says that "too much favorable comment cannot be made about the .220-250." The .220-250 will not use the standard .220 Swift ammunition as the Swift is much smaller in the body of the case, and is also longer. But the .220-250 Gipson will use the .22 Varminter ammunition as made up by the late J. B. Smith, and the rifle is chambered to much the same dimensions as the Varminter. This means the standard .22 Varminter, which many others call the .22-250.

THE .219 GIPSON WASP

Byron Cottrell of the Gipson firm, says that the .219 Wasp has been over ballyhooed but it is not over rated in accomplishment. They claim that one of these rifles, correctly made up and loaded, will shoot plenty of groups of 5/8 inch at 100 yards —these being ten-shot groups and not five-shot, and this degree of accuracy appears to be expected in a very fine rifle of this caliber. Gipson's say that they have made some which will shoot 100 shots into less than an inch at 100 yards. This is a condition far more difficult to accomplish than to find a rifle which will shoot ten, ten-shot groups averaging one inch in diameter, or even so that all ten are an inch or less each.

July 21, 1947, in what was one of his earlier letters on the subject of Gipson developments, Cottrell said, "The .219 Wasp does give very moderate pressures. With a case full of 3031, —about 27 grains; or 4320, which weighs 30 grains, and a 55-grain bullet, the pressure appears to be less than any cartridge of which we have knowledge. The .219 Zipper is right in the same class, and will handle 35 grains of 4320. We are also making a .220 Wasp, very little shorter than the regular Wasp and of the same capacity. It is made from .220 Swift cases, and uses the same loads as the .219 Wasp. It requires no altering of the bolt face. All of these cartridges are very accurate if the right ammunition is used.

"We generally use a 14-inch twist in these rifles, but we have made them with 16-inch twist that would really shoot. The groove diameter should be a full .224 inch as we have never seen one of these .22's shoot its best with a tight barrel. In fact, the best-shooting one we have made lately in a sporter barrel, has a groove diameter of nearly .2247 inch. The 16-inch twist will give results with a 50-grain bullet and possibly with a 55-grain missile. We had one that did!

We have seen many ten-shot groups fired at 500 yards, that measured under five inches, both with the Wasp and with the .220-250."

Cottrell mentions that he owns a .219 Wasp rifle made up on a Savage Model 99 lever action. The action was made up originally for the .22 H.P. cartridge and is fitted with a 22-inch light weight barrel chambered for the .219 Wasp cartridge. The action handles this cartridge perfectly, he reports, and the rifle shoots with fine accuracy.

It is in his opinion, a "swell little rifle." It makes a fine hunting rifle, being short, light, easy to carry on those steep hills and mountains in Potter County, Pennsylvania — many of them are round, sugar-loaf hills with not a thing on them but the usual fourteen to fifteen pounds per square inch of air pressure. A good deal of this area is "mostly up and down."

It is a rifle he expects to use a lot for wild turkey hunting, and when loaded with reduced loads, for squirrels. He obtained this action from Savage when he worked there in the Savage plant, and also a stock for it of the RS type, and a Model T forearm. It is equipped with target scope blocks and no iron sights.

He uses on it a Unertl 4X small game scope — which is relatively a small, light, rather short top-of-the-barrel type of
scope, suitable for general hunting, but made much better if
fitted by Unertl objective of about 5-1/2 power and a size of
1-3/8 to 1-1/2 inches.

SPEER CASES FOR .20 AND .35 NEWTON

Cottrell mentioned also that Speer has made up some .30
Newton and .35 Newton calibers of cartridge cases, and has
them for sale at $5.00 per box of 20, cases are empty and un-
primed. That figures out as 25 cents each, just for the cases.
These were ready in the spring of 1949.

Under date of August 6, 1948, Cottrell said, in a communi-
cation, "The .220 Swift Improved — the .220 Swift with a sharp
shoulder — seems like a very fine cartridge. The first one we
made of this caliber shot less than 1-inch groups at 100 yards,
right from the start. After we changed the load a little, we were
able to keep the bullet holes in 3/4 inch. We sent this rifle up to
J. B. Smith for testing, and it was there when he died, so we
never received a report upon it.

"Our Improved .220 Swift is a sharp shoulder, and can use
the factory ammunition. We did this wildcatting without increasing the case capacity any more than possible, as we already consider the case too large — especially for the short, light .22
bullets.

"As to chucks, we do not have the numbers of chucks you
ran across in Ontario, but last year two of the boys went into a
farmer's field in Potter County and saw 28 woodchucks at one
time. They only killed an even dozen and quit with chucks still
watching them. I often use a .270, and the rifle I used this trip
(1948) was a .270 bull gun, — for the most of my shooting, anyway.

"We are getting our barrel machinery in shape as fast as
possible — we have Pratt & Whitney barrel drill and reaming
machines. We have drills for all calibers from .170 to .50 caliber, and have most of the rifling heads and the rest on order.
Someday, before long, we will get into production on the .170
caliber, as well as the others.

"The .170 might make a fine wild turkey rifle. The ranges
are usually well under 200 yards, and a fellow doesn't want to
blow them all to pieces. Turkeys take plenty of killing, but the
meat mangles and tears rather easily."

.256 GIPSON MAGNUM

There always will be shooters who will prefer to use a rifle of larger caliber than .22 for woodchuck shooting. The longer, larger diameter, heavier bullets are better wind-buckers and in many localities, wind-bucking is more important than recoil or report. Also, there are those who feel a bit effeminate unless the rifle report has considerable "wham" to it.

While the late Charles Newton has been credited principally with introducing the .256-caliber rifle to the public, especially the American shooters, the facts are that long before the .256 Newton came out here, the 6.5 m.m. Mannlicher was the standard small caliber, high velocity, center fire cartridge in central and southern Europe, and almost all over Africa, and where it wasn't they used the 7 m.m. or .275-caliber. The 7 m.m. was the Mauser small caliber. All Spanish speaking countries use them, and many others.

The .256 Gipson Magnum cartridge is based on the .275 Holland & Holland cartridge case. But it can also be made from the .300 Magnum brass. The rifle for the .256 Magnum usually is made with a 10-inch twist. The velocities developed with a 26-inch barrel having 10-inch twist, are as follows:

.256 Gipson Magnum

130-grain Barnes bullet, 60.0 grs. I.M.R. No. 4350,— Vel. 3,315 f.s.
150-grain Barnes bullet, 58.0 grs. ''   No. 4350,— Vel. 3,150 f.s.

Be sure to observe the weight of the bullet when considering the above figures.

This is one of the finest all-around, long range game cartridges suitable for both woodchucks and most big game, as well as superb for western coyote and wolf shooting, or for the same in Canada or Alaska. The rifleman using this must be able to load his ammunition and have equipment for doing so, or make arrangements with some commercial hand-loader to supply him.

This caliber is one of Fred N. Barnes' favorite hunting rifles. It is reportedly his choice for long range mountain marmot hunting, which is the western woodchuck shooting far up in the tablelands and valleys of the high altitude Rockies. It is good for anything up to elk.

A couple of years ago, Gipson fitted a .256 Gipson Magnum barrel which he had also chambered, to an action for Fred Barnes. This rifle has a 6-inch twist. In this rifle he uses 200-

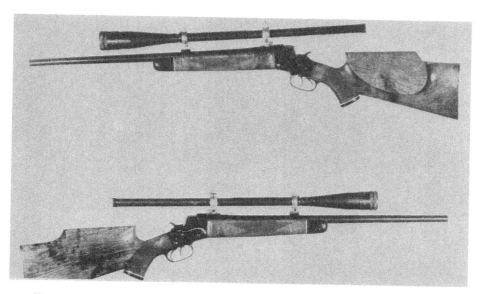

Remington-Hepburn action with Ackley-made Myrtle wood stock.

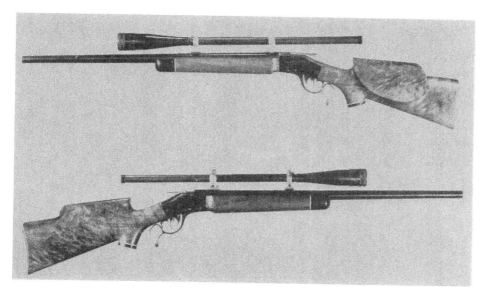

Sharps-Borchardt single shot, Ackley high-comb cheek piece stock.

.224 belted Ackley express bolt action rock chuck rifle.

Five of the Steve Gallt woodchuck cartridges. *L to R:* R-2 Gallt improved; .200 Asp Express; .224 Asp Express; Gallt version .219 Wasp; Gallt version .22-250.

grain bullets of his own manufacture, and a charge of special slow powder, not on the market, to obtain a velocity a bit above 2500 f.s. Remember this is with a 200-grain very small caliber bullet. He wrote Cottrell since the last elk season to say that he had killed an elk with it, also, a friend of his killed an elk with the same rifle. Barnes remarked that he had never seen a rifle that held its energy better at long range, or which would shoot any flatter.

The powder he used was 50-caliber machine gun powder. This 50-caliber machine gun powder and the nitrocellulose coated rifle powder for .30-1906 ammunition used in World War II by the U. S. forces, were of the same chemical composition and general form, except that the 50-caliber machine gun powder was, of course, much the coarser in granulation. Obviously, this very coarse grained nitrocellulose 50-caliber machine gun powder would burn slowly and with lower pressures in a magnum rifle cartridge. Both DuPont and Hercules made this 50-caliber machine gun powder. It is not on the market regularly, however, for reloaders. And it is unlikely either company ever made a complete set of loading tests for such use in rifles, if they made any.

Cottrell says that it seems impossible to use too much of it in any ordinary cartridge. In a large .280 Magnum cartridge they used 84 grains of it, with the 180-grain Barnes bullet, and pressures seemed to be less than in standard Krag loads. After-dark shooting and long range trajectory tests indicated the powder was burning uniformly.

THE .25-1906 GIPSON

This cartridge is made from the .30-1906 case, expanded at the shoulder and necked to .25 caliber. Three thousand foot seconds velocity was obtained with this case, from a 26-inch barrel with 9-inch pitch of rifling, using a 125-grain Barnes bullet ahead of 53.0 grains of DuPont 4350. It is a case suitable for use with coarse grained powder and heavy bullets.

All such cases can be used with lighter bullets, such as 87 and 101 grain, but in that instance, the twist should be 12 or 14 inches, and the case will be found larger than desirable for a light .25-caliber bullet as somewhat better results could be obtained with light bullets, if a smaller cartridge case were used.

This case is claimed to give target accuracy with good 117-grain bullets and 38.0 grains of DuPont No. 3031.

A fast twist, 9 inches or so, will be needed for that bullet also.

Not very many present day 100- or 101-grain bullets will stand up for the full load in this case. These were designed for velocities developed by cases like the .25-35 and the .25 Remington. When good bullets are available, either commercial, like Western, or hand-made, this caliber makes a fine, long range woodchuck or coyote rifle. With the 125-grain Barnes bullet it is a good deer rifle. The drop from line of sight when sighted in at 200 yards, and fired at 500 yards, is only 3 feet, 2 inches, by actual shooting.

If the rifle be sighted for 200 yards, and big game is sighted at 500 yards, by aiming a foot and a half over the top of the back, a kill might be expected.

The most accurate load Cottrell has as yet used in it is the 100-grain Barnes bullet and 30.0 grains of DuPont No. 4198. He believes the velocity is between 2300 and 2500 f.s. He worked up this load for use on wild turkeys. Just before the open season they sighted in this rifle at 200 yards to find out what sight setting it would take. The rifle required but three minutes increase which would suggest that the velocity was up around 2500 f.s. They also found it easy to make groups round and under 2 inches. In fact, Cottrell says, all of the 200-yard groups were under 1-1/2 inches. This is even better accuracy than he obtained with 38.0 grains of No. 3031 and the 117-grain bullets. He feels that the 9-inch twist is about right for this long, sharp-pointed 100-grain bullet at the above velocities.

.276 CARLSON MAGNUM

The case for this cartridge was designed by Richard Carlson, of Hamilton, Montana, and the reamers for the chamber made up by Gipson. It is a fine, all-around big game cartridge and a very effective long range load on woodchucks. It can be shot at short range just as well, but may mangle the chuck, and the arm makes a lot of noise for shooting in settled areas.

The velocity figures, chronographed by H. P. White Company of Cleveland, Ohio, for a rifle with 9-inch twist, follows:

.276 Carlson

160-grain Barnes bullet 59.5 grains of 4350 lot 9C Vel. 3015 f.s.
180-grain Barnes bullet 57.0 grains of 4350 lot 9C Vel. 2830 f.s.
195-grain Barnes bullet 54.0 grains of 4350 lot 9C Vel. 2657 f.s.

.270-4000 GIPSON

This one was made up on the Newton case. Some claim it is the best .270 wildcat ever designed. But it is not of much use until .30 Newton cases are available as it used only the .30 Newton case. There have been rumors that Western might again make up a lot of .30 Newton cases, so if and when someone does make .30 Newton cases available, here is the data. Gipson has one in this caliber, as they had a small quantity of such brass on hand, and they recently made up another for a customer who had some cases.

This caliber is claimed to be accurate with all loads listed, and to give target accuracy with reduced loads. The loads listed were chronographed in the old Niedner plant by Gipson. Ten-or twelve-inch twists are satisfactory but 11-inch twist is recommended to those who wish to use a wide variety of bullet weights. Velocities listed were obtained in a rifle with 26-inch barrel.

.270-4000 Gipson

130-grain Western bullet, 66.0 grs. 4350, Vel. 3419 f.s.
130-grain   "   "   68.0 grs.   "   "   3500 f.s.
145 W.T. & C.W. bullet, 64.0 grs. "   "   3133 f.s.
150 Western   65.0 grs. "   "   3177 f.s.
160 Barnes .270 Mag. Bu. 61.0 grs. "   "   3025 f.s.

For the reader's information, and as a definite comparison of results, below are the ballistics of the .270 Winchester factory ammunition.

Note the great ballistic advantages of the .270-4000. Remember too, that .270 factory ammunition should not be tried in the .270-4000 chamber.

.270 FACTORY WINCHESTER AMMUNITION

130-grain factory bullet 3120 f.s.
150-grain factory bullet 2770 f.s.
100-grain factory bullet 3540 f.s.

For all practical purposes, the .270-4000 Gipson starts off a 130-grain bullet as fast as the factory .270 Winchester starts a 100-grain bullet. Or, it starts a 130-grain bullet 300 to 380 f.s. faster. Or, it starts a 150-grain bullet 57 f.s. faster than the .270 W.C.F. drives a 130-grain bullet. The pressure is likely higher, the report is louder and sharper, it gives more blast at the muzzle, but this cartridge throws a bullet on a materially flatter trajectory than the 1/2 inch over 100 yards, 2 inches over 200 yards, and 5 inches over 300 yards of the factory .270 W.C.F.

To refresh your memory, the .270 W.C.F. factory cartridge is for all essential purposes, the .30-1906 case necked down to fit a .275-inch bullet. Therefore, you cannot take .30-1906 brass and use it instead of .30 Newton brass and expect to obtain .30 Newton-270 results. All you would get is factory .270 results, if fired in a chamber that fits a .30-1906 case necked to .270.

Some will ask, ''Why shoot a cannon like this at an eight pound woodchuck, ''In like manner, why not ask, ''Why shoot a 12-gauge shotgun at reedbirds, or even at woodcock?''

Some of the boys are going to do so, in spite of high winds and foul weather. They want to make something roar that will reach out 500 yards, lift that woodchuck up in the air and slam it down! The joker of the whole affair is to get bullets made now of a jacket thickness to expand properly on an elk or a moose, to expand with equal facility and in an infinitesimal interval of time, on a woodchuck. Usually they don't, they romp right on through and expend their energy on the surrounding turf.

I recall with mingled feelings of astonishment and chagrin, how I once shot a woodchuck squarely through the lungs and heart, at a distance of about 50 yards or less, on a green meadow near a narrow lane, on a farm in Delaware. The chuck was nibbling grass. It never even stopped nibbling. Gave no immediate sign of having been struck or of even having heard the .30-1906 caliber rifle which had driven a 172-grain bullet through it. After a few moments it suddenly seemed startled, then gave signs of being uncomfortable — as it was bleeding into the lungs, then it rushed for the den, and before getting down, fell over. It can be said truthfully, we were both surprised!

THE .300 MAGNUM SPECIAL

The .300 Magnum Special Gipson cartridge was made by reforming the .375 Magnum cases, or by firing .300 Magnum cases in a rifle chambered for the .300 Magnum Special. The firm recommends making them from .375 brass. They say they have not so far had any of the .300 Magnum cases split in the larger, sharper-shoulder chamber, upon firing, but it could happen.

The first .300 Magnum Special Gipson rifle was made up for David Drew of Caswell, Alaska. With the same load and hold, the rifle, he reported, would not miss a wolf between 200 and 400 yards, due to trajectory.

So far as known, the rifle has not so far been chronographed. The following loads were worked out by Mr. Drew who reportedly said that they all gave moderate pressures insofar as could be determined.

.300 MAGNUM SPECIAL.

Winchester No. 120 primer used with all of these charges.
150-grain Open Point bullet, 77.0 grs. 4350. Shoots into 1-1/2 minutes of angle.

172-grain B.T.	75.0 grs. 4350.	
180-grain B.T.	45.0 grs. HiVel No. 2.	An accurate but moderate velocity target load.
220-grain bullet	70.0 grs. 4350.	Powerful and accurate.

The rifle was made up with 12-inch twist in a 28-inch barrel. Gipson has made up a number of these rifles, some with 12-inch twist and some with standard 10-inch twist. It is, in their opinion, the best .300 Magnum cartridge. It has a good shape and shoulder angle, and is not too large. It is also made of good brass.

As a woodchuck cartridge it is, of course, much too powerful for most shooting, that is, it is unnecessarily powerful and noisy; also, the rifle gives materially more recoil than the .30-1906 rifles of equal weight because the arm uses 25 to 30 grains more powder. However, there are places, in central New York State, in north eastern New York, a few places in Ontario, and almost any place in plains country, where such a rifle would be very effective at long range on coyotes and wolves. But shooting a woodchuck with such a cartridge is ballistically much the same as transporting an 8-inch rifled cannon up on a portable mount and carriage, to kill a single sniper in the opposing lines. The results on a direct hit are quite effective and immediate, and also, very messy, but it does seem like using a broad-axe with a six-pound head to drive a single six-ounce tack.

A RESUME OF VERNOR GIPSON'S

WILDCAT RIFLE DEVELOPMENTS

The most popular cartridges for which Gipson chambered rifles during 1948 and 1949, were the .219 Wasp, the .220-250, .220 Wasp, .219 Improved Zipper, and the Lovell G-3. He also had some demand for the .220 Krag and the .224 Lightning.

The .219 Wasp is an extremely accurate and efficient little cartridge, and at present is the most popular cartridge for which they chamber .22-caliber center fire woodchuck rifles. It normally gives velocities of 3500 to 3700 f.s. with 55-grain and with 50-grain bullets. It is a very good all-around cartridge for shooting crows and woodchucks. Like all modern cartridges, it is at its best when used in a good bolt action rifle, but being a rimmed case it should be considered a single shot proposition only. A few have been made up as repeaters but generally they do not work too well when so supplied. The bolt face has to be altered for the larger rim and then cannot again be used for standard diameter rimless cases.

For those who want a rifle for a rimless case, the Gipson .220 Wasp is provided. This was designed to duplicate the .219 Wasp in a standard rimless case — the case used is the .220 Swift — which is rimless, and it has the same powder capacity (30 grains) as the .219 Wasp. It gives just about the same degree of accuracy, but better still, it produces one hundred foot seconds greater muzzle velocity to its bullet, using the same loads. J. Bushnell Smith chronographed a variety of loads for the .220 Wasp, for Gipson, with the following results:

27.5 grs. 4895 and 55-grain 8S bullet gives 3625 f.s. muzzle vel.
30.0 grs. 4895 and 50-grain 8S bullet gives 3820 f.s.   "   "
30.0 grs. 4320 and 50-grain 8S bullet gives 3750 f.s.   "   "

I have shot the equivalent of this load in a .22 Varminter rifle, cartridge case size in both instances considered, the ammunition was loaded by Bushnell Smith and it shot very accurately and consistently — 30.0 grains of 3031 and 50-grain 8S bullet, 3820 f.s.m.v.

This cartridge should also be considered as a single shot proposition as none of these short cartridges load well when used in a bolt action repeater with standard size magazine and a long bolt throw.

When a rifleman wants an arm to work properly as a repeater, the best of the Gipson .22 wildcats which are powerful combinations is the .220-250. This cartridge is too well known to need much comment other than to say that it is just as accurate and reliable as it was ten or twelve years ago. The cases are readily obtained and easy to form; and when proper ammunition used in a good rifle, it is a hard combination to outshoot. muzzle velocity of the more accurate loads lies between 3600 f.s. with the 55-grain Sisk bullet to 3900 f.s. for the 50-grain size.

The .22 Lovell is still popular with those shooters who do most of their shooting in thickly settled or at least moderately settled farming country where the least noise is desirable and the woodchucks are often plentiful and generally also — smart! Gipson's most popular version is the G-3, a maximum capacity case along the lines of the Hervey Lovell "Maximum Lovell" case. This wad made up in at least three different designs, originally, the G-1, G-2, and the G-3, they varied mostly in the shoulder angle, this differing from 17 to 23 degrees, the G-3 having the latter. The G-3 will hold 2 or 2-1/2 grains more powder than the usual 15-degree slope R-2 cartridge. Dick Simmons says that Gipson's Maximum Lovell cartridge was the first of many similar shape cases ever received by him.

THE GIPSON IMPROVED HORNET

Vernor Gipson took the .22 Hornet cartridge, lengthened the body and gave the shoulder a more abrupt shoulder angle and then straightened the neck to hold the bullet parallel its full length. It looks something like his G-3 Lovell and also like Kilbourn's K-Hornet, yet there appears to be some difference in general contours.

Cases are formed by the firing of regular .22 Hornet ammunition in this Improved Hornet chamber. It will use about the same powder charges and bullets as any other of the K-Hornet types of .22 cartridges in the wildcat family.

I found the .22 Hornet to be very accurate and highly deadly on woodchucks in Ontario, in 1946, when shot in a K-Hornet type of chamber put in a single shot rifle by Mr. G. B. Crandall of Woodstock, Ontario. While some men who buy Improved Hornets use only factory ammunition for rather close range shots, I used it for shots at all ranges to which a Hornet will normally be introduced and it made good.

There are a few gunsmiths, the most outspoken of which is Charles Parkinson, who claim that a lot of good .22 Hornet rifles have been somewhat ruined in accuracy by chambering them for the K-Hornet type of ammunition but I have not had such complaints from other correspondents. Nor have I heard it about K-Hornet types of rifles put out in the United States.

THE .220 KRAG

This cartridge was designed by Vernor Gipson to give the same type of ballistics as the .220-250, but from a rimmed case that could be used in Winchester single shot actions; these do not handle rimless cartridges to good advantage, as compared to rimmed cases. Harvey Donaldson used one of the first .220 Krag rifles made by Gipson, and called it the .22-4500. Gipson never claimed any higher velocities for this cartridge than were delivered by the standard Varminter — the .22-250-3000. Mr. Donaldson, according to the rifle's makers, used loads which swelled the chamber of the rifle and so they suggest it is probable he obtained velocities in the general neighborhood of the figure mentioned.

The .224 Lightning is a good cartridge for use in single shot actions, as the head of the case is large and the case capacity is high. Most of the old .30-40 Krag ammunition has badly split necks as of this date, and new .30-40 cases are no better than any of the others. The cartridge would be a better .22 caliber with a smaller capacity cartridge case. The .303 British case is slightly smaller capacity, and as they had millions of rounds of that caliber with very heavy cases for aircraft machine gun use, the .303 of that type would make a better .224 Lightning than the old .30-40 Krag cases.

GIPSON'S AND COTTRELL'S IDEAS ON RIFLE ACTIONS

FOR WILDCATS

In the making up of a fine .22 high velocity varmint rifle or one for use as a target rifle or for rest shooting work, Gipson and Cottrell recommend a good strong bolt action with a good lock action. Also, they suggest the use of a high grade telescope sight. It is not possible to obtain the best from one of these rifles with any hunting telescope they ever used or saw used. They suggest the higher powers — from 10X on up, of the fine target scopes with large front sections. Large objectives, that is. Also, good bullets are very, very important. In fact, their importance cannot be over estimated. Without the very finest grade of custom-made .22 bullets, the worth of the very finest precision job of rifle making is thrown away. The fine rifle without the finest bullets cannot ever be a top performer, and the fine bullets without the fine rifle are also only ordinary result getters. The twain must meet!

DIFFERENT ACTIONS

As to actions, Gipson's believe the best action today is the Winchester Model 70, or 54. This is not because of any better design, but because of better steel that is correctly heat-treated, and fine workmanship. They prefer any of the good American actions to the Mauser. They say, they have no fault to find with the design of the Mauser action, but the material is not as good as that which United States Manufacturers have used for the past twenty years. If the Mauser is correctly heat-treated, it is okay, but a test made on the outside of those received does not guarantee that the lug seats are of the correct hardness. They had not had any trouble with Springfield or Enfield actions. The Remington Model 30 and 30S class right along with the Enfield; they are very strong, good actions, but are unnecessarily large for most varmint rifles.

The Winchester S.S., Stevens 44-1/2, Sharps-Borchardt, are all good actions and will make satisfactory hunting rifles, but they are not as rigid as the bolt action with its one-piece stock, and will not, as a rule, give as fine accuracy. They report that they do not know of a single shot rifle made up on a single shot action that will shoot equal to the Wasp on a good bolt action. Everything considered, they believe the Winchester S.S. is the best. The Stevens 44-1/2 has a poor firing pin arrangement and it is impossible to completely correct it.

They have had many Mausers, which were apparently all right when viewed, fail to hold their headspace. They have had several cases, so they advise me, where the proof load would set the lug seats back from four to ten thousandths, but they have never had that happen with a Winchester 70 or 54, or a Springfield or an Enfield. They have had to replace the receivers of nearly a dozen Mausers, due to setting back in the lug seats.

CHAMBER THROAT DIMENSIONS

Gipson says, ''As to the throat of a rifle barrel: The purpose of the throat is to get the bullet into the bore with the least possible deformation of the bullet, and with as little loss of gas as possible. This deformation of the bullet is of the most importance in .22 caliber — and of course in the still smaller .170 caliber, as these bullets are easily deformed and are readily bent sidewise with small amount of pressure.''

He also said ''There is no such thing as special or secret throat — they are simply good common sense and careful workmanship. Of course they are cut differently for different types of bullets having points which are dissimilar.''

When a customer desires the greatest possible accuracy, Gipson recommends the heavy, straight taper barrel of not less than 26 inches and up to 30 inches in length to insure uniform burning of the propellent.

For all ordinary purposes, including woodchuck shooting up to 300 yards or so, the heavy sporter barrel will deliver the goods. It is surprising how accurate a really light barrel is, if it is turned down properly so that it is perfectly straight. A really good sporter weight barrel of a .22 varmint rifle may be deadly on woodchucks at 400 yards. The really accurate barrel should have the bore concentric with the outside for the whole length of the barrel. Gipson reports that he made a 20-inch barrel for the .220-250 cartridge, which, when equipped with scope blocks and target scope, would make one-inch ten-shot group at 100 yards.

They admit that the heavy barrel is of course more reliable on the average, omitting exceptional barrels which might be of any weight, but the heavy barrel is the better selection for target work, for ammunition testing, of for best work on crows up to 300 to 350 yards. I do not believe that a heavy rifle is necessary or satisfactory for the woodchuck hunter who must go over hills and across fields, carrying his own equipment.

Gipson says, ''We have tried three different twists of rifling, 14-inch, 15-inch and 16-inch, and find no great difference in them, but none have proved any better than the 14-inch and this is what we generally use. The 15-inch might as well be forgotten as there is little enough difference between 14-and 16-inch twist performance.

''It is quite common for our .22's (varmint rifles) to make minute-of-angle groups at 500 yards, under favorable weather conditions of course.''

STRAIGHTNESS OF RIFLE BARRELS

"We believe that any good reputation that our barrels may have is due in no small part to the fact that they are straight. It is surprising how many rifle barrels are turned out and sold that are definitely lacking in straightness of the long axis. Our barrels are straight inside and outside, and they are concentric their entire length. The chamber is carefully cut and in line with the bore in each barrel. The layman assumes these things are so in all custom rifles, and for that matter, in all rifles. But such is not the case. Some gunsmiths do not even have a method of checking barrel straightness. Certain crooked barrels may shoot remarkably well, especially until they become heated up and tend to change the direction of their long axis; but straightness is to be desired."

It is interesting to note Mr. Gipson's emphasis on the straightness and concentricity of the rifle barrel and on precision rifle making. This proper cartridge design, accurate loading of ammunition, target sights (telescopic) suitable for a woodchuck rifle, and the assembly and making of the whole so that the small-caliber, high-velocity bullet may be projected from the rifleman to the woodchuck in a parabola which travels in but one plane, is the aim of any conscientious rifle manufacturer who combines correct engineering principles with consummate mechanical skill.

CHAPTER 17

Steve Gallt's Small Caliber Cartridges

THE woodchucks we have in central New York State are big handsome fellows, especially when hunted in the late summer and fall. They appear first in mid-March after a four-or-five-month period of hibernation. They are not usually too handsome when they first appear, but good feeding on the farmer's best clover and alfalfa soon puts Mr. Monax in shape.

I have noticed a number of peculiarities and individual characteristics about woodchucks. For instance, a pasture chuck is much more wary than a meadow chuck. He never attains the glossy coat or the size of his fellows in the feed lots. The pasture chuck will usually outwait the hunter but the well-fed meadow chuck will usually pop up to see how things are in less than five minutes. Another peculiarity of the chuck is that if you encounter one when he has been driven out of his den, or is traveling from his den to another chuck hole, he will not run but will give fight.

Last summer I sat on a knoll where I could see for some distance in all directions, and had with me my most excellent B & L 7 x 35 Zephyr binoculars — which are the best glasses I have ever used for woodchucks. I noticed a chuck walking along a small meadow knoll about 500 yards off; keeping the glasses on him I watched his progress for over half an hour. When I first saw him in the glasses, he was walking slowly toward a hole about 50 yards off. He walked to the den mouth, stopped a moment, and then went in to investigate. In about a minute he came out on the dead run, with another very angry chuck nipping at his heels. At that range I was unable to tell whether this other chuck was of the same, or opposite sex. He never stopped running until he had gone about 50 or 60 feet, but the pursuing chuck stopped within 10 or 15 feet. He sat up and surveyed the countryside for about five minutes and then returned to the safety of his abode, minus his visitor.

Another peculiarity of the woodchuck——about 10 miles from where I live is an old abandoned stone quarry at the edge of a small woods, and just inside, perhaps 50 feet from the open fields, are about 20 chuck holes in a circle of 50 or 60 feet, and all seemed to be occupied. I decided to return later that day to see whether I could spot any of these fellows. It was nearly 7 p. m. when we got there, and to our great surprise there were 12 or 15 chucks when we spotted them from a distance of about 20 yards. Being too close for a shot, we watched them for about ten minutes. I never before have seen such a bunch of chucks in one group, they were like a prairie dog town or convention. Some were playing with much growling and grating of teeth. Suddenly one of them evidently winded me because he then gave a piercing whistle and all of the chucks started pell-mell for their dens. I noticed that they went by one hole, each to get to his den. One old gray chuck was left sitting straight up, about 60 feet from me. He would turn slowly, surveying the entire open field ahead, but not seeming to care about the woods directly back of him. Finally, I whistled and he dropped from sight where he had been sitting on a vertical hole all the time. I have been back several times for a look and have always refrained from shooting because the average range was only about 50 feet, and I was more interested in watching their habits than in making close range kills having no sporting feature. I never saw only one or two chucks out at that quarry, there were always 12 to 15 or more out at one time. I have been watching this place for four summers, including this last summer, and the group still gathers there. I have never seen a woodchuck den in low, swampy ground. They are always above high water mark. How they know where this lies, I am unable to perceive.

THE WORK OF DIFFERENT RIFLES ON CHUCKS

I have used many rifles on chucks, and will enter below the notes made from their testing and performance.

The .22 Hornet

The Hornet does a very good job on chucks up to 100 yards —in many cases, to 125 yards. The .22 Hornet of course will kill up to 200 yards, or maybe further, but chuck shots at that distance are not bench-rest shots and unless one makes a heart or head shot, you may leave a wounded or suffering chuck down the den, and that leaves the wrong sort of memories.

Hand-loading your Hornet ammunition does help but when we do reload the .22 Hornet for chucks, we find the lighter bullets work in the better due to the very material increase in muzzle velocity and that out to at least 100 yards. This higher velocity gives a greater explosive or at least lacerating effect.

Listed here are some of our favorite loads for the .22 Hornet, some of them are on the high pressure side, and these should be used only in a good strong bolt action rifle.

.22 Hornet Loads

Primer	Bullet	Powder	Muzzle Velocity
Rem. 6-1/2	40-grain Sisk	11 grains 2400	2600 f.s.
Rem. 6-1/2	35-grain Sisk	9.8 grains 4227	2250 f.s. Squirrel or S.R. chuck load
Rem. 6-1/2	45-grain Sisk	10.6 grains 2400	App. 2600 f.s.

The Improved Hornet or .22 K-Hornet has slight advantage over our regular .22 Hornet on chucks at distances of 100 to 125 yards, but I doubt that our Improved Hornet will do as good killing at 150 yards as the regular .22 Hornet at 100 yards.

I own an Improved Hornet on a 44-1/2 Stevens single shot action, with 22-inch barrel that was a very convenient car gun for chucks, easy to carry when hunting in the fields, convenient to handle getting in and out of a car. This rifle with 4X scope has often produced better groups than Improved Hornets with heavier barrels and these on bolt action rifles. Verily, some strange things happen in the rifle game. The .22 Hornet class of rifles are most desirable in this community where the farmer does not appreciate your scaring his stock with the louder reports of the big .22's, or with the 25's and heavier calibers.

Our best loads for the Improved Hornet rifles are the following:

Primer	Bullet	Powder	M.V.
Rem. 6-1/2	50-grain Sisk Lovell	11.0 grains 4227	2600 f.s.
Rem. 6-1/2	41-grain Sisk	13.2 grains 4227	3000 f.s.
Rem. 6-1/2	50-grain Sisk Lovell	11.3 grains 4227	2775 f.s.

The .22-3000 Lovell is in itself a wonderful chuck cartridge and is the father of two more — the R-2 and the Imp. R-2 Lovell. To Hervey Lovell should go the credit from chuck hunters for the .22-3000 Lovell and the later Imp. R-2 Lovell, as the idea for the latter sprang from the former, and ways to adapt it to the I.M.R. powders. In itself, the .22-3000 takes over where the .22 Improved Hornet leaves off. Our favorite load for this cartridge is 16.3 grains of 4198 compressed by a 50-grain Sisk-Lovell bullet and these in front of the Remington No. 6-1/2 primer.

The R-2 Lovell is a very efficient little case. We used this caliber until we acquired reamers for the Improved R-2, or the so-called .22 Maximum Lovell which for a time, had quite a vogue. Personally we much prefer to use this caliber as long as we are going to improve the .22-3000 — why not go all the way and get the maximum performance with the efficient 30-degree shoulder and the stepped up muzzle velocity? Our Maximum Lovell works the best in good strong action and when fully loaded perhaps a little on the heavy side. We have a hi-side Winchester single shot which shoots wonderfully when loaded to its maximum capacity. This rifle was originally a Winder musket and contrary to all opinions that it should not perform well when using its original .22 short cartridge, listed here is the best load; and I have seen a friend shoot 3/4-inch groups with it at 100 yards. The rifle was equipped with a Weaver J4 scope in a Redfield mount. The J4 as you know, is a cheaper grade of Weaver.

The load we use in this outfit is 18.3 grains of 4198, Remington No. 6-1/2 primer and the 50-grain Wotkyns-Morse bullet. This is about all the powder we can get in the case. Perhaps the K-Lovell's own Maximum Lovell case will accept 18.5 grains of 4198 but we are unable to get that much powder in our case by sifting or the use of a long drop tube. With the 18.3 grains we have to jar the case several times before taking it from the drop tube and even then powder comes up level full to the case mouth and the bullet must compress the powder. (I do not recommend this load for any other rifle action although the case shows no excessive pressure.)

Rifles chambered for this cartridge are most always accepted by the farmers as safe around their farms here in central New York State. But ring in a .25-06, or some of the others which burn materially more powder and produce a much sharper and louder report, and it is claimed immediately that you have curdled the cow's milk, scared the chickens off the nest, and likely have also curdled the farmer's disposition and have scared his wife, and if she has a hair-trigger temper she throws a conniption. Most times, that leaves you walking hurriedly over to your car to drive away.

We have used the finer-grained powders in the Maximum Lovell — such powders as 4117, but find the cartridge develops its best accuracy with woodchuck bullets when using the long grain 4198.

Our next cartridge in size and for use in the less settled districts is our .22 made on a shortened Zipper case. I can also use the .22 Hi-power, the .25-35, or the .30-30 cases. Our case is 1.750 inches overall, with a .250-inch neck and a 30-degree shoulder slope. We fire-form the case which leaves a body taper of 0.017 inch. Its accuracy seems to leave nothing to be desired although its report is rather snappy. A Southern shooter has us chamber one for him, using an F.N. action and a .2242-inch barrel blank by Adair who is located at Roseburg, Oregon. He sent me some targets showing 5/8-inch groups made while fire-forming the cases for this rifle, and the barrel and action in a military stock. With a new and well-bedded stock and formed cases we should be able to materially reduce the size of his groups by a fair amount.

The reason we like this rifle so well for chucks is its flat shooting, most desirable feature on long shots; a good supply of brass is always available; also it is adapted to any type of action. The killing power on chucks seems to put it right up in the class of the .220 Swift, .22-250, .22 Improved Zipper, and similar cartridges. In penetration tests, this little case does the same things with 28 grains of 3031 that we can do with 36 grains of 4320 in our .22-250. The latter, of course, is a slower powder. So far the case seems to be fully as versatile as the .22-250, as it shows good accuracy with all loads from one extreme to the other. We find that a grain or two under the maximum load gives the best results. Good loads with this case are:

Primer	Bullet	Powder	Case swaged down
Rem. 9-1/2	55-grain W-M.	28.0 grains 3031	Win. .25-35
Rem. 9-1/2	Humphrey 50 grains	28.0 grains 4895	Win. .219 Zipper
Rem. 9-1/2 (best)	50-grain Morse	28.5 grains 3031	.219 Super X

We feel that too many loads keeps a fellow in a quandary

and that you are then testing powder and bullets most of the time instead of finding a good load and then shooting it.

I ran across a peculiar incident in the fall of 1948. A chuck was sitting at his den mouth, at a range of 238 paces from point of firing. I was observing the shot through binoculars. The bullet hit the sandy loam three inches under the chuck's stomach. Upon the impact of the bullet, he bounced into the air about two feet or so. He came down on top of the hole and remained there. What killed this chuck we will never know. There was no break in his hide that we could find, and not a sign of blood, not a drop. Was the kill due to the explosive effect of the bullet or because the ground flew up and struck him, possibly over the heart? Or was it fright?

We have seen this little cartridge kill a fox at better than 300 yards. The 50-grain W-M bullet entered the left hip from the rear ranging up the chest through the body, where everything in its path was a mass of shattered flesh and tissue.

The Improved Zipper and the .22-250 seem to perform much the same. As far as we can find, the loads are interchangeable although the .22-250 will accept a greater variety of loads which prove accurate. I prefer either to the .220 Swift. For the bolt action rifles I would choose the .22-250, and the single shot, to use the .219 Zipper Imp. A friend, Ed McNally, has an Improved Zipper on a Springfield action and the rifle shoots like a house afire.

We much prefer to have both of the above mentioned cases with a 30-degree shoulder taper or slope, the .22-250 to retain its regular body taper and the Imp. Zipper .012-inch body taper.

Loads for these rifles can be found in Sharpe's Complete Guide to Handloading, or in the Ideal Hand Book. Our best load is 36.0 grains of 3031 behind a good 55-grain bullet and the charge ignited by the Remington 9-1/2 primer. We seem to get better results with this primer than with others. For the Improved Zipper, use 34.5 grains of 4320 and a 55-grain bullet with the same No. 9-1/2 primer.

Our idea of a good high-speed .22-caliber woodchuck rifle includes the following: A short, squatty case of 20 to 30 grains powder capacity (you would have it in the Lindahl .22 Chucker), a body taper 0.010 to 0.012-inch with a neck 0.250-inch long, a 28- or 30-degree shoulder slope, a hot primer, a good bullet, one of our modern powders, and no graphite or other wad. Why raise the breech pressure if it can be avoided?

We prefer to use Winchester Super-Speed or Western Super-X cases entirely. And by all means use a good Mauser action, or if available, a Model 70 Winchester action, with an 8X or 10X Unertl scope and their good external mounts, with the lock type adjustments. I would add a stock with a proper height comb and a well-bedded barrel. I do not see the need of carrying a sling around in the field, and to use it, one has a tendency to pull the forestock away from the barrel, with some mountings of the swivel.

THE .200 ASP EXPRESS CARTRIDGE

The .200 Asp Express is a high velocity, relatively large capacity, very small bore, belted cartridge for woodchucks. It was developed by Mr. Steve Gallt, a steel erection man and rifle crank, of Lafayette, New York. I like the lines of this cartridge which is very similar in contours to my own cartridge design made from a shortened .22-250 Varminter, necked to .170 caliber and called the .170-4000 Landis Express. The difference is in the larger caliber of the .200 Asp. The .170-4000 is a rimless job and the .200 Asp of Gallt's design has a belted head.

Mr. Gallt's article will show riflemen what is possible in a woodchuck cartridge between the .170 Express cartridges in the lower bore size, and the larger and more powerful .22 Express cartridges; the .236's and the .240's. The .200 Asp uses powder charges between those of the K-Hornet and R-2 on one side, and the .219 Donaldson and .22-250 on the other. By driving a 45-grain bullet of good sectional density it will give very flat trajectory over 250 to 350 yards.

The .200 Asp was conceived some time ago as an alternative to the regular high velocity .22's and also in response to the average farmer's plea for low report chuck rifles, and often his insistence upon the use on his place, especially within hearing distance of the buildings, of a rifle with less report than the .22 Express rifles. He also desires positive disintegration of the bullet, thus eliminating ricochets.

After due deliberation, and also after trying the smaller size cases in .170 caliber, it was decided that a rifle should be developed and a very accurate cartridge for it, that would produce a muzzle velocity of 3750 f.s. with a good weight of bullet in proportion to the caliber, while developing a muzzle energy of about 1400 ft. lbs. This is to be with a medium power load. The top load to give a little better than 4000 f.s.m.v.

To arrive at these figures it was necessary to get out our reliable stone tablet, hammer and chisel to do the intricate and involved figuring required to produce a super-super woodchuck cartridge.

The first and primary step is to eliminate the report, so the search was begun for a noiseless rifle powder. The initial results were a true phenomenon. A relatively fair degree of honesty impels us to report that while the search was most interesting, sometimes startling, we were in the end compelled to admit that we had not produced a truly noiseless propellent which was explosive. It was then decided to use some of the more common existing powders such as DuPont No. 3031, 4320, and 4198. These we had found in previous experiments to give very good accuracy and velocity even though the report was above a whisper, especially with a full load.

The average person would have said, "That — with all this figuring. Let's get a good .22 Varminter or Improved Zipper and our figuring has all been done for us and much of the experimenting as well." But we, being of a different nature felt that something new should be developed. The first problem was insurmountable by us and we even approached some very learned men about this, and after a few remarks to cover their obvious lack of personal interest, we decided to drop that line of investigation and adopt another tack.

We have rifles that will give the desired muzzle velocity, along with sufficient foot pounds of energy, so the only thing left for us to do was to see if we couldn't do something about flattening the trajectory. It is a very important feature if the rifle you have is capable of shooting beyond 100 yards with any degree of accuracy and likelihood of hitting the skull of a woodchuck. We figured that if we could lessen the amount of drop out at 200 and at 300 yards, it would be a great help. A help to all but the woodchuck. It is likely to hasten his final hibernation.

Looking at the standard ballistic tables put out by the leading cartridge companies, we find that the .270 caliber with the 150-grain bullet out-performs the .30-1906 caliber with the same weight of bullet (because, of course, it has a higher sectional density and retains its velocity better after it speeds away from the rifle).

The above mentioned figures led me to believe that we should take the regular .22-caliber bullet and reduce its diameter not to .170 caliber but to a size in the ratio of the reduction from the .30 to the .270, which after all, is .275 or .276 inch, and then we would have a bullet of quite flat trajectory and yet sufficient mass and weight that it might do a bit better in the wind, and impart a sharper "smack" on the woodchuck.

Basing our figures on this, we had a Ackley barrel bored to an even .200 inch diameter. After many letters between rifle cranks and gun bugs and myself, it was decided that a 10-inch twist would be fast enough to stabilize a 45- or a 50-grain bullet of this size. The greenhill formula states that a twist of slightly over nine inches would be required to spin the bullet properly. My utmost respect to Mr. Greenhill and his formula but I have greater respect for the experience of Mr. Landis and others who have spent years developing, designing and shooting modern high velocity rifles. Many have found that a twist one or two inches on either side of a given rate of twist will give most excellent results and sometimes with materially higher velocity and also definitely lower breech pressure and less wear on the barrel.

The barrel was duly bored and rifled to .206 inch diameter while, the outside was tapered from 7/8 (which is 14/16) inch, to 13/16 inch, in a length of 25 inches. This we felt would give us the proper weight for a varmint rifle.

The action selected was a G 33/40 Mauser with the small receiver ring.

After dismantling and throwing away the stock we really began to be generous and tossed the barrel and bolt away also, replacing the bolt with an F.N. bolt altered for low scope mounting. Checking the receiver in the lathe we used a tool-post grinder to smooth up the front of the receiver shoulder for a good barrel fit.

The stock, of necessity, should be a blank that would not warp first one way and then the other, so, after due deliberation and correspondence we finally decided to use a 3/8-inch piece of select, straight grain walnut to which was glued two pieces of fine figured curly maple, each an inch and a quarter thick. This little procedure had a tendency to stop or counteract warpage. In jig time this was hacked, whittled, rasped, sanded, and cussed into a very beautiful stock with smoother lines than displayed by any Miss America that I have so far glimpsed.

Trigger to heel is an even 13-1/2 inches, and from the front guard screw to the fore-end is another 13-inches, giving us a total stock length of 33 inches. The beavertail forearm is 2-5/8 inches in the widest part and is brought back in sweeping lines to blend in with the pistol grip and cheek piece. The grip is of the Wundhammer type, or very similar to that style, and is also quite like those found on some of the fancy custom rifles. Checkering is, of course, 16 lines per inch, not because it is easier to do, but because it gives one something to feel and the diamonds are sharp and clean and provide a condition that one is unable to have in a 24 line-to-the-inch checkering.

All of the stock work was by Jack Himes who is in ability, one of the leading stockers in the country today.

The design of the case required serious thought. A rifle is a rifle not so much because of the rifle itself, but because of the ballistic and physical characteristics of its cartridge. Our first consideration was to have a case with a top capacity of 25 grains of powder back of a 45- or 50-grain bullet of .20 caliber. In doing some figuring on paper the capacity was increased slightly to allow us to use powders like 4320, 4064, and 4350 along with the easily and inexpensively obtained 4895, or the versatile 3031. Having decided on case capacity, the problem of selecting the right brass gave us a lot to think about. It would be impractical to make new brass without the excessive expenditure required for punch presses and other equipment, so this had to go the way of noiseless gun or rifle powder.

Our next move was to take one of our existing cases, commercial or wildcat and alter it to fit our needs. This still didn't give us the case that we felt would safely handle the load we wished. Our slide rule was getting so much wear that we had to hurry and decide whether the .300 H & H shortened would work better than the .30-1906 case or would the rimmed Zipper be the one. Whether to use a short, fat case, or a long, thin case, bolt thrust, pressure, extraction, boiled like dry ice in water. Lo and behold like manna from Heaven, came a letter from Parker O. Ackley containing one of his latest creations, the .30-1906 case belted.

To belt the .30-1906 case, Ackley had reduced the body of the cartridge up to the solid part of the head by .026-inch, leaving the case with a belt very similar to that on the present Magnum case.

This gave us a stronger case, also a very definite way to

head space accurately. The rest of the case dimensions follow: Head to edge of belt, .235 inch; diameter of the head, .474-inch; diameter of the case at the belt, .450-inch. Diameter at shoulder, .440-inch; neck diameter, .248-inch; case length to shoulder 1.5312 inches; neck length, .312-inch; and made with a 30-degree shoulder slope that gave an overall case length of 1.9687-inches.

The amount of work hardening involved in belting this case really did the trick giving us a much stronger case than could be had by any other known method. Annealing the shoulder and neck was comparatively easy. Just dip the end of the case in molten lead for a moment or long enough to bring the case to the same temperature as the lead bath. You can almost hold the case in your fingers while annealing, so you know that the heads are not being annealed. I use a pair of tweezers to hold the cases and as soon as they are the right heat in the lead bath, drop them in a pan of water.

Case forming was comparatively easy. A threaded die blank knurled and threaded on the outside to a NF 7/8 x 14 inches was chambered with the regular chambering reamer and cut off to the exact length desired. After screwing this die into our press it was easy to form and trim the cases correctly.

Bullets were a problem from the start. I thought that I could swage some regular .224-inch 45-grain bullets down to .206-inch. We did, but not too successfully. Then we tried to make good bullets of our own design. These worked fairly well and even worked better from the second set of dies after we got away from the idea of pencil-shaped points on the bullets. We now have two sources of bullets: our own, which we like, but they are hard and slow to make; and the 45-grain bullets made for us by Parker Ackley. These are of the soft-swaged type with heavy jackets to stand high velocity.

CHAMBERING

Chambering is so easy that to cover it here will take only a moment. The necessary equipment and essentials are one engine lathe equipped with a steady-rest and the roughing and finishing reamers also a good twist drill smaller in diameter than the shoulder of the roughing reamer, plus a good Jacobs chuck in which to hold them.

This is the way we do the work. It may not be the easiest

way, but at least it works fairly well. I have never particularly liked to use a chuck with a hollow in the headstock large enough to handle the barrel, so we put on the face plate and use a center upon which we mount the barrel, the other end in a steady rest which we try to have perfectly in line with the center. Now comes the problem of turning the barrel without having it slip off the center. To overcome this, we made a lathe dog with two ears instead of one which is usual, and on the end of the other ear we threaded it for a 1/4 x 20 inch thread so we could fasten it to the face plate, then screwing down the regular set screw while holding the barrel tightly against the center it gave us a nice, straight-line operation.

We are now ready to turn down the breech end of the barrel for threading. It's a good idea to cut the same number of threads on the barrel that are in the receiver. We try to get a fit on the threads that requires quite a lot of handpower to turn the barrel up to the shoulder on the receiver. We twist drill one thousandth smaller than the bore in the barrel to guide the drill in a straight line. Using this drill we hog out the steel to within 1/8 inch of the chamber depth. Now exchange drill for the roughing reamer to increase the chamber depth to within 1/16 inch. Here we substitute the Jacobs chuck for a live or ball-bearing center in the tail stock.

Taking the barrel from the lathe, screw the action on the barrel using a good husky wrench with a little power and then mark the underside of the barrel and receiver with a witness mark so that the barrel can be removed and replaced with some assurance of having it in the same depth. Now put the barrel back in the lathe and using the finish reamer with an extension which we hold in our hand, move by screwing with the tail stock. We cut and try until we can close the bolt on the minimum head space gauge. During these operations we try to keep plenty of good cutting oil on the drill and reamers and of course clean the chamber well between operations. We prefer to use an integral throater on our finishing reamer.

It is a nice thing to have a stopper on the reamers to control the depth, but then again the next chambering job will probably be on a Springfield so it will then be necessary to take the stopper off anyhow.

Crowning the barrel is done by reversing the barrel in the steady rest. Using a good sharp tool, we face the end of the barrel and then take a cut part way across the barrel leaving the rest of the steel for protection against jamming the rifling. Most people seeing this remark that we have placed a sleeve in the barrel.

ATTACHING SCOPE BLOCKS

Scope blocks are easy to put on if you keep them in line directly on top of the barrel, the correct distance apart, and you are careful not to drill a hole all the way through the barrel into the bore while you are busy watching the alignment of the holes. It is also a very good idea not to break off over two or three taps because you might be unable to get them all out. Then, what to do?

Bluing the rifle is done much easier if the barrel and action are completely taken apart. We use the salt bath method and if this procedure isn't followed, the salt is bound to work out the cracks requiring a lot of watching and wiping and grumbling.

After all this enjoyable work we are now ready to do actual testing of the results.

G. B. CRANDALL'S MORE RECENT CHUCK CARTRIDGE
DEVELOPMENTS, AND AUSTRALIAN VARMINT
RIFLE CARTRIDGES

G. B. Crandall, of G. B. Crandall & Son, gunsmiths, of Woodstock, Ontario, is the dean of Canadian varmint rifle custom gunsmiths. Mr. Crandall recently built a new gun plant on his property on which his residence is also located. This has individual motors for each lathe, press or whatnot, and modern lighting.

George Crandall was the developer of the .22-303 Varmint-R cartridge, and of the K-Hornet, with Lysle Kilbourn. The .22-303 Varmint-R is made from the heavy brass .303 British anti-aircraft cartridges, cut off and swaged down.

In recent letters he remarked as follows: "We have developed a real .25-caliber cartridge out of the rimmed .303 Savage case used in the Model 1899 deer rifle of the lever action, highly popular, easy-to-carry sporting type, so popular for years among Canadian sportsmen. Factory barrels are no longer available in this caliber and consequently we take a .303 Savage action and stock with a rusted out barrel, and rebarrel it with a new .25-caliber barrel chambered for this .25-303 Savage case.''

I have done considerable field shooting with a .250-3000 Savage in the Model 99 action, fitted first with one of the original semi-heavy barrels, and later with a 24-inch lighter barrel when that one developed a swollen chamber. My son used it much more than I did, and we both liked it fine, especially with the longer, heavier barrel. Crandall can supply any length or weight of barrel on the Savage action with this new .25-303 Varmint-R cartridge.

AUSTRALIAN VARMINT RIFLE CARTRIDGES AND SHOOTING

Some of the .22-303 Varmint-R rifles got over into Australia and New Zealand, and on their part over there, they developed about three different .22-303's of their own. A letter from Mr. Eric Lamont, custom riflesmith, who rebarrels and restocks varmint rifles, and whose shop is in Ashfield, New South Wales, Australia, to G. B. Crandall, reads as follows: ''As far as varmints go, we are well supplied, taking into consideration the various definitions of the word varmint. They range from the lowly rabbit to a bull camel. (How would you like to shoot an angry bull camel with a breath like an open sewer?) All imported animals seem to turn out to be pests in this country. The rabbit is only valued for his fur, and as severe penalties are incurred by land owners for infestation above a certain number per acre, the method of extermination is of no great importance so long as the animals are destroyed, so that crops may be harvested.

''To date with a Varmint R I have shot everything from rabbits to deer with excellent results, the bag to date consisting of foxes, dingoes (a type of coyote), kangeroos, wallabies, fallow and red deer, brumbies, which in your lingo would be wild horses, donkies, scrub bulls, and a bull camel. I had to take a .318 Accelerated Express to finish off the camel. These are tough hombres. I have found this caliber to be most effective on Johnstoni Crocodile as found in the upper Barwon River. The best method I have found of hunting and shooting them is to use a canoe at night with a spotlight mounted directly under the rifle barrel.

''Under separate cover I am sending you the fired case of the V-R (Varmint-R), as requested and I have also included several other cases in which I felt you might be interested. The two Sprinter cases are a semi-commercial production inasmuch as the firm, Small Arms & Accessories Ltd. make up rifles on the SMLE action and supply ammunition for them. Incidentally, they make their own barrels. I do a lot of the ballistic work for this firm. Another firm in a semi-commercial way is Naughton & Co., Melbourne, N. S. W., who produce a rifle known as the Falcon. This is a full length .22-303 with a Bisley (British) barrel on an SMLE action. Their ammunition is made at a government arsenal, hence the absence of head stampings.

"Another case in which I feel you will be interested is the Australian version of the .219 Donaldson Wasp. This is made up from the .303 British case. Examples of this case are included in the packet. This of course requires extensive drawing operations.

"Evidently my own reamers must be very close in dimensions to those of your own. Landis gives your cartridge neck length as .325 inch. I felt that was a little too short and increased it to .350 inch as you have done. I notice that your fired cases are being held to a shoulder dimension three or four thousandths smaller than those given by Landis.*

"Also I would like to point out that the dimension forward of the rim varies considerably. In Australian-made ammunition it varies and averages .455 to .456 inch, whereas Winchester cases seem to average .453 to .4555 inch. Consequently, I find it necessary to allow a larger tolerance here than you do. Most of the gunsmiths out here have agreed on the present dimensions and we have found that we can interchange. The same thing occurs with our Wasp which was originated by W. Harrison of Earlwood. Most of the cases out here are of the Berdan type of priming but are much cheaper than those that could be imported.†

*Author's Note: Two draftsmen, including myself, took these dimensions all from cases supplied at the time by Mr. Crandall, which were form fired cases —hence would be larger. We used a specially selected micrometer, without play, and these measurements were accurate for the cases at hand. Each dimension was checked and double checked.

†Author's Note: The late George Schnerring's method of decapping Berdan primed cases would be helpful in Australia. He simply filled the case to the brim with water, placed a close-fitting brass or steel rod vertically over the neck and tapped suddenly with a mallet. The pressure was transmitted through the water to the Berdan primer, and if not oxidized to the brass of the case, it promptly popped out. The case was thus decapped without fuss or feathers and could be reloaded with Berdan primers.

"Frankly, in the .25-caliber sizes, my favorite rifle is the .242 Vickers, which under our conditions I find gives much better results than many of the lauded American .25's. A better rifle even than this, is the Holland and Holland .240 Apex, as it has much better sectional density than any U. S. .25 caliber."

So, reader, when all you see is No Trespass signs, don't shoot off or near the highway, don't carry a loaded rifle along a highway, your actual small game season is limited to two weeks or a month, deer to ten days or two weeks, and even the crows caw at you in derision, get yourself a book or two of travelers' checks, hop a plane for Australia, and get all the assorted varmint shooting you may want.

CHAPTER 18

Notes from Frank Wallace

Among the more experienced varmint and woodchuck hunters of north eastern Pennsylvania, is Mr. Frank R. Wallace, of Wilkes Barre, who is an enthusiast on the subject of the .219 Improved Zipper. Mr. Wallace has had considerable experience as a hunter, both as a bird hunter and as a rifleman. In a breezy letter received November 12, 1949, he comments on various subjects as follows:

I was certainly pleased to receive your long interesting letter. I am sure that I cannot return a similar one but at any rate here it is for what it is worth.

I have had no vacation and consequently very little time in which to conduct a shooter's activities. While I killed thirty-five or forty chucks this summer I neglected the photographic angle and consequently have nothing additional to send you. While I am not getting any phenomenal groups with my Improved Zipper, I am continually impressed with its value as a practical field rifle within reasonable velocity limits and it very thoroughly satisfies me. Actually, since I do not have the opportunity and time for it anyway, I am more interested in field shooting than in bench rest effort other than load testing. It is my inexpert opinion that the Improved Zipper is inherently as accurate as the highly-touted .219 Donaldson Wasp if as much attention were given to it. To me the value of the Improved Zipper is its use of factory ammunition with the subsequent ease of formation of improved Zipper cases.

My hunting this fall likewise has been sketchy. Fortunately I have an excellent dog and when I do have an opportunity to get out I have reasonable luck. On opening day, in 90 degree temperature a friend and I killed a limit bag of woodcock, all local birds. Since I have been unable to hunt during the week, I have been running up across the border into New York State where Sunday hunting is permitted. There, two weeks ago we ran into

340

a flight of woodcock, and enjoyed some excellent shooting and dog work. Since the weather remained mild I revisited that cover a week later and again took four woodcock in short order. I then turned my attention to grouse and had one of those shooting days you remember for a long time, particularly in our covers here. I had five possibles and scored on three of them in an hour. I was forced to stop hunting with a mixed limit bag of four woodcock and three grouse.

THE K-HORNET

One of the early 54 Winchesters in the Hornet caliber with the now obsolete Lyman 438 scope served me with complete satisfaction for a number of years. Groundhogs were plentiful in the areas I hunted and I was generally able to keep my shots within 150 yards. Within that range the regular Hornet cartridge was a dependable killer if the shots were placed in the head, neck or chest cavity. I never seemed to have any trouble with changes in zero. This rifle, a standard model, always shot good groups with either the soft point or the hollow point ammunition. In my experience the hollow point fodder was the better killer. For this size case, standard barrel weight provides fine accuracy, and there seems to be no point in burdening oneself with extra barrel weight.

As my interest in the sport widened I added a better scope. This and the growing scarcity of chucks tempted me to take longer shots. It was then that I began to notice sensitivity to wind and a lack of dependable killing power at ranges beyond about 175 yards. This induced me to rechamber for the K-Hornet cartridge in order to add a few hundred foot seconds velocity and achieve a reduction in sensitivity to wind.

From bench rest I had the experience shared by some others of obtaining even smaller groups with factory ammunition in the K chamber than in the standard chamber. Then began that quest for an equally good hand load which took me through a variety of primers, both rifle and pistol, and a variety of nondescript wartime and prior bullets. When shooting is to be done we must shoot what is available, but in my opinion it is never a mistake to match cases with similar make primers when supplies are available. While I have not yet by any means run the gamut of loads which can be worked out for the K-Hornet I have so far been unable to match the groups obtained with factory ammunition. However, many groups run close to an inch which is good varmint rifle grouping in any league.

My reloading involves a careful glass inspection of cases, trimming and neck reaming when necessary, and weighing each powder charge on a Pacific balance. However, one does not need to shoot half-inch or even one-inch groups to have a dependable varmint rifle. In catch-as-catch-can shooting in the field there are a number of variables which serve to cancel one another and even with a two-inch rifle and load a good rifleman can do a workmanlike job on woodchucks.

I would not, however, return to the standard cartridge because with the additional velocity a 40-grain bullet can be used with equal or better killing power and a flatter trajectory.

Apparently the factory policy in the case of the Hornet cartridge is to use a slightly over-size bullet which gives exceptionally good accuracy at the velocities loaded. Thinking that the additional velocity of the K-Hornet might require a smaller bullet diameter, I tried some .223 inch bullets. These, however, would not group at all in my rifle. For field shooting I have standardized on 12.5 grains of 2400 with the Sisk 40-grain .224 inch bullet in Winchester cases and 13 grains of 4227 in Remington cases.

I have never been interested in working up reduced loads for the K-Hornet since I have no use for them. All my shooting, even small bore work, has been directed toward a practical application of it in the field on woodchucks, crows, hawks, etc.

Those that have shot the Swift and other high velocity calibers have undoubtedly noticed the moisture almost like dust, that is drawn from the carcass when a chuck is hit solidly. The stepped-up velocity of the K-Hornet at times gives similar results. Until I understood this I thought I had missed several shots as the result of seeing what I thought was dust from the bullet's impact which shots, upon investigation, proved to be clean kills.

THE IMPROVED ZIPPER

My Improved Zipper was built on a Mauser action with a medium weight 27-inch barrel and a well-proportioned stock with plenty of wood out front. The installation of a better trigger, a side safety to clear the scope, and a Winchester adjustable fore-end stop set me up in business to test a new wildcat at the bench and in the field.

Frank Wallace testing ammunition from a shooting bench. The rifle is a Model 70 Winchester cal. .22-250, and the scope a 1¼" Fecker.

Vernor Gipson, custom gunsmith of North Salem, Ind., chambering a barrel.

A nice pair. CREDIT: FRANK WALLACE.

Black chuck and gray chuck shot by Frank Wallace. CREDIT: FRANK WALLACE.

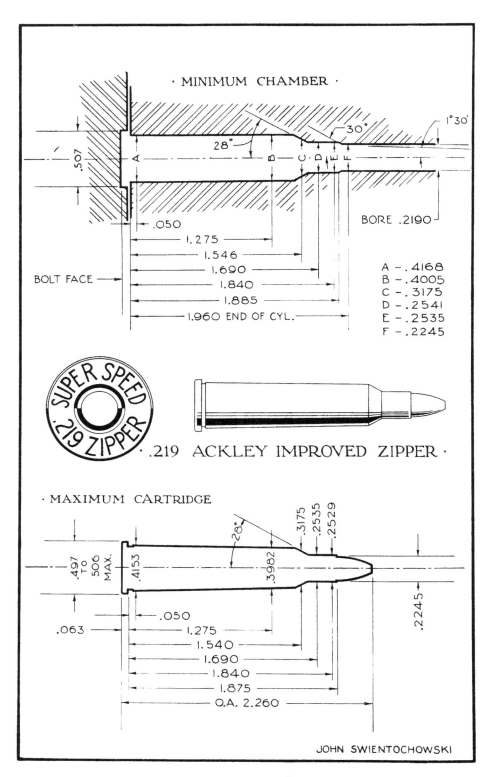

· MINIMUM CHAMBER ·

1°30'

28°   30°

.507

A B C D E F

.050

BORE .2190

BOLT FACE

1.275
1.546
1.690
1.840
1.885
1.960 END OF CYL.

A – .4168
B – .4005
C – .3175
D – .2541
E – .2535
F – .2245

SUPER SPEED .219 ZIPPER

· .219 ACKLEY IMPROVED ZIPPER ·

· MAXIMUM CARTRIDGE

28°

.3175
.2535
.2529

.3982

.497 TO 506 MAX.

.4153

.2245

.050
.063
1.275
1.540
1.690
1.840
1.875
O.A. 2.260

JOHN SWIENTOCHOWSKI

.219 Ackley improved Zipper.

The factory 56-grain load shot well enough; most of the groups running about an inch and a half. Even at the reported loss of a couple of hundred foot seconds velocity the factory load was sudden death on chucks when fairly hit. Often the animal would not show any indication of being struck and an instant later simply collapse. Compared with the K-Hornet 40-grain load the heavier 56-grain bullet was undoubtedly causing the difference.

This led me to the conclusion that assuming satisfactory accuracy I should use the heavier weight bullets because the Improved Zipper case provided sufficient powder capacity to push them along at a good velocity.

I began with 4320 powder, the Morse 55-grain bullet, Winchester super-speed cases and Winchester 115 primers. While with the K-Hornet I was unable to duplicate groups made with factory ammunition, I was delighted to find the exact opposite true of the Improved Zipper. Almost immediately the hand load groups beat those made with the factory ammunition.

Half-grain variations from 31 to 33 grains of 4320 all shot well. The best shot groups, however, appeared with 31.5 grains. This would undoubtedly be considered a light load for the Improved Zipper, giving a velocity of somewhere in the neighborhood of 3300 foot seconds, but I am more interested in hairline accuracy than velocity and this velocity carries the 55-grain bullet along well at the longer ranges.

I find it best to ream the necks and trim after the third firing. Necks appear to thicken more than lengthen. Incidentally, for this trimming and reaming job Wilson tools are excellent.

Sometimes I become a little skeptical about this 400-yard chuck and crow shooting. I use a ten power scope, and I believe my eyes are average. I don't kill any woodchucks at 400 yards or even 300. As a matter of fact, I do not shoot at them at those ranges. Beyond 250 yards (which is a long way across a clover field) what with wind, trajectory and my own holding, there is too much chance for error for me, at least, and while I might secretly aspire to such marksmanship I do not attempt it.

But back to the 31.5 grains of 4320. This quantity of powder when poured rather slowly comes to the bottom of the neck and with an .046 grease wad and the depth necessary to seat the 55-grain bullet seems to provide a well-balanced load. I shall standardize on this load for my summer's shooting and test it thoroughly in the field.

Meredith has shown that 3031 powder is the most efficient powder to use in the Zipper case when considering velocity versus pressure. While this may be true, 3031 has not given as good accuracy in my loading.

We read of phenomenally small groups shot by some wildcats and by some shooters. Perhaps we are inclined to feel disappointed when we have invested a round sum in a rifle components and loading tool which do not give us similar results. But we shouldn't feel discouraged. Compared with the few of unlimited time, money and the ability to tinker with bedding, throating and so on, there are thousands of run-of-the-mine fellows who load and shoot and let it go at that except for the occasional advice possibly of some gunsmith or fellow shooter. When these average fellows sit down at a bench rest or lie prone behind a rolled mat or sandbag and shoot groups of somewhere in the neighborhood of an inch at 100 yards, plagued with all the variables that can haunt a reloader, they are doing all right.

When you have a good load shoot some five-shot groups. They are a great comfort and dandy to display proudly to your friends. For your more lucid moments, however, shoot some ten-shot groups. They are good discipline. And also for discipline keep all your groups. Your average may not show up so well but you will know more about your rifle, loads and your loading. Mark your groups with the weather and lighting conditions. They will contribute an interesting diary.

The shape of the Zipper case is one to inspire confidence and enthusiasm by its very appearance. The report is authoritative but not at all unpleasant and the noise sufficiently mild to cause no concern amongst the landowners. Shot side by side, the Improved Zipper seems to have no more report than the K-Hornet. The .22 Hornet case is my first love and I shall continue to use it, but the Improved Zipper is fast supplanting it in my esteem. It just seems to be a grand in-between case with plenty of killing power, excellent accuracy, sensible powder consumption and long barrel life.

There is apparently considerable variation in the dimensions of the Improved Zipper case as chambered by various gunsmiths. Corson mentions 38 grains and some of the loads recommended by Ackley reach this weight. The maximum for my version would appear to be about 35 grains. This case appears to possess sufficient favorable ballistic characteristics to justify standardization and possible factory adoption. It shoots right along in the class of the .22 Varminter and other wildcats which require case forming or trimming before reloading.

So far this season I have shot 13 chucks with 55-grain Sisk and 31.5 grains of 4320 which shows excellent tearing qualities at 150 yards and beyond.

CHAPTER 19

Hooper, Risley Work

M R. M. S. RISLEY, of Earlville, New York, is one of the pioneers in the building of modern .22-caliber high velocity woodchuck and target rifles in the United States. With G. B. Crandall of Woodstock, Ontario, he developed the R-2 or sharp-shoulder version of the .22-3000 Hervey Lovell woodchuck and winged varmint cartridge in the late 1930's. He has worked with Harvey Donaldson on the production of a number of his ideas. Mr. Risley has built a good many hi-side and low-side Winchester single shot rifles, bushed the firing pin, made the stock, and otherwise custom-built many .22- and .25-caliber chuck rifles. He worked on the metal work of many of Bob Owen's famous sporters — Risley doing the metal work, Kornbrath the engraving, Owen the stocking. Mr. Risley's comments upon building chuck rifles are, therefore, of far more than ordinary worth.

The building of a modern high velocity woodchuck and target rifle consists of several steps, namely:

1. Selection of the action.
2. Selection of the barrel blank.
3. Choosing of the stock blank or wood for the stock.
4. Selection of the scope and its mounts, and the determination of the positions of the blocks on the barrel and receiver of the rifle.

As to actions, the Winchester Single Shot, Stevens No. 44-1/2, Sharps-Borchardt, Farquharson, and some of the German falling-block rifle actions are all satisfactory, some of them very much so.

Of the bolt actions, the Springfield and the Winchester Model 70, Mauser, and the Enfield, and the Remington Model 721 and 722 are most used. There are quite a number of private barrel makers who turn out gilt-edged blanks, and there are of course the old reliable, Winchester barrel blanks.

Most gunsmiths like a certain make or brand best but I find that they all respond to good gunsmithing in the fitting and chambering process and nearly all are capable of making excellent groups.

WOOD FOR STOCKS

Of the wood for stocks, I prefer air-seasoned imported walnut. Second choice is some of our native black walnut, much of which is good wood and is quite satisfactory. The third choice is curly maple, which is the hardest to find in a piece satisfactory for a custom rifle stock but when the right tree or blank is located, then curly maple is very satisfactory and makes up into a beautiful stock.

KILN DRYING

Kiln drying has its good points and some wood would be worthless unless kiln dried. But on the other hand, regardless of what may be said, you lose a certain amount of tensile strength by kiln drying, which strength is most desirable in a gun stock. For this reason, properly air-dried stock blanks are to be preferred when available.

BARREL BEDDING

Barrel bedding—that deep dark secret process, will be brought out into the open, when barrels and actions and stocks fit.

When you assemble some rifles, especially bolt actions with one-piece stocks and feel the barrel and action actually bend when the guard screws are fully taken up, the rifle cannot be expected to perform in any but an unsatisfactory manner. This is the reason why so many of the so-called "inletted and finished stocks" do not produce a rifle which will shoot.

SCOPES FOR WOODCHUCK RIFLES

Scopes of two classes are used on woodchuck rifles: target scopes and hunting scopes. Target scopes and mounts are preferred by most chuck hunters as they want to own as deadly a combination as possible. Some few hunters are satisfied to use the regular high-grade hunting scopes in both low and high power. In fact, quite a number are using four, six and eight power hunting scopes.

CHAMBERING

As to chambering, it goes without saying that close chambering and heading go hand in hand with accuracy. Most prefer about .002 inch tolerence on chamber neck, and resize to hold the bullet firm on each reloading of the case. Best results are obtained with reamed case necks and bullets of uniform diameter. These can be obtained today in several makes.

THE TWO GROUPS OF VARMINT CARTRIDGES

I would divide the ideal varmint and woodchuck rifles into two groups:

First Group: Those using the smaller cases such as the .22 Hornet, 2-R Lovell, .218 Bee, .222 Remington and so forth.

Second Group: .220 Swift, .219 Improved Zipper, .219 Donaldson, .22 Varminter or .22-250, .250 Donaldson Ace, and similar cartridges.

The first group cartridges are satisfactory for the hunter who is satisfied to be able to reach out to 250 yards with the more powerful cases of this group. I consider the shooting of chucks as little less than mass killing at this range when one of the best long range outfits is used and the man shooting is a real expert.

The second group will do the same at these ranges and these are capable of killing chucks consistently between 250 and 400 yards, with occasional kills at greater distances, all due to the higher velocity and flatter trajectory. But on these longer shots it is a real sporting proposition in the matter of hits and misses as the chuck has a little chance — although with some riflemen, not a great deal.

There is a strong tendency today to try some other caliber than the .22, probably for the reason that the American rifleman is always after something new, regardless of how well what he has has served him. The grass is always greener in the distance or on the other side of the hill. The .236, .240 and the .250 calibers are coming into their own again. We can look for a large number of these rifles in the tryout at the Johnstown, New York Bench Rest Shoot this coming fall.

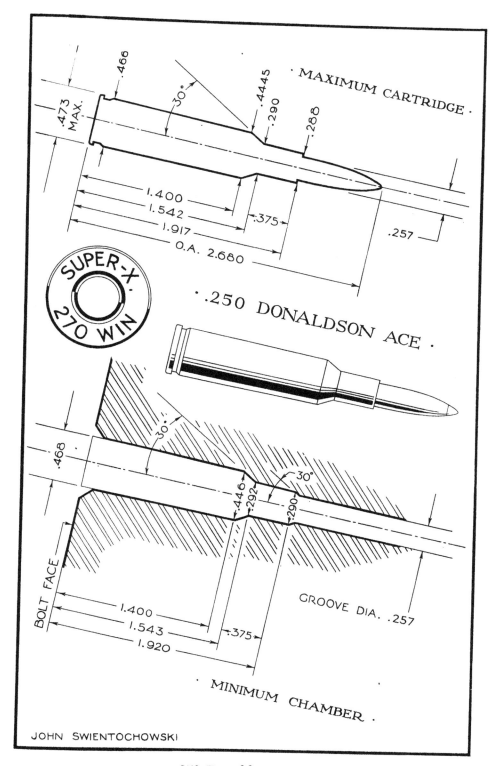

. MAXIMUM CARTRIDGE .

.466
.473 MAX.
30°
.4445
.290
.288
1.400
1.542
.375
1.917
.257
O.A. 2.680

SUPER-X
270 WIN

. .250 DONALDSON ACE .

.468
30°
.446
.292
30°
.290
BOLT FACE
1.400
1.543
.375
1.920
GROOVE DIA. .257

. MINIMUM CHAMBER .

JOHN SWIENTOCHOWSKI

.250 Donaldson Ace.

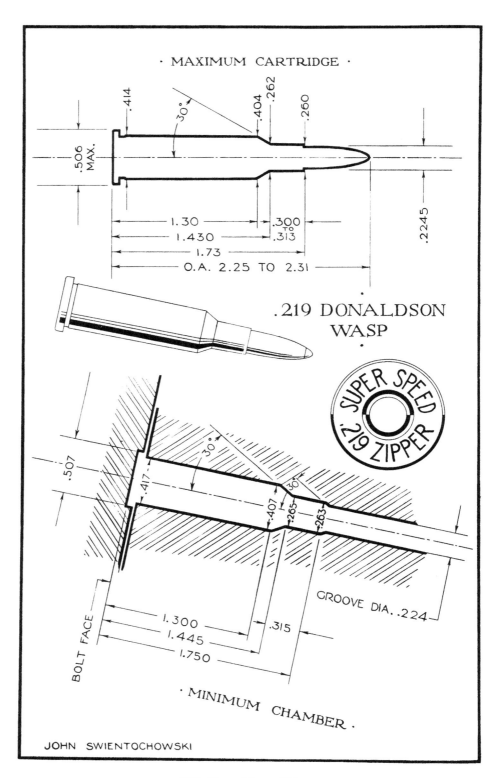

· MAXIMUM CARTRIDGE ·

.219 DONALDSON
WASP

· MINIMUM CHAMBER ·

JOHN SWIENTOCHOWSKI

.219 Donaldson Wasp.

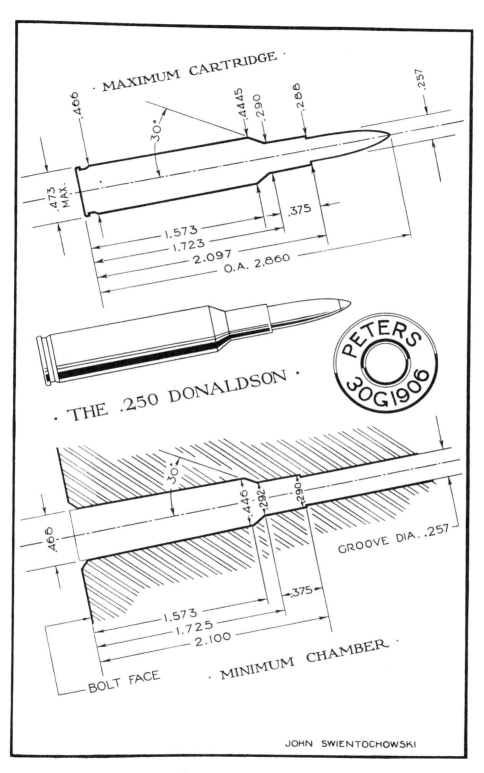

The .250 Donaldson.

Model 70 chuck rifle owned by Tom Higgins of Irwin, Pa., re-barreled by Wallack for the .22 H & W Improved Swift, 24X Unertl 2″ scope.

.250 Donaldson caliber bench rest rifle by Wallack on the fine shooting stand manufactured by Gene Beecher.

Woodchuck rifle built on Winchester Hi-wall single shot action barrel work by L. R. Wallack, R2 Donaldson caliber, Fecker "Woodchucker" scope.

Chuck rifle by L. R. Wallack, cal. .22-250, Wallack #2 stock, FN Mauser action. Capable of one-hole accuracy. CREDIT: NOEL BOGHETTI.

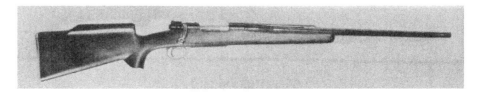

Woodchuck rifle built by L. R. Wallack on 98 Mauser action, cal. .22-250, scope rib, special stock with offset comb. DENSHAM & SCHILL.

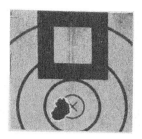 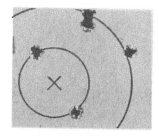

Two groups fired by Gene Hudgins of Philadelphia with a .250 Donaldson Ace built by Bob Wallack on a Winchester 70 action. Both are 5-shot groups and are reproduced exact size. First was fired at 100 yards, the second at 300 meters. A Douglas barrel blank was used and the load was 35 grains of 4895 with the excellent 100-grain Sierra bullet.

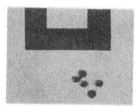

This 5-shot 200-yard group with a .22-250 rifle was fired by Bob Wallack in a rifle he made. When fired (1948) it was a world record for that distance. Fired in competition and reproduced exact size. Load was 37 grains of 4320, Western 8½ primer, 55-grain RCBS bullets.

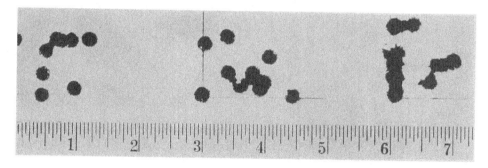

Sample groups fired with new varmint loads at 100 yards, Mann barrel. *Left to Right:* .250 Savage, .270 Winchester, .30-06 Springfield. CREDIT: WESTERN CARTRIDGE CO.

Frank Hubbard, of New York State, using a bench rest to sight in a chuck rifle.

Custom gunsmith Bob Wallack of Langhorne, Pa., chambers one of his super accurate rifles.

Manley Butts, of Bradford, Pa., the bench rest shooter, discussing accuracy with Harvey Donaldson at the Johnstown, N. Y., range, September, 1949. CREDIT: CHARLES TRAVIS, JR.

Harvey Donaldson, one of the greatest cartridge case designers, responsible for the .219 Donaldson, R2 Donaldson, and 25 Donaldson cases.

Left to Right: Al Marciante, designer of the .22 Marciante Blue Streak chuck cartridge; Col. Townsend Whelen, who has written extensively on varmints and chucks; and Joel Hodge, President of the Bench Rest Shooters Association (1950). CREDIT: CHARLES TRAVIS, JR.

Charles Parkinson holds a chuck shot with a tiny 25-grain Sisk soft point bullet. CREDIT: C. S. LANDIS.

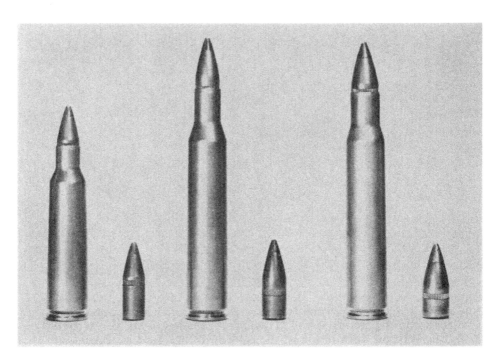

New varmint soft point loads. *L to R:* 250 Savage 87-grain, 270 Winchester 100-grain, 30-06 Springfield 110-grain.

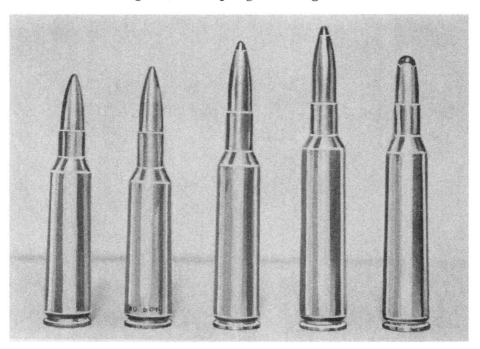

Some 25 caliber cartridges Wallack is tooled up for. *L to R:* .250-3000 Savage, .250 Donaldson Ace, .250 Donaldson, .250 Donaldson Helldiver, and .257 Roberts. CREDIT: JOHN B. CHRISTMAN.

The main or principal reason for the swing to the larger caliber is for better wind-bucking characteristics as the .22 caliber at longer range is affected by wind more than the larger caliber bullets of nearly the same velocity.*

On the other hand, the .240 and the .257 caliber produce a greater volume of sound, and in many areas, this is definitely not desirable in hunting woodchucks. The recoil also is definitely greater. Going down still farther to the .17 calibers, the recoil, report and percentage of dangerous ricochets is materially less, hence more desirable in certain settled areas. The whole thing sums up to the condition that the rifle, its cartridge, bullet, powder charge, report must all be chosen as being most ideally adapted to the work at hand. You must have the greatest number of advantages and the fewest number of disadvantages — and these will vary with the locality — to be top man in your chosen sport.

*Author's Note: This is due to the higher specific gravity of the larger caliber bullets. The core is greater in mass and weight in proportion to the core of the .22 bullet, and the copper jacket, and the specific gravity of the two combined is higher, because the specific gravity of lead is much greater than that of copper or its alloys. This assumes the two to be of comparable lengths and weights. Also, a larger mass of anything seems to drift less in a side wind, than a small mass, like gravel or fine stone.

 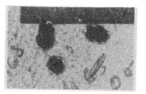

These two groups, fired at 200 yards by Al Barr with a .250 Donaldson rifle chambered by Wallack give an indication of the accuracy of this cartridge in a properly built rifle. Load was 44 grains of 4350 (approx. 3200 fps) and 97.5-grain RCBS bullet. Reproduced exact size.

Three 10-shot groups at 100 yards by Sam Clark, Jr., of Oakland, Maine. Shot with heavy .219 Donaldson rifle. Load used was 25.6 grains of 4895 and 55-grain RCBS bullet. These are among the smallest 10-shot groups ever fired. Reproduced exact size.

CHAPTER 20

Gunsmiths and Chuck Rifles

CHUCK RIFLES FROM A GUNSMITH'S ANGLE

by

L. R. Wallack

CHUCK hunters demand a high standard of accuracy in their rifles; therefore they require a rifle built to exacting specifications and of the best materials. We have learned a lot about rifles, cases, bullets, loads, stocks and shooting from bench rest matches. Bench rest and woodchuck rifles are closely allied, and bench-rest shooting has shown us why some rifles are accurate and why others are not.

I believe the way to tackle a problem is to break it down into sections; therefore the first section of this article will be in reference to actions suitable for woodchuck rifles. The action is the basic element of a rifle, and we must have a good foundation with which to begin. It has been definitely proved that bolt action rifles show a higher standard of accuracy than single shots. This does not mean that occasional single shots will not perform satisfactory, for they will. But I am speaking of averages, and bolt actions do average better. Bolt actions to be used may be Mauser, Springfield, Enfield, Model 54 and 70, Remington 720, 721 and 722, FN Mauser and a few others. These should be closely inspected by the riflemaker before being barreled to insure their serviceable and safe condition. Bolt actions permit a closer breeching than single shot actions, have less "spring" and better camming and extracting power which is a help when using "hot" loads during chuck hunting.

I am not condemning single shot actions for they will give excellent accuracy for a woodchuck rifle. Note carefully that I do not recommend them for bench-rest rifles. Bench rest shows that single shots perform very well, but as you probably know, bench-rest shooters demand a standard of accuracy that will put all shots into a quarter of an inch at 100 yards. As yet, we

350

haven't arrived at that, but we're coming! A good single shot rifle will shoot into one minute-of-angle, (one inch at 100 yards, two inches at 200 yards, etc.). This accuracy is demanded and is needed for chucks as they are small targets at long range; crows an even smaller target when stripped of their plumage.

Among the better single shots are the Winchester, Hepburn, Borchardt, Stevens 44-1/2, and some of the imported German actions. The old Ballard, the prettiest of all in my opinion, is not suitable for any conversion except the .22 long rifle due to the split breech block. The Winchester is among the best and is my favorite for conversion; however, it requires a lot of work to make it perfectly safe for modern high speed chuck cartridges. It must have the block bushed, which involves drilling and tapping a large hole in its face, a tool steel plug threaded and tightly screwed into this hole and the whole block hardened and tempered. It also needs a safety type firing pin made and installed so in the event of a primer leak, the gases and pin cannot blow into the shooter's face. Coil spring actions also need a new link made so the hammer will be cammed back during the first downward movement of the lever before the block moves down. This will allow the firing pin spring to retract the pin; otherwise it will be broken. When these operations are done to the Winchester single shot, you have a good action, and one to be prized.

There are several types of Winchester actions. The low side wall model is suitable for cases of Hornet capacity and no more. The high wall comes in both thick and thin wall versions and both are acceptable for barreling to chuck cartridges if in excellent condition. Occasionally, one will find an action that has been cut away to facilitate loading of .22 long rifle cartridges. These actions are not acceptable for rebarreling as this cutting away of the receiver walls weakens them.

The Remington Hepburn is also a fine strong action for a chuck rifle foundation. It has a drawback in its tang however, as this does not permit proper stocking without alteration. The Hepburn block must also be bushed as the Winchester, and fitted with a safety firing pin. It is recommended that the upper tang be cut off and lower tang bent; also that a stock bolt be employed to hold butt stock in place.

The Sharps-Borchardt action makes a good rifle but has a rather unusual firing pin condition in that there is no retractor. This requires a shorter protrusion of firing pin. The action also requires bushing, as explained before. The Borchardt has an excellent stock drawbolt and is an easy rifle to stock.

Summing up single shots, I would say that the Winchester would be the best one to convert because it is among the strongest, if not the strongest, and there are probably more of them in circulation so that spare parts may be obtained by cannibalization.

Barrels come under discussion next, and rather than go into a lengthy discourse on technical aspects of barreling, I'll discuss the various shapes that can be utilized. A great many bench-rest shooters use their heavy rifles for chucks using 20 power scopes! This is a lot of work—toting a 17-pound rifle around, then spending several minutes finding the chuck in that small field of view 20X scope. These shooters usually have a lighter rifle, which they call their "chuck rifle." Many times this rifle is made from a bench-rest rifle barrel that has lost its gilt edge for the matches and is turned down to smaller dimensions. There's another type of shooter who likes to have a "compromise" rifle; that is, one which may be used for both target shooting or bench rest, and which also is light enough to carry in the field as a chuck rifle. Such a rifle will weigh about 13 pounds with scope. Then we have a true chuck rifle, weighing from 10 to 12 pounds. This rifle will have a lighter barrel than the bench gun or the compromise rifle. We have a standard barrel which we call No. 4 Varmint barrel, 24 to 26 inches long, 1-1/8 inches at breech, straight cylindrical for 2 inches, then straight taper to a 3/4-inch muzzle. Harvey Donaldson uses a barrel of these dimensions; 26 inches long, 1-1/8 inch breech, straight for 5 inches, then straight taper to 5/8-inch muzzle. This is a little lighter than our No. 4 barrel. The straight action in both these barrels makes them stiffer. Any barrel lighter than this would be a sporter, and I might add that sporter barrels in properly built rifles give a very high standard of accuracy. We have built a good number of sporter rifles in varmint calibers that will average better than minute-of-angle on the bench rest, even with 6X scopes.

I would suggest a barrel similar to our No. 4 in dimension for woodchuck shooting. It will give excellent accuracy and has enough weight to allow it to be held steadily for long shots. Naturally we have many customers who have their own ideas about barrel dimensions. We always try to give them what they want as long as they will be safe and we think they will give good accuracy.

There are many cases which give good accuracy in wood-chuck rifles. I would suggest that the more popular ones are the .22-250, .219 Donaldson and the .250 Donaldson. The .22-250 is one of the finest cases ever developed combining excellent accuracy with flexibility — it shoots well with almost any load. The .219 Donaldson is more critical than the .22-250, but has a very slight edge in accuracy. Being a rimmed case (built on Zipper case) it is suitable for single shot actions, while the .22-250 is not. I also highly recommend the .219 Imp. Zipper for single shot action use. This case has about the same ballistics as the .22-250, but is of course on a rimmed case. These three cases (.22-250, .219 Donaldson and .219 Imp. Zipper) are excellent for woodchucks up to 300 yards. For a shorter range chuck rifle, and one which makes less noise, a desirable feature in many localities, there is the R2 Donaldson (also known as .22-3000R2) a smaller case built on the .25-20 single shot case. This case will give good results on chucks to 200 yards, and fair results to 300 yards.

The newest wildcat in the Donaldson "family" is the .250 Donaldson; this case is built on .257 brass and is shortened slightly and blown out to a fatter body shape with 30-degree shoulder angle. Bench-rest tests of these rifles have shown remarkable accuracy with maximum loads — loads which will drive a 100-grain 25-caliber bullet faster than 3300 f.p.s. (chronographed at Remington Arms) combining about one half minute-of-angle of accuracy in heavy bench rifles and one minute in lighter rifles. We use 45 grains 4350 powder in this case, not a maximum load, but a hot one. This load gives the accuracy described above. .250 Donaldson rifles may be loaded with 60-grain bullets such as the Hornady, and driven by 45 to 46 grains 3031 at 4250 f.p.s. (estimated). While these rifles will not give the velocity of the Magnums, they will give two things the Magnums lack — accuracy and barrel life.

We use barrels of 14-inch twist for these .250 Donaldson rifles, and suggest the use of this cartridge for woodchucks that have been educated to riflemen. They have ample accuracy for crows and chucks at very long ranges; the 100-grain bullet traveling at 3307 muzzle velocity packs a real wallop. We also recommend this rifle for deer hunting. In sporter rifles it has excellent accuracy, and will give the hunter the blasting effect that small game hunters have realized for several years with high power .22 calibers.

Accuracy in chuck rifles being of paramount importance, I'll describe my method of finding the proper load for a .219 Donaldson rifle. The same method with different loads may be applied to any caliber. First I must have good bullets, otherwise there is no use trying. At this writing (early 1950) I'd use either RCBS home-made bullets or Sierra factory bullets in either 50- or 55-grain weight. I would now load five cartridges with each of the following loads: 26 grains 3031, 24 grains of 4895, 29 grains 4320 and 17 grains 4198. Now I would fire four groups, one with each load; results usually indicate that one of these loads will shoot better than the rest. Let us assume that the 3031 load gave the best results. Now we'll go back and reload with 3031 and slowly work up or down whichever seems to be indicated. When we arrive at the best the rifle will do with this load, we may be satisfied and we may not. If not, we will then try with different bullets. For this shooting I strongly suggest five-shot groups, and all should be from bench or sandbag rest. Five-shot groups will not indicate that a rifle will shoot, but they will tell if a rifle will not shoot. After we have something that looks like an accurate load with five-shot groups, we'll try a ten-shot groups. This will begin to tell the story. Shoot three ten-shot groups if possible. Ten shots must be under one inch (at 100 yards) or we do not have either bench rest or chuck accuracy.

It is now in order to fire at least three consecutive ten-shot groups at 100 yards under perfect weather conditions — 100 yards because we are testing rifles rather than riflemen, and perfect weather for the same reason. We will use the best load for this test which is the acid test. If all groups are one inch, we have a good rifle, if under a half inch we have a "bumble bee" that should be saved for matches and never fired indiscriminately. If the rifle does not keep these groups under one inch, proceed with another load exactly as you have done with the first one. In my opinion, a woodchuck rifle should keep all its shots under one inch from a bench rest.

Another feature to be kept in mind when working up a load is seating depth. This is arrived at easily and there is no mystery about it. First, be sure the rifle is on safe, that is so the bolt may be opened without being able to fire. It is sometimes advisable to remove the firing pin and bolt sleeve for this test. Load a cartridge with the bullet well out. Try this in the rifle — you should be able to feel the bolt when the bullet touches the rifling — keep screwing in the seating plug until you have bullets seated to a depth that will just allow the rifling to touch and slightly engrave the bullet. It is not necessary to smoke bullets or anything like that — you will be able to see the faint marks made by the rifling on the bullet. Don't forget that different bullets will require the different seating depths.

Summing up, I would like to state that woodchuck rifles need bench-rest accuracy, and that woodchuck hunters should demand this type of accuracy, for no matter what sort of killing power a rifle has, it is entirely useless if the bullet doesn't hit its mark. If possible, woodchuck hunters should select a bolt action for their chuck rifle for the slight increase in accuracy. I've enclosed drawings of the .219 and .250 Donaldson cartridges; these are the correct sizes, and are directly from Mr. Donaldson. I would like to add that our firm was selected by Donaldson to be the first to use this new .250 case.

Be on the lookout for a new woodchuck cartridge — that will soon be available — the .22 GW special. It has all the accuracy and velocity of the .22-250, and has more barrel life. Standard .22-250 dies are used for reloading.

Testing Bench Rest Rifles: I make the following guarantee for my bench-rest rifles of proven accuracy — "I guarantee this rifle to have fired the groups furnished (three consecutive ten-shot groups at 100 yards, under minute-of-angle) but I cannot guarantee that the customer will shoot minute-of-angle groups. Perhaps this sounds rather self-centered, but it is the only legitimate guarantee a riflemaker can make with regard to accuracy. No man can tell if a rifle will fire a group under one minute-of-angle! He can prove that a given rifle has done so in the past, but what it will do in the future is something else. There is no way of knowing when a stock causes a bedding shift until too late. Bench-rest accuracy is often uncertain and rifles are fickle. Generally speaking, when we build a rifle for a bench-rest shooter, we know it will shoot. We know this because we use the best materials in action, barrel and stock properly fitted. If assembled correctly it has to shoot — usually requiring adjustment in loads only. But, once we test a rifle we do not know that the tests can be duplicated — we only hope they can; to date they have.

When we test a rifle in this manner, making no attempt to find the proper load, it will be a fine accurate rifle when worked up properly. We have two reasons for not suiting the load to the rifle. First, not as in Pope's day, these barrels with hot-jacketed bullet loads wear out barrels fast; with the old black powder loads, a rifle was good for years. We are reluctant to fire these rifles more than necessary. Second, we feel that the customer will want the thrill of this testing himself. When he has taken the trouble to suit his loads to the rifle, he will be a hot competitor in the bench-rest shoots, probably winning many matches with quarter-inch groups or smaller.

Testing woodchuck rifles is quite similar to testing bench-rest rifles, although I make no guarantee for them in the way of accuracy. These rifles (with No. 4 barrel) are built exactly as bench-rest rifles are. The same regard is given to actions; barrels are rifled the same and stocks are made from the same quality of wood. Therefore, these rifles will shoot as well or almost as well as a bench-rest rifle. I say "almost as well" because ever since a tube was first rifled, the fact has been pretty well established that the heavier the rifle, the better the accuracy. Prime reason for this, in my opinion, is that the heavier rifle may be held more steadily. Heavier barrel is of course a bit stiffer which holds muzzle flip to a minimum. In a lighter rifle, as barrel and stock warm up, the more limber barrel will begin to flip more than a heavy bench-rest barrel.

When a properly built woodchuck rifle is fired by a good rifleman, with a good scope and under good conditions, it will perform like a bench-rest rifle. I place no reservations on this statement, but it's important to note that everything must be right before the shooting is begun. It is also important to fire these shots slowly, and not to let the barrel become too warm.

One further thought in connection with the comparison of chuck and bench-rest guns — be it ever remembered that you can never shoot better than you can see. The bench-rest shooter performs with a scope often running to 20 or 25 power. The chuck hunter usually performs with around a 10 power. Both choices are correct for the purpose, but for the sake of rifle comparison, both should be fired with the same power scope. The lad with the 10 power is definitely underscoped when it comes to grouping ability regardless of what the rifle may be capable of doing.

I have mentioned that woodchuck rifles are built with the same care as bench-rest rifles. I might add that sporting or hunting rifles are built with the same care and also show marvelous accuracy. It is now up to the shooter to be careful of a few things before he goes hunting. Be sure guard screws are tight on a bolt gun and tang screws (or stock draw bolt in single shots). If you make changes in any of these screws it will behoove you to check the rifle on the range, for this tightening often changes the center of impact. One of the most common troubles is scope mounts and scope base screws. Scope base screws should be tightened securely; best way to do this is to remove screws, place a drop of shellac on each screw and draw up tightly — they will stay put. Scope mounts should be tight on bases. Use a large coin for this and check before going either to the range or hunting.

Every chuck hunter should stick a target or two in his pocket before he leaves the house. Before hunting, select a likely spot where your bullet won't ricochet, tack up the target and back up 100 yards. Now try your rifle. There's nothing like confidence in your rifle; you want it to be built right; you want a cartridge that will kill the game with dispatch; you want the bullet to go where you aim it. This sort of an outfit will give you confidence; a shot or two before squaring off on a chuck will tell you for sure. Good Luck.

LOADS FOR DONALDSON WOODCHUCK CARTRIDGES

Mr. L. R. Wallack has suggested the following loads for use in the cartridges mentioned. As different custom rifles will vary in chambering in the manner in which chambering reamers differ in dimensions, and the use each reamer has had, also the depth to which the reamers are run when chambering the rifle, another rifle of a similar designated caliber may vary considerably or possibly only a little in the depth of shoulder, diameter of chamber at any point, and also the shape and depth of the throat, with free-boring if any. Consequently, no one suggesting loads can tell how they will perform in another man's rifle.

The loads below are believed to be all right but they are not guaranteed and may not be satisfactory at all in your rifle. Start in with the lighter loads and develop your charges, increasing the load but a few tenths of a grain at a time, until you find a satisfactory charge in your rifle.

.250 Donaldson: Winchester No. 120 primer, 42 to 45 grains of DuPont No. 4350, and the 100-grain bullets have shown best results. When using the 87-grain bullets, spire point or other, 33 to 34 grains of 4895 (lot 25136) and Western No. 8-1/2 primer have been good. Also, 4064 should work well, so should 4320, and in lighter charges, 3031, especially should 3031 work well in lighter charges with the 87-grain bullets.

.250 Donaldson Ace: 34 to 37 grains of 4895 or 40 to 41 grains 4350, with the 100-grain bullet. Western 8-1/2 primer. For the 87-grain bullet, about 29 to 31 grains of 4895 could be tried. Go easy and don't try a maximum load at the start.

.250 Donaldson Helldiver: 50 to 52 grains of 4350 has done very well with the 100-grain bullet. Powerful and very accurate results reported.

.22 G. W.: This Gundersen-Wallack design is quite similar to the .22-250 or .22 Varminter but it has a considerably longer case neck, and the case is made up from the .257 Roberts case rather than the .250-3000 Savage brass. Presumably a case with a longer neck will give longer barrel life.

Don't overdo things when you start to load. Give the rifle and your own eyes a chance. A more moderate load, provided it burns the powder cleanly, almost always is the more accurate; it has a lower pitched and less sharp muzzle blast; hence for both reasons, you will shoot it better and your rifle will wear longer when using it.

CHAMBERING DIMENSIONS

AS USED IN CHAMBERING WOODCHUCK RIFLES

by

L. R. Wallack

.250 Donaldson Cartridge

Overall length (case)	2.100″
Length of body of case	1.573″
Length of neck	.375″
Angle of shoulder	30°
Diameter front of body of case	.446″
Diameter rear of body	.468″
Diameter front of neck	.290″
Diameter rear of neck	.292″
Groove diameter of rifle barrel	.257″
Twist of rifling, one turn in	14″
Bullet diameter	.257″

.250 Donaldson Ace Cartridge

Overall length (case)	1.920"
Length of body	1.400"
Length of neck	.375"
Angle of shoulder	30°
Diameter front of body of case	.446"
Diameter rear of body	.468"
Diameter front of neck	.290"
Diameter rear of neck	.292"
Groove diameter of rifle barrel	.257"
Twist of rifling, one turn in	14"
Bullet diameter	.257"

As will be noted, the Ace is 0.18 inch shorter in over-all length; body of case is .173 inch shorter. Other dimensions the same.

.250 Donaldson Helldiver

Overall length (case) full length .257 Roberts
Angle of shoulder	30°
Diameter front of body	.446"
Diameter rear of body	.468"
Groove diameter of rifle barrel	.257"
Twist of rifling, one turn in	10" to 14"
Bullet diameter	.257"

.257 Roberts rifles can be rechambered to Helldiver and factory ammunition can be fired in the Helldiver chamber.

.219 Donaldson Cartridge

Overall length of cartridge	1.750"
Head to shoulder	1.300"
Length of neck	.315"
Diameter of rim	.506"
Diameter head of case body	.417"
Diameter of shoulder (latest dimension)	.407"
Angle of shoulder	30°
Groove diameter of rifle barrel	.224"
Twist of rifling, one turn in	14"
Bullet diameter	.224"

.22 GW Special

Overall length of cartridge	1.987″
Length of body	1.500″
Length of neck	.312″
Angle of shoulder	28°
Diameter front of body of case	.414″
Diameter rear of body	.468″
Diameter, neck	.256″
Groove diameter of rifle barrel	.224″
Twist of rifling, one turn in	14″
Bullet diameter	.224″

.22-250

Overall length of cartridge	1.920″
Length of body	1.500″
Length of neck	.270″
Angle of shoulder	28°
Diameter front of body of case	.414″
Diameter rear of body	.468″
Diameter, neck	.256″
Groove diameter of rifle barrel	.224″
Twist of rifling, one turn in	14″
Bullet diameter	.224″

CHAPTER 21

Working at Home

SINCE the demise of R. F. Sedgley & Co. in Philadelphia, there seems to be no available supply of new Winchester single shot rifle actions, as Sedgley bought the whole available supply when Winchester closed out these actions — a supply, as I recall, of some 5000 new hi-side Winchester receivers and actions. All of these were later sold for scrap, and they are lost.

The Winchester single set trigger actions have often at times caused trouble in different ways, usually by giving non-uniform trigger pull — and an abnormally hard trigger pull when shot unset. There were other troubles too. One was the unexpected firing of the rifle when this was most embarassing to the rifle's owner.

On a single woodchuck hunting trip, I recently was present when three of these hi-side Winchesters with single set trigger, each fired twice, accidentally. One man had his rifle fire twice directly across the hood of his automobile, and in the first instance he narrowly missed the top of the engine. Both shots startled three hunters and gave the rifleman a very red face. The rifle was an R-2.

Another man had his rifle fire once when laying it carefully on the ground. It put a geyser of dirt and stones right back in his eyes. Another hunter narrowly missed the top of his auto. At any rate, it seems unnecessary to add here that such occurrences can be both embarassing and dangerous.

One possible cause is a too-light setting of the set trigger action, which had not been the case in any of the six accidental shots mentioned.

Another cause is the fly on the hammer. The fly — which has been made in at least two models, is a small irregular piece that sets into the back of the hammer and normally allows the hammer to ride over the half-cock notch when the trigger is pulled. The fly rides on a small pin in the back of the hammer.

If the point of the fly which protrudes to the rear wears off too much, or the small pin which goes through a small hole in the fly near its bottom edge comes loose, your rifle will misfire every time because the hammer will strike and block in the half-cock notch, and you can pull and keep on pulling until your fingers are sore, and that rifle still won't fire. Incidentally, the action may be irregular, one time your rifle will fire properly, with a light, even pull; next time it may stick and give a bit, and then fire. The third time it is like pulling against a four-horse team. Your rifle will not shoot.

Consequently, to save the energy of all those who have a habit of expressing their feelings when things go wrong, I am going to take the space to tell you here exactly how a new fly is made and installed in a Winchester single shot action. Or rather, we will let a friend tell it in his own language, as he ''gave being'' to a new hand-made Winchester single shot action fly and reports are that he had been married almost exactly 25 years when this earth-shattering event was accomplished.

Before we let him loose in this book, let me explain that the one style of Winchester single set trigger fly, probably the first one, was very small and delicate. It was only about 1/32 inch thickness, and the hole in it, which was supposed to contain a minute pin on which it was to ride for its lifetime, was about the size of the eye — but a round eye, in a needle, having a very small eye.

This tiny fly was followed by the later fly, which is approximately 1/16 or 0.0625 inch in thickness, and is of such a size that four together cover the whole surface of one side of a dime.

Enter now, Mr. A. C. Calm, of Philadelphia, mechanical engineer and trade school expert, and the author of training courses in mechanical trades, who took pity on a friend and spent three hours of hard work in producing a hand-made fly. Wrote Mr. Calm:

MAKING A NEW HAMMER FLY FOR A WINCHESTER HI-SIDE, SINGLE SHOT RIFLE ACTION, WITH SINGLE SET TRIGGER.

by A. C. Calm

There are times when sympathy overcomes our better judgment and causes us to offer our services to the forlorn — widows with a friendly nod excepted. And so, when I found friend C. S. Landis, close to the wailing wall and having rifle trouble, and bemoaning the fact that many Canadian chucks were still digging dens, and thus making and setting booby traps for both men and horses, because the hammer of one of his rifles stopped at the half-cock notch on the way down, I was overcome by sympathy and quite rashly volunteered to use my limited skill to design and make a new fly, and thus allow that hammer to go home after its installation.

This Buffalo Gun of Landis', a lever action Winchester hi-side (vintage of God-knows-when), rebarreled and chambered for a mite of a .170 cartridge, was disassembled, inspected, and found to have a mutilated "fly." All sportsmen will recognize the serious possibilities of this, especially when the rifleman goes on a 2500-mile safari with an arm firing a 25-grain bullet.

However, the "fly" in question is a cam-shaped piece which is pinned in a slot in the lower end of the hammer, at a location midway between the half-cock and full cock sears. Its function is to block off the half-cock sear when the piece is fired, permitting the hammer to fall to its extreme limit of travel.

The business end of this fly was found to be sharply beveled to a cold chisel point, which may have been due to wear, but because the part was hardened, it looked more as though someone had dropped his pick and shovel a sufficient length of time to try his hand at the emery wheel. Anyhow, the fly was too short to function properly and could not be salvaged. Since a replacement part for this damaged part could not readily be located, it was necessary to make a new part by hand.

Knowing that the fly had to be heat-treated, we looked around for proper material, and Landis located a 2 by 2-inch piece of Disston saw blade stock, which incidentally was 1/16-inch thick and slightly thicker than required.

A sample was cut from the piece of blade to permit experimenting with its hardening qualities, the chemical characteristics and physical or molecular structure of the piece being unknown.

Having no hardness testing equipment in our dog house we checked the hardness of the defunct fly with a file and, finding that the piece of metal was only slightly scratched, we decided on the temper by consulting a tempering color chart. Since wood bits and saws are drawn to purple (520° F) and still can be readily filed, we decided to try tempering the same to a bronze color (490° F).

The sample was heated to bright cherry red and quenched in room temperature water. Test with a file showed it to be glass-hard. After polishing with emery cloth, the piece was tempered to the selected color by laying it on a scrap piece of 1/2-inch thick iron, and heating slowly to assure even temper. It was quenched when the bronze color was attained and a subsequent file test showed its hardness to be very close to that of the previous fly on that hammer.

A piece of the saw stock, 1/16-inch thick was then roughed out to approximate shape and draw-filed to proper thickness. The pin hole was drilled and the old fly pinned to the new piece. It was then a simple matter to file the piece of saw blade to the profile of the fly, making necessary allowance for the point which was missing on the old fly but which was badly needed on the new fly.

The latest fly was then fitted into the action and found to work satisfactorily, after which it was removed, hardened, and tempered as was the original sample and was then reinstalled.

The whole job took about three hours, which is not begrudged if it stops a full grown man from mourning some chucks that whistled in derision at a half-cocked rifle.

Considering the extreme importance of small and apparently unimportant parts to the mechanism of a varmint rifle, the above description may help others to plan and manufacture, or have made, a new part to any one of the old rifle actions, so that they can keep their favorite arm in serviceable and satisfactory condition.

Considering also, that most of the more widely known gunsmiths today are making deliveries six months to two years or more after receipt of the order, and often also, after they had promised or assured the rifleman customer they would make delivery in a very much shorter interval, the importance of knowing how to make your own repairs to rifles, or the proper procedure so that you can induce a tool-maker or mechanic or mechanical engineer among your friends to make it for you, is obvious. Either you make your own rifle serviceable, or you do not shoot that rifle today — for a very extended period in far too many instances.

MALFUNCTIONS WITH THE WINCHESTER
HI-WALL ACTIONS

Mr. Harold C. Wood, Allentown, Pennsylvania, has had a lot of experiences with Winchester hi-wall set trigger actions on woodchuck rifles and wrote this letter in June of 1948 when I had difficulty in Ontario with my hi-wall action twice shedding its set trigger fly. Mr. Wood was then of the opinion that probably the metal parts were binding against the wood on the inside of the stock, which might have swelled due to rainy weather. Wrote Mr. Wood:

I have had numerous experiences similar to the one you spoke of to me. I have had a number of Winchester single shot actions and every one I owned had a single set trigger. It it did not have one when I bought it, I soon had one installed as I used to think I could not shoot a chuck rifle unless it had a set trigger, and I always preferred the single set action. I only had one rifle I can recall that had a double set trigger, although plenty of my friends had them, and I am familiar with the Schuetzen double set triggers.

I had a .257 Roberts built on a Mauser action that had a double set trigger. I did not keep it long. I had one experience with it in Greene County. I was driving along a back road and saw a chuck lying on top of his hole about 100 yards off, so I stopped, took a bead on the chuck and thought I would set the set trigger. I thought it set very hard and all of a sudden the rifle went "boom." Instead of pulling the set trigger I was heaving on the regular trigger. Luckily it was pointed in the direction of the chuck and at that only shot over its head about two inches. But this sort of soured me, and while it was not the fault of the rifle, yet that sort of set trigger being partly responsible for this sort of a shot, made me lose interest in using that action.

About two years ago I bought a dolled-up hi-wall Winchester s.s. from O. H. Elliott of rifle fame, in caliber .224 Donaldson Krag Lightning. This rifle had been built up for some doctor by M. S. Risley. It was then a speed action with skeletonized hammer and stiff main spring. The hammer throw was then only a fraction of an inch. It had the half-cock notch taken off entirely and Mann-Neidner firing pin, hammer rested directly on the firing pin and the firing pin on the primer. Doesn't sound so hot from a mechanical design standpoint, does it? It didn't to me.

If I had been home when Elliott delivered the rifle, I would have let him take it with him. But the more I looked it over the more I thought I would like it, so I finally kept it.

When I carried this rifle out in the field, I always had the finger lever about one-third way open. It had a single set trigger which was in the habit of working itself lighter in pull as time went on and one had to adjust it every so often to keep it just right. There was no chance of it catching in a half-cock notch, having none, and when you touched that baby she went off, "boom!"

As I mentioned previously, I have had a dozen Winchester hi-walls and never had one of them go off before I wanted it to fire, but this action had me on tenterhooks half the time, and it did fire twice for me, unexpectedly, in one week's hunting in New York State. Both times I was in the car and both times I inadvertently touched the trigger when it was set. Once I was just getting set to shoot a chuck. I had the rifle trained on the chuck and it went down, as they often do, unexpectedly, so in waiting a moment and in moving around to get a better position from which to fire, I touched the trigger unexpectedly. Luckily the bullet went in a safe direction near where the chuck had been sitting.

Another time I was crawling along a hedge trying to find a place where I could see through the hedge growth to shoot at a chuck in a hayfield beyond. The same thing happened again. I had a bead on the chuck, and he dropped down. So, as he was down, I decided to change to a better position before firing. In moving I touched the trigger and the rifle fired. I should have told you it happened three times with that rifle, for it happened again that same day, within a half hour. We started to drive on out the back road, my brother and I; he was driving his car at the time when we saw some crows on a side hill not over 100 yards away. We stopped and they paid not the slightest attention to us. I got all set for the shot and was just about to pull the trigger, when my brother said, "Down there comes a car," so I opened the finger lever and pulled the rifle in.

After the car passed a safe interval, and the crows still stayed there, I stuck the rifle out and closed the finger lever, forgetting about the trigger being set and in jockeying around for a good shooting position, safe and steady, the rifle fired again. Of course it was aimed in the general direction of the crows as I was just moving it a hair to get into a steadier position, and from a better angle. While the firing of the rifle wasn't a matter of danger to anyone, it gave me the jitters. Two accidental firings in one day were too much for me. I wanted things more dependable.

That all came about by the rifle not having a half-cock notch and me not wanting to rest the hammer directly on the firing pin, which in turn as previously mentioned, rested on the primer. The theory of the thing was okay and also the workmanship, as the firing pin had, or was supposed to have had, a spring strong enough to resist the pressure of the hammer, but it did not altogether do so as you would occasionally see a very small dent in the primer, especially if you had a primer not seated to its full depth.

Anyhow, I got a new hammer and took it up to Risley and had him install it. I wanted Risley to put in a heavier spring. He didn't do this; he claimed it was okay as it was. So he put in a new hammer and left the half-cock notch on it. I drove up to his place in New York State over a week end. I left the rifle and he said he would have it by the next week end. My brother was going up the following week end for something he had left with Risley and he picked up the rifle and shipped it to me.

When I got the box I took the rifle out to see how it worked. It would fire okay with the regular trigger but not with the set trigger — it caught in the half-cock notch every time. Was I burned up!

The next week end I high-tailed it back to Risley's. He said it was very unusual and that the rifle had worked all right when it left his place. I handed it to him and he worked it several times and we never thought to try it when we put the stock on it as it worked okay in the metal parts. Well he was stumped as here we were with an assembled rifle that wouldn't work. He said he would have to grind down the spring, and did so, and that didn't work. He tried this and he tried that. Finally my brother said, "Shirley, we are all going at the thing wrong. It works without the stock and it won't work with the stock on the metal. Possibly there is too much wood sticking out inside somewhere, which catches the sear or something," he picked up the stock and looked it over. He said, "Here is the trouble right here, — you can see where the sear is hitting the wood." He took a penknife and shaved the wood out a bit and then everything seemed fine. But by that time I was disgusted with all this plus the long journeys to get the rifle working properly, so I sold the rifle. I had driven over 800 miles on the two trips and had I looked I would have seen that just a bit of wood sticking in too far has caused the trouble.

My .170* did the same thing when it came back from Parkinson and I had the same trouble. I simply took the stock off and it fired fine with the stock off, so I knew the stock was the culprit. About two minutes with the small blade of my pocket knife and no one would want to have a finer rifle.

I bought a .219 Zipper built by Winchester on a hi-wall action and the first time I tried it out, it would not fire at all when using the set trigger. This was about 1945 when I did not know too much about the mysteries of the single set trigger. I took this Zipper to a competent gunsmith and he would not touch it— said he was too old to learn. So I took it home and went to work on it myself. I soon discovered the trigger spring, the one that works the set trigger, was too weak to hold the sear up out of engagement with the half-cock notch. Not being in a position to retemper the spring and not having a new one at hand, I conceived the idea of placing a small shim of wood block under the front end of the spring thereby putting it on a shorter purchase and consequently giving a much stronger push against the cam that works the sear. It has worked fine ever since.

Last year I sold my last hi-wall action and vowed I was through with them but now I have two of them again. I have two very nice actions. The one that Parkinson barreled up for me has the milled out sides and the other has the heavy sides.

Since thousands of woodchuck hunters use hi-side Winchester single shot actions and there are no new ones anymore, or few factory parts, and as the years go by, and chuck hunters find theirs wearing out, and more and more difficult to service, this data has been set down here to help you rebuild and readjust your old Winchester hi-side action so that as a woodchuck rifle it may continue to function long after old man Winchester ever thought it would.

Also, your son or grandson may need to have a rifle stuck in his hands and be turned loose to develop a sufficiently strong physical frame to go through this life, and most likely he would never make the grade with out a good safe and substantial rifle.

*Author's Note: Mr. Wood suggested I look for that swollen wood in my hi-side and he said that probably there were only two things that could be wrong with it. Either the set trigger spring is weak or the wood is touching. That is, if the rifle will fire regularly when using the trigger unset.

FITTING UP SPEED ACTION, BOLT ACTIONS
WITH SPECIAL SAFETIES FOR USE WITH
LARGE DIAMETER TELESCOPE SIGHTS

Sometimes a Springfield or a Mauser action will give some trouble with a speed action firing when the safety is snapped off. What to do? I have both Redfield and also a Buehler safety to use whichever works best on a Cramer speed action Springfield .22-250, which at times has given this difficulty, likely because of being set too light.

Mr. C. J. Henninger of the Cramer Bullet Mould Company wrote me as follows on how to make a suitable speed action adjustment.

"In the Cramer speed action the forward adjustment screw controls the amount of spring tension exerted against the trigger itself. The adjustment screw on the forward side of the center portion of the trigger is the adjustment for back slap and the adjustment screw on the rear of the center portion of the trigger is for the sear contact. Combinations of these three adjustments will result in trigger pulls from 8 ounces to as heavy as 6 pounds." (I had mine set at 1-1/2 pounds, at which point the pull was very fast and very smooth.)

"I am sure the difficulty you have experienced is due to the change-over from the standard Springfield safety to the Redfield safety (which will work with the large diameter scope barrel, which the Springfield safety will not clear — the Redfield and the Buehler, whichever is used, are each on the right side of the scope barrel and don't need to go under it).

"Your gunsmiths, Wurzer & Peterson, should be able to make the necessary adjustment which is easily accomplished by grinding off the contact surface of the sear on the trigger itself. Probably an additional clearance of .005 to .010 inch would make the Redfield safety operative."

This for those who may run into a similar situation. Other speed actions, or speed actions with set triggers, may have slightly different adjustments to give them a sufficient bite and to result in proper bearing of trigger and sear.

Charles Parkinson, custom gunsmith of London, Ontario, wrote me as follows, on June 17, 1950, regarding the operation of the safety and speed action on his .22-250 Springfield sporter.

"It looks as if your rifle has not sufficient clearance between cocking piece and sear. The safety should cam the cocking piece back clear of the sear when safety is on and when released it should move slightly forward to again engage the trigger sear. When it fires on releasing the safety it shows that there is not enough clearance between sear face and the cocking piece face and this will not allow the trigger sear to come up and engage cocking piece. One of these engaging surfaces will have to be ground or stoned off to allow them to contact properly.

"I have not had too much experience with the Springfield action, but on the Mauser, more common here in Ontario, I find that as the safety comes from the maker only about 10 per cent of them will work without some stoning.

"The Buehler is to my mind, the safety which is more likely to work on your Cramer speed action fitted to a Springfield."

DETAILS TO WATCH CAREFULLY IN THE MAKING
OF HOME-MADE BULLETS

by

Fred T. Huntington

My first thought along the line of making accurate bullets would be concerning the necessary forming dies and tools used in doing the work. These dies must be machined and made as carefully as possible and to the finest degree of accuracy possible. If you are going to make your own dies, then it will mean a "trial and error method" until you are "lucky" to get one good set of dies. My first attempt seemed so easy to complete that I became overconfident and decided to make a lot of them. I found it took nine more sets before I finished another suitable one. Matching up head ogives with body sections is really a job! It may seem easy up to the point of heat-treating, but most generally after the heat-treating, it is necessary to either start all over again, or correct the poor alignment caused by the movement of the metal during this process.

The movement of the metal can perhaps be more clearly described as the molecular movement within the mass of the metal. Metals under heat-treatment seem to grow or increase in mass which means the molecules grow in size. This growing of the metal causes warpage which is extremely hard to overcome. Metals such as steel and most alloys increase in length, width, and volume as the temperature goes up. During the quenching process there is a tendency for this metal to warp or stay in the enlarged state. Even as the metals cool and do decrease in length, width, and volume, they do not return to their former state as before heat-treating. To overcome this growing or warping is one of the most perplexing problems we have to face. Metals with the least tendency to this molecular movement are the most satisfactory for this type of die making and are the types of metals we are using in our R.C.B.S. dies.

Many metals have been tried in an effort to overcome this difficulty, and each one was supposed to be the answer. However, of fifteen different metals used, we have found none as yet that will not move slightly during heat-treating. We have the finest type of heat-treating furnace and fine temperature controls and although factory recommendations have been followed, all of the metals give some trouble in movement during the hardening process.

I would recommend my Rock Chuck Bullet Swages, but for you readers, there are other forming dies to be considered. We have found, however, that other types of dies do not repeat in concentricity of the bullet formed. Also, many of these dies do not produce a real, perfectly round bullet. Our dies are finished, ground inside and out after hardening and therefore, are as nearly perfect as possible to make. With the type of mechanical threading between the ogive section and the body of the die (a patented feature) we find it is an easy matter to make these dies repeat to a nearly 100 per cent perfect bullet, each time. The finished product, of course, is up to the bullet-maker, himself, and he can either make a good or bad bullet even with a good set of dies.

In starting out and using the best dies, do not expect to make perfect bullets. Bullet making is comparable to running a lathe for the first time. One cannot learn by reading a book and then going to work. Learning to make accurate bullets is acquired by trial and error and trying all conceivable methods. Then, there is the problem of guns and bores of the rifle barrels. One bullet is found to shoot well in a particular rifle while another does not seem to do well at all. Why? All we can do is guess and try something else. One rifle may shoot better with a particular shape of bullet than another. There are available several shapes of bullets and dies furnished in various diameters, according to the wants of the bullet-swager, for making differently designed bullets. We make a 4S shape which has a short ogive, designed especially for Hornets and similar rifles where the bullets are made to feed through a magazine. This bullet would be very accurate though in any rifle of proper fitting bore because it has a short point and would be concentric from base to point. It has a shape similar to that of the Remington 45-grain S.P. bullet. We also make the 6S ogive which is a 6-caliber head with an approximate shape of the 55-grain Express Sisk or Sierra Spitzer bullet. This is at its best in about 50 grains weight. However, it does well in many rifles from 45 to 55 grains weight or heavier, if desired. The third shape of bullet is a 7S and is similar in outline to the pointed spitzer type Sierra bullet. This bullet is best in soft swaging around 55-grain weight and for pointed, fully formed bullets of 55 grain weight and above. These described are all in .22 caliber in diameters from .222 to .2285.

The first step in making home-made bullets is to have available a lead cutter which we make at $7.00. This tool cuts the lead cores into nearly even weight slugs which act as the core to put into the bullet jacket. It is a shearlike tool and does not necessarily have to be made with extreme accuracy because in following up this operation with the next recommended step one of our Core Extruders selling for $12 will be used. This die is used by cutting your lead slugs overweight a grain or two and then forming in this die under pressure where it extrudes the excess weight of lead, making nearly even weight cores formed properly for the bullet jackets. These lead cores will hardly show a variation in weight on a fine scale and this is considered to be one of the best additions to a set of bullet-making dies as it eliminates hand segregation of the cut cores and weighing them for evenness in weight. There is a great deal of ballyhoo about various other dies costing nearly twice as much, but you will find this die will make weight cores as evenly and in turn will work with a core swager to the very best advantage in making a final nearly perfect bullet.

One important item, which should be mentioned before core swaging, is the bullet jacket metal and the jackets used. The jackets should be of a gilding metal, made especially for bullet jackets. Plain copper cups will not do as they are too soft. We always carry bullet jackets from .22 to .30 caliber. The .22 calibers which seem to work best are as follows:

.575-inch length (which make from 35- to 48-grain bullets); .657-inch length (which make from 48- to 52-grain); and .705-inch length (for bullets of 52 to 55 grains and the longest length, at this writing); .735-inch length (which is the most suitable for "soft swaging" around 55 grain weight and for pointed bullets of heavier than 55 grain weight). In .25 calibers, we have .886, .912, and .939 and .997-inch lengths for bullets from about 87 grain to 125 grain weight. These seem to be the most popular lengths and form the best in these weight classes. Each die will perform a little differently with the respective lengths and in that case there is no ironclad rule to follow. In ordering, until you know definitely what lengths are needed for the exact weight of bullets desired, it is best to order, for instance, 1000 of each length for trial purposes and then reorder the lengths you find work best in your dies and for your rifle. We then take this extruded even weight core and place it in the bullet jacket. This jacket is then reworked in the core swaging die, which sells for $10 complete. This tool expands the core in the proper way in the jacket without getting it out of shape or oversize. We make this die a little on the small diameter size so if the jackets are oversize, by using an extra small punch (which is furnished) it forces the jacket into the die first—this punch is then removed and the regular punch is used to upset the lead core into the jacket. It must be remembered that all you are trying to do is upset the lead core uniformly so it will not come out of the jacket during the next operation and the elimination of trapped air in the base of the bullet is assured. The diameter of the core is made to the exact proper size and shape in order to do the job of core swaging in the most efficient way. Excessive pressure at this point does no good and does do harm to the good work preceding the operation. All that is wanted is to upset the lead evenly. Each core and jacket being alike, the lead does not want to be forced down around the forming punch—only upset to the walls of the jacket in order to exclude the air from the jacket base and sidewalls so you will be assured that it will not move further during the bullet-forming operation except by pressure used in the forming die itself. This operation is often done by hand with a hand punch and light hammer but is a poor substitute and if real accuracy is desired, follow each recommended step carefully.

During all of the preceding operations care must be taken to work on a clean bench. All dies and jackets must be kept absolutely clean and free from dust and dirt. If the necessary precautions are not used, it will be found that dirty components act as a lap in the die bores and gradually scratch and lap out the dies to larger diameters. With properly kept components the wear on our dies is practically none at all. Many dies have produced from 25 to 50 thousand bullets before being worn out.

The above paragraph is most important in the forming operation which is to be described as we go along.

Our .22-caliber forming dies sell for $32.50 per set including the ram for the Pacific, Easton, or Universal Tools. It also includes the forming punch which is held by the ram in the particular tool and the forming die which is actually a two-piece die brought together by a combination of interrupted and continous thread, requiring about one full turn of the head section to remove it from the body section. The Pacific Tool seems to be the one the die works more easily in and gives the greatest satisfaction. However, the dies are adaptable to the Easton or Universal Tools. In .243, .25 caliber and 6.5 caliber the dies are $40 per set and include in addition to the above-named items, a heavier handle and toggle assembly for the Pacific Tool only, which increases the leverage about 40 per cent and still does not cut the stroke of the ram down to any appreciable degree. As the diameters go up, the leverage required multiplies greatly — the .25 calibers taking about 30 per cent more leverage than the .22 calibers, and the .270 would, of course, take about 30 per cent more than the .25 calibers and so on until .30 calibers and above are reached the pressure required to form an accurate bullet becomes a major item to consider. Pressure can be cut down by venting dies and casting preformed cores but this takes away the accuracy instead of increasing the potential accuracy of the bullet. As the only concern is extreme accuracy, the thought of vented dies will not be included in this article.

In making bullets you must decide whether you want to form "soft swaged bullets" for target shooting or fully pointed bullets for varmint shooting. It is generally conceded that soft swaged bullets, which work the jacket an extreme minimum during the forming operation, are the most accurate. However, many feel the fully pointed bullets are more accurate and all agree that the fully formed bullets carry up the best on long-range shooting. I would suggest that both types of bullets be tried in order to determine how each will act in your rifle. Diameter of the bullet as pertaining to the bore and groove diameters is very important. Usually, if you intend to load to maximum, the bullet should be just under the groove diameter. If for target or bench rest accuracy, it is believed that a bullet from approximately .0001 inch undersize to .0002 inch oversize will work the best. It would be best to start just a little undersize of the groove diameter, which can be determined by slugging the bore of your rifle with a soft piece of lead, upsetting it with two cleaning rods and then pushing it from the chamber-end to the muzzle. Send this slug with your order and it will help materially to get your dies in a more nearly proper diameter and the final results should be better. If your dies are a little undersize, they are then easily lapped out to proper diameter but if they are oversize, there is nothing that can be done to bring them back and down to proper diameter.

In soft swaging, you must by the trial and error method figure out how much lead is to be used with each particular jacket. There is no set rule on this. Generally speaking, if you want to make soft-swaged bullets of 50 grain weight, a .705 inch jacket would be used and if 55 grain weight is desired then a .735 inch jacket would be considered the best. Soft swaging in simple wording is not putting enough pressure on the core and jacket to form a pointed or lead tipped bullet. Many prefer a wide opening in the end of the bullet or hollow point of about 1/8-inch opening and others prefer a much smaller opening. Again, you must determine in your own rifle which one will shoot the best and follow this type accordingly. In the soft swaging method, if the extruded cores and properly swaged cores in the jackets are placed properly, work the jacket to a minimum and also the cores. If these are disarranged to any great degree, the accuracy of the bullet then falls off.

Soft swaging takes much less pressure and is easier on the tools, dies and the operator, which is a factor many consider to be important. Personally, I prefer the small lead tipped fully-formed bullet. However, I am not a bench rest group shooter. My shooting is confined mostly to hunting varmints and as a consequence I prefer the streamlined bullet with a small amount of lead showing. This type of bullet has good wind-bucking ability and looks well when loaded into these modern cartridges. They also expand extremely well at all ranges if the speed is sufficient. I suggest the hollow point type of bullet for those wanting a bullet to expand more easily, especially at long ranges and when the full tip bullet is not suitable to your needs.

In forming fully pointed bullets and also the soft-swaged type, we recommend a slight trace of lubrication to be applied to the jackets on the outside only. Some use cadmium plated jackets and "swear by them," others use the cadmium and "swear at them," feeling that it does scale off into the pores of the rifle barrel eventually causing a building up of metal in the bore, which is almost impossible to remove. For this reason, cadmium plating of the jackets is not recommended. They will do no damage to the dies so it is immaterial whether they are used. However, approach this angle with extreme caution, as rifle barrels are expensive and extremely accurate ones are few and far between. Speaking of lubrication, there are several ways of giving it properly. Rubbing the outside of the jacket on a bar of Ivory, Swan, or White King soap, is probably the best lubricant. It will take longer but in the final analysis cause less trouble. Other lubricants recommended are a good grade of deep drawing extruding oil, available from any major oil company; but it does come in large amounts, most generally. We (R.C.B. S. Co.,) furnish it in small 2 ounce bottles for 50¢ per bottle, postpaid. Lanolin, which can be obtained from any drug store can be used but sparingly—thin this with gasoline or solvent. It is best to rub it into a clean cloth and then roll the jackets on the cloth. Only a slight trace of lubricant should be used, regardless of what is used. Good grades of lubricating oil can also be used following the above instructions. Many find Hoppe's No. 9, used sparingly, to be very good. Another lubricant highly recommended is Molykote which is a molybdenum sulphide product made by the Alpha Corporation of Greenfield, Massachusetts. It is a fine powdered substance that looks and acts somewhat like a powdered graphite but is undoubtedly a finer product with more lubricating properties. It is also advisable to clean the dies occasionally with Hoppe's No. 9, using a fiber bristle cleaning rod.

Now, we are ready for the actual forming operation: —first, try the punch, by hand, in the dies to be sure it is perfectly free and does not bind. You must watch these punches carefully. If dropped on the floor at any time, be sure to inspect the forming end for roughness and deformation. They must be hard and tough so they do not bend, and under such circumstances scratch the die body. If this happens it might ruin a good set of dies and be the fault of no one.

Place the core swaged jacket, which has the open end upwards, on top of the forming punch and guide it carefully into the die by raising the lever of the tool. In the case of soft swaging you can bring the handle right up and over the dead center position, take the head off carefully and push your formed bullet out. When fully forming bullets for small lead tips, it is best to approach the final pressure setting with extreme caution. When this setting is just right, you can then either bring the lever up most of the way and then vent or bring it clear over dead center, release the pressure and then vent your dies. Bring the lever over dead center again and release the pressure again. Take the head section off carefully and with the push-out plug, carefully force the fully formed bullet out of the die. I always rerun the formed bullet back through the die carefully in order to complete the final smoothing up of the bullet. This can be done later or in many cases does not have to be done at all. I recommend this extra operation for uniformity and after all, that is what we are striving for.

Handle your finished bullets with care, especially if you plan bench-rest shooting with them. Tough handling after the bullet has been formed, will often damage their potential accuracy.

I would like to especially call your attention to the amount of pressure used when forming bullets. This is one of the most important items to watch in making bench-rest bullets. The least amount of pressure will perhaps make the most accurate bullets because it keeps the jacket and lead in the original state as near as possible.

It has been found that in a soft-swaged bullet the amount of pressure required to form such a bullet is at a real minimum. These soft-swaged bullets are the ones that are winning the bench-rest shoots today and it is felt that such formed bullets are more accurate because of the minimum amount of pressure used in the forming operation. In each case it is necessary to try each type of bullet to determine exactly which is the most accurate in your particular rifle, but even if you find a pointed bullet to work the best, be sure to use only enough pressure to just form the desired point—no more. It is possible to make fully pointed bullets with resulting round even bases and this nicely rounded base seems to give the best results. To clear this point, we furnish a flat face punch and when you have used the correct amount of pressure in forming the bullet, you will have a nice flat base and still have evenly rounded edges on the base.

No definite or specific information is available on just what happens during the forming operation; however, it is felt that under the pressure of punch and ram, the jacket metal actually tends to flow toward and get heavier in the base portion of the jacket. It is this flowing that we want to hold to an absolute minimum, especially with the type of leverage available on the standard tools today. This type of leverage is actually not enough to do the job satisfactorily unless you soft swage. The ram tends to slow in its travel and often stops, so you can get another pull on the ram to make it go over dead center. In our new R.C. B.S. Bullet Forming Press and Combination Reloading Tool, the leverage has been greatly increased and is actually compounded so the ram operates in a slow, deliberate manner from start to finish of stroke. This slow, deliberate action along with proper lubrication is what is needed to form the best bullets. It is entirely possible with this new press and our dies to form nicely pointed noses and still keep a nice flat base with proper rounded edges.

In all of our dies, we work from a smaller diameter up to a larger diameter in each operation. In so doing, there should be little or no spring out of the jacket or core as it is released from the die.

Perhaps the most interesting thing in connection with this hobby is when you have the so-called perfect dies, the perfect barrel, the special chambering job, fancy stock and combinations of best possible loads and you still find that you cannot put the bullets all in one small hole. Then all you have to do is convince your wife that you should have a new barrel chambered for an entirely new caliber in which to further your research efforts, and it gives you a chance to go through this interesting process all over again. Oh, yes! Don't forget that you should also have another new different style or caliber — a complete set of bullet dies to go along with the new barrel!

R.C.B.S. LARGE CALIBER BULLET FORMING DIES

The demand is ever increasing for all caliber bullet forming dies so we have given the larger caliber dies considerable thought. One of the main things encountered which has given trouble is the life of the dies expressed in number of bullets you can make out of a given set of dies. The .22 calibers, because of the amount of metal around the bore and the pressure required to form bullets have given extremely satisfactory service. However, when you get above .257 or 6.5 caliber, the pressure multiplies greatly and of course the bore of the die increases so the pressure per square inch becomes an important factor. The metal not only wears but it does stretch or expand with continued use of forming pressure till the dies become oversize and useless. We have found that to increase the Rockwell hardness of the die does no good and often does harm because if they become too hard they are also brittle and have a tendency to break during forming operations.

To overcome this breakage and excessive wear angle, we have increased the outside diameter of the die to 1-1/4 inches which will help very materially. It might appear that we want to just be contrary about this and made the dies larger so that they could not be used in standard available tools. However, the above explanation is the real reason. We do not want to produce dies that later will give trouble because there is really much time and expense in the making of a good set of our type bullet dies and when necessary to replace on an adjustment basis, we lose considerably each time. We want to build dies that will give proper service and last, and dies we can stand behind.

All of the available presses of reloading nature lack strength, leverage, and resistance to spring off the main frame of the tool. With these thoughts in mind we have tried to develop such a tool which will be built to stand the job, and still be suitable for a reloading press also. We feel this has been accomplished in our new R.C.B.S. Bullet Forming Press and Combination Reloading Tool, which is described in our literature.

Our .270, 7m.m., .30 and larger caliber dies will all have a thread diameter of 1-1/4 inches and be made especially to fit our new press. The new press will have a suitable bushing so you can still use the regular 7/8-inch diameter dies. Our .22, .243, .257 and 6.5 diameter dies will still be made to fit the 7/8-inch thread of all standard tools and can be used in our new press by the use of the mentioned bushing from 1-1/4 to 7/8-inch.

Our larger caliber dies will work much the same way as our smaller diameter dies. What we are trying to attain is extreme accuracy in repeating each bullet to 100 per cent concentricity and uniformity. So far, our dies have not been touched in these particulars. Other dies give more speed and possibly more ease of operation but they do not repeat in concentricity and uniformity like the R.C.B.S. dies.

We could overcome the pressure angle by venting the dies

but uniform bases with uniform points would be impossible. This being the case, we feel that to get the best results it is necessary to use a die of our type construction, which is an un- vented type of die. This type of die of course builds up more pressure than the vented type of dies and takes more pressure to do the forming operation. It is a known fact that few bench- rest records have been won by the sleeve type or vented type of die. The best commercial bullets available are made in a proc- ess very similar to the one we recommend, namely cutting cores accurately, extruding excess lead to a very accurate degree, core swaging properly, and finally, the best possible forming die operation.

For those who just want to form bullets for their own use and do not expect to do competitive bench-rest shooting with them, we plan some more reasonably priced dies which will be of cheaper construction and be of a vented type die but in all probability will only make the hollow point type of bullet which does not require as much pressure to form a bullet. These dies also will be made for standard tools of 7/8-inch thread diameter,

Our point or ogive styles will be of the semi-spitzer type of point which seems to be in most demand for flat trajectory, game or target shooting. It is specially to be noted that an ogive of not too long a radius is by far the best for all around use because you can make a wider range of weights of bullets in each set of dies in each caliber. In the .270 caliber we want to pro- duce a die which will make bullets in ranges from 100 up to 160 grains if desired. In .30 caliber we intend to make the style of ogive suitable for bullets from 150 to 220 grain weight. In this way they will please the greatest majority of shooters as these are the popular bullet weights in the respective calibers. Diam- eters of dies will be standard for the caliber desired unless a special diameter is ordered for a particular bore. We will fur- nish special diameters subject to some delay of course, depend- ing on which dies are in production.

UNCLE GEORGE'S STORY OF THE WOODCHUCK

(AS TOLD TO M. S. RISLEY BY GEORGE WILCOX)

In this day and age of super-accurate woodchuck and var- mint rifles equipped with modern telescopic sights, it is a far cry from the 1870's when Uncle George Wilcox first was bitten by the woodchuck craze.

As told me by Uncle George it went like this: "I used to spend part of my time with Granther and Grandma Wilcox. Granther Aaron Wilcox lived on the old farm back in the land of 'stiddy habits.' Some called it 'Egypt,' but I liked the first name best.

"Grandther had an old Springfield flint lock musket of the year 1808. It had been transformed by screwing a plug and nipple in the barrel and a piece of recessed steel had been set in the jaws where the flint originally had been placed.

"When I was about ten years old, I developed a hankering to fire the old gun, and asked Granther if he would let me.

"He said I wasn't quite old enough and besides the gun was loaded with a heavy charge for wolf and he couldn't be bothered to fire it himself, thereby wasting the wolf load and of necessity then putting a boy's load in and then reloading for wolves before returning the gun to the horn rack back of the kitchen stove.

"One warm spring day when the snow was partly gone and Granther was boiling sap in the sugar bush, I saw the biggest woodchuck sunning himself on the old stone wall back of the hog pen. He looked as large as a fairly well-grown Jersey calf to me. I ran into the house, looked around and saw that Grandma was not in sight. I got a chair and eased the old musket off the horns behind the stove and ran into the back yard. I couldn't hope to hold the gun at arms length as I was pretty small and light for my age, but I saw an old whopper of an ant hill, so I lay down on my belly and rested the old musket across the top of the ant hill.

"I got both hands on the hammer and pulled her back as far as she would go and drew a bead on that chuck. I took two or three breaths and yanked. The old gun let out a beller and drove me back about four feet. I slid along on my belly and then discovered the gun had dug a gash in the sod where the toe of the butt plate had rested on the sod. The gun finally came to rest behind me after whirling over backwards.

"I thought my arm and shoulder were broken but someone grabbed me by the scruff of the neck and I heard Grandma telling me what Grandther Aaron would do to me when he found out I had fired Old Betsy. She also laid it on with a heavy hand where it would do the most good and I would appreciate it least.

"As soon as she had returned to the house with Old Betsy, I made for the stone wall to see what had happened out there. I peeked over the wall where the woodchuck had been sitting and there, deader than a salt mackerel, was the gol-dingdest shrivelled up, scrunty little woodchuck I had ever seen just out of his winter's hibernation.

"I took another good look at that tiny woodchuck which had looked as big as a well-grown calf when it lay on the wall, and which was actually not much bigger than a swamp rabbit as it lay there dead, and I turned around and looked again at the spot on the wall, and I said, right out loud, 'Aw, Shucks! Could the game have shrunk that much, had Granther been shooting at a wolf? Aw, Shucks — I still don't believe it! I must have killed the wrong woodchuck!' Maybe, at some time or other, so have we all. They always look so much bigger snoozing out there on the wall or sitting, 300 yards away, out in the pasture field.

"With that I turned around and walked slowly back to the house, thinking of what Grandther would likely do to me, and I said to myself, 'Aw Shucks!'

W. H. BOYD SPINS SOME YARNS

Mr. W. H. Boyd is the Registrar of Firearms in the Province of Ontario. He is a woodchuck shooter when he has opportunity, is an archer by choice of hobbies, and is also a pistol shooter. Fortunately for riflemen in that area, he sees the firearms problems from the shooter's angle as well as that of an official. Here is his story.

Your book on woodchucks and woodchuck hunting should be very interesting. I do not know of a better sport than groundhog hunting. Alex Rutherford of whom you may have known, but deceased since 1933, and I used to hunt woodchucks almost every day. He was a printer by trade and read almost every book he could get his hands upon.

Alex and I started out first to hunt ground hogs with .303 Ross rifles. We used army ammunition and bored the points with an 1/8-inch drill. There is an aluminum point in front of the lead under the jacket and we used to drill through this until we struck lead. The doctored bullet would practically blow a hog to pieces. It would not ricochet on anything short of a large stone. It would then make quite a noise but would not ricochet very far.

We found that with these rifles we soon ran out of hogs as about three trips on a nice day would clean them out if we hunted all in one area. We then began using B. S. A. .22-caliber target rifles with high speed, hollow point bullets. It required a hit in the head, most times, to stop the chuck outside the hole. Most body shots permitted the animal to get into the den out of sight, from where we could hear it lamenting and know it was suffering. This did not appeal to us. We then started to shoot them with .455-caliber service revolvers using the wad-cutter bullets. These proved to be good stoppers but we still had a large number of chucks getting down the hole when hit and when we went up to the den we could hear them complaining.

During the years we shot together we had many amusing experiences. I believe the funniest and one which might have turned into a tragedy, occurred one day when we were shooting in the Caledon Hills on some farms that had been worked out and then turned into ranch land. We had just crossed a hilltop when we spied a big hog on a stone sunning himself. The animal was about 200 yards away; we watched and saw it move along the top of the rock. It presented a perfect shot.

On opportunities of this sort we were in the habit of using a hard-nose bullet and aiming about 2 inches or more below the hog in order that the bullet would be deformed on the rock and bounce into the chuck and kill it instantly. It would often bounce him as much as a foot into the air and the laceration was considerable, in addition to which the chuck absorbed quite a bit of bullet energy.

Alex won the toss and took the shot. He was using a long Ross with four power scope. The shot was perfect and the hog, instead of bouncing into the air sailed out like a clay pigeon. When Alex made this shot at the chuck on a rock after the chuck sailed through the air, out bounced an old tramp who had been having a snooze in the sun. Presumably he had seen and heard enough for one day. We were too far away to catch the expression on his face but his antics were really funny! We watched him, keeping low meanwhile so that he could not see us, until we were fully satisfied that he was quite uninjured and then, like two Arabs in the night, we stole away. I would have liked to have obtained a motion picture of this shot and its most unexpected results.

A number of our group were great practical jokers and often used much careful planning in carrying out a joke. One of the best I know of, and which backfired in an amusing manner, occurred as follows.

A chap whom we will call Norm was a very enthusiastic

chuck hunter but he worked in a sporting goods store where the wage level was low and he could not afford a car. One day he talked a more wealthy customer into going ground hog shooting on a Saturday afternoon just when the grass was still short and the shooting perfect. They drove to a section of the country which was used for pasturage, but which also contained a few very good clover fields. Stopping on the road in front of a large brick farmhouse, the clerk went in to ask permission to engage in woodchuck shooting on that farm. Because of the damage done to grass and hay by chucks, this is usually readily forthcoming.

The farmer gave him a good reception and permission to kill all the ground hogs he wished, provided he was careful and did not shoot in the direction of the house or in any direction which might be dangerous. As he was leaving he asked the lad from town if he would do him a favor and shoot an old horse that was in the back pasture several fields from the house, as the animal was so old and his teeth so worn down, he could no longer eat. It had been a pet of the children and was very gentle as well as being a good driver and saddle horse. They did not have the heart to send it to a glue factory nor a fox farm and no one living on the farm had the grit to put it out of its misery.

Norm returned to the car in high spirits and said he had received permission to shoot woodchucks and they were to drive down the side road and go to work on them. They drove down the road for three fields and Norm said, "This is the place." After getting all their shooting equipment on their persons they crossed the fence and went up a hill. From the top of the hill a number of ground hogs could be seen and about 100 yards off the old horse stood with bent head. He was, as a matter of fact, a rather pitiful sight. "Look at the old horse!" remarked Norm. "I am going to shoot the darned old thing. It is too old to be any good. It's a sin to let it stand there and suffer!" Before his friend could say a word or raise a hand to stop him, he took a quick aim and when the rifle cracked, down went the horse as if poleaxed. His guest looked at him as if he had suddenly gone mad and, turning on his heel, he raced to his car and drove as rapidly as he could clear into Toronto, leaving Norm thirty miles above Toronto without transportation home. Next time he saw him, he refused to speak. This was one case where a joke backfired tremendously. Try bumming a ride, some time, in rural Ontario, with a rifle over your shoulder, dressed in old clothing and having no money. Every motorist who comes along

will take a look and step on the gas so that the pedal goes clear
down to the floor. Norm admits that was the longest and loneli-
est walk he ever had, and since then he has shot no more horses.

The antics of a ground hog when just nipped by a bullet, and
is suddenly startled in this manner, are sometimes quite amusing to watch. On one occasion I shot a hog lying asleep on top of
a large rock. I was using ammunition with hard nose bullet. The
ground hog jumped up and ran in circles around its hole which
was beside the rock and gave a better display of speed than a
race horse. After about a dozen circles it then dashed into its
hole. Examination of the shot mark showed that the bullet had
gone between its stomach and rock giving it a good brush burn
but it did not draw blood. A short time later I killed a chuck
from the same den, and this most likely was the same animal,
as it had a pronounced streak across its stomach.

Numerous other incidents could be related had we the space,
but these few may suggest that not every shooting misplay is
unfortunate. Many of them are so amusing at the time that they
add something to the joys of a shooting excursion into the woodchuck fields. More and more amusing and really good shooting
to you.

Appendix

MANUFACTURERS AND SUPPLIERS
OF CHUCK HUNTING EQUIPMENT

Custom Gunsmiths: Individual gunsmiths and firms who build complete custom-made woodchuck rifles: turn, thread and chamber barrels; fit barrels or rechamber to new calibers; rework actions or make speed actions; apply set triggers and fit custom stocks of their own or roughturned blanks. They fit telescope or metallic sights and sling swivels; bore sight and target rifles; convert factory rifles into wildcats.

P. O. Ackley, Inc., R. D. Trinidad, Colo.
Jack Ashurst, Grangeville, Idaho
Maurice Atkinson, Streetsville, Ont., Canada
Brown & Edgar, 10320 Stagg St., Roscoe 3, Calif.
Floyd Butler, R. D. #2, Poultney, Vt.
Kenneth E. Clark, Box 95, Madera, Calif.
G. B. Crandall & Son, Woodstock, Ont., Canada
Vernor Gipson, Box 156, North Salem, Ind.
Roy Gradle, 205 W. Islay St., Santa Barbara, Calif.
Griffin & Howe, 202 E. 44th. St., New York 17, N. Y.
Hollywood Gun Shop, 6032 Hollywood Blvd., Hollywood 28, Calif.
Kenneth L. Hooper, Eureka, Mont.
Al Hoyer, Yeagertown, Pa.
Paul Jaeger, Jenkintown, Pa.
Charles C. Johnson, R. D. #3, Springfield, Ohio
Robert Keel, South St., South Bethlehem, N. Y.
Lysle D. Kilbourn, Whitesboro, N. Y.
R. W. Lathrop, 110-1/2 Broadway No., Seattle, Wash.
E. V. Leach, 168 St. Patrick St., Stratford, Ont., Canada
Hervey Lovell, 925 Water St., Port Townsend, Wash.
Lindahl Gun Company, Central City, Nebr.
Al Marciante, 1216 Princeton Ave., Trenton, N. J.
Mashburn Arms Company, 1220 N. Blackwelder St., Oklahoma City, Okla.

Elmer McConnell, Delhi, Ont., Canada
Raymond J. Overbaugh, R. D. #3, Amsterdam, N. Y.
Pachmayr Gun Works, 1220 S. Grand Ave., Los Angeles, Calif.
Charles Parkinson, 473 Charlotte St., London, Ont., Canada
Pfeifer Rifle Co., Inc., 11252 Penrose St., Sun Valley, Calif.
David G. Poyer, 2520 W. Koenig, Gand Island, Nebr.
Frank M. Riddle, 214 Imperial St., Oil City, Pa.
M. S. Risley, Earlville, N. Y.
I. O. Stone, 23540 W. Eleven Mile Road, Birmingham, Mich.
W. A. Sukalle, 1120 E. Washington St., Phoenix, Ariz.
Taylor & Robbins, Rixford, Pa.
Roy Vail, Warwick, N. Y.
W. F. Vickery, 123 Peasley St., Boise, Idaho
L. R. Wallack, Jr., Langhorne, Pa.
Edgar L. Warner, S. Madison St., Port Clinton, Ohio
Weatherby's, 8823 Long Beach Blvd., South Gate, Calif.
Wurzer & Peterson, 5239 N. 5th St., Philadelphia, Pa.

Barrel Blank Manufacturers: These are manufacturers of bored and rifled .22-, .25-, .270- and .30-caliber barrels in the form of turned and rifled blanks, not chambered, threaded or finished. They are sold to custom gunsmiths and shooters prepared to complete and fit them. These barrels are often turned out, hundreds of the same caliber on a set-up of the machines, and the customer wishing one to a dozen unfinished barrels of a different caliber may have to wait a few weeks if his caliber is not then in production in the shop of his favorite barrel borer, or if he wishes a different rate of twist than the barrel man is cutting.

P. O. Ackley, Inc., R. D., Trinidad, Colo. (Also makes .170 barrels.)
James D. Adair, R. D. #1, Roseburg, Ore.
J. R. Buhmiller, Kalispell, Mont. (Probably has largest volume of woodchuck rifle barrels.)
G. R. Douglas, R. D. #3, Charleston, W. Va.
C. R. Pederson & Son, Ludington, Mich.
Pfeifer Rifle Co., Inc., 11252 Penrose St., Sun Valley, Calif.
Ralph F. Pride, 10140 S. E. Market St., Portland 16, Ore.
John L. Gregoire, P. O. Box 412, Chester, Conn. (Has had unusual success with bench-rest barrels.)
W. A. Sukalle, 1120 E. Washington St., Phoenix, Ariz.

Custom Rifle Barrel Manufacturers: These men and firms make complete turned, bored, threaded, chambered, and blued rifle barrels suitable for the finest accuracy in woodchuck shooting. They cut extractor slots, bush firing pins, and fit new firing pins; skeletonize hammers and tune up actions. Most of them will lap a barrel, when advisable, straighten a barrel, or chamber for a wildcat cartridge. When unavailable, select someone from the list of custom gunsmiths.

P. O. Ackley, Inc., R. D., Trinidad, Colo.
G. R. Douglas, R. D. #3, Charleston, W. Va.
John L. Gregoire, M. E., P. O. Box 412, Chester, Conn.
C. R. Pederson & Son, Ludington, Mich.
Pfeifer Rifle Barrel Co., 11252 Penrose St., Sun Valley, Calif.
Ralph F. Pride, 10140 S. E. Market St., Portland 16, Ore.
W. A. Sukalle, 1120 E. Washington St., Phoenix, Ariz.

Below are the custom rifle barrel manufacturers specializing largely on .22 long rifle rim-fire barrels. In many areas the .22 rim-fires, and the .170 Woodsman with the .22 Hornet, are about all one can use without being chased. Over short and medium ranges they are all good killers, with proper aim.

Eric Johnson, 115 Carleton St., Hamden, Conn.
George Titherington, 1321 S. American St., Stockton, Calif.

Custom Stockers of Woodchuck Rifles:

P. O. Ackley, Inc., R. D., Trinidad, Colo.
Maurice Atkinson, Streetsville, Ont., Canada
L. M. Brownell, Sheridan, Wyo.
G. B. Crandall & Son, Woodstock, Ont., Canada
Vernor Gipson, Box 156, North Salem, Ind.
Griffin & Howe, 202 E. 44th St., New York 17, N. Y.
Hal Hartley, R. D. #4, Lenoir, N. C.
John Hutton, 1720 N. Barton St., Arlington, Va.
A. L. Knight, Fort Worth, Tex.
M. E. McGlothlin & George W. Reynolds, P. O. Box, Mesa, Ariz.
Pachmayr Gun Works, 1220 S. Grand Ave., Los Angeles, Calif.
Frank M. Riddle, 214 Imperial St., Oil City, Pa.
Thomas Shelhammer, Dowagiac, Mich.
Keith Stegall, Gunnison, Colo.
Taylor & Robbins, Rixford, Pa.

Roy Vail, Warwick, N. Y.
Edgar L. Warner, S. Madison St., Port Clinton, Ohio
Weatherby's, 8823 Long Beach Blvd., South Gate, Calif.
Wurzer & Peterson, 5239 N. 5th St., Philadelphia, Pa.

Engravers:

A. Griebel, 4724 N. Keystone Ave., Chicago 30, Ill.

Manufacturers or Importers of Checkering Tools:

Frank Mittermeier, 3577 E. Tremont St., Bronx 61, N. Y.
Warner Products, Baldwinsville 1, N. Y.

Custom Checkering of Rifle Stocks:

E. R. Briggs, 4555 N. 17th St., Philadelphia, Pa.
Edgar L. Warner, South Madison St., Port Clinton, Ohio

Importers or Suppliers of Rifle Stock Blanks:

E. C. Bishop & Son, Warsaw, Mo. (Missouri walnut)
Herter's, Inc., Waseca, Wis. (Laminated, and also walnut blanks)
R. G. (Bob) Owen, P. O. Box 131, Port Clinton, Ohio (French
    walnut)
Roy Vail, Warwick, N. Y. (French Walnut Blanks)

Partially Inletted Rifle Stock Blanks:

E. C. Bishop & Son, Warsaw, Mo.
Central Pattern Works, Racine, Wis.
Flaig's, Millvale, Pa.
Herter's, Inc., Waseca, Wis.
W. R. Hutchings, 4504 W. Washington Blvd., Los Angeles, Calif.

Manufacturers of Speed Actions for Bolt Action Rifles:

J. C. Bogut, Hudson, Wis.
M. H. Canjar, 4476 Pennsylvania St., Denver, Colo. (Canjar
    Trigger)
Kenneth E. Clark, River Route, Madera, Calif.

Cramer Micromovement Trigger — Carl B. Cramer, Cramer
    Bullet Mould Co., 11625 Van Owen St., North Hollywood, Calif.
Dick's Gun Shop, Luck, Wis. (Dick's Trigger)
Paul Jaeger, Jenkintown, Pa.
Mashburn Arms Co., 1220 N. Blackwelder St., Oklahoma City,
    Okla.
Viggo Miller, 4340 Charles St., Omaha, Nebr.
M. L. Smith, Bryan, Tex. (Slick triggers, speed action.)

    Manufacturers or Importers of Schuetzen double set trig-
gers: For Mauser and other bolt actions, and
Single Set Triggers:* For bolt actions and single shots they will
fit.

Flaig's, Millvale, Pa. (Double set triggers for Mausers.)
Paul Jaeger, Jenkintown, Pa. (Single set triggers for bolt actions.
    Also speed actions for bolt actions.)
Chester Nikodym Industries, Chagrin Falls, Ohio. (Double set
    triggers for Springfield bolt actions, Enfields and Mausers.
    He also has Mauser actions complete, with or without set
    triggers.)

    Manufacturers of Chambering Reamers for Wildcats: Also
other calibers suitable for woodchuck rifles.

Christy Gun Works, 875 57th St., Sacramento, Calif.
R. K. (Red) Elliott, Ramona, Calif. (His reamers are finished
    perfectly.)
Otto Fritz, Arcadia, Mich.
Fuller Tool Co., 3950 West Eleven Mile Road, Berkley, Mich.
H. & M. Tool Co., 250 E. Nine Mile Road, Ferndale 20, Mich.
Redford Reamer Co., Box 141, Redford Station, Detroit 19, Mich.

    Manufacturers of Rifle Headspace Gauges:

R. K. (Red) Elliott, Ramona, Calif.
Femco Speciality Mfg., 1115 N. E. 60th St., Portland 13, Ore.
Forster Brothers, Lanark, Ill.
Otto Fritz, Arcadia, Mich.
H. & M. Tool Co., 250 E. Nine Mile Road, Ferndale 20, Mich.
Redford Reamer Co., Box 141, Redford Station, Detroit 19, Mich.
L. E. Wilson, Cashmere, Wash.

*Author's Note: Nothing is so important on a woodchuck rifle as a very fast
action and a perfect trigger pull.

Rifle Bolts Bent and Otherwise Altered for a Telescope:

Vinton A. Kellar, Big Run, Pa.
Kess Arms Company, 1004 W. Center St., Milwaukee, Wis.

A majority of the custom gunsmiths listed farther forward in this directory are prepared to do this work, also.

Manufacturers of Special Safeties for bolt action rifles:
Fitted so as to be to the right of large diameter rifle telescopes. The standard Springfield and Mauser military safeties cannot be turned over under the barrel of the telescope. If used, the scope must be moved forward and finally backward before firing. This may disturb the center of impact because the scope may then not lie in the same position in the mounts, thus the line of sight be changed.

Anderson Gun Shop, 1203 Broadway, Yakima, Wash. (Their safety is for model 99 Savage .250-3000 etc.)
Maynard P. Buehler, Orinda, Calif. (Buehler Safety)
Redfield Gun Sight Company, 3315 Gilpin St., Denver 5, Colo.

In the use of such safeties with some of the speed actions it is very necessary to grind or stone off the contact surface of the sear on the trigger itself, by as much as .005" to .010" or the rifle may fire when you snap off the safety. With a Swift or a Varminter this is likely to be a bit disconcerting.

Manufacturers of Trigger Shoes: These are usually applied to the trigger of a pistol or a revolver. Because they increase the surface on which the finger rests, and also tend to localize the spot on which the trigger finger presses, they may be very helpful on rifles, especially to those who are inclined to flinch and who will shoot better if the rifle fires a fraction of a second before the expected instant.

Flaig's, Millvale, Pa. (Ace shoe)
Harvey E. Henshaw, 818-20 Oakwood St., Pittsburgh 21, Pa.

Manufacturers of Rifle Telescope Sights:

P. O. Ackley, Inc., R. D., Trinidad, Colo. (Ackley bought out the Malcolm Co. and can supply some parts for, and repairs on these rifle telescopes.)

Argus, Inc., Ann Arbor, Mich. (Spotting scopes)

Bausch & Lomb Optical Co., Rochester, N. Y. (Rifle and Spotting Scopes)

Davidson Mfg. Co., 5146 Alhambra Ave., Los Angeles, Calif.

Edwards Sight & Optical Co., 631 N. Columbia St., Union City, Ind.

J. W. Fecker, Inc., 2016 Perrysville Ave., Pittsburgh 14, Pa.

Leupold & Stevens Instruments, 4445 N. E. Glisan St., Portland 13, Ore.

R. A. Litschert, Winchester, Ind.

Lyman Gun Sight Corp., Middlefield, Conn.

Norman, Ford & Co., 1312 W. Erwin St., Tyler, Tex.

R. Noske, San Carlos, Calif.

Pachmayr Gun Works, 1220 S. Grand Ave., Los Angeles 5, Calif.

Stith Mounts (Bear Cub Scopes), 300 Transit Tower, San Antonio, Tex.

John Unertl Optical Co., 3551 East St., Pittsburgh 14, Pa.

Wollensak Optical Co., Rochester 5, N. Y. (Spotting Scopes)

Carl Zeiss, Inc., 485 Fifth Ave., New York, N. Y.

Manufacturers of Rifle Telescope Mounts: Of these, there seems to be no end. Most scope manufacturers make rifle scopes of 5/8″, 3/4″, 7/8″, and 1″ in main tube diameter. Mounts must be of the correct ring diameter, or they won't fit. Objective and eye piece diameters are usually greater. In any case the rings must be opened or the eye piece removed to get the main tube into the mount rings. Parts are then replaced and the cross hairs refocused. There are both top mount and side mounts. Get the former if possible. Target mounts are better than the bobtailed mounts, although not as handy to carry. They permit more accurate placing of the center of impact of the group.

P. O. Ackley, Inc., R. D., Trinidad, Colo.

Maynard P. Buehler, 110 Orinda Highway, Orinda, Calif.

Kenneth Clark, Madera, Calif.

J. W. Fecker, Inc., 2016 Perrysville Ave., Pittsburgh 14, Pa.

Griffin & Howe, Inc., 202 E. 44th St., New York, N. Y. (Hunting scope, side mount)

E. C. Herkner, Boise, Idaho

Clarence A. Hill, Dixon, Ill.

Paul Jaeger, Jenkintown, Pa.

King Gun Sight Co., 667 Howard St., San Francisco, Calif.

R. A. Litschert, Winchester, Ind.
Lyman Gun Sight Corp., Middlefield, Conn.
Mashburn Arms Co., Oklahoma City 6, Okla.
Miller Arms Laboratory, Box 91, Poughkeepsie, N. Y.
MyKrom Company, 1335 S. W. Morrison St., Portland 5, Ore.
R. Noske, San Carlos, Calif.
Pachmayr Gun Works, 1220 S. Grand Ave., Los Angeles 13, Calif.
Redfield Gun Sight Corp., 3315 Gilpin Ave., Denver, Colo. (Redfield Jr. a most excellent mount for short scopes.)
Stith Mounts, 500 Transit Tower, San Antonio, Tex. (Stith mount a very good one for short, hunting scopes.)
Tilden Manufacturing Co., 2750 N. Speer Blvd., Denver, Colo.
Timney Scope-Mount, 5832 Oliva Ave., Bellflower, Calif.
John Unertl Optical Co., 3551 East St., Pittsburgh 14, Pa.
W. R. Weaver Co., El Paso, Tex.
Williams Gun Shop, 7387 Lapeer Road, Davison, Mich.
Carl Zeiss, 485 Fifth Ave., New York, N. Y.

Custom Loaders of Woodchuck Rifle Ammunition: There are thousands of riflemen whose time and facilities for preparing ammunition for woodchuck hunting is limited. Many of these are severely handicapped in the keeping of small quantities of smokeless powders or primers by ridiculous, unreasonable, or prohibitive storage regulations; by excessive fire insurance rates; by police snooping and by nonsensical interstate transportation laws. Consequently they'd rather pay someone to hand-load their ammunition and ship it to them in one package. Fifteen to thirty dollars worth of loaded wildcat ammunition will last the average chap one to five years, and, if stored sensibly, should keep in good condition for five to twenty years. Why therefore purchase one hundred dollars worth of reloading tools and components, and build an expensive storage magazine?

It is rather difficult to compile a complete or proper list of custom loaders. You cannot surmise properly as to some of it until you have shot it, or have hunted with others who have. But most of it shoots better than most commercial ammunition, if properly made. In addition to the list shown below, most custom gunsmiths will reload 100 or 200 rounds for you, or will know of someone who can do this properly. Most wildcatters have acquired reloading tools for three to ten cartridges, and sometimes can be prevailed upon to do a kindly act. Ask your sporting goods dealer to advise you of any such who may live close by. We have tried in the list given here, to put down only those who can supply accurate charges. The calibers they are prepared to sell you, may change somewhat from year to year.

P. O. Ackley, Inc., R. D., Trinidad, Colo.
H. D. Adams, Mt. Morrison, Colo.
Addington Custom Loader, 2539 A. St., San Diego, Calif.
J. R. Appleby, Estevan, Sask., Canada
Buey's Reloading Service, 5438 Christian St., Philadelphia 43, Pa.
Harold Burnett, 6035 E. Grand River, Howell, Mich.
L. M. Coates, 1422 E. Union St., Seattle 22, Wash.
O. E. Coleman, Post Falls, Idaho
G. B. Crandall & Son, Woodstock, Ont., Canada
E. G. Dahl, R. D. #4, Billings, Mont.
L. P. Fisher, Presidio, Tex.
F. J. Fox, 143 Ferry St., Easton, Pa.
Hanson's Custom Loading, Bonner Springs, Kan.
Phil. V. Hershey, Ashland, Ohio
E. A. James, Naples, Tex.
F. R. Krouse, 305 E. Iron Ave., Albuquerque, N. M.
Kroeckel's Custom Loads, Pendleton, Ind.
P. G. Mansfield, New Boston, N. H.
Bob Moody, Helena, Mont.
Charles H. Morse, 517 Prescott St., Herkimer, N. Y. (also Wotkyns-Morse bullets)
Charles Parkinson, 473 Charlotte St., London, Ont., Canada
Schwartz's Custom Loads, 109 Lockwood Ave., Woodbridge, N. J.
Sequin's Custom Loads, 2218 Tower Ave., Superior, Wis.
Bert Shay, Wurtsboro, N. Y.
Van's Custom Loads, William Van Nostrand, 55 Walnut St., Gloversville, N. Y.
L. R. Wallack, Jr., Langhorne, Pa. (He employs a man to do this.)
J. G. Wilkinson, 1209 Lincoln Ave., Peoria, Ill.

Manufacturers of metal-cased soft point, or metal-cased hollow point bullets for woodchuck shooting: They sell direct to the customer.

P. O. Ackley, Inc., R. D., Trinidad, Colo.
Harris Machine Co., Rivera, Calif. (Sierra Bullets)
George Hensley, of Hensley & Gibbs, 2692 E St., San Diego, Calif.
Milo Hill, Caledonia, Ohio (Hill bullets)

J. W. Hornady, 216 W. Fourth St., Grand Island, Nebr.
H. Guy Loverin, Lancaster, Mass. (Cast bullets)
M. G. S. Bullet Company, Hollydale, Calif.
Charles H. Morse, 517 Prescott St., Herkimer, N. Y.
Pearson's Precision Bullets, Pearson's Gun Shop, 4180 College
    Ave., Indianapolis, Ind.
R. B. Sisk, Iowa Park, Tex. (Sisk bullets)
Speer Products Co., Lewiston, Idaho (Speer bullets)

Many of these bullets are carried in stock by your principal
local sporting goods dealer, or by dealers who advertise sportsmen's supplies.

Manufacturers of Reloading Tools for Commercial and for
Wildcat Cartridges: Also, gadgets used in reloading.

Belding & Mull, Inc., N. Front St., Philipsburg, Pa.
Brown & Ball, 1206 "B" Ave., La Grange, Ore. (Outside neck
    reamers)
Cramer Bullet Mould Co., 11625 Van Owen St., North Hollywood,
    Calif.
Easton Engineering Co., 225 S. State St., Salt Lake City, Utah
Earl Gibbs, 1620 Sheridan Blvd., Denver, Colo.
Harris Machine Co., 312 E. Bermudez, Rivera, Calif.
Hensley & Gibbs, 2692 E. St., San Diego, Calif.
Hollywood Gun Shop, 6116 Hollywood Blvd., Hollywood 28, Calif.
Fred Huntington, 1365 7th Ave., Oroville, Calif. (R.C.B.S. Bul-
    let dies and bullet-making tools)
Charles C. Johnson, R. D. #3, Springfield, Ohio
Lyman Gun Sight Corp., Middlefield, Conn.
Masters Machine Works, Brookville, Pa. (Jordan Reloading Tool)
Meepos Machine Shop, 135 N. Western Ave., Los Angeles 4,
    Calif.
Modern-Bond Corp., 813 W. 5th St., Wilmington, Dela.
Pacific Gun Sight Co., 355 Hayes St., San Francisco 2, Calif.
Charles Parkinson, 473 Charlotte St., London, Ont., Canada (.170
    tools)
Potter Engineering Co., 10 Albany St., Cazenovia, N. Y.
The Redding Company, Box 524, Cortland, N. Y.
Santa Anita Eng. Co., 10 Albany St., Cazenovia, N. Y.
C. V. Schmitt, 459 Sexton Bldg., Minneapolis, Minn.
G. T. Smiley Co., Clipper Gap, Calif. (Cartridge case trimmers)
Star Machine Works, 418 10th Ave., San Diego, Calif.

W. S. Vickerman, 208 S. Ruby St., Ellensburg, Wash. (Bullet
   seaters)
L. E. Wilson, Cashmere, Wash.
Yankee Specialty Co., 851 E. 6th St., Erie, Pa.

Lead Wire for Jacketed Bullets:

Rochester Lead Works, Rochester 8, N. Y.

Woodchuck Rifle Rest for Field Shooting:

Murphy's, 236 W. Locust St., Butler, Pa.

Cross Hair Dots for Rifle Telescopes:

T. K. (Tackhole) Lee, P. O. Box 2123, Birmingham, Ala.
Robert S. Thomas, (Tommy Dots), 8402 Fenton St., Silver Spring,
   Md.
T. W. Stein, 854 S. Washington St., Butte, Mont.

General Supplies for Gunsmiths and Riflemen:

Frank M. Mittermeier, 3577 E. Tremont Ave., Bronx 61, N. Y.

ADDITIONAL INFORMATION ON THE DISTRIBUTION OF

DIFFERENT VARIETIES OF WOODCHUCKS IN CANADA

The Following from the Ontario Dept. of Lands and Forests

Dear Sir,
        This will acknowledge receipt of your letter of March
29, 1950, with reference to the distribution of woodchucks in
Canada. The Marmota Monax Canadensis (The Canada Woodchuck) inhabits the forested part of Ontario, being found in clearings and natural openings, but although it has a wide distribution, it is never abundant and could never be so in forested
country.

From the Wildlife Division, Department of Resources and Development, Ottawa, Ont.

Dear Sir,
        This will acknowledge your letter of March 29, 1950,
regarding woodchucks, (Marmota Monax) in Canada.

The authority generally accepted in Canada for distribution of mammal species is R. M. Anderson, Catalogue of Canadian Recent Mammals, National Museum of Canada, Bulletin No. 102. Dr. Anderson lists six subspecies of woodchucks in the Marmota Monax group. As you suggested, Marmota Monax Canadensis is the most widely distributed of the subspecies. Mr. Anderson extends its range to all areas of Canada except British Columbia, the Yukon Territory, Newfoundland and Prince Edward Island. Marmota Monax Ignava is peculiar to Labrador and northern Quebec. Marmota Monax Johnsoni is known from the Gaspe Peninsula. Marmota Monax Ochracea is found in northern British Columbia and the Yukon Territory. Marmota Monax Petrensis is found in the interior ranges of southern British Columbia. Marmota Monax Rufescens is found in southern Ontario north to the Ottawa River.

Letters on Woodchuck Distribution

From Lloyd Melville (veteran guide, sportsman and rifleman, of Siderite, Ontario).

Siderite, Ont.
April 7, 1950

Dear Mr. Landis,

Before I received the letters in '46, '47 and '48 telling me about your chuck hunting with Crandall, Epps, and others, and before reading some other accounts of chucks in other parts of southern Ontario, I thought that we had pretty good country east of Georgian Bay and the north end of Lake Huron. Several years ago I thought I did something when I shot 50 woodchucks in a whole summer. But I have learned that a party would get that many in a couple of days in some sections farther south.

Woodchucks are not plentiful in the wilderness but I have seen individuals, never more than one at a time, across northern Ontario and Quebec, and up the east coast of James Bay just south of Hudson Bay, almost to the northern limit of timber. Along the coast of the Bay, the ones that I saw had their homes in the piles of driftwood that the wildest storms had driven farthest inland. They were the most wary chucks that I have ever seen anywhere and would run for cover the moment one of our party made the slightest move. The chucks around my old home seldom hurried if forty yards separated them from a man. I made a 400 mile canoe trip from Moose Factory around the south end of the Bay and up the east coast as far as the Misa-gattee River in 1934 and camped in several places on the beach-es. Had several opportunities on this trip to study them.

The ordinary chucks with which you and I are familiar range as far north as the Height of Land — the dividing line between the St. Lawrence watershed and the Hudson Bay watershed. But we did not see many of them north of the dividing line. Those to the north appear to me to be a distinctly different species. They are smaller and slimmer than the southern chucks. The longer winters and different types of food might account for this physi-cal difference. But the northern animals have a much heavier growth of hair on their tummies. It is very red.

I got around the peninsula of Michigan that runs up between Lakes Huron and Michigan quite a lot during the years that I was head guide for a set of boys' camps. We skirted an endless number of deserted farms and farms that should have been de-serted, but people were still trying to make a living on them, or at least they were living there. We canoed along the shores of several inland lakes and also 60 miles of the Au Sable River. Never saw a single chuck, or the burrow of a chuck in that area. This territory is west of Lake Huron. I have a very good friend who owns a part interest in a 1,200 acre private hunting pre-serve there. I am writing to him for more information and will let you know what I hear from him. The Laurentian Hills form a belt one hundred miles wide north of the Soo and there is very little farming there until you reach the Clay Belt. Am sorry that I do not know anything about the chucks among the farming settlements up there. Have canoed lake and rivers from the Ka-washkagama which is 150 miles west of the A. C. R. east into Quebec, and saw lone specimens here and there. Saw a few red-bellied woodchucks on the banks of the Albany River.

Sincerely,

Lloyd Melville.

Siderite, Ont.
April 9, 1950

Dear Mr. Landis,

Since mailing you my letter of April 7, with notes on the distribution of woodchucks in Ontario and Quebec, I met a couple of farmers from the Clay Belt at Hearst who are familiar with the conditions pretty well over Ontario east to the boundary with the Province of Quebec. They came originally from the Ottawa valley.* These farmers, of course, know something about chuck conditions in southern Ontario.

They told me that woodchucks are well distributed through all the farming communities of the Clay Belt, along the Canadian National Railway from Hearst east to Cochrane. From Hearst east to Cochrane is about 140 miles. They said that they knew nothing about the chuck situation farther east than Cochrane along the same C. N. R. railroad. They had never been there. In the fall of 1925 I was over in P. Q. along the C. N. R. and around La Rein and saw there some of the finest farms that I have ever seen anywhere in the north. But it was September and October — too late in the year to see woodchucks as they had denned up for the winter.

A local nimrod in any of the farming sections from Sudbury (in the mining area) to the Soo, and again in the Clay Belt of northern Ontario should be reasonably sure of getting five or six chucks in a day. Occasionally he may up that figure considerably; other days it will be lower. The big bags taken in certain sections of southern Ontario are impossible in the north. My farm east of the Soo was on the bank of the Thessalon River, in good average chuck country for the north. The field was 220 rods (1210 yards) long, 100 rods (550 yards) wide at one end and 50 rods (275 yards) wide at the other. I raised crops that chucks love, and I eliminated the chucks thoroughly. They used to move in, in the Spring, and set up housekeeping. There would be Pa, Ma, and four or five young chucks in a den. The best years, four or five seasons, I averaged about 50 chucks a year.

In the earlier years of my chuck shooting I used a .22 W.R. F., Model 1890 Winchester, and liked it better than the regular

*Author's Note: The Ottawa River divides southern Ontario from Province of Quebec, and I have ridden 50 or 60 miles west to north along the Ottawa. The road is on the south side of the river, in Ontario after you drive relatively a few miles west of Montreal. There is then no road there going west or northward in Quebec, or even in that whole section of P. Q., as it is traversed by the Laurentian Mountains or their offshoots and the muskegs between. These lie among the sharply sloped, steep, forested ridges covered with ash, maple, oak and some evergreens which is deer country. The drainage is mostly into the Ottawa River, from both sides, and thence east into the St. Lawrence at Montreal. The Gatineau River runs south into the Ottawa River just east of Ottawa. It was too late in the year then, to see woodchucks as in October they had been denned up about two months. The Valley of the St. Lawrence extends from hundreds of yards to·several miles north and south from the St. Lawrence, the most chucks being on the southern side of the river. North of there is forest and muskeg for hundreds of miles.

.22's. That was in the days of black powder and none of the .22 ammunitions had been improved. For the last few years that I was there on the farm, I used the .30-1906 Springfield exclusively, with reduced loads; the 169-grain Squibb gas check bullet and 25.0 grains of Lightning No. 1; the 110-grain Remington Hi-Speed bullet, or the 172-grain F.A. Bullet (the point doctored and the weight reduced to 169-1/2 grains). Both loads with 43.5 grains DuPont 4350. All three loads were good killers at the short ranges at which I used them, — 50 yards was the greatest range at which I ever shot a chuck in those days.

I have never seen or heard of a real, scope-sighted varmint rifle being used north of Sudbury, though some may exist. The majority of the hunters in that area, then, could not have spared the sheckels required to obtain one. I doubt if a dozen chucks have ever been killed at more than 100 yards in any 50-mile stretch of country mentioned.

The redbellies — the redbellied woodchucks, of farther north, are distinctly museum class. On a 700-mile canoe trip down the Albany (which flows generally eastward into the James Bay), and the west coast of James Bay, I saw less than a dozen redbellied woodchucks. On the 400-mile trip up the east coast, I saw seven or eight woodchucks.

One might say therefore, that while it is true that the two varieties of eastern Canadian woodchuck (other than those found in a restricted area in Labrador) are found scattered over an area at least 600 to 800 miles eastward from a line drawn due north from the Soo, but in a few areas in this immense section are they really very numerous, except south and east of the upper shore of Lake Huron, and in the farming, dairying and horse breeding sections of Ontario, and slightly into the tobacco section but not much into the fruit and vineyard sections close to the north shores of Lakes Erie and Ontario. It is in the warmest, richest and most highly cultivated areas devoted to various types of farming, haying and grazing, and not in the rougher and more heavily forested areas, in which Canada has most of its woodchucks. As in the States, it is not in the deer, moose and grouse areas in which we have the best woodchuck shooting, but in the more highly developed agricultural areas and in the less thickly settled sections on the north fringe of such townships.

Sincerely,

Lloyd Melville.

Ode to "Chuck Huntin"

I've sat around the campfire in Ontario's lonesome pines
To plan the 'morrow's deer hunt with the Redbone's anxious whine
I've hunted Mallards on the prairie when thousands blacked the sky
Where a double barrel shotgun got the limit at one try

Now some would go to Africa for lion on the veldt
Or spend a fortune on safari to get a zebra's pelt
While others hunt the grizzly in the Province of B. C.
Or tramp for miles in winter gales the timber wolf to see

In Tennessee we hunt the boar through briars with sweat and toil
Above the timberline we search the mountain sheep so wild
We all agree that South Dakota's pheasant hunts are nice
And if it's thrills you're looking for a cornered cougar will suffice

Nearly all the wild life in the land is hunted with a zest
And every nimrod will insist that his game is the best
For he loads the old jalopy with tent and cooking gear
His choice of decoy, axe and stove is made with cautious care

He must have matches, extra socks, wool coat and frost bite kit
Sleeping bag and pressure lantern, hunting knife and shooting mit
He freezes hours on a stand for a moose to cross the bay
The old Winchester weighs a ton and the camp is miles away

Now you who've hunted see these lines and know just what I mean
To hunt where shooting's guaranteed would be just like a dream
Some overlook a little varmint always out when weather's fine
You can hunt him at your leisure in the good old summertime

All you need is that "pet" rifle and a hat to shade your eyes
The farmer always gives consent for the groundhog's quick demise
This marmot eats the rural crops, he's an obese, crafty yegg
Who leaves a large and hidden hole to break the horse's leg

So you hunt him in your shirt sleeves and you scan a certain mound
There's no danger if you miss him with that soft dirt all around
You forget the office pressure and you bask in nature's shade
Some might call it lazy huntin' but for me it's heaven made

No pot hunter lurks the forest to mistake you for a deer
No trigger happy tyro planting buckshot in your rear
You boys can sit in camp and drink or try your luck at cards
I'm looking for that smart old "chuck" at about three hundred yards

Who hibernates 'til Groundhog Day on February two
Then shuffles back to tell his spouse the winter's nearly through
Marmota Monax is his name and edible is he
Just "Whistle Pig" is what they called him back in Eighty Three

You will never catch him napping he's a cunning little one
I often stalk him close enough for muzzle loading gun
He's prolific, he's terrific and with any kind of luck
I'll be three score ten and plenty when I shoot my last woodchuck.

D. M. MOROUGHAN

CPSIA information can be obtained at www.ICGtesting.com
Printed in the USA
BVOW09s1236200515

401114BV00005B/183/P

9 781614 272489